Legal Artifices: Ten Essays on Roman Law in the Present Tense

ENCOUNTERS IN LAW AND PHILOSOPHY
SERIES EDITORS: Thanos Zartaloudis and Anton Schütz

This series interrogates, historically and theoretically, the encounters between philosophy and law. Each volume published takes a unique approach and challenges traditional systemic approaches to law and philosophy. The series is designed to expand the environment for law and thought.

Titles available in the series

STASIS: Civil War as a Political Paradigm
Giorgio Agamben

On the Idea of Potency: Juridical and Theological Roots of the Western Cultural Tradition
Emanuele Castrucci

Political Theology: Demystifying the Universal
Anton Schütz and Marinos Diamantides

The Birth of Nomos
Thanos Zartaloudis

Leibniz: A Contribution to the Archaeology of Power
Stephen Connelly

General Advisor
Giorgio Agamben

Advisory Board
Clemens Pornschlegel, Institut für Germanistik, Universität München, Germany
Emmanuele Coccia, Ecole des Hautes Etudes en Sciences Sociales, France
Jessica Whyte, University of Western Sydney, School of Humanities and Communication Arts, Australia
Peter Goodrich, Cardozo Law School, Yeshiva University, New York, USA
Alain Pottage, Kent Law School, University of Kent, UK and Sciences Po, Paris
Justin Clemens, University of Melbourne, Faculty of Arts, Australia
Robert Young, NYU, English, USA
Nathan Moore, Birkbeck College, Law School, University of London, UK
Alexander Murray, Queen's University Belfast, UK
Piyel Haldar, Birkbeck College, Law School, University of London, UK
Anne Bottomley, Law School, University of Kent, UK
Oren Ben-Dor, Law School, University of Southampton, UK

edinburghuniversitypress.com/series/enlp

Legal Artifices: Ten Essays on Roman Law in the Present Tense

Yan Thomas

Translated by:
Chantal Schütz & Anton Schütz

Edited by:
Thanos Zartaloudis, with Cooper Francis

Foreword:
Anton Schütz & Thanos Zartaloudis

Afterword:
Alain Pottage

EDINBURGH
University Press

Edinburgh University Press is one of the leading university presses in the UK. We publish academic books and journals in our selected subject areas across the humanities and social sciences, combining cutting-edge scholarship with high editorial and production values to produce academic works of lasting importance. For more information visit our website: edinburghuniversitypress.com

Edinburgh University Press Ltd
The Tun – Holyrood Road
12(2f) Jackson's Entry
Edinburgh EH8 8PJ

First published in hardback by Edinburgh University Press 2021

Typeset in 11/13 Palatino by
Servis Filmsetting Ltd, Stockport, Cheshire, and
printed and bound by CPI Group UK Ltd, Croydon, CR0 4YY

A CIP record for this book is available from the British Library

ISBN 978 1 4744 4667 9 (hardback)
ISBN 978 1 4744 4668 6 (paperback)
ISBN 978 1 4744 4669 3 (webready PDF)
ISBN 978 1 4744 4670 9 (epub)

Contents

Copyright Acknowledgements

Abbreviations

— *C.J.*, for Justinian's *Codex*, his compilation of imperial laws (534).
— *D.*, for Justinian's *Digest*, a didactic treatise of Roman law (533).
— *I.*, for Justinian's *Institutes*, a didactic treatise of Roman law (533).
— *X*, for the *Decretals of Gregory IX* (also known as *Liber Extra*) a compilation of papal decretals (1234).
— *VI*, for the *Liber Sextus*, a compilation of papal decretals going back to Bonifacius VIII (1298).
— *Extrav.*, for the *Extravagantes*, a collection compiled by Jean XXII (1317).
— *on, in,* or *gl.*, for glosses and comments of medieval jurists on a passage of Roman or canon law.
— *c.* for *canon*.
— *pr.* for *proemium*, the introductive paragraph of a juridical text.
— *s.v.* for *sub verbo* (in reference to words, which mark a comment or a gloss).
— *eod. loc.* (refers to a passage quoted shortly beforehand).

Foreword

Operations and Artifices: The Art of the Oldest Legal Professionals

Anton Schütz and Thanos Zartaloudis

I.

Yan Thomas (1943–2008), French legal historian, thinker and specialist in Roman law, has had a significant and lasting influence in legal historical research and legal thought, which reverberated across the social sciences and humanities.[1] His aversion to 'doctrinal interpretations'[2] (Marta Madero) meant that his rigorous historical philology was driven by a rejection of modern aspiration-guided conceptions of law and stale or comforting interpretative formulas, often produced in the name of the wider illusion that presumes 'law' is characterised by the evolution of a universal meaning.[3]

The ten essays collected in the present volume have been published over more than three decades, between 1973 and 2005. At least equally significant is the thematic distance between the pieces. There are essays on parricide in Rome; on a Roman father's right over life and death of his sons; on the ways Roman private law infiltrates and structures views and practices on crime, guilt and fault; on modern labour law and its differences, as well as commonalities, with rented slave work in Rome; on structuralist and Marxist history writing and views of evolution in relation to Roman law; on how a legal order that fails to refer to responsibility has managed to function as a legal order; on modes in which historians of Rome have chosen to relate to legal historians of Rome (and vice versa); on what remains of Roman history and law today, if one sections them from what has been their imperialist message and colonialist mission throughout many centuries; and on how the 'linguistic turn' has (or should have) changed the profile of Roman legal scholarship. Each of the ten chapters offers a separate contribution to Roman law. At the same time, all relate to contemporary problems and matters, some directly, where the reference to Roman law scholarship is triggered by current events (as most notably Chapter 6), others indirectly, when the question of expounding and understanding the decisions and reasons of Roman law is asked anew in the light that is shed on them by current events, cases, or debates.

The *Corpus Iuris Civilis*, today sometimes celebrated as the West's second bible, looks back to a millennium and more of existence as a discipline. In the history of world private law, Roman law figures effectively as a unique achievement relating to ways of dealing with life-world-structuring issues in a vast field of matters including ownership, possession, damage, contract, heritage. The long sequence of historical 'repetitions' of Roman law, forming a key artery of institutional transmission over the European continent, and via multiple ramifications worldwide, is owed, Thomas's work insists, to the structural dependence of law and legal argument on *reasons* and/or *references*. What is the difference? Why do lawyers content themselves with references? Invoking reasons supposes a human subject that is keen to know. Such a subject is prominently supposed in philosophy, starting from the first sentence of the First book of Aristotle's *Metaphysics*, which claims that, by its very nature, the human being desires to know. But does it? Proof to the contrary is abundant, at least outside philosophy. The operations of law are a cautious reaction to the hyperbolic reliance embodied in the philosophical trust that people can be expected to wish to know. For Thomas outlining the culture of Western law and jurisprudence and the status of the Roman jurists in it, almost nothing is as important as the need to take note of the fact that jurists had (and continue to have) other problems and exigencies than those of the philosophers.

The history-covering glory of Roman private law has not been about teaching those eager to be taught, not about being known or understood as enlightening, but about offering solutions that work even below the level of teaching or understanding. Legal references are successfully cited or invoked in litigation; and litigation is where Roman private law's success story unfolds, what it covers; 'the all-covering' (*pandectae*) was the name of the main compilation of classical juristic writing (another name was *Digest*, meaning that which is 'unfolded' or 'dealt with'). Reasons were formally defined, but 'Reason' was not the problem law claimed to solve. According to juristic teaching and convention, Reason was present in the legal text because it was written into it (Roman law being, notably according to the Middle Ages, *ratio scripta*, 'written reason'). Jurists dealing with private law litigation delivered their goods by making arguments based on *references*.

The triumphal procession of classical Roman law was not simply fuelled by the writing of the classical jurists (dating from the first century BCE to the third century CE), but also by the collection that was in itself already the first in the long series of its repetitions, the late – and famously fudged – standard version of classical Roman law which is known to us as the 'Body of Civil Law' (*Corpus Iuris Civilis*); and which was put together in the earlier sixth century (a half millennium, more or less, after its sources) by a commission of law professors appointed by Emperor Justinian in Byzantium. Despite a spectacular over-abundance of solemn imperial proclamations, exhortations and recommendations, the underlying idea for the commission was simple enough: to create once again the conditions of legal life to emerge, self-reliant and viable by its own means, to recreate the dynamic of classical Roman law, now under Christian auspices. Hence, a key point is omnipresent in Thomas's writing: the success story of Roman law is the result of a protracted institutional process, answering the endlessly growing demand of litigation to which it gave rise. This is a process of multiplication of legal demand that finds its final and most effective accomplishment a further half-millennium after Justinian's professorial commission, starting from the eleventh and twelfth centuries, with the birth and growth of Roman law teaching in the West.

The assumption of the intrinsic perfection of Roman private law, encompassed the European world for a long time. It was the product of the late eleventh- and early twelfth-century creation of an institution that centre-staged the reference to Roman law. The law school of Bologna, and a whole network

xi

of law schools in its wake, provided a site in which, generation after generation, student intake after student intake, medieval Roman law-scholars and their students went ceaselessly through the *Institutes* (an official textbook for first-year-students), the *Digest* (the already mentioned selection of classical juristic writing, which forms the largest and most momentous component of the *Corpus*, and at once the sole source of non-statute law), as well as the *Codex* and the *Novellae Constitutiones* (collections of imperial statutes ancient and recent). Providing Roman law with a site of permanence and continuous reprogramming, the Bologna institution, or more exactly the fact that Roman law was hitherto in operation, and would be so 'for good', transformed Roman law's so far merely textual existence into a new 'process-reality' (as philosopher A. N. Whitehead called it a century ago). It was in other words both operational and permanent. Product of a symbiosis between the newly emerged specialised teaching institution and the *Corpus Iuris Civilis*, whose study it steadily reiterated, transforming it into an open-ended programme, the Bologna law school structured the societal fate of the European continent.

Roman law carries, embodied in what it refers to as its origins, a claim to timeless knowledge. The source of this knowledge is most generally referred to by the word *natura*. Thomas, as the reader will discover, devotes to this notion some of the most decisive pages of the present volume. The notion that legal precepts are endowed with an origin but with no end, that law is, then, a matter both of an initial decree and of timeless validity, has lent its general framework to the reasoning of Roman jurists and, in their wake, of generations of civil lawyers. One can wonder whether it was this that prompted Thomas to come up with what can clearly be qualified as the sharpest resistance to the radically naturalist position of the Roman jurists that he studied. His claim that the accomplishment of the classical Roman jurists lies in their art of contingent yet precisely argued operations is a direct reply to their reliance upon *natura*, a reliance that served as the source of the legitimacy with which they provided their work.

When Thomas, whose sense of historical accuracy has been honed by his resistance to the methodological a-historicism that so often takes hold of the minds of lawyers (and, contrary to what William Maitland thought, not only in England),[4] encounters the classical juridical concept of *natura*, this also opens up some perspectives on French intellectual history. Those who are familiar with Michel Foucault's pleadings to historicise the claims presented by all official views, e.g. of medicine and psychiatry, might be tempted to notice affinities in Thomas's suggestions to historically reassess classical civil law. The nature of their trade imposes upon jurists in Rome – as a thousand years later, in the great era of Bologna – the need either to dislodge the disquieting spectre of contingency, or to render it invisible. Roman private law has been about positing rights (in common law parlance, supplying legal remedies) working under the uncanny condition that everything that happens could just as well happen otherwise, or not at all. Uncanny and unwanted, this contingent condition must be cured. Unfortunately, the remedies and devices to domesticate such disquieting contingency, are an equally contingent artefact. They boil down to covering in an apparel of naturalness the artificiality and contingency of legal problem-solving, yet through operations that are themselves bound to involve more of the same. It is tempting to understand the whole quid-pro-quo as something like a large-scale venture of 'contingency-laundering'. Law can, if not 'solve social problems', resolve a paralysing state of indecision by replacing the two (of the number of parties in a litigation) with the one (of a judgment). To do so, it must mobilise the contingent operation of decision-making. Except that openly admitted contingency does not bode well for the decision's authority.

The decision's 'also otherwise possible' is the dangerous *pars destruens*, the price to be paid for the decision's virtuous, unifying *pars construens*. Only decisions can solve disputes, which thus can only be redeemed at the price of contingency – a blemish from which they can be cleansed and rehabilitated only by means of yet another, supplementary, contingent operation. The name of this operation is naturalisation. The Roman jurists being experts in this travesty, the cloak in which the hope to conceal the contingency of juristic operations is invested, is, already since the *Digest*, nature. Thomas, with his radically historicist view of the civil law's founding operations, will be led to draw attention precisely to the contingent, artificial operations that the naturalist sleight of hand strives to cover up. Thomas's own reconstruction of classical Roman jurisprudence describes it as a specialised professional debate, an industry of artificial moves and contingent operations. But that is only one of two sides. Equally fundamental is, according to Thomas's outline, the jurisconsults' move of clutching to 'nature' as to the inexhaustible spring of their decisions' legitimacy. It is by borrowing nature's voice that they succeed in resolving tangled and complex situations. Yet the nature at stake is a highly artificial and contingent one that unfolds in the contrivances and arguments of a small group of classical Roman jurists.

Historical relevance distracts from legal relevance in that, centre-staging not decision but knowledge, it focuses on the past's potential to be presented as a narrative. Legal relevance distracts from historical relevance in that, centre-staging decision, it focuses on the past's potential to decide present disputes. The tension between the two component matters of legal history is easily grasped. Thomas is aware of its implications: for instance, the dream – and it is a dream that was very popular with the pandectists, the classical German nineteenth-century professors of Roman law – of engaging in some trans-historic dialogue with Ulpian, born in 170 CE, to discuss with him cases and concepts of supposedly timeless Roman private law can of course be dreamt, but a true debate would suppose two jurists exposed to the same set of historical conditions. Equally inadequate would be an attempt to dissolve Roman law into a sequence of diachronic events, leaving behind the systemic or synchronic aspect constituting what had been called all the way since Justinian's time, 'a body of law'.

II.

Thematically, the ten chapters of this collection document interventions in numerous fields and controversies. The two shortest essays, Chapters 1 and 2, have both been written as an introduction to a collective volume. Chapter 1 (Buenos Aires, 1999) is the introduction to a collection of selected Thomas publications entitled *Los Artificios de las Instituciones*. Thomas focuses on the fact that legal forms of social life are constructed rather than 'natural' or spontaneous, and allocates to those in charge of the construction work what he calls an art, *ars iuris*, the art of law. Its distinctive feature with respect to other arts and their respective practitioners resides in the fact that lawyers construe their edifices equipped with a *capacity of giving existence to that which they affirm*. The products of the *ars iuris* are performative utterances, made of mere words ('montages'), but carrying the rather singular performative virtue of delivering the conditions of their realisation. In this sense, what is called 'law', approached each time only by approximation, is understood as 'the medium *par excellence*' for the artful fabrication of the institutional entities from which social organisations are formed.

Chapter 2 (2002) is likewise an introduction, this time to a collective volume edited by Thomas, a special issue of the prestigious French historical periodical *Les Annales*. It contains contributions by several historians devoting themselves to historical specialities that often overlap with those of ancient or medieval legal history. The volume focuses on the divide between history and legal history. The question that Thomas asks his co-contributors is how law relates to the *other* social sciences (assuming that law is one among them, which is not an assumption that goes for everyone). Is there something by which law, understood as a social science, stands out as anomalous? Such a particularity might exist, but if it does, it is to be seen neither as a natural endowment, nor as one part of the famous distinction between the *is* and the *ought*. The discovery of the 'duality between facts and norms' fails to exhaust the question of law and its history, Thomas stresses. Instead, legal orders are a matter of production. Rather than irremediable facts, the outcome of some underlying regularity, they are contingent artefacts, obtained by means of ever-more specialised procedures. Law is, both today and during the times of classical Roman jurists, the exercise of legal professionals. But this is only one side of the coin. The principal discursive effort is that of conjuring away the fear that springs up, with irresistible necessity, from that which is just a matter of decision, given that the very form of the decision spells out that, no matter what is decided and how it is, it could have been, or could be, decided otherwise. In order to assure that contingency, the inevitable by-product of decision making, is compatible with stability, in order for the wound of contingency to heal, decisions need to be covered by a layer of event-less, decision-free naturalness. The reference to *natura* serves to upgrade that which is construed and decided, by supplementing it with the most insuperable of surplus values.

This is also why a legal order consists, in Thomas's words, of 'accumulated layers of congealed decisions'. The chemistry allowing the freezing of the contingent materials of legal decisions into a sustainable dispositive is discussed by unrelenting analyses of the interventions of the classical Roman jurists. Everything looks as if, in order to fit the mute and polymorphous reality of the 'facts' into both quotable and performative legally sustainable words, Rome's pioneering jurists, in order to describe their way of proceeding, could have borrowed, a millennium and half in advance, the terms used by philosopher René Descartes: *'larvatus prodeo'* ('I advance under a mask'). The Roman lawyers rarely speak about 'facts', in the style of twentieth-century social sciences: what counts for them is the entire situation of a 'whole case' or issue, the 'thing' (*res*). While foundational elements of Roman law such as the person, contract, property, point to a semantic history that is relevant up to our times, for Thomas the key point is that these juridical elements are units in a process of formatting and categorisation that involves its own specific coherence, different from, but comparable to, what will happen in many later legal orders. Hence, the legal historian needs to appreciate these elements not as information, ideas or social phenomena, but as keys to the formal organisation of law that gives rise to a social world of its own.

Both chapters discuss, from different directions, the same fundamental question: what can be learnt from legal history and especially Roman legal history, today? Chapter 1 focuses on Roman law's prominent presence over two millennia. The Roman-law schooled professional decision-maker speaks in its name, yet Roman law itself pretends that its argument is ultimately rooted in *natura*. Roman jurists stick to the lesson that they fare better deciding and speaking in nature's name, rather than their own. Let us keep in mind that the space given to *natura* within the legal text makes of it a positive concept in its own right. While insisting on his indifference to legal theory, heavily overdone in his view with respect to legal history, Thomas sides with 'positivist' (and against 'naturalist') legal-theoretical pleas, not because of any claim to have discovered a legal 'naturalistic fallacy' (confusing indicatives with imperatives, taking an 'ought' for an 'is'), but rather because of legal history's anti-naturalist lesson. Legal history shows that law thrives courtesy of positive artifices and operations, not of uplifting theoretical explanations. More or less fraudulent attempts of selling positive law *as* natural law have accompanied law at all times. In addition, the standard positivist explanation, having accomplished its promise as soon as it arrives at law's positive or decision-based sources, appears as a rather jejune endeavour, even if, admittedly, it has helped many a legal practitioner to organise their routines by supplying them with a grill of some minimal realistic consistency. Explanations in law are generally justifications (there is no need of being a Nietzschean to recognise this, which Thomas, a historian and not a genealogist, incidentally was not absolutely). A historical view, on the other hand, can deliver a faithful portrayal, based upon an independent and reliable account of law's position in its social context. Only legal historians, not theorists, have access e.g. to the fact that positive law only outsources the reference to nature; it never definitively escapes a meta-law explaining/justifying it in the name of silent nature.

Moreover, it is well-known that the study of legal theory, a field established in the undecided region between explanation and justification, is and has always been an integrating part of the study of law. But if this is so, if legal theory is a reliant sidekick rather than an independent observer of law, the question that imposes itself is where a more trustworthy yardstick, if any, to appraise law and its social role, might be located? Thomas's roadmap features legal phenomena inclusive of their here and there, based on the choice that it is less instructive to excogitate the universal properties of law, the conceptual (timeless) horizon that law authorises under no matter what circumstances, than to study the transitory, momentary, 'mortal' features of this or that law in particular that has effectively existed. Even if knowledge is better served by the historical approach, there is a price to be paid for leaving the church of theory (or philosophy) for the sect of history, and it is a price to be paid in the crucial currency of communicative performance, empowerment, plausibility ('number of followers', in the language of social media users). Historical knowledge is predicated upon intimate familiarity with concrete, event-related, observer-dependent information. As we have seen, for both Thomas and Maitland, knowledge of law's history is not necessarily to be found on the checklist of the indispensable abilities of a successful lawyer. Does this make of the historical study of law an overstated ancillary pastime? As we know, there are cases where the best that can be done is to indicate the point of rupture or bifurcation, where everyone chooses their side.

Historians and lawyers differ in their approach to the past. Being divided between 'two different logics, the logic of authority, and the logic of evidence', they remain subject to a spell that Maitland has expressed thus: 'what the lawyer wants is authority and the newer the better; what the historian wants is evidence and the older the better'.[5] Thomas's writing shows that the lawyerly preference for new authority over old evidence, far from being limited to the historical research of English law, includes Roman law. The duties of successful legal professionals are subject to carrot and stick in both regimes. Decisions, cases to deal with, involve the continuous possibility of winning or losing, which partly explains the propensity for 'authority', even if today we would rather speak of 'plausibility'. Historians, as well, are exposed to success or its absence. There is, however, one momentous difference. The echo, whether acclaiming or repudiating, that greets a historian's intervention, will never obtain the legal force of a *res iudicata*, as is the case in law. There is no such thing as a historical interpretation that is given or denied validity. That practitioners of history prefer evidence to authority, while practitioners of law make the opposite choice, could well be related to this functional heteromorphism between validity-sustained disciplines and those that are not. As observed by Maitland, for historians, the best evidence is that which comes from closest to the event; for lawyers, the best authority comes from closest to the validity-triggering verdict. Thomas points to the tensions that haunt the practice of legal history, torn between its two component vectors. Legal historians, like Maitland or, a century later, Thomas, understand law as one of the sites in which society acts in the guise of a laboratory of its own 'historical variations'. Topics of legal history find their *Sitz-im-Leben* in this laboratory. In Chapter 2, once more, Thomas addresses the Maitlandian problem, the legal-historical square of the circle as it might be called, this time turning to a public not of lawyers but historians. He charges the tacit postulate according to which all historical topics are equal – different in content, but equal in complexity and significance: law's performative prowess constitutes a surplus value, to which legal history needs to stick uncompromisingly. It excludes referring to matters legal in the same way as to any other aspect of cultural or societal reality.

Legal history in Thomas's rigorous sense carves its way by means of its relentless effort to avoid both insufficiencies: with respect to history *and* with respect to law. Both argumentative movements are essential. Addressing lawyers, Thomas underscores that Roman law has to be understood as one transient historical object. Roman law's unique bi-millennial success story offers no exception to Foucault's claim that there is no such thing as a 'transhistorical object' for the historian. Turning to historians, Thomas claims that law's performative sway over society's evolution requires the centre-staging of Roman law, including for a historian gifted with the most unsparing mastery of Roman law. In this manner, Chapter 1 turns to a public of Roman-law schooled jurists: Thomas doubles down against any trans-historicising hypostasis; Roman law is a historical topic in the same way as any other. In Chapter 2, staging a discussion with historians, Thomas explains how and to what extent law and matters legal fail to fit into the conventional mapping system used by historians in dealing with the objects of their research, as well as how law's societal endowment and intrinsic complexity provide it with an impact and a historical role different from that of other historical objects.

In Chapter 3, *The Language of Roman Law: Problems and Methods* (1973; fundamentally a review article) the same ambition of deconstructing the overarching effects of the jurists' operations is applied to the language of Roman law. Thomas follows the footsteps of a now largely forgotten Italian linguist and legal historian, Antonio Carcaterra, publishing from the 1960s to the 1990s who, simply on the base of Thomas's quotes, has a claim to the credit of having introduced the major twentieth-century discovery known as the *linguistic turn* within the study of Roman law. Like Carcaterra, Thomas questions the standard narrative of the relationship between Roman law and its non-legal origins and antecedents. A large majority of Roman law specialists, throughout the nineteenth and twentieth century, believed that classical Roman law integrated numerous concepts that had previously existed outside of law, e.g. in religion or philosophy; and that legal discourse subsequently appropriated them, charged them with legal meaning and transformed them into legal concepts.

The widespread idea that a substantial fraction of the language of Roman law results from the appropriation, by lawyerly exchanges and the jurists' communication, of a semantic realm that looks back to a long lease of non-legal pre-life, is, according to Carcaterra and Thomas, based upon a misunderstanding of how legal language works, of what happens when it kicks in, of how it re-initialises a word it uses, charging it with specific functions, obliterating (or not) its past semantic sense. For Thomas and Carcaterra, the assumption that a legal nomenclature comes into existence as a supplement, by merely adding a new scope, new harmonics as it were, to a language that has already existed before and that continues to exist outside of law, misses the point. The effort of the Roman jurists was one of offering a formally dependable, articulated mechanics of interconnected levers, an order of selective conditions, dependences and relevancies – a consistent network of meanings, not a sophisticated appendix to common sense.

The origin of a legal term is to be found within law, and not in some extra-legal pre-history. Jurists charge words with an argumentative function absent from those same words when they are used in ethics, philosophy, religion and so on, let alone vernacular Latin. But neither did this lead jurists to develop a mere legal *terminology*. The supplementary layer of sophistication is not the salient point, legal language functions as a language, and by means of arguments. To downgrade function, scheme and rationality of words to a mere terminology is to misconstrue legal language. A legal argument is carried, not by *nomina iuris* (legal names) but by discourse (sentences). What makes language legal are the stakes. The only constitutive difference of the language of Roman jurists is that they communicate only with fellow jurists – not with neo-platonic scholarchs, homeless cynics, stoic preceptors, members of a college of Roman *pontifices*, or indeed Christian preachers, nor indeed with an undefined anyone. As Thomas puts it: 'All the words of a legal proposition . . . need to be presumed to include a specific legal meaning'. Even where, as in the case of *fides*, the extra-legal existence of a legal term is beyond doubt, the extra-legal origins of the law term have been emptied of what Thomas calls their religious or moral *aura*, as soon as it is part of a legal argument. Once a term is used and contextualised as a legal term, all that is triggered are the legal distinctions, any reference to vestigial 'natural' or 'pre-legal' associations boiling down to a moot point. What vanishes in communications between Roman jurists, is the ecumenic use, in Thomas's words: the 'axiological common value' of the words at stake.

Thomas insists that the language of the Roman jurists is indeed a full-blown language, not a sub-species of common Latin, nor a terminology plugged into it. The arid language of the classical jurists exists simultaneously with classical common Latin. Even the metamorphosis that their texts undergo when, in 530, they are cut and pasted into Christian Emperor Justinian's *Corpus Iuris* (courtesy of which we know most of what we know about them) is less a Christian 'moralisation' of classical law, than legal language assimilating any external, moral or other extra-legal elements, into its own argumentative structure.

In close proximity, Chapter 4, *The Law Between Words and Things: Rhetoric and Case Law in Rome* (1978) offers an inquiry in what is called *ars juris*, legal art. It shows that, if the powerful Latin of the legendary Roman proto-legislation, the *Twelve Tables*, had been easier to translate, twentieth-century theory of speech acts and performative utterances would perhaps seem less original. '*Uti lingua nuncupassit, ita ius esto*', 'that which has been said, let it be law' or, 'shall be right what the mouth has claimed'. But neither are, in Thomas's view, a number of common Marxist explanations likely to do justice to the teaching of Roman classical jurists. The question is

less whether 'reification' or 'fetishism' are fitting conceptual
instruments to study the legal order's ways of encoding the
social world in language; rather, what looks problematic is the
sway of some undeclared form of evolutionary universalism.
What Thomas criticises more than the compulsory reference
to such concepts is the evolutionary hypothesis underlying
Marxist explanations (and quite a few liberal ones, to boot).
While the conservative belief dominant among the specialists
of Roman law tends to locate the wealth of meaning boasted
by Roman law either in the atemporal nature of the juridical
mind, or in 'humanity's choice' of following the Western,
i.e. the Roman model, Thomas attributes it to proximities
between the actions and ways of the classical Roman jurists
and that of contemporary legal practitioners. Rather than
some trans-historically stable identity, we find a line connecting over time two distant legal orders and juristic practices,
both involved in the social effort of dealing with cases. The
unfolding over time of legal orders has been an object of interest since far earlier than modernity and its study of classical
law. In Rome itself, the official narrative features an account
of law presenting it as subject to continuous improvement.
The gesture of overcoming outdated past law was inbuilt
in the legal present tense. Older, stricter, more rigidly lit-
eralistic or ritualistic legal ways, yielded to more modern,
user-friendly, rational, flexible ones. This self-interpretation
of legal evolution has prevailed since the first century BCE.

Meanwhile, rhetoric has generated an art of classifying
ways of speaking, and a flourishing of doctrines of legal
analysis, known in Rome as theories of *genus* and *status*.
Thomas shows how rhetoric makes itself indispensable in
many fields: those gifted for a career of political leadership
are necessarily orators, concerned with the business of combining things and words. This involved a toolbox of rhetorical
operations: the search for ideas (*inventio*), their appropriate
articulation (*dispositio*), finally the fact of putting them in the
form of a discourse (*elocutio*) staged in the demonstrative, the
deliberative, the judicial, i.e. in each of the three genres of
speech. Also, the newly emerging professional bodies – the
jurists, the rhetoricians, those in charge of operations of economic exchange and generally matters of value – participate
here in one common effort. It is decisive to understand this

effort as a cognitive exercise, rather than some mastery allowing the imposition of judgments; it is as *cognitive arts* that they produce a new architecture of abstractions, norms, and arts of mediation. Thomas shows how the writing of classical Roman jurists involves a metaphysics of the object. The old legal-theoretical habit of finding fault with 'formalism' fails sufficiently to individualise the 'arts' that, from antiquity to the present, enabled law to impose its reason, be it via mental transformation, via technical language accelerating the internal communication between jurists, or via the law's key performative privilege of conferring existence upon its own utterances.

Chapter 5, *Artifices of Truth in the Medieval* ius Commune (2005), is a study on metamorphoses of Roman law under Christian auspices during the Western Middle Ages, about a millennium after the flourishing of the classical Roman jurists. The very title offers a valuable opportunity to realise that the 'common'-word, in reference to normative and justice-related matters, is barely a precision instrument. Although Thomas fails to bring up the matter, the medieval *ius commune* is a challenge to the English common law – despite the narrow commonality between the two laws that bear the reference to the common in their coat of arms. It is not tempting to take Thomas's study of *ius commune* as an occasion to further overfeed the already bursting file of inquiries in the history of the common law. Yet, one crucial clarification regarding the divergence between the continental and the insular style of referring to normative realities is of the essence. The continental *ius commune* and the insular common law refer to different normative realities. The first claims to be a species, not of law, Latin *lex*, but of *ius* – it claims to be a common *right*. It is *as a* common *right* that the normative culture created by the Roman jurists, compiled by the Byzantine emperor, recycled by the medieval jurists of Bologna, has provided the framework of legal life on a large part of the European continent during most of the second millennium CE. This is why it would be disastrous to translate *ius commune* as 'common law'. Popular as this expression is, the gesture toward which it points is different, more ambitious and also more ambiguous. Locating the commonality on the *law*-level moves the issue toward the question *Whose* law? Thus, toward an inquiry about who makes the law, about the author or origin of collectively binding norms, historically, to a dispositive of independence. *Ius commune*, on the other hand, provides a dispositive of knowledge, a science of rights, where no 'whose-' or 'who-' questions show up.

As the sphere of normative phenomena finds its societal *Sitz-im-Leben* in the realm of discourse, it is unsurprising that the most decisive legal discussions populating the relevant centuries – mainly the twelfth to the fourteenth – were not wary of turning to the notion of truth. Thomas explains how the Roman professionalisation of the normative realm can be understood in terms of an industry producing artificial truths. Out of nature, or so they pretended, the jurists spun an artifice in the service of juridical institutions. The realm of the counterfactual was subjected, by the classical jurists, to what would tend to appear today as the space of a continuous invasion, or a relentless process of colonisation. Legal problems that appeared in direct confrontation as unsolvable, allowed of a solution as soon as some additional liberty, some 'as if' was allowed in, subverting the factual. The general title of these enabling operations, giving rise to the juristic invention of a form of 'deficit spending', long before the word was coined, was that of 'fiction', an operation already known to the classical jurists but not yet subject to any particular theoretical reflection. In the name of *fictio*, Thomas notes, Roman civil law had forged gods (*consecratio*), sons (*adoptio*), transformed death into life (*restitutio*) and persons into things (*diminutio status*). Law's alchemic power is, Thomas writes, that it can 'transform the order of things' and, crucially, by the mere exercise of an ultimately linguistic capacity, control the real. It was up to their medieval and Christian followers to forge a notion of fiction that would encompass, with theoretic stringency, competent conceptual tools to deal with the realm of what medieval jurists were able to do through the medium of *fictio*.

In Chapter 6, *The Subject of Right, the Person, Nature: Remarks on the Current Criticism of the Legal Subject* (1998), Thomas centre-stages a contemporary topic, the case of Nicolas Perruche, born in 1983 heavily disabled after a pregnancy during which his mother had contracted rubella, a disease known to be dangerous to a foetus. The mother is told, by medical error, that she had developed antibodies against the disease, which prevents her from having her pregnancy terminated. The case, which turns on the admissibility of what is soon called the *harm of being born*, and on whether this is covered by the category of what French law calls 'reparable harm', is dealt with by diverse French and European courts (1989 to 2000). It is finally decided in favour of the child being awarded indemnities. It is extensively discussed in France under diverse headings (disability; responsibility; abortion; right-to-life; eugenics). In 2002, Thomas also co-authors a critical work about the case.[6] Indicative of the fact that the matter has not reached a stage of consensus is a French bill in 2002, known as the 'loi anti-Perruche', which excludes any further claim to compensation for the harm suffered by the simple fact of being born. Going far beyond this single matter, Thomas presents a re-evaluation of the longstanding critical topic, less of the 'legal subject' properly speaking than of the *subject of rights*. Moving past the Perruche case while unfolding its lessons, he speaks for his own purposes demolishing the opinion according to which the fact of being interested in the past goes along with a preference for the past over the present, and according to which historians, insofar as they are professionally dealing with the past, are naturally conservative.

Such conclusions, Thomas explains, are unfounded. No doubt that a pre-existing nostalgic or conservative bent in a person can be aggravated by superficial historical notions; but historians are equipped to reliably resist half-baked arguments that foist upon the past, or this or that particular past, the role of a model for the present. Thomas sharply rejects the 'identity' approach to the past. Hence, historians whose grasp of their topic is not superficial are recognised by their 'differentialist' view. Instead of locating, in the bygone period they study, something like a root, an origin, an ancestor, an *archē* of the present, they recognise in it a twin of the present – something that was, at its moment, equally complete, equally satisfied with itself, equally uninterested in what lies beyond its borders, as is the period in which unfolds, now, their own lifetime. The study of history or especially legal history does not have the task of providing later generations with an earlier ideal to identify with. It helps to acknowledge identities, but it does so by supplying examples of difference and otherness. Roman law unfolds, Thomas recognises, according to genealogical 'precedent'. Yet, law's reliance on internal operations, its extreme plasticity, its increasing technicity, the emerging of a legal language (cf. Chapter 3 above), the resulting 'professional closure' (legalising ever-increasing degrees of 'denaturalisation'), let him put less weight on genealogical dependences than e.g. Foucault. Diverse accesses to the distance separating the horizons of one's lifetime from those defining the lifetime available under the late Republic and the early Empire, are provided by legal, rhetorical, literary and ideological observations of classical Rome.

Today, while common-sense historicism continues to identify, with Cicero, in the present the pupil (of the past, epitomised as its teacher), discoveries in biotechnology and genetics have imposed a moratorium on these conservative values, e.g. on absolutising 'filiation' – as Thomas calls it, following Pierre Legendre, in his polemics against this author.[7] Alongside Perruche, Thomas also evokes the legal issues brought about by sex-reassignment surgery. In the view of its adversaries, these interventions, marked by a double excess of individual desire and marketability, ought to be outlawed by further 'inalienability clauses', further extensions of the list of *res extra commercium* (=things subtracted from commodity exchange). Thomas's reply to this is another list. He catalogues the desired and commodified goods the exchange of which has long since been liberally admitted, such as the private appropriation of scarce resources, regardless of its sweeping social consequences. In comparison, he argues, the most recent bio-technological advances appear innocuous.

The history of 'subjective rights' is also that of the *subject of rights*. However, this issue appears to be far less straightforward than is often assumed. On the one hand, up to the sixteenth century, the term *subjectum iuris* referred, not at all to persons or their relationship to their rights. Instead, *subjectum iuris* referred to a theme, a question, a topic of discussion (a 'subject', precisely). On the other hand, and far more importantly, the issue of the subject of rights embodies what Thomas believes to be the most tenacious of urban myths. The advent of the 'legal subject' is habitually centre-staged as a historical watershed, the birth of legal modernity; indeed, the legal form of the opposition of the ancients to the moderns (a long-standing cultural artefact in which Thomas, however, recognises only an ideological 'product of liberalism'). That 'power-to-act', whose creation is, Thomas claims, falsely attributed to legal modernity, has in reality already been the most lasting achievement of the Roman jurists, medieval and indeed ancient, who, celebrated as champions of a rather legendary 'classical natural right doctrine', had instead *already* reformed the reference to nature, pre-empting by positivising *natura* – 'denaturing' (Thomas) it – into a device, a 'supplementary instrument' of civil law in the making.

Chapter 7, *Vitae Necisque Potestas: The Father, the State, Death* (1982/1985), the longest and most elaborated of the texts contained in this volume, offers a ground-breaking discussion of the power that Roman fathers held over their sons. It equally refers to Roman 'domestic jurisdiction'. Thomas encounters the latter in the context of his discussion of the statutory power held by a Roman father (and one should never forget that this directly concerns, as is the case of many Roman institutions, a rather small minority at the top of society) to kill his son. There is a point here that has not been understood by many specialists of Roman law, and that Thomas puts right at the centre of his inquiry: *vitae necisque potestas* was not conceived as a sanction: it was conceived as a definition. It defines a social-structural matter – namely, the question what is a father, and what a son – and thereby provides a rationale of the relation between social categories. Essential here is the fact that the paternal power of taking the son's life is not conditional on any behaviour or action of the son; it is therefore foreign to criminal law and cannot be integrated in its functioning. This is also, claims Thomas, why there is no possible overlap with jurisdictional issues. Note that both of these claims conflict with the consensus about the juridical and social context of *potestas vitae necisque*.

The category most often suggested as an overarching category is that of 'domestic jurisdiction' (which, not to be found in the sources, is yet widely accepted among twentieth-century specialists of Roman law). It boils down to the notion that, in Republican times, powerful Roman families enjoyed a socially and publicly accepted capacity to judge serious cases of outlawed behaviour right inside the family – within the 'house' – and have their judgments executed with the help of public agents. Thomas does recognise one common element between penal practices and the killing of a son according to *potestas vitae necisque*. This is the extraordinary degree of cruelty expressing itself here and there. From all other vantage points, paternal *potestas vitae necisque* over sons was categorically detached from matters of criminal law, as it required no judgment pronounced over the son, no misdeed committed by the son, no reference to the son's behaviour. The exercise of *potestas vitae necisque* is free to him who holds it (this is why it is, strictly speaking, not even an 'exercise'). While the *potestas vitae necisque* enables fathers to deal death or let live, what one searches for in vain, are any 'implementing rules'. This is why Thomas sees in *potestas vitae necisque* a definition of the respective personal legal status of Roman fathers and sons. The father's power deprives the son during his father's lifetime of any legal status, any right.

Notwithstanding this, most specialists do allocate the father's *potestas vitae necisque* over his son in the category of 'domestic jurisdiction', some claiming that it falls into the same category as, e.g., the capital punishment of the adulterous woman (the killing of the disobedient slave did not require a particular legal provision). Thomas argues, first of all, that the notion of 'domestic jurisdiction' poses the well-known historical problems attached to the retrospective use of a novel terminology: with no echo in the accessible source material, it remains, according to Thomas, questionable as to its historical legitimacy. The present chapter, as well as the following one, on parricide (in short, Chapters 7 and 8) suggest that the respective status of fathers and sons in Rome has provided one of the ground rules determining the life of wealthy Romans throughout the Republican and early imperial era, that the total disjunction without overlap of these two positions forms one of the key issues both of the evolution of Rome and the history of Roman law. Father and son: Thomas subjects the relation to a series of interrogations focusing on the relationship between public *imperium* and private *potestas*. In many cultures, the fact of dealing death carries a structural value. But Rome seems to be alone in featuring a specific legal structure in which the power of dealing death gives positive shape to the specific, 'inimitable' social bond between father and son. It is the bond itself that matters for Thomas, as it durably – and relatively independently from the events to which it gives rise – contributes to the structure of social life in Rome.

Seen through contemporary eyes, this chapter also lifts the lid upon what might be, in structural terms, the most harassing incertitude for modern observers of Roman law doctrine: has there been, as we are 'naturally' inclined to assume, such a thing as an 'integrity of law' in classical Roman times, in the way there is (or so we assume) in our own? Did classical Roman private law and Roman institutions add up to something comparable to what modern legal theorists call a 'legal *order*'? Or is the fine line separating the (neatly juridified) world as we know it, from the society of Roman antiquity located, precisely, between the modern understanding of law as a legal order covering the entirety of social relations, and the conditions of Roman society, where law might have played a very different, and possibly far less encompassing role?

It is striking, incidentally, to observe how closely Thomas's teaching on the understanding of Roman political and normative history is related to the epistemic preferences at work in Foucault. In order to discuss the pastoral-practical-ethical teaching of the Hellenistic and Roman age, Foucault sets out to emancipate the entire scope of relevant sources from the role assigned to them by the consensually accepted doctrine of the later twentieth century, which tended to reduce the issue to one single point of discussion: the transition from pagan Antiquity to early Christianity. In order to break the stalemate, Foucault refused to subject himself to the claim that constituted the compromise at its base: the overriding importance of the emergence of Christianism. In rejecting the notion of 'domestic jurisdiction', Thomas commits himself to a comparable move: that of parting with the traditional assumption of Roman law scholarship according to which Roman law and institutions form a rational and indeed responsible political-legal totality – an assumption which in turn invested the historians of Roman law with the duty of delivering their unending *laudatio* of the process of rational self-transformation triggered by Roman law.

Next to the father's power over the son's life and death, we find, among the themes of this collection, the equally quintessentially Roman preoccupation with parricide. This forms the topic of Chapter 8: *On Parricide: Political Interdiction and the Institution of the Subject* (1995). Qualified at the time as the 'unbelievable' (*incredibile*) crime, as a thing struck with unreality, having an institutionalised rejection attached to the very possibility that it could ever be imagined to happen, parricide was, at once – and apparently without the contradiction being perceived as problematic – centre-staged as all-too overly present, indeed as an event eminently and constantly haunting Roman society. Drawing the lessons of this schizoid status of a crime at the crossroad of a fanciful fixation, and a danger to the life of a whole class of Roman citizens (virtually every father of a son), Thomas moves his inquiry beyond the point at which the perspective bounces back, as it were, from the specifically outlawed parricidal deed to the action of its outlawing, of casting it into a specific crime, or from the perpetration of the parricidal act to the law prohibiting it (just as if the law, not its violation, caused the trouble, or in other words, just as if what deserved attention, was less the crime than its 'criminalisation').

Reflecting on this quid-pro-quo, Thomas branches off to a micro-study focusing upon a figure of thought familiar to many observers of law including Plato. This is a move away from fighting crime, from defending and enforcing the law, toward *accusing law*, suspecting it of effectively centre-staging that which it claims to fight; indeed, in the most extreme and accomplished version of the argument, of being the agent of the misdeed it outlaws, crime's effective origin. Obviously, Roman parricide is here only part of a much larger file. At some point, triggered by the limited success of public crime-control, which no longer appears to provide a reliable degree of prevention, it is supplemented and sidelined by a competing view that no longer asks the question of crime, but of law's combat against crime. Where law and law enforcement do not convey the notion of being successful, where the outlawed behaviour goes on unabated, where the law fails to provide an efficient way of effectively diminishing undesirable forms of behaviour, what becomes questionable is the very idea of qualifying a particular behaviour as a crime. Thomas quotes many Roman writers who all subscribe to the notion that it was *not* a good idea to make a crime of parricide: the multiplication of parricides is, they hold, the answer to its having been conceived as a crime, as the object of an explicit prohibition. Now, a prohibition that fails at the single task at which it was meant to be helpful stands in urgent need of rethinking. The task itself has not disappeared: the difficulty, for society, of coexisting with parricide, remains a major one. Is there a better chance of coming to grips with parricide through some other channel than a law against parricide? The stakes at issue are obvious enough: a society in which the relation of sons and fathers becomes unliveable is a society in danger, its social bond in crisis.

What should the *potestas vitae necisque* be compared to in current society? What is it that, today, could come close to the utter dissymmetry of the relationship between fathers and sons prevailing in Cicero's times, or Hadrian's? The question is an instance of *non liquet*, or 'doesn't flow', to cite the formula in which a classical Roman judge expressed his incapacity to decide. Preoccupations are dated: for instance, the lack of equality between men and women was not a conflictual matter in Rome, though it is today. Conversely, a father's right to deal death to his son strikes a current observer as outlandish and demented; in Rome, it defined the fundamental social bond, and any challenge would wreck the public order. Constitutions are dated as well: the Roman political entity, the city as a permanent 'public thing', is derived from the *cives* (citizens), and was an abstraction without 'subjective identity' or 'moral personality' (whereas the opposite was true of the Greek *polis*: the relation between *polis* and *polites* being based, or so he claims, upon the collective entity; the *polis* was first). Moreover, the Romans, in dealing with their city, knew of no 'metaphor', 'fiction', or proper-name based institution. Finally, the Roman lawyers were, for Thomas, not the pioneers of any 'functionalist' view of legal institutions – contrary to certain modern sociological commonplace genealogies.

Chapter 9, *Act, Agent, Society: Fault and Guilt in Roman Legal Thinking*, is the second earliest piece of the collection. Published in 1977, it was written in the context, or at the very least in the aftermath of the Paris 1968 revolution, a fact that might provide a hint toward the astonishing admission that the human person and its acts are concepts that 'remain foreign to the world of law', and subject, instead, to the definitional power of society. Thomas here takes the concept of responsibility as a testing probe and as an indicator of the way in which change and repetition, innovation and continuation, intervene in continental legal history, first within the evolution of classical Roman law, then through the consecutive cohorts of jurists and interpretational practitioners that have successively been dealing with the Roman legal *'Ur-Text'*: glossators of the twelfth and thirteenth, commentators of the fourteenth and fifteenth, humanists of the sixteenth, adepts of *usus modernus pandectarum* of the seventeenth, natural lawyers of the seventeenth and eighteenth, and pandectists of the nineteenth century.

It is well known that the Roman law has, starting with its classical original writers (way before its official compilation in the *Corpus iuris civilis*), protested its undisturbed identity. Yet, an object of 2,000 years of readings and misreadings, the evolution of Roman law has gradually bred the power *enabling law to leave Roman law behind*. The chapter offers a youthfully adventurous account of this paradoxical manoeuvre and of the eminent role that repetition plays in the history of the legal transmission in Europe. Thomas sees it as a sequence of serial re-readings of even earlier re-readings. The text, largely unchanged since the *Corpus iuris*, is overlaid by ever new strata that mediatise the reader's access. In this way, rather than as a flypaper which any legal variation or evolution is bound to get stuck on, the text functions as an enabling device, indeed as a device for enriching the text with new possibilities, functioning both as a measure and a generator of distance. Thomas, thus, suggests that Roman law never succeeded in establishing itself as a stable long-term rule (otherwise than for its name), nor in imposing an identical and invariable discipline unto every generation of young lawyers that ruminated it. For Franz Kafka, it was the sawdust, already pre-chewed by numberless earlier intakes, that every new generation of law students had to re-chew once again. For Thomas, it is a device, at once, to increase every successive generation's *distance* from the original model, and to *measure* this distance – allowing the determination of how far we have already made it on our way out of it, on our road to liberation and modernity, but also to accomplishment and perfection – toward the omnipresent, though unwritten, goal of a society-wide promotion of law.

The dimension in which Thomas shows this long process of improvement and working-through unfolding is that of responsibility. Its emergence marks the decisive step in which older sources of identity, immanent or transcendent, such as family, blood/descent, divinity, have given way to the ideal of the *homo juridicus*, a notion that is abstract, smooth, widely applicable, and able to give rise to ever newer (and more performing) societal arrangements. The *homo juridicus* – a recent, thoroughly modern, yet unscrupulously ante-dated notion that, despite its Latin name (Article 1382 of the French Civil Code, which burdens the author of a culpable action with all damages that result from it, is quoted as its exemplary expression) – heralds the advent of the age of responsibility. But responsibility is not an easy, even less an unequivocal, concept. Having channelled it through its fundamental, yet also fragile and ambivalent eighteenth-century premises, Thomas draws on the linguist Emile Benveniste and the Hellenist Jean-Pierre Vernant and their attempts of throwing light into the maze of agency, agent names and action names. Manmade events can be described as actions, which, if relevant, crystallise in things – in being. But, as well as being analysed as actions, manmade events can also be attributed to an agent, and expressed, not in terms of being, but of having.

Thomas introduces a polarity, that had not yet been carried through in the field of Latin studies, between things, that shape the actions of agents, and actions to which one relates as to something that one 'has'. This polarity between the auxiliaries to be and to have is, Thomas argues, powerfully present in Rome. The interest focuses on one or other sort of 'having'. What is fascinating is that this characteristic link between the result of an action and someone who 'has' (acted) it, involves neither responsibility (according to the term's current meaning), nor even the qualifications as deeds or misdeeds. Of the latter, the evolution of Roman law's narrative boasts a term that has survived down to our own crime-related terminology. This is the notion of a *delictum*. A *delictum* is, Thomas explains, conceived, in Rome, not as an action, but as an omission. Strictly speaking, it is necessarily the product of a lack. 'Committing a crime'; the wording fails to fit the Roman way of imagining what a crime is. Criminal (delictual) behaviour was the purloining of what belongs from where it belongs. Someone omits to leave a thing where it was. The 'external' vision, Thomas explains, of an act or omission, does not generate a generic concept of fault, nor an organising individual, or an internal responsibility or universal agency. This explains why Roman law proceeds with lists, cataloguing the different juridical *topoi*, multiplying in time, synthesising each time an act to an agent. The individual is, hence, not a 'separate' psychological or moral being.

In the final essay, Chapter 10, *The Slave's Body and its Work in Rome: On Analysing a Juridical Dissociation* (2002), Thomas establishes an astonishing intersection between the history of ancient slavery and modern labour law. While a lot of research had been done on ancient slavery and slave labour in antiquity, another more complicated question has not received any comparable amount of attention: what is it that has prevented ancient, especially Roman society, from construing a dependable, load-based rather than pain-based, concept of work? The answer to this, as Thomas presents it, is not simple.

The analysis of the classical Roman jurists' dealings with the issue shows that work was, to some hitherto unsuspected extent, a massive reality in Rome, that it was at stake in a large number of everyday transactions, which jurists were continuously involved in arranging, homogenising, rationalising and conceptualising. At the same time, slavery and slave labour were for a long time the dominating themes of historical and legal historical research. This foregrounded the dichotomy between societies based on slavery and societies without slavery. A gaze into the current context poses the question as to what extent the claimed bipartition of the slavery-societies of past and present post-abolition societies has the side-effect of obfuscating relevant empirical features and situations. Working conditions in Amazon warehouses, to take only one out of numberless instances, appear to indicate the subtleness of the transitions between slavery conditions and non-slavery conditions, and a certain indifference to other features. The main question, however, is whether it had been premature to celebrate the successful abolition of slavery as long as not all the aspirations inherent in the abolitionist agenda are realised plainly and without remainder. Thomas's inquiry into the pre-history, in classical Roman law, of certain limited yet essential fractions of modern labour law, focuses, based upon extensive documentation, on the correspondences between the efforts of the Roman jurists to organise and juridify the respective rights in a slave, held partly by the owner of the slave and partly by the renter of the slave's workforce, in comparison to the efforts of modern labour law to define the rights a worker can claim, in their own person, against their employer. This should not be understood only or principally as a relativisation of the boundary between the fate of the Roman working slaves (whose duties and work conditions are negotiated exclusively between their two masters) and that of employees negotiating with their employer, but as an exercise in empirical juridical genealogy, as an opening to unexpected but possibly enlightening family resemblances, and as a challenge to – and a resistance against – cross-cultural blind spots (or *epistemological obstacles*). Comparing nowadays contracts over work between workers and employers, with Roman contracts over work between slave employers and slave owners, is predicated upon steering clear of the one issue that had been considered for centuries as the decisive one: slavery or freedom, having or not having the right of speaking for oneself. What allows Thomas to draw, in the space of a few pages, the axis aligning work-related disputes then and now, is to keep this question in suspense. Roman slave-owners, negotiating the working conditions of their slave with the renter of their workforce, indisputably share with modern and current workers, acting and speaking for themselves, a common interest in maintaining health and other conditions indispensable for the work to be completed. The originality of Thomas's approach is doubtlessly proportionate to the issue of slavery, the abolition that very recently put an end to it, the revulsion it causes, the emergence of modern slavery, slavery's afterlife as racism, and the light cast on ancient slavery by all of these. The superabundantly justified horror of including ancient slavery (despite the absence in it of race and racism) had put a lid on the study of Roman work.

The linguistic references themselves, the Latin *labor*, the

Greek *ponos*, were seen as exclusively connected to slavery by a one-to-one-relation. Pain alone was considered the measure of work – not workload, output, or value. The subordination of the worker under the master's unlimited power over the workforce embodied in his slave labourer was centre-staged. Though no one doubts that the slave at work was monitored, not by the owner/master, but by a manager in charge (generally another slave), what caught and kept modern historians' attention were the property rights in the labourer-slave. Was this because they fitted so well into the simple category 'infra-' vs 'superstructure'? At any rate, the word *operae*, designating the product-, result- and task-related activity, based on function and subject to complex legal definitions concerning the features that fall today under the notion of 'work', is rarely referred to. Twentieth-century writers on Roman society and its relation to work generally choose to follow and elaborate the notion that work and slavery are indissolubly intertwined in Roman antiquity. This is in part mythological; even so, it might be the best way to proceed if one wishes to focus on the distance of present and past, which many consider as the historian's key task. The relationship between slavery and the *operae* contract is effectively complex. Free persons, in full control of their own free status, can legally enter *operae* contracts, by leasing their workforce. Thomas's interest as a historian is not that of deepening the distance between 'them' and 'us', the classical Romans and the modern. What retains his attention, are the unsuspected proximities as much as the distances. This is why he was attracted by the correspondences between the functional and juridical autonomy that defines the sphere of work in our days, and the Roman way of dealing with work.

Thomas's main topic in the Roman culture of work was not *labor*, the painful exaction, but work, specifically the *operae* contract and the legal relationship involving a certain workload to be delivered. *Operae* contracts admitted human beings of two different status: free persons willing to sign an *operae* contract over their own workforce, and slaves, subject to an *operae* contract between a slave owner and a slave renter (or sometimes between two slave renters). In both cases, there is an agreement about human workforce. As far as slaves are concerned, most such transactions passed through the Roman legal concept of *ususfructus*. Yet, based on juristic ground-work that dates from the time of Emperor Augustus, just on the threshold between BCE and CE, the domain of *ususfructus* is itself split into two neatly separated subsets, one referring to in-house use (*usus*); the slave is in this case serving in the owner's family (the category is 'enjoyment'); the other one, *fructus*, refers to the 'fruit' of work properly speaking. Only work, having its price on the market, is a matter of profit and can be the object of an *operae* contract.

This collection, thus, presents ten essays devoted by French jurist and Roman law scholar Yan Thomas to as many different Romanist debates and problem structures of the past decades. They provide kaleidoscopic evidence of the vast realm of potential lessons to be learnt about humankind and human beings as subjects of law and politics, lessons kept in store by the in-depth study of earlier normative formations, such as Roman law (classical, medieval, modern). They also show an exemplarily innovative thinker at the height of his acumen and audacity, and a resolute sceptic with respect to the sacrosanct sufficiency that always claims to be inbuilt in the state of scholarship-as-it-stands. Roman law scholarship has not always been a field predestined for 'risky' innovative research. Being built upon the overpowering achievements of earlier pioneers, it again and again struggles with a structural debt crisis, and the resulting inertia. The attempt, on the other hand, to simply graft onto the study of past normative orders the protocols of modern science, only gives rise to the rather colonial vision of the still-unknown as a borderless continent awaiting its discovery by 'scientific mastery' – a vision which amalgamates a utopian project with a dystopian phantasm. Law is gifted with a well-nigh infectious ability of making sense. The past, in comparison, is small fry. But Roman law, as traditional legal history sees it, cumulates both sense-making attributions, being quintessentially law, and, given its unequalled perfection, equally quintessentially prevented from ever joining the past. There are opponents; they loudly denounce here an attitude of Roman-centric exceptionalism and privilege. We know their counter-suggestion: to forget Roman law altogether. Thomas proposes a third way. Roman law makes sense *because* it is past. Being different from the law 'as we know it', while offering itself as an object of study, it supplies its students precisely with the opportunity of getting knowledge of the law of which we claim that it is the law 'as we know it'.

Notes

1. For a bibliography of Thomas's work, see http://cenj.ehess.fr/ index.php?291.
2. 2012, p. 103.
3. See, for instance, Thomas, 1973.
4. 1888.
5. Ibid., p. 14.
6. Thomas and Cayla, 2002.
7. Legendre, 1996.

Bibliography

Legendre, P. (1996) *Filiation − Fondement généalogique de la psychanalyse*, par A. Papageorgiou-Legendre, Paris, Fayard.

Madero, M. (2012) 'Interpreting the Western Legal Tradition: Reading the Work of Yan Thomas', trans. Kathleen Guilloux, 67 *Annales. Histoire, Sciences Sociales*, pp. 103–32.

Maitland, F. W. (1888) *Why the History of the English Law Is Not Written*, Inaugural Lecture, Cambridge, Cambridge University Press.

Thomas, Y. and O. Cayla (2002) *Du droit de ne pas naître. À propos de l'affaire Perruche*, Paris, Gallimard.

Thomas, Y. (1973) 'La langue du droit romain. Problèmes et méthodes', 18 *Archives de philosophie du droit*, pp. 103–25.

One

The Contrivances of Legal Institutions: Studies in Roman Law

This volume deals with the institution. Its object is thus the notion that the forms of social life are constructed forms, not spontaneous forms. The institution, as seen from the point of view of a jurist, is at the heart of my work. Throughout Western history, the law has served as the medium par excellence for institutional construction work, construing montages made of words. These words affirm what they affirm. Yet, in addition, they are also equipped with the singular capacity of giving existence to that which they affirm, provided they are uttered by holders of the power to do so. In such a way that the social relations they construe, appear to boil down to one single compassing discourse, at once coherent, rational and effective.

In order to put a label on this effect of the law, the tradition – Latin, Roman, medieval – generally makes use of the formula *ars iuris*. The 'juridical art' to which this refers, was both a systematic body of knowledge that has its foundation in the act of relating and ordering texts, and a technical know-how to put its interpretations in the service of practice. This 'Law as art' is thus to understand both as the exercise of giving form to social objects, as a remodelling of reality by means of verbal artifice used in alliance with the special powers of effect-generating speech, and at the same time as the creation and the ordering of a social world that proceeds by a steady effort of redefining and requalifying its components. Such an effort, to be sure, does not happen by means of any immediate experience. Rather, it happens in explicit opposition and in direct contrast to the hypothesis of immediate experience, in contrast especially to any notion of an immediate common social sense. As will be shown, law separates that which appears as indistinct, divides up that which the claim of such a social sense common to all ventures tends to amalgamate in one undifferentiated totality.

The inquiries that I am conducting in these studies are committed to this wager. It is by referring to the tradition of Roman law that they intend to underline an essential feature of Western social organisation, a feature that historical anthropology, far more preoccupied with archaic foundations than with modernity, has, at large, been rather inclined to leave aside. What these studies try to deliver is an account, both technically concrete and methodically conscientious, of the manner in which law's multiple separations and disjunctions proceed, when they try to institute the social bond in a rationalised world – a world which is one of separation, rather than of fusion. My work is conducted through the analysis of the ways and moves through which concrete juridical objects have been construed. What manifests itself in this choice is surely a taste for the concrete. Yet, at the same time, what has guided me, as well, was my conviction that any purely theoretical – or in other words purely doctrinal – attempt to understand politics and law inevitably leads to the impasse of generalisation, not to mention the lethal banality that all general approaches necessarily end up with. Rather than offering any all-inclusive lessons, the task that seemed to me desirable is that of multiplying specific lines of attack. It is after all a well-known fact that, as soon as one comes up with a general theory of law, of politics, etc., it so happens that the aspiration of carefully connecting all the features of a topic, only gives rise, in the end, to some comprehensive interpretation of the world at large, in other words to a meta-discourse, and as everyone knows, for a meta-discourse, any other meta-discourse can effortlessly substitute itself. At the same time, this reasoning allowed me to spare my readers all accounts of what law is, of what law is needed for, etc. All that awaits them are piecemeal analyses of this or that specific legal construction, where each bit is taken out from (and trying to elucidate, in return) this or that specific moment within a specific history, chosen according to the efforts of imagination and complexity, that these histories, in their making, depended upon.

Historical disciplines, and the human sciences in particular, surely strive to establish that, of the factors determining the career of societies, none lies beyond the reach of the highly sophisticated elaborations which are manufactured by culture. This is true even where, as is the case here, the term 'culture' is used in the restrictive sense in which it only applies to so-called 'erudite culture'. It is, however, the world of institutions that allows us to get access to a far higher level of consciousness of artifice. Here, society reveals itself as being fabricated from the outside, as it were, employing the equipment of a machinery. The decisive aspect of this machinery, the mythological one, is only ever encountered by the various well-known theories of sovereignty. What we are interested in, is, on the contrary, the properly technical dimension of the matter. In the world of institutions, there is nothing that can claim the indisputable status of a 'fact'. The very idea of a social fact (and, a fortiori, that of a total social fact) simply makes no sense, once one looks at it from this perspective. From the institutional angle, a social fact exists at best to the extent that it is qualified and pre-formed according to categories that relate to a judgement dealing with value, a practical judgement in other words. In order to judge, it is necessary to distinguish; in order to act, it is necessary to separate. In an inquiry like this there is no way to connect its objects apart from supposing that they form unending chains of interdependencies. Facts are constrained by heteronomous signifiers. It is through the latter alone that they are constituted as distinct entities. Which is precisely the point that we need to understand.

It surely cannot be the legal historian's aim to skip these construction works under the excuse that they are but arti-ficial stage settings, or that they screen and obscure a state of things which might otherwise enable us to grasp reality unvarnished, in other words to capture the naked truth of reality, itself being understood as a matter of pure essence. A whole mythology that dates back to the nineteenth century, and that has its roots in particular in German idealism, still exercises its censorship today, even within current legal-historical studies: we only have to look at doctrines such as that of the spontaneity of law, of its immanence in the social, of the roots of law in an immemorial and fundamental cul-tural ground. Think of the myth of legal custom having grown out of the ancestral soil, of the myth of organic communities, or of this whole dream, in no way especially democratic, according to which the social per se is a thing that is unmediated and transparent. What legal history provides us with is, on the contrary, a pathway to a disenchanted world, in which collective destiny manifests the arbitrary nature of its practices, and to a knowledge that is increasingly specialised and increasingly inaccessible to all. It is a world that has indeed been prepared and fabricated for a long time, starting in Roman antiquity, passing through medieval scholasticism, ending up in the laboratory of the jurists as specialists and technicians of division/separation. Among other topics, our investigations address the divide between labour and work, the distinction between body and commodity, those through which the subject has been instituted as the subject of prohibitions or divisions – divisions between father and son, between father and mother, between citizen and foreigner, etc. Above all, they try to examine the divisions between the legal and the illegal, law and its transgression, power and its subjects. To summarise matters, I would say that the point I am most interested in is the impact of the fact itself, the element of arbitrariness that is always assumed as such in processes of decision making, looking at a world that is not only one of knowledge but, first of all, one of decision. The ultimate aim of my attempts therefore addresses the constitutive arbitrariness of the juridical art, and the question of what distinguishes these power techniques from the methods of speculative knowledge acquisition.

In sum, my task is to study – up-close, as through a magnifying glass – a number of very ancient institutional objects, forged within the Western scholarly tradition in the studies of the jurists. This notion of an *object* in law is among those that I will especially insist on. Legal history, I think, should busy itself with objects much more than with ideas. This is not meant in the sense that it has to be a sociologising history. We never get access to unmediated social relations or social practices; what we do get access to are formal entities: nature, the person, the subject, work, filiation, prohibition, law, etc., and, within them, the infinitely numerous heterogeneous relations to which they give rise. Yet, these entities are given by the law and the jurists a unity of qualification and significance which renders possible judgement and rational decision, and which, at the same time, makes of them genuine entities, autonomous objects that are, as such, no less real than others. It is for this reason that I did not want to write a history of ideas nor, even less, a history of doctrines. Instead, I wanted to show how institutional objects, such as nature, such as the person, the subject, prohibition, filiation, origin, law, were brought into existence, and how they were awarded a real existence – an existence that has governed our own existence for a long time. I am therefore always striving to contextual-ise, to precisely trace the contours of the objects with which I am engaging. It is, however, true that all one can expect to be given through these objects is no more than a partial approxi-mation of what is called law.

One count on which my work surely has no claim to deliver any contribution is an ability to define anthropological or cultural invariants, or to determine their gradual build-up over time. Instead, my aim is to depict ancient models for the construction of singular institutional objects, whose manner of elaboration, more than their content, are of interest to us today. Consider, for example, the theme of the construction of law as an emancipation from a natural order of things, or the theme of the construction of the juridical fiction as an instrument destined to act counter to reality, to subject reality to negation; consider the theme of the constitution of legal agents as *persons*, which results in unfolding a second layer over the layer of that of distinct individuals – a fold enabling each of us to pass from the singular to the univer-sal and from the concrete to the abstract. Or consider the reification of labour as a 'thing', separate from the working body. Or the apparatus of the traditional subjective economy that, by means of filiation, locks every legal subject between the two opposite poles of autonomy and heteronomy – cf. the autonomy of the father in relation to the heteronomy of the son, itself taking place inside an equally constructed division of the sexes. The bond of filiation inscribes itself in a vast network of genealogical montages that allow us to follow up their trace until we reach the idea of *origin*, which, as a form, is incidentally more ancient than that of nationality.

The material that we encounter in all of these corresponds to a textual tradition. It is in other words a nearly permanent continuity of texts – of texts that are themselves compositions made of slightly older texts; in sum, a vast history of interpretations that proceed by means of combinations and approximations of allegations and arguments that reach beyond any age. Of particular importance are the texts of the *Corpus iuris civilis*, jurisprudential and legislative texts redacted between the first and the third century CE, and later – during the first third of the sixth century – compiled by Emperor Justinian, to be, much later again, since the twelfth century, continuously glossed and commented upon in Western universities, until being finally incorporated into all of the juridical, political and even philosophical literature of modern continental Europe, during the era of national codifications, which spans from the late eighteenth to the latest nineteenth century. In the development of this ancient body, a common foundation is slowly constructed, arranged, woven together out of accumulated references. Juridical erudition precisely aims to bring to light some of these Roman-Scholastic references, even if such elaborations were later covered over and hidden by other constructions, especially that of the national, centralised state. This is archaeological work. Legal historians should be attentive to the history of the codified material that serves to fabricate those institutional things out of which social organisations are formed. They must also encounter, beneath what this or that author says, those minuscule elements whose meaning has not ceased to change over time, but which, nevertheless, constitute one continuous subtext. Their method is necessarily a method of juridical philology. It privileges those notions inscribed in words and even more those formulas transported from one text to another, those abstractions taken from the ideological contexts within which words and formulas are re-employed. There is no doubt that this codified material puts us in constant contact with a history of the elements of which institutions are built. Any 'ideas' crossing the skies over them are already flying in their service.

Two

Legal History for Historians: A Presentation

Like any sociologist or historian, the legal historian studies social practices, law being unquestionably a social practice. And yet, whether they are arguing the case of law or against it, identifying agents or actions is not properly speaking the task that legal historians assign themselves; on the contrary, they are loath to be peddlers of a transparency that would only obfuscate, precisely, the division between law and reality, between norms and facts, between representation and presence. It is this transparency to which legal historians object; if they choose to make the law their object of study, it is in order to expose it. Far from venturing to uncover, beneath the law's abstractions (rules, procedures, concepts, systems of categories), the reality of a social game in which the irreducible singularity of its actors and the irreducible reality of their relations are finally given full visibility, legal historians suspend and temporarily set aside this singularity as well as this reality. They do so, not, of course, because they would deny that the law is connected to concrete referents, which would be an absurd thing to do. They do so in order to describe the practical effects of all the formal mediations that are provided by the law between subjects and other subjects, between society and itself. The legal historian, in short, describes the work by which the law acts upon these referents, and reacts to them, by which it effectively transforms them – in the manner in which every social technique transforms the society to which it refers, and upon which, at the same time, it operates.

It is clear to everyone today that law touches all aspects of social life: economic, cultural, religious, technical, even scientific, as well as virtually anything that is produced or made to happen in our societies. Yet, it is from a very specific point of view that law pertains to these. It defines the elementary forms to which, in the eyes of a judge, the otherwise numberless quantity of factual situations from which legal disputes arise, needs to be reduced. It is relatively easy to discern that legal disputes are decided by means of rules. This aspect of normativity, inescapably evident to anyone, has long been instrumental in fostering the belief that in order to identify the legal practices which are relevant for sociologists and historians, it is sufficient to juxtapose the description of norms with the description of their social fields of application. The description of the disparities between the two registers, plus the analysis of the ways in which the subjects internalise norms and learn to achieve strategic mastery over them (according e.g. to the theory developed by Pierre Bourdieu) has served for a long time, and still serves today, as the panacea wielded by those who attempt to integrate law into the human sciences. The jurists for their part, especially the positivist jurists of the Kelsenian school, were, from this point of view, barely more advanced: the concept of *standards* (or *norms*) *of conduct*, of Kantian inspiration, considers the duality of *is* and *ought* from the angle of a pressure exercised by the second over the first, in a way that might be more or less successful or effective according to the situation. But the question of the law is far from exhausted once one has discovered the duality of facts and norms, or even tried to smooth it. The difficulty of law – and of its history – lies elsewhere. It is a corollary of the logic at work wherever norms are put into operation. Their operation is the reformatting of facts – the facts that are brought before the courts. For norms do not apply directly to facts, which are infinitely diverse and polymorphous; just as norms do not immediately address subjects, who are irreducibly singular. Rather, norms apply to the paradigmatic situations to which legal interpreters reduce the facts by imposing upon them a form that makes them suitable to a rule, at the same time as they project the rule's outlines upon them. Similarly, norms are applied to legal subjects, who are different from the empirical individuals themselves, just as, grammatically, the subject of a sentence is different from the singular person that it refers to. The juridical operation does not consist in foisting law upon facts, which would be unthinkable and impossible. Rather, the

8

juridical operation is an exercise in reconfiguration: it remodels the facts in order to qualify them so as to make them fit into the practical value judgement it imposes. This operation can be analysed from a nominalist point of view: the facts do not receive a name that corresponds to their nature, but one that suits the treatment to which one wants to subject them.[1] However, it can also be analysed from the point of view of the effectiveness of the juridical operation and of the forms it gives rise to, independently from the constraint the law exercises over it. Juridical qualification provides social life with a form, it cuts out and defines entities and relations, such as the person, commodity, property, contract, work, representation, etc., each of which is necessary to enable law's variable practical operations, which thereby become reality.

The difficulty of conceiving the concrete level of reality in which these forms operate is all the greater because they are less concepts than instruments. Effectively, the categories of qualification do not serve to know things but rather to evaluate things in order to settle the disputes that have arisen over them – and thus to *produce things differently* from what they are outside of the law and its narrow and precise measure. Even the very notion of a *legal category*, routinely used by lawyers, is quite misleading, since it tends to substitute, for law's practical action of evaluation and decision-making, a concept of something that is happening at the level of pure knowledge. To the simplification delivered by the duality of *is* and *ought* that dissolves the legal object in the irreducible distance between facts and norms (and regardless of the fact that this duality itself is a historical construction with effects that have been decisive within Western evolution, as has been shown by Alain Boureau), a second simplification is now added, one that carries the risk of reducing the legal object to its linguistic representations. Even if it borrows from the methods of historical semantics – and it can barely avoid doing so – it is not the case that legal history counts among its callings the discovery of meanings, whether for the sake of deciphering the modes of representation of the world, or of furthering our knowledge of the world. For while its most tenacious element-units (person, property, contract, etc.) also turn out to be concepts with a very long linguistic history, we must not lose sight of what they are in law – namely, first and foremost, accumulated layers of congealed decisions. Nor is the idea of a conceptual history in the sense of Koselleck any more fitted to the specific exigencies of law, than is the history of the divisions that rule the relation between reality and normativity.

There are, in our societies, other procedures of qualification, outside of the law, as well. These co-exist with legal qualifications. Lawyers in France sometimes qualify them as 'pre-qualifications'. There exist other formats or other manners of reformatting, other non-legal ways of producing typical situations – including non-legal ways of realising values authorised by judgements (as shown by the work of Boltanski and Thevenot).[2] All of this goes without saying. What one calls the law is particular in the sense that it relates to a specific inclusive order of formatting, the one that applies to situations destined to be judged legally and only legally. This refers less to a state monopoly of power than to a method of producing such a coherence of qualifications as required by the task of rendering ultimate judgements about values. Wherever in a given political entity, in Western societies at least, a conflict sets in opposition, not only individuals or groups (whose disputes refer to an order of qualification and evaluation), but also those very norms and qualifications themselves, it falls into the exclusive purview of the law to deliver a decision. What constitutes the matter of law is thus the bulk of procedures and categories of qualification, in the broadest sense. They constitute – up to this day, at least – the political kernel of things legal.

That these procedures find their place in society goes once again without saying, and the observation that, this being so, they are 'social', is so obvious and so general that it does not advance us any further than the tautology *'ubi societas ibi ius* (where society, there law)', which everyone knows by heart. What is at stake when we are dealing with law is not law's indisputable social nature, it is the legal shape of societies – of some of them at least, ours certainly included. Now, that which today appears as obvious to the contributors of this special issue of the *Annales*, had not been obvious yesterday – certainly not in those trends of legal historiography which, under the pretext of doing history, have developed an entire ideology of the social spontaneity of law. For a long time, the law has constituted a world neglected by historians. They thought that what was to be found in it are but a number of immediately available sources to be used by the history of social practices, by the history of institutions and politics, or indeed by the history of ideas. For lack of the ability to transcend an approach that takes texts as mere documents carrying information, or for lack of paying attention to the very forms – the procedures and schemes of qualification – that are in charge of channelling and filtering the facts to assure the practical enforcement of legal decisions, one neglected the task of fully appraising the scope of law understood as a formal organisation, which, far beyond simply describing the world, served first of all to produce it. Time and again, researchers, subject to the belief that law was a means of gaining access to the knowledge of the practices, the mentalities, or the ideas which tended to constitute the object of their studies, lost sight of the immediately operative (only indirectly cognitive) significance of the legal texts they used, failing to take into account that these practices, mentalities and ideas, operate on a wholly different level than where they located them. Historians have sometimes produced great books writing under this misunderstanding, but a misunderstanding it was nonetheless.

The attention given to the law's formal operations, and to the procedural and practical contexts where these operations are located, is what brought the authors of the present issue of the revue *Annales* together. If one refuses to apportion this particular attention to forms and operations, one considers legal history in a way that mistakes its object for something it is not. The question of what continues to distinguish jurists who are interested in history – traditionally called legal historians – from historians who are interested in law, is still an open one. Legal historians, in the restrictive and traditional sense of the word that is relevant in this context, are – irrespective of whether or not they so claim – not historians of society, not historians of the economy, of culture, of science, of religion, of aesthetic productions or any other aspect of human practice. Are legal historians properly speaking only those dealing with the finite number of *forms* put into action for the task of submitting the facts that arise, in each and every one of these fields of activity, from their subjection to the unique overall category of jurisdiction and the qualifications thereby obtained? The historical knowledge of law is, in other words, but the knowledge of the historical expressions that these forms, their connections, their systems perhaps, have taken. As to the *historians* who are interested in law, who alone may be called 'generalists', it can be said that, even where they are interested in law just because of the weirdness, or the narrowness, of the law's approach to things, this interest in law remains for them subordinated to the imperatives of comparison. They alone are able to undertake the work required by this interest in the comparison with other, competing normative approaches, to which they are devoting themselves, with respect to each of the societies they study, including our own.

Any effort that lawyers make in order to help historians to get hold of the nature of this or that new perspective of their own historic discipline, will be returned to them a hundredfold.

Notes

1. See Olivier Cayla, 'La qualification, ou la vérité du droit', *Droits. Revue française de théorie juridique*, 18, 1994, pp. 3–18.
2. Luc Boltanski and Laurent Thévenot, *De la justification. Les économies de la grandeur*, Paris (Gallimard) 1991.

Three

The Language of Roman Law: Problems and Methods

Rare are the jurists who are aware of the methodological cul-de-sac where they are led by the refusal to accept a linguistic approach to the law. Italian linguist Antonio Carcaterra's substantial work on the subject draws its significance from this situation. Carcaterra's oeuvre, the novel perspective it imparts on legal research at large, but in particular on the research on Roman law, its exemplary presentation of a resolutely semantics-based approach to Roman law, deserves an extensive presentation in this special issue addressing law and language, of the *Archives d'histoire du droit*.

By their attempt to bring to light the meaning of fundamental concepts of Roman law, Carcaterra's studies venture to lift them out of the deep ruts into which they had sunk under the weight of the exercise of traditional legal-dogmatic attitudes. His studies of possession, good faith, deceit,[1] illustrate the defining features of a new way of studying Roman law. Its originality is owed, less to any achievements in the usual repetition of questions already discussed a thousand times (as happens often in the field), than to the challenge it poses to the general refusal to address certain preliminary issues, and the effect of this refusal, which consists in keeping the scientific effort a prisoner of its own initial errors.

The huge progress that the systematic application of the most elaborated philological methods has brought to the knowledge of Roman law is no secret to anyone. Great German and Italian scholars have been successful by means of a rigorous inquiry into the issue of interpolations – that is, in establishing, with some certainty, what had been the classical state of the texts compiled under Justinian, as opposed to the text presented in Justinian's compilation itself. On the basis of more certain material it had become possible to unveil the essential features of such fundamental institutions as, for example, the system of contracts, transfers, easements, procedural mechanisms, etc., knowledge of which had previously been beset with uncertainty. And yet, with some fortunate exceptions, and despite the limits imposed upon anachronism by the available knowledge today relating to the numerous historical layers concealed below the more tumultuous aspect of the texts, many works, although highly qualified otherwise, have been smothered by the weight of the very problems that they ventured to solve. All of this was, in a sense, natural. The questions were such that the mere ability to formulate them presupposed the fact that a range of far more difficult and more necessary questions had been previously resolved.

Roman law texts were interrogated,[2] generally speaking, in a way that suggested that it was up to them to shoulder the burden of answering for the existence of the past-related problems that posed themselves today. Seen from this angle, Roman law appeared in the guise of the law's youth, its prime seed. Contract, the autonomy of the will, the capacity of the legal subject, subjective rights,[3] all of these elements, essential insofar as without them a culture of law cannot effectively exist, hovered in the limbo of a marvellous infancy; courtesy of its future developments, it was fated to live up, one day, to the beautifully mature definitive stage that shines from the pages of the French Civil Code. For the specialists of Roman law, the task had been that of discovering the origin of the dogmas of their own time in a golden age of law, hence to solemnly enshrine, at the price of the abolition of history, the spirit of law with its eternal logic, the eternal axiology of the principles of law, from where the liberal ideology draws the entirety of its metaphysics.[4]

On a purely methodological level, what one finds in these weighty debates are attempts to answer a range of questions that starts with the one, ever-unformulated question of the very existence of the problems under scrutiny – a question that steadfastly refuses to present itself. We note an extremely rich body of science and erudition, suspended within a space of paradisiac absence of a problem (though you can say, as well – the result being the same in both cases – within a space that is so overcrowded with problems, there is no one who cares enough to check whether there exists any compelling reason for a problem to be posed).[5]

One of the merits of Carcaterra's work resides precisely in the fact that he proposes a rigorous method to define the object that a specialist of Roman law intends to study; more exactly, that he poses the question that is relevant for this view. A researcher dealing with the texts of the *Corpus iuris* finds himself immediately confronted with problems of meaning: the question of the question is, therefore, necessarily a semantic one, a question that makes necessary a recourse, however succinct, to the resources of linguistics.

Thus, the prejudgement sees in *dolus bonus* a reference, emanating from the legal order, to a set of behaviours that are admitted in the environing social conceptions. This hypothesis (not unlike the case of that which epitomises, in French law, the standard of a *'bon père de famille* [good family father]' is based upon a simple impression: that *bonus/bon*/good is not a legal term; if *bonus* is not a legal term – or so it is concluded – it can find its referent only in some common pool of moral values. One can easily see how this solution, reasonable in appearance, leaves unsolved the preliminary question: *is 'bonus'* a legal term? The fact is that Antonio Carcaterra, to whose work the present study tries to draw attention, shows that this adjective, *'bonus'*, denotes, in the Roman legal text, very exactly the quality of what is conformable to the norms of positive law that rule the matter at stake.[6] The call to a 'social conscience', is only a product of the *pandektistische Schule*; in our view, and even without at all touching the issue of 'ideology', it is the result of an elementary epistemological mistake: that of narrowing one's own horizon by identifying it with the limits of 'good sense'.[7]

The same error, though here with considerably heavier consequences, prevails over the case of faith (*fides*) and of the actions in good faith attached to the *fides*. Here, it was tempting to stick to that which seems, at first sight, obvious: *fides*, a religious and moral value, reinforced by *bona*, is conflated, in the language of law, with one of the basic concepts of the Roman axiological vocabulary. Since it goes without saying that a legal obligation cannot arise from a legal norm, in the absence of a *lex*, good faith (*bona fides*) is cast in the role of the source from where springs an *oportere* (a 'needs to be done'), i.e. the moral standard that springs up as a supplement where the law remains silent. Thus, once the old legitimate actions have revealed themselves to be insufficient, the *praetor* had to allow that relations lacking a legal sanction be invested with the legal protection of which they stood in need. There remains the question of the base upon which the ensuing considerable expansion of law (and let us not forget that we were dealing with such staple matters as sale, lease, mandate, etc.) is implemented? On the base, obviously, of that very same good faith. The action *formulae* give us a hint of their importance:

> *Quidquid ob eam rem N. Negidium A. Agerio dare facere oportet ex fide bona, id . . . condemna* (Judge, condemn NN to hand over to, or perform for, AA anything that he owes him by good faith . . .).

This position, prevalent within the doctrinal debate,[8] is based on the postulate according to which it is excluded that an autonomous legal meaning can operate under the cover of a word that is borrowed from the lexicon of religious and moral values; this postulate involves the following corollary: failing any other civil source of obligation, it is morality that can be used directly[9] as a valid legal foundation.[10] Once again, the starting point is not discussed. This starting point is the question of whether there is not a specific meaning of *fides* whenever it is used in legal contexts? In such contexts, does the *bona fides* not lose its religious and moral aura? Is it not transformed, by the language of the law, into a purely technical concept, one that is – at best – very distantly related to the more elevated and noble extra-legal *fides*, and which there is no longer occasion to invoke in this context?

This is the fundamental problem to which Carcaterra has seen himself confronted. A rigorous in-depth study of semantics, unprecedented in this context, allows him to conclude that the *oportere ex fide bona* of the formula does not refer to an extra-legal notion of good faith: the *fides bona* does not give rise to a non-legal *oportere*. Instead, it is a hermeneutic device, a criterion that is imposed on the judge by the *praetor*.[11] The interpretation of the *negotium*, the transaction subjected to his judgment, will have to obey the legal criterion of good faith,

which is a criterion in the service of extensive interpretation (*interpretatio plenior*, as opposed to a criterion of strict
interpretation).

The good faith of the *bonae fidei iudicia*, i.e., the judgments
according to good faith, is thus, technically speaking, exactly
the interpretational criterion that is conformable to the *summa
vis*[12] (the fullest significance, the entire scope) of the legal
action formula that contains, this time, all the elements of
the dispute, the *quid actum est* (what has happened), the deal
(*negotium*) itself in all its aspects (and not only the solemn
formula, i.e. the words alone, as it is the case of the actions of
strict law).

The 'myth of good faith'[13] has thus been debunked. This
ineffable good faith, of which no Roman law scholar has ever
been able to give a definition other than in the vaguest of
terms,[14] is treated by the author in reply to a preliminary question: suppose the term refers back to the sense defined by the
legal order itself, how can its meaning be recognised? Cicero,
Gaius, the compilers of the *Digest*, have left us a number of
legal definitions:[15] yet, most of the decisive Roman legal terms
(e.g. *possessio, oportere, res, causa*, etc.) remain in shadow, more
exactly in the state of implicit definitions. It is up to the legal
interpreter to discover the meaning, by way of a systematic
study of the contexts, or by establishing the relations to the
various institutions, or else through meaningful hypotheses;
inevitably, this will lead him up to a semantic analysis, and
therefore require him to tackle the problems which only a
preliminary theoretical reflection enables the researcher to
confront. Thus, in matters of good faith, the question of the
question is: does the existence, within the legal terminology,
of a word borrowed from the axiological vocabulary, necessarily imply, on the side of the legal order, a semantic referral
to the axiological 'common value' of this word? Or, more
generally speaking, do the legal terms derived from common
language (cf. words rooted in the religious, moral, social, conventional, etc., sphere) retain their original meaning, when
they are used in their new legal context? Are they not, on the
contrary, once they are part of the law, replaced with what
one might call a social-meaning-derived legal neologism?

These are questions of method. The problem with
which Antonio Carcaterra has been confronted is one of

epistemology. Starting from a number of limited inquiries in specific institutions and concepts, he had to commit himself to a preliminary work, in order to base his results on serious foundations. This – locating one's first object in the language of law – is indeed the task to which a legal historian should devote his first efforts. In Carcaterra's case, it has resulted in two important works, which carry an immense weight for the Roman law scholar. Both of them are dedicated to the study of law as a specific language and to linguistic method as a channel for law's singularity.[16]

These two works are not analytically dissociable. Together, they form a coherent set whose spirit we shall try to respect in broaching the points that appear essential in our eyes, as they constitute the frame of their respective developments. To this end, and to avoid repetitions and overlaps, but especially to restore the intrinsic order of the problems studied, we opt to reduce the outline of their presentation to their basic components which, subject to the tortuosities of a thought subject to returns and anticipations, is not in all instances visible in all its clarity.

I. Causes of the distance between common Latin and the Latin of the Roman legal system

There is, at first sight, no such thing as a particular way of speaking that would be specific to law. A lawyer who has to deal with a litigant unhappy about the use of jargon that he fails to understand, will only reply that, within a profession, one has to call things by their name – a medical practitioner, after all, does not proceed otherwise. But the debate, thus far, deals in its entirety with those technical terms that any vocational activity, from a certain level of complexity onward, cannot help grafting upon the common language: it does not question that this inelegant appendix remains within the order of that which is common to all. It is in this inherited linguistic pool that the law, without changing anything about it, draws, at once, its morphology, its syntax, its vocabulary.[17] The only items that deserve, from this view-point, the jurists' attention, would be those *nomina iuris* which punctuate their discourse.[18] In other words, a good scholar of Roman law is a lawyer armed with a solid formation as a philologist.

Etymology and context suffice to master the task of dealing with any problematic terms.[19]

Such a position, however, is not grounded upon serious foundations. Rather, it is the fruit of an impression that has chosen to take itself for granted. Not only does it mix up language and terminology (the fact is that, for a vast number of lawyers, the horizon of language limits itself to that of vocabulary); it also surrenders to the snare of focusing on the 'literal sense' of an utterance, of forgetting, that is, that the understanding of speech is predicated upon the knowledge of a language which exceeds by a long way the provisional moment of any 'context' properly so-called. The meaning of a legal utterance depends on items that are, in Carcaterra's words, '*in absentia*', as much as it does on items '*in praesentia*'.[20]

That which is *in praesentia* limits itself to an isolated proposition. While the mastery of Latin makes us believe that we can decipher its meaning, the proposition forms in reality an integral part of a legal system which, in its entirety, makes sure that its effective meaning lies outside its literal meaning. Roman law is a structure with a content, the latter manifesting itself in a linguistic structure (Latin). Common language, thus, delivers a primary literal sense as a supplement to a secondary legal sense. The 'juridical' reading of a legal proposition can then only be achieved by means of rules that are part of the metalanguage of law. It is effectively the latter which possesses the structural characters that are at the origin of the distance between legal language and common language – a distance that, pace B. Biondi and M. Kaser, is not exceptional, but rather omnipresent.

A. – The first specific feature of legal language resides in the fact that any legal system is, first of all, *preceptive*. This preceptive character of any legal utterance is compatible with the fact that certain legal propositions might appear, at first glance, as simple descriptions or pure opinions which do not imply a commandment. The *Digest* contains any number of philosophical and literary passages, mostly from Greek sources.[21] What is the meaning to be recognised in these borrowings? Do they retain their original scope, merely subjective, descriptive, constative, once they are inserted into a legal codification? Do they not feature themselves the power of obligatory precepts, as soon as they are put into the legal context? For the layman – yet also for numerous specialists of Roman law – the definition of the law that Marcianus has borrowed from Demosthenes and Chrysippus (*D.* 1.3.2) has no other value apart from its philosophical one. Effectively, according to an opinion going back to the stoic philosopher Chrysippus – a mere opinion with which, thus, one might agree or not – the law is the universal queen to which all living beings are subject.[22] For Justinian, no doubt already for the jurist Marcianus, who mentions this excerpt in his *Institutes*, this is not only an opinion but a principle of constitutional law: all subjects of the Empire have to obey the law. The juridical implantation has made a precept out of an opinion, an objective norm out of a subjective statement, and this without in the least modifying that which the proposition allows to be perceived.

B. – The preceptive character of legal propositions is reinforced by their performative property.[23] Performative utterances are particularly frequent in Roman law. One finds them everywhere, in the solemn *formulae* of the very ancient strata of law, in declarations made in the course of the law case, or in the *tria verba* of the praetor (*do, dico, addico*). To a layperson, things might look as though what such declarations do is only take note of an already existing situation of law or fact (for instance: *'aio hunc hominem meum esse*/I say that this slave is mine'). In reality, however, it is the declaration, the formula, that creates the right.[24]

C. – The abstract character[25] of any legal utterance imposes the translation in general terms of what is expressed in particular and concrete terms. Thus, the precept of the XII Tables: *si calvitur pedemque struit, manus endo iacito* expresses, with the images and the rhythm of a song (*carmen*), the rule according to which a triable litigant, who is the object of a judiciary summons, can be brought to the tribunal forcefully, if he resists. These fundamental characters impose, between the literal and the juridical meaning of a proposition, a distance that is as important as it is evident. A message interpreted without invoking the rules of hermeneutics conferred upon it by a legal order is, for the jurist, nothing but a group of signs deprived of their meaning. It is, so to speak, an irrelevant message, a dead letter capable of being resuscitated only by reading it in the light of the linguistic structure of the law. And this linguistic structure of the law, notwithstanding the twofold nature of law's characters – preceptive and performative – belongs to the law alone, exclusively of any other normative system, because what is at stake in this linguistic structure derives its force, its institutional properties, only from an order of positive law.

This first result alone, by emphasising the general aspects of the legal language, which require a solidary interpretation of a legal system in its totality, as an item defined by its linguistic characters, demonstrates the insufficiency of any only terminology-based view-point.

D. – The issue of terminology remains essential nonetheless. For if the legal modes, properly speaking, are limited in number and easily circumscribed, one cannot say the same about the countless objects and concepts to which refers the legal vocabulary, and these possess a consummate skill of eluding their interpreter, by concealing their operations under the power of their signs. Roman law, as is the case with any historical legal system, rests upon a certain general way of shaping the world, a *Weltanschauung*. This legal *découpage* of the world – which never exactly corresponds to the one realised by the common language – bases itself upon a number of fundamental principles and elements (the principal legal categories) which, in their totality, form a structure,[26] and it is to this structure that all the other elements of the system refer. We are dealing here with invariants which, during a given historical period, define a legal order. These invariants present themselves in the form of headwords. In order to get access to any other aspect of law, an exact understanding of these is indispensable.[27] They express an original vision of the world,[28] a vision which provides the very measure of the specificity of the legal rules with respect to those of other normative systems.

This is also why, contrary to a very widespread preconception to the opposite, the invasion to be found in Justinian's law, of terms rooted in the vocabulary of morals (*caritas, aequitas, humanitas, benignitas*, etc.), does not correspond to an intrusion of morals into the law.[29] What they indicate is much rather an assimilation, by the law, of a pre-existing ethical terminology, that thus becomes the base of new legal meanings. Morality, in the law of Justinian just as in classical Roman law, is nothing more than a common ground made of values to which the positive law directly refers: these values are transformed and institutionalised; they indicate features specific to the legal order, regardless of the fact that, among the linguistic signs which it brings into play, some are also to be found in non-legal contexts.[30] Observed from this angle, the eternal question of the relations between morality and law reveals itself as a part of the far wider issue of the autonomy of legal language.

Pushing the analysis further yet, Carcaterra notices that the language of law, as opposed to the so-called 'technical' languages,[31] does not content itself to graft onto an unchanged common ground a group of specifically juridical terms (as one finds in biology, physics, informatics, etc.). Rather, the field of words carrying a particular juridical meaning extends far beyond the relatively limited circle of *nomina iuris*:[32] in addition to the lexemes and syntagmas indicating a legal institution (examples: *lex, hereditas, emptio venditio, indicium,* etc.), it includes an incalculable number of diverse terms which, reputedly non-juridical (or not *properly* juridical) because referring to such concepts (examples: *fides, dolus, habere,* etc.) or objects (*fundus, ager, aqua pluvia,* etc.) as also occur outside of the law, are nonetheless subject to a particular treatment, be it because they receive a specific definition,[33] because they feature in legal contexts that exercise a semantic attraction over them,[34] or because, more generally, in the absence of any reference in the ordinary or common sense, they have to undergo an interpretation that is conformable to legal hermeneutics and which agrees with the structure of the legal order in which they are integrated.[35] Hence, what needs to be presumed is that each single word of a legal proposition includes a specific legal meaning, the law constituting an autonomous language, one that corresponds to a global vision of things, the like of which other, so-called 'technical' languages, are incapable of proposing. As Carcaterra has noticed, only religion shares with law the privilege of being endowed with a language (constituted, to be sure, by general terms stemming from common resources) to which the non-initiated have no access.[36] To that *Weltanschauung* of law and to its language corresponds a linguistic code, made of rules of interpretation and of transformation, and of a system of fundamental concepts used in every research of meaning, etc., all of which are open and in need of deciphering.

One readily perceives how much the philosophy of law can gain from such an approach. Rather than contemplating the legal phenomenon from the outside, comparing it to other, nearby phenomena (politics, morals, economy), this approach allows it to be considered from the inside, in its linguistic structure. The question of what is law thereby gains in technicity what it loses in breadth of perspective. It can now be formulated in this manner: what are the proceedings that make it possible to decipher a legal utterance, a legal message? How can the relevant linguistic elements, to which law owes its linguistic status, be discovered?

II. Methods of linguistic analysis of law

The hypothesis according to which law manifests in the form of a language has a claim to be tested by means of proceedings of the sort of those used in linguistics. To start with, one needs to acknowledge, with Antonio Carcaterra, that jurists – and first of all, legal historians, whose task is obviously an even more demanding one – are inclined to deal with questions of meaning in complete ignorance of what the use of the methods of general semantics could contribute to their task.

Carcaterra, in view of these medieval jurists and how to relate to this issue, first draws attention to a powerful tradition of indifference. Contrary to the jurisconsults of Roman antiquity, who were exceedingly familiar with the linguistic theories of their times,[37] the professors of medieval universities assert that they had been subjected to an 'Aristotelian imperialism' which, for several centuries, had made them forget, or so they claimed, the stoic doctrine of semantics and its fertile contributions, thereby limiting the business of legal interpretation to the exclusive model of logic (to which, by the way, grammar paid obedience, as well) and leaving no attention for language and its particularities. The narrative fits the advent of a hermeneutics in the style of that of Savigny,[38] to which numerous generations of jurists were to remain faithful – generations who crossed without noticing the major current that, starting from Humboldt, was to give rise, via Saussure, to contemporary semantics. Without sectarian preconceptions, Antonio Carcaterra draws, from linguists pertaining to the most diverse schools, the recipes of semantic analysis that allow the production of answers to the principal difficulties of legal language.

Once the solution of limiting the specificity of legal language to *nomina iuris* is discarded, what remains is to discover the non-empirical criteria which allow us to account for the distance existing between common and legal meaning. The principle according to which, in the absence of any explicit definition by the legislator,[39] the interpreter is under the duty to suppose that the reference is to the common meaning of a word, is barely satisfactory: it is predicated upon a refusal to consider the existence of a hermeneutic code proper to law, a refusal to assume a foundational conceptual framework into which all legal concepts are eventually fated to coalesce. We have, thus, to consider in each lexeme the distinctive element or feature which, by adding to or subtracting from the meaning which it conveys in the common language a number of unities of meaning ('semes'), succeeds in endowing it with its particular legal standing. But this meticulous treatment should be preceded by an inquiry destined to bring to light the structural elements of this or that particular legal system. The point being that of releasing the main semantic fields or 'classemes'[40] inside which we witness lexical unities organising further lexical units, whose meaning depends on the legal function of these categories. Carcaterra limits his study to a number of examples (including person, thing, duty, power, faculty, conformity, causing, changing). These, however, are sufficient to convince us of the fact that there are structures, and that, what at first looks very much like an inextricable lexical chaos, derives from them.

But perhaps we need to push the analysis even further and ask whether those classemes are not articulated in an order that is consistent with the legal order, once one understands the latter as a system of organised relations. In this respect, the distinction, suggested by Gaius (*Institutes*), between persons, things and actions,[41] supplies an example of a *summa divisio* of a scope that might transcend an exclusively didactic level. Indeed, each of these *genera* is endowed with a function (actors of the exchanges, objects of the exchanges, recognised forms of the exchanges)[42] that necessarily affects the meaning of the elements that compose them. To put it differently, the Romans would have had the intuition that a structural description of their lexicon is indispensable to triggering a precise juridical meaning. The existence of such classemes as defined by law itself allows the charting of the semantic values of terms that, as long as they are considered in isolation from each other, seem to refer to some 'common' sense (as in the case of *paterfamilias*, cf. *infra*). In a more general manner, these classemes (of which Carcaterra points out, correctly, that they ought to be the privileged field of application of the general theory of law) constitute the legal framework around which aggregate, in order to be dubbed with legal character, the countless unities of which the lexicon is composed – a lexicon which is always open and subject to the continuing evolution of a legal system, according to the historical moment under consideration. A semantic analysis, regardless of which type, has necessarily to refer to it as to the first and indispensable resource of the legal reading of the propositions at stake. Mind that this code is *not* established according to the same rules as those to which one refers on the level of a 'literal interpretation'.[43] Here again, we find, therefore, the distinction, proposed by Carcaterra, between context and structure, between that which is *in praesentia* and that which is *in absentia*. To have forgotten this distinction constitutes effectively the major insufficiency of the traditional interpretation.[44]

The semic analysis properly speaking is an inquiry into differential semantic elements allowing distinctions to be established between the meanings of lexemes and, more particularly, in the field that is of interest to us, between their respective uses, 'legal' and 'common'. We shall have to raise the differential features that oppose and characterise the values within one word according to whether or not it belongs to a legal proposition. Hence, a semic analysis of *pater* allows the specific difference which produces a legal sense (x semes ± a,b,c, . . . semes) from a given ordinary sense (function of x semes) to be established with precision.

Ordinary sense = S1 (a human being) + S2 (male) + S3 (adult) + S4 (has children)

Legal sense = S1 (human being) + S2 (male) ± S3 (adult or not) ± S4 (has children or not) + S5 (Roman citizen) + S6 (*sui iuris* [subject to his own authority alone]) + S7 (exercises his *potestas* over such persons as: *filii familias*/sons within the family; *uxor*/wife; slaves).

The specific difference of the *pater familias* in legal language is thus analysed in the following fashion: / + S5, S6, S7 – (potentially) S3, S4/.[45]

The examples that show the precision with which the Romans were practising this type of analysis include a summary of the distinctive features of *possessio, fundus, ager* (*D.* 50.16.115), *villa* (or *aedes, D.* 50.16.211, etc.). As a rule, divisions in *genera, species*,[46] etc., lead up to those distinctive features that one needs to know in order to grasp the legal meaning contained in the *definitio*. One arrives, in this way, at establishing an extremely vast legal vocabulary, or, on the level of the lexicon, at determining a language that corresponds to the original division of things and concepts. It was essential to show that any such division is organised from an autonomous structure of semantic relations.[47]

Yet, methodologically, the difficulties and the limits of the proceeding need to be admitted. The venture that Carcaterra attempts to start along the lines of his componential analysis risks remaining applicable, exclusively, to fields conceptually organised in *genera* and *species*. Even the semic analysis of contracts and contractual obligations[48] shows the insufficiencies of the componential proceeding – which, in the end, will only formalise the results, supplementing them with didactic expositions drawn from the Romans themselves. In the venture to reduce legal semantics to a seme-related organisation of what is already legally organised, there lurks, it seems, the danger of remaining in the circle of a mere tautology. The risk is that of superimposing, upon the already existing divisions, a more refined taxonomy which, regardless, would prove unable to endow science with being anything more or other than a general system of commonplaces. Ultimately, it is only through componential analysis that the results based upon mere certainties can be examined systematically. Yet, this mostly has to be preceded by research aiming exactly at establishing the distinctive features that it works around, in their factuality. In other words, such an approach cannot do more than record the results that have been achieved and put them into some consistent order. Which is precisely the point. Many of the essential concepts of the Roman legal system are marred, to this day, by a lack of accurate understanding (*actio, res, causa*, etc.). It makes no sense to apply to them a method that treats as well known what remains to be discovered. Instead, one needs to follow up the diverse meanings corresponding to the respective categories of a term's uses. The number of these linguistic contexts is sometimes impressive; their treatment, however, generally leads us to some ranking order where certain emergent types of syntagmatic relations deliver the key to the meaning of the phrase under consideration. But if it is not always the case that the meaning of a word boils down, according to the formula of the linguist Antoine Meillet, to the middle value of its uses, this is so because the uses are distributed in classes that, often enough, cannot be reduced to a common genre. It remains true that only the use determines the meaning, and that therefore a systematically conducted distributional study is the indispensable preliminary of any serious research about any legal concept, whether unknown or believed to be known.

This analysis is all the more necessary in Roman law, since the key words of the juridical lexicon mostly correspond to institutions, that is to say, to types of relations, to which the legal order assigns both a well-defined status and a well-defined function. These functions, however, appear only in interactions with, thus together with, the other pieces of the system, within a network of syntagmatic relations that they sustain with their 'partner' pieces. In this respect, the linguistic dimension faithfully reflects the proper dynamic of any given legal system. As an institution defines itself by its functions, a word defines itself by its uses. In the play of their uses in the service of a law that is at work, meaning and function conflate in a way to define a conceptual unity. A componential analysis, such as the one to which Carcaterra invites us, supposes a closed system, frozen in its static order; in contrast, a distributional study has the advantage of letting us discover the moving parts of an open order in perpetual evolution in their interdependence and their movement. Both methods compete in establishing – through the required linguistic analysis – what would be the specificity of a law that is considered as language.

This specificity does not manifest alone at the sole level of the lexicon. There exists also a legal syntax. It is circumscribed by studies in deontic logic,[49] to which Carcaterra devotes striking developments.[50] For this occasion, the author makes himself a disciple of Chomsky, whose principle he adapts to the syntactic analysis of Roman legal propositions. In particular, it shows that the categories of classical grammar fail to take into account the deep structure of normative utterances, and that an interpreter, having recourse to logical analysis – in dealing, for instance, with a proposition like *viam muniunto* (XII Tables, 7, 7) – prevents himself from grasping its deep structure, the one present in its original state, before the process of enunciation has succeeded in making it appear at the surface of the statement. Rather, normative utterances come forward in the following way:

/if there are riparian owners/
= they need to build and maintain the road (*viam muniunto*).

Restituting the deep structure by using the rules of transformation backward presupposes the basic syntactic structure featured by Roman legal norms. They result from the combination of two propositions: a conditional one (where we find posed a condition, premises, a case), and a principal one (which contains the precept, in other words, the juridical conclusion).

Examples:
– XII Tables:

> *si calvitur pedemque struit, / manus endo iacito*
> *si adgnatus nec escit, / gentiles familiam habento*
> The triable litigant, who is the object of a judiciary summons, can be brought to the tribunal forcefully, if he resists.
> If no relatives on the father's side can be found, let the family estate pass to a member of his *gens*.

– Praetor's Edict:

> *Si quis id quod traditur*
> *ex iusta causa et mondum / iudicium dabo*
> *usucaptum petet,*

Pacta conventa, que neque dolo malo,
/servabo
neque adversus leges etc. . . . . facta erunt,

Mind that this structure (case or condition + sanction) is identical to that of the *formulae* of action on the base of which the judge is invited to issue his sentence:

si paret . . . / condemna (if [xy] turns out to be the case . . . / condemn)
si non paret . . . / absolve. (if [xy] turns out not to be the case . . . / discharge)

The jurisconsults themselves, in their *responsa* and their *opiniones*, comply with this characteristic structure of the Roman rule: exposition of the *casus* + solution. Consider the following example, one among thousands:
– Ulpian, *D.* XII.4.6.

Si extraneus pro muliere dotem dedisset et pactus esset, ut, quoquo modo finitum esset matrimonium, dos ei redderetur, nec fuerint nuptiae secutae (casus)
condictionem patri competere Marcellus ait (Marcellus' solution)
If a stranger has given a dower to a woman under the condition that the dower returns to him once the marriage ends (no matter how), suppose the marriage has not occurred (*casus*)
M. argues: thus, if the dower has been the father's, then he can claim it back (Marcellus' solution.)

– Neratius, *D.* XIX, 5.6.

insulam in hoc modo, ut aliam insulam reficeres, vendidi (casus)
respondit nullam esse venditionem, sed civili intentione incerti agendum est (responsum of Neratius).

Roman law is entirely construed on case law. It is based upon case law that the *leges*, the edict of the *praetor*, the action *formulae*, the reasons given by judges, all draw the rules and the solutions that present themselves, logically and syntactically, presupposing that they are directly derived from the premises, as the juridical sanction that attaches to a determined *causa*. The external aspect under which a statement is presented is then of no particular importance. Effectively, for all types of reasons, including stylistic ones, the way it is presented can give rise to misleading appearances, as happens in the case of an explicit legal solution that solves an implicit *casus*. Indeed, it can present itself in the guise of a merely objective definition, without any apparent normative dimension.[51]

Despite their limited number, these examples suffice to show that the statements of jurists bring into play, on the syntactic as well as on the lexical level, a list of original rules of interpretation resulting in a code which is distinct from the code that serves to decipher the statements produced by common language. It is this distinctive code, built as it is on the particular structure of a particular legal system, but also, far more generally, upon the structure of law as a system of institutionalised rules, that delivers the key to the totality of linguistic signs by which the law manifests itself. Signs marked by the particularity that they belong to two overlaid languages which simultaneously belong to two registers of meaning, registers that only knowledge of both can enable them to be distinguished. We are not dealing, therefore, with two juxtaposed orders, as it is supposed by the restrictive theory of *nomina iuris* and of 'technical terms': this erroneous idea – from which, incidentally, legal practitioners escape, courtesy of their intuition and pragmatism – is owed, essentially, to the refusal of legal theorists (and even more, legal historians) to recur to linguistic procedures in dealing with a question that they cannot envisage otherwise than in some empiricist and punctilious manner. The result of this refusal is the widespread unawareness of the fact that the law can be treated as a language, and that the language of law is an issue that needs to be answered as a preliminary one, before even the merest problem of meaning comes up.

We, therefore, find here the reason why, in Roman law, any inquiry – whatever its object – needs to be preceded by an inquiry into that object in its own terms, why, in other words, there is no way of discovering anything that the researcher has not first construed by their own means. Legal concepts are not to be seen as pre-existing data, in such a way that one only needs to take them into account for what they are. Instead, they are the result of a set of interrogations to which legal language has given rise following its own chaotic ways. And these interrogations are all the more necessary in Roman law as in this field we are dealing with a language that is doubly problematic: as a language of law, distinct from mere Latin; and as the language of Roman law, which means that any simple 'intuition' is excluded from providing a method of discovery of how its concepts might have been produced. In both respects, an analysis of the linguistic type can hedge both against the temptations of excessive facility and against the inherent dangers of an empiricism that arms itself with an alleged common sense. The latter is the more formidable as, in outlining its horizon, it has nothing but itself to rely on.

In this perspective, the work of Antonio Carcaterra indicates a path – a path that is difficult to master and likely to repel those in search of seductive hypotheses and brilliant paradoxes. In order to realise the ambition of providing an insight into what a great scholar of the nineteenth century, Rudolph von Jhering, called 'the spirit of Roman law', scores of painstaking and rigorous semantic inquiries will need to be conducted with utter attention.

Notes

1. See in particular: on good faith, *Intorno ai bonae fidei indicia*, 1965, and, answering the objection of Max Kaser, 'Ancora sulla fides', *SDHI* (*Studia et documenta historiae et iuris*) p. 33, as well as, on deceit, *Dolus Malus*, 1970.

2. The imperfect form, 'were questioned', is meant as a reference as much to the past, as to a surpassed present. Yet, the best studies today envision Roman law as a historical topic, which is most fortunate. See for instance, on archaic and classical law, the works of M. Kaser, W. Kunkel, A. Magdelain, L. Labruna. In the margin of these middle-of-the-road researches, we find the emerging of a style of inquiry that adopts an epistemological approach, and to which Carcaterra's works will contribute a whole problematic that, hitherto, had remained in the shadow.

3. In a more or less disguised fashion (see, for instance, the *autonomia privata*, standing in for the autonomy of the will), these concepts cast their shadow upon the articulation of the

great treatises of law. See, for instance, significant from this angle, those of the towering romanist Emilio Betti (*Diritto romano*, 1935; *Istituzioni di diritto romano*, 1960). The domain of public law is not immune to these dogmatic deformations; see, for instance, dealing with the political implications of M. Wlassak's work, the remarks of G. Broggini, *Index arbiterve*, 1957, p. 5 and note 3: Wlassak's interpretation of the *litis contestatio* shows the partisan view of this great scholar, his centre-staging of the liberal doctrine of contract explaining his minimisation of the (essential) role of the praetor within the stages of appeal *in iure*. Equally remarkable are the reflections of Giuliano Grifò, 'Attività normativa del senato in età repubblicana', *B.I.D.R.* (*Bullettino dell'Istituto di diritto romano*), pp. 31 ff., according to whom discussions about the powers of the Senate and the sources of Roman law find their appropriate location in the framework of the separation of powers (a claim that involves a double anachronism).

4. The situation of legal history is, in this view, similar to that of scientific history: the progresses of the human spirit punctuate with errors – always later corrected – the pathway that leads to *truth*. As G. Canguilhem shows in his *Etudes d'Histoire et de Philosophie des Sciences*, 1968, the research of precursors (that is to say, in law, that of the genesis of an institution, featuring predecessors, origins, developments, etc., etc.) consists in joining successive episodes, then claiming that they are stages of one single path, finally extracting a thought from its history and grafting it onto another history. One thus creates a reversible intellectual space where that which is true always ends up victorious over that which is false. In our discipline, on the contrary, it so happens that its starting point is no other than classical Roman law. We are moving within some kind of tilted circle on whose uppermost point the end coincides with the start. And much would remain to be said about the ideological function of Roman law in the *pandektistische Schule* and in the German university of the nineteenth century.

5. Some select examples should suffice here:
    (*a*) Despite the works of P. Bonfante and E. Albertario, the doctrine of contract understood as an abstract constellation of law is still alive and kicking. P. Voci, for instance (*La dottrina romana del contratto*, 1946), notwithstanding the fact that the texts in which *contractus* is used in the generic sense are established as interpolations, treats the contract as an agreement of wills constituting an obligatory relationship.

The will, regardless of the fact that it has been shown not to constitute an indispensable element of the existence of a *contractus* (cf. Arangio-Ruiz, Bonfante, De Francisci), is still treated, by P. Voci and many others (including E. Betti and E. Wunner, the author of the last general study dedicated to the topic) as the building premises on which the contract is grounded, and as the ultimate reason of its legal nature.

(*b*) Subjective right remains in place as the fundamental presupposition of the field of rights within the Roman legal system (as to the *actio*, see the classical work by G. Pugliese, *Actio e diritto subiettivo*, 1939, greeted with quasi-unanimous approval). The controversy has been revived by the audacious studies of M. Villey, who, starting from a semantic inquiry into *ius* and *res* in the classical texts (and specifically in Gaius), has concluded that this category had no currency in Roman law. As they are based on the refusal to consider the importance of language, the criticisms to which this thesis has given rise (Pugliese, 'Res corporales, res incorporales e il problema del diritto soggettivo', *R.I.S.G. (Rivista italiana per le scienze giuridiche)*, 1951; Betti, 'Falsa impostazione della questione storica, dependente da erronea diagnosi giuridica', *Studi Arangio-Ruiz*, IV, pp. 81 ff.) can barely be relied on: indeed, according to their authors, the categories of legal dogmatics exist independently of their expression in legal language. This is an unacceptable claim, whose only merit is to highlight, by way of contrast, that the key to the problem is, precisely, an essentially linguistic one. Yet, even so, the last studies devoted to the issue continue to paint their object in accordance to this claim (C. Gioffredi, 'Osservazioni sul problema del diritto soggettivo nel diritto romano', *Studi Sforza*, 1968; R. Orestano, 'Diritti soggettivi e diritti senza soggetto', *I.U.R.A (Rivista internazional di diritto romano ed antico)*, 1960, pp. 149 ff.; R. Coing, *Zur Geschichte des Privatrechtssystems*, 1962).

(*c*) One can ask oneself – while acknowledging its immense historical value and importance – whether the work of M. Kaser on Roman ownership, predicated as it is upon the refusal to consider the question from a dogmatic angle, does not bear out the implication that a subjective right to ownership had first appeared, in its absolute form, toward the end of the archaic period. In our view, the seductive hypothesis consists in arguing that a right, which has been 'relative' in its beginnings, extends over the entire classical period. This is particularly true if one considers that the sources do not confirm the use of *'ius'*, or only within the limits of controversy and process (cf. *ex iure quiritium meum esse aio . . . ius feci . . .* for the *sacramentum in rem*; and for the formulary process, *si paret hominem ex iure quiritium Auli Agerii esse . . .*). Related to the system of proofs, this relative right corresponds in reality to the attribution of a good that can be grasped only at the end of the trial: thus, the law intervenes at the borderline between opposite interests, on the level of controversies and exchanges. But within the scope of what we call the exercise of the right of property (and the very expression 'right of ownership' has a meaning only inside this realm), the Roman texts, while it does mention private powers or *potestates* galore (*mancipium, dominium*, etc.), fail to mention rights: this is why, in order to take account of the Roman language, one would have to invert the terms of our expression, and speak, rather than of a law of ownership, of an ownership of law. If one decides to adopt this use of language, the question of an absolute right no longer poses itself.

6. Understood in this way, *bonus iudex* no longer refers to the good judge, but to the judge who abstains from violating the regulatory duties of his *officium* (to the judge, that is, who does not make his own the law-case that he has to judge about). The *bona fides* is not the 'good' faith; it is a bond, the nature of which belongs to the category of a legal duty, which thereby gathers, without apparently in the least referring to ethical norms, all the elements that characterise, in law, the obligation contained in the *fides* (cf. *infra*).

7. For an example of an approach that goes in directly the opposite direction, see the whole epistemological work of G. Bachelard.

8. W. Kunkel, in *Festschrift Koschaker*, II, pp. 1 ff.; M. Kaser, *Das altrömische Jus*, 1949, pp. 290 ff.; *Römisches Privatrecht* I, pp. 162, 406; C. Gioffredi, 'Ius, lex, praetor', *S.D.H.I.* (*Studia et documenta historiae et iuris*), 1949, pp. 110 ff.; A. Magdelain, *Les actions civiles*, 1954, pp. 46 ff.; G. Broggini, *Index arbiterve*, 1957, pp. 185, 194, 214, 231; F. Wieacker, 'Zum Ursprung der *bonae fidei iudicia*', Z.S.S. (*Zeitschrift der Savigny-Stiftung für Rechtsgeschichte*), 1963, pp. 1 ff.

9. Which is to say, without being subjected to any transformation at the moment of passing into the law.

10. Cf. Broggini, op. cit., p. 194: 'The *bona fides*, the *aequum bonum*, that he (the *praetor*) uses as a foundation of the new legal relationship . . . are meta-legal concepts that are slowly

assimilated into the legal order'; and: 'It is not the law but the *aequum bonum*, the *bona fides* [incidentally, it is already abusive to assimilate these two concepts, YT] that the *arbiter* is supposed to apply: the *bona fides*, as a foundation of the mutually owed duties'.

11. The word 'ex' here carrying the sense of *'secundum'* (= according to).

12. Cf. Cicero, *De off.*, 3, 17, 70: *'Sed, quid sint "boni", et quid sit "bene agi"* (this deals with the formula of the fiduciary action, which carries the clause: *ut inter bonos bene agi oportet*), *magna quaestio est. Q. quidem Scaevola, pontifex maximus, summam vim esse dicebat in omnibus iis arbitriis, in quibus adderetur ex fide bona, fideique bonae nomen existimabat manare latissime . . .'* (But what is meant by *'boni'* and what, by *'bene agi'*? This is a big question . . . The high priest Quintus Scaevola used to say that those arbiter-decisions, where you find the formula 'according to good faith' added, carried a very high power, and held that the name 'good faith' was widely in use). On the interpretation of this passage, against most currently admitted translations, cf. Carcaterra, *Intorno ai b.f. iudicia*, pp. 18 ff.

13. Cf. Carcaterra, op. cit., pp. 158 ff.

14. Cf. Carcaterra, op. cit., pp. 159 ff.: multiple examples of these definitions, among which one can quote Arangio-Ruiz ('sentimento giuridico popolare'), Betti ('correttezza e lealtà'), Kaser ('Bedürfnis des Lebens'), A. Levi ('soggettiva interna regolarità della conscienza'). The controversy (are we dealing with a fact of psychology? of ethics?) that has been moved in the last century (Waechter vs Bruns), and that has been taken up by Bonfante, Arangio-Ruiz, Beseler, Betti; Biondi, Dulckeit, etc., represents the perfect type of a mode of discussions where the imagination is allowed to express itself in well-hewn formulas. One finds nonetheless some renewal of the relevant perspectives in J. Imbert, *Studi Arangio-Ruiz*, I, pp. 339 ff.; A. Piganiol, *R.I.D.A. (Revue internationale des droits de l'antiquité)*, 1950, pp. 346 ff., and in the consummate studies of G. Dumézil (*La religion romaine archaïque*, 1966, pp. 150 ff., 201 ff. and 'Credo et fides', in *Latomus*, XLIV, 58; 'Fides romana et la vie internationale', Institut de France, séance publique des Cinq Académies, 25 October 1962, pp. 1–16; 'Les Romains, peuple de la fides', *Lettres d'Humanité*, 23, 1964, pp. 419 ff.). The last great synthesis of a jurist on this question takes into account the religious and sociological viewpoints thanks to which the

historians just mentioned have deepened our knowledge of the topic (L. Lombardi, *Dalla 'fides' alla 'bona fides'*, 1961).

15. Cf. A. Carcaterra, *Le definizioni dei giuristi romani*, 1966.

16. *Struttura de l linguaggio giuridico-precettivo romano*, Bari 1968; *Semantica degli enunziati normativo-giuridici romani: Interpretatio iuris*, Bari 1972.

17. This is the thesis of Roman law scholar B. Biondi, 'la terminologia romana come prima dommatica giuridica', in *Scritti giuridici*, vol. 1 (see Antonio Carcaterra's severe criticisms, in *Struttura . . .*, pp. 16 ff.) It underlies Savigny's thesis of interpretation which, in turn, implicitly founds the largest part of the terminological studies that have been taken up during the nineteenth century. Thus, it is pervasive in the writing of the great specialists of Roman law, P. Bonfante, E. Albertario, E. Betti, or M. Kaser, but as well in that of legal theorists and logicians, as, for example, in G. Kalinowski, *Introduction à la logique juridique*, p. 45. For Kalinowski, legal language 'derives' from 'natural' language, but the nature of this derivation and its implications as to the structure of legal language are, as Carcaterra reminds us (op. cit., pp. 14 ff.), covered in dark shadows.

18. The theory of *nomina iuris*, inchoately present in Biondi, has given rise to a remarkable study by M. Kaser, 'Zur juristischen Terminologie der Römer', *Studi Biondi* I, 1963, pp. 97 ff. Carcaterra acknowledges Kaser's merit of having drawn a distinction between the authentic language of Roman law (conceived on the level of technical terminology) and the artificial language that has been introduced in the nineteenth century by the pandectists, who, striving to impose the form of a system onto a law foreign to the spirit of the great German treatises, succeeded in endowing it with their rationality. This is witnessed by the presence, in the German treatises of *Pandektenrecht*, of numerous nouns that are formed by using verbal infinitives while removing the verbal suffix of the infinitive, and that can still be found in numerous textbooks today. But M. Kaser fails to offer a precise criterion for distinguishing a legal term from a word that is 'borrowed' from common language.

19. Cf. the excellent plea for the respective contributions of classical philology and Roman law in C. Georgescu, *Study of Juridical Philology and Roman Law*, 1940. But the absence of all preliminary reflection on the specific characters of the language of Roman law marks the limits of a method that results, in a patient and documented study of the *causa*, in

a heterogeneous *tableau*, based upon the literary meanings of a word (efficient cause/final cause), and fails to account for the legal functions that the concept accomplishes in the system, and language, of Roman law. Equally well known is the interest that Roman law scholarship has in etymologies (see especially the studies of Bonfante, Noailles, de Visscher, Kaser, Gioffredi, de Francisci, etc.). Yet, such inquiries, indispensable as they are in order to isolate extremely ancient states of the meaning of a word (see, for example, the relevant work of G. Dumézil, in his *Idées romaines . . .*, op. cit., and É. Benveniste, especially his *Vocabulaire des institutions indo-européennes*, 2 vols, 1969) are divested of their interest with every evolution of the law enriching its first elements with new correlations (see on this topic the remarks of E. Bréal, *Essai de sémantique*, 1924, pp. 143 ff., and, more generally, in view of the insufficiency of traditional etymology, Kurt Badinger, 'L'étymologie hier et aujourd'hui', in *Cahiers de l'Association*, n. 11, May 1959, pp. 239 ff., which, taking up an idea developed by M. von Wartburg in 1922, insists on the necessary transition from an '*etymologie-origine*' to an '*etymologie-biographie*' of the word at stake, as well as on the structural orientation that is at work in this new approach.)

20. The expression 'language of law' that underlies these remarks, obviously refers, not to 'the Latin', but to Roman law. The refusal to consider the Roman legal system under this aspect results in the insufficiency of systematic studies in the sole domain of terminology. Generally, one contents oneself to notice, empirically as it were, a group of contexts that prove sufficient to circumscribe, by way of comparison, an approximative meaning. The very structure of privileged semantic fields remains almost *terra incognita* for most studies, and if one limits oneself to the case of this or that particular word, even less is to be reported about examples of an exhaustive research of its distributions. To take only some peculiar instances, and without prejudice to their vast historical and juridical importance, the studies devoted to such fundamental concepts as *ius* (a), *iurisdictio* (b), *actio* (c), etc., suffer from the absence of a rigorous semantic introduction, to which the insufficiency of their material (constituted principally by the *meaning* of these words) condemns them right from the start, which explains the uncertainty or approximative character of their theoretic conclusions.

(*a*) On the topic of *ius* the literature is massive. Cf., for example, C. Gioffredi, '*Ius, lex*, praetor', *S.D.H.I.*, 1947, pp. 19 ff;

Diritto et processo nelle antiche forme giuridiche romane, 1955; M. Kaser, *Altrömisches ius*, pp. 22 ff.; pp. 35 ff., pp. 101 ff.; A. d'Ors, 'Aspectos objectivos y subjectivos del concepto de ius', *Studi d'Albertario*, pp. 277 ff.; F. Bozza, 'Ius quiritium', *Studi senesi*, pp. 1 ff. None of these studies contains a structured chart of the ramifications of *ius*.

(*b*) Semantic aspects of *iurisdictio* are treated on an empirical level by F. de Martino, *Giuridizione*, 1937, pp. 139 ff.; C. Gioffredi (as quoted above); S. Pugliese, *Il processo civile romano*, I, 1961, pp. 144 ff., II, 1963, pp. 155 ff.

(*c*) Wlassak, *Römische Prozessgesetze*, I, 1888, pp. 31 ff. and 72 ff. (fundamental study about the respective meanings of *actio* and *iudicium*); G. Pugliese, *Actio e diritto subiettivo*, op. cit., pp. 18 ff. Against the subjectivist interpretation of G. Pugliese, a first glimpse of its relations, both syntagmatic (*actio* plus its diverse constitutive factors which indicate the list of its key species, such as the *actio empti venditi, actio furti*, etc.), as well as associative (such as in the many contexts in which *actio* and *causa* are interchangeable) where the term *actio*, as it is present in the language of Roman law, is such that it recommends the conclusion that it is its 'objective' features that carry a fundamental importance. Most frequently, *actio* appears in the sense of the typical case of a legal remedy that the 'objective law' makes available to particulars, for the purpose of sanctioning a typical legal relationship which is equally recognised by the law (*causa*).

21. Cf. Antonio Carcaterra, *Struttura . . .*, pp. 130 ff.
22. According to M. Pertolongo, 'Lex nel diritto romano e nella legislazione giustinianea', *Annali dell'Università di Perugia*, Fac. Giur, 49, pp. 275 ff., who attributes to this text only a simple rhetorical value. The normative character of certain legal definitions is correctly underlined by G. Kalinowski, A.P.D., 1971, p. 496.
23. Carcaterra, *Struttura . . .*, pp. 103 ff. The discovery of the 'performance' is owed to J.L. Austin ('Performatif-constatif', in *Cahiers de Royaumont*, Philosophie IV, 1962). This fundamental aspect of language, taken up by J. O. Urmson ('Histoire de l'analyse', in *Cahiers de lexicologie* 4, 1962) has been deepened in a critical sense by E. Benveniste, 'La philosophie analytique et le langage', *Problèmes de linguistique générale*, pp. 267 ff. E. Benveniste offers an essential contribution to the analysis of legal discourse. He establishes the characteristics of the *performative* (authentication as an 'act' based on the factual circumstances that endow a proposition with

performativity; property of being self-referential, which distinguishes it from the imperative – the latter, far from identifying the act performed, aims solely at giving rise to a behaviour). Among the conclusions authorised by these studies we find: the fact that it fails to use the imperative does not necessarily make of an utterance a constative utterance; it might create a new situation, to which the members of the political community find themselves necessarily subjected. Conversely, a legal norm does not necessarily present itself as destined to act upon behaviours.

24. This interpretation bases itself upon the rule of the XII Tables: *uti lingua nuncupassit, ita ius esto* ('According as he has named by word of mouth, so shall right hold good', cf. the tr. of E. H. Warmington, *Remains of Old Latin* III: *Lucilius* and The *Twelve Tables*, Loeb Classical Library 1938; 'According as he specified with his tongue, so shall be the law', according to the tr. of Johnson, Coleman-Norton and Bourne, *Ancient Roman Statutes*, Austin, 1961, pp. 9–18, n. 8); the tongue has pronounced, so the *ius* shall be). This principle, the uttering of which was part of certain solemn legal acts (*cum nexum mancipiumque faciet* / when making a debt pledge and a transfer declaration) needs to be considered as a general hermeneutic rule. Positive law establishes a rule according to which every declaration, if made in certain specific conditions, will create law. The performative character is, thus, less an effect of the transparency of language, than a result intended by the law (this point sheds some more light on the analysis Benveniste has offered of the 'circumstances' that are indispensable in order to become performative. Such circumstances are, in reality, present within the will underlying the legislation). This aspect of the particular linguistic structure of Roman law is here combined with a consequence rooted in an institutional (non-linguistic) situation. Even leaving behind the circle of solemn formulas, one could argue that what the *responsa-writing* jurisconsults are expected to come up with, within the limit of their competences (which, whenever they hold the right to officially reply to any law-related question, the *ius publice respondendi*, are of some importance), is not simply an opinion. When having considered a *casus*, they settle the dispute, by declaring e.g.: *esse actionem – esse obligationem – posse abiri ab emptione* (X does have an *actio*; an obligation does exist; Y is entitled to cancel his purchase). The jurists neither simply decide upon an existing legal solution, nor do they limit

themselves to expressing their personal opinion. In reality, what they do is: *say the law*. They create, for those asking for their advice, a new legal situation, one that, in the *casus*, had only been inchoately present.

25. Carcaterra, *Struttura* . . ., pp. 109 ff.
26. There is a layer of secondary concepts that function according to the rules of the system to which they belong, grafting themselves onto this structure. *Possidere*, for instance, necessarily refers, within a legal context, to a legal persona (*paterfamilias*) on the side of the subject, and, on the object side, to a *res corporalis in commercio*, a corporal thing that is the object of business transactions. The proposition that a slave (not a legal *persona*) possesses moral virtues (not a corporeal thing subject to legal exchangeability or *commercium*) would, in Roman law, be encumbered by a twofold absurdity, as it fails to feature the basic relational terms that are implied by possession (*persona-res*). What we here call 'structure' is a system of concepts each of which is endowed with a function that proves its necessity within the integrity of a network: thus, the meaning of *persona* cannot be dissociated from its function in the exchange of goods (*res*). Usually, the word *structure* is used, in law, in a very vague sense. For the jurisconsults, 'structure' is just the sum of determinations of a given legal institution. It is, in this sense, only a preliminary stage of what one then calls, not without confusion, legal 'nature' (see regarding this notion of legal nature the embarrassed explanations of P. Collinet, *La nature des actions des interdits et des exceptions dans l'oeuvre de Justinien*, pp. 29 ff., developing an extremely obscure definition given by A. Esmein – in *Revue historique de droit français et étranger*, 1900, p. 492: 'The legal nature of an institution boils down to the legal categories by means of which the law realises and sanctions the general idea that serves this institution as its principle'). This boils down to the notion that legal structure is a compound of differential elements. In turn, this notion, which lacks all theoretical coherence, maintains a practical ambition that is itself inspired by the need for definition and classification. Incidentally, the purely scholastic use of 'structure' appears in our eyes as perfectly justifying the comparison with another notion, born in the Byzantine schools of the late Empire, and invested with an equivalent function which is, precisely, that of 'nature'. There is no secret as to the high esteem that taxonomy enjoyed with the Byzantines. The reference to *natura* (as in *natura contrac-*

tus, natura actionis, etc.) allowed them precisely to express the particularities of an institution, its distinctive features, which define its 'nature' by opposition to neighbouring institutions (what we would call 'relevant features' today). It would be interesting to establish an inventory of the uses, in the writing of jurists (and especially of specialists of Roman law), of *structure* and *nature*. Our impression is that of a very large imprecision in the way these terms are used, often interchangeably.

27. It goes without saying that the study of these 'witness-words' (for the term, cf. the lexicologist G. Matoré) is meaningful only as long as it integrates itself into a synchronic order. Any merely linear study of a legal term would be, in our view, of little interest. (Incidentally, one wonders even more what one might say in this respect about the history of legal concepts fabricated in the nineteenth century?) First, because there is less of an evolution to be found than, rather, fractures of meaning, but more importantly still, because these ruptures themselves result from a modification of the general economy of the system. For instance, the modern meaning of contract will appear only in direct correlation with the emerging of the legal subject capable of contracting, in other words of a virtual holder of a subjective right of ownership, that is, it appears at the moment when the needs of a market economy will produce a philosophy of natural right which will give rise, as it did in Roman legal language, to a genuine thrust of reordering. As has been magisterially demonstrated by M. Villey's studies on the meaning and the function of *persona, res,* and *actio* (which is to say, of the three pillars of the Roman legal system) this trinity will refuse to work in the very moment in which the word *ius* will take up the meaning which certain specialists of Roman law still continue to endow it with, today.

28. In the sense in which Sapir and Whorf understood the relation between language and culture. The architecture that the law imposes upon the social reality and the world of moral ideas is particularly well established by Antonio Carcaterra, *Struttura . . .,* pp. 144 ff., 192 ff., and *Semantica . . .,* pp. 29 ff.

29. This thesis is professed by E. Albertario, 'Etica e diritto nel mondo classico latino', in *Studi di diritto romano,* III, and has been severely criticised by Antonio Carcaterra, *Struttura . . .,* p. 147 ff. Notwithstanding this criticism it still represents an almost unanimous opinion: F. Schulz, *Prinzipien des*

römischen Rechts, 1934; S. Riccobono, 'Humanitas', *Atti cong. internaz. dir. rom.*, II, Verona 1953, pp. 209 ff.; B. Biondi, *Il diritto romano cristiano*, 3 vols, 1952–4; A. Guarino, 'Equità. Diritto romano', *Novissimo Digesto Italiano*, VI, pp. 619 ff.

30. *Caritas*, in the *Novellae* of Justinian, thus becomes in Antonio Carcaterra's view (loc. cit.) a proper legal concept; the extension of its use fails to coincide with the *absolute* scope of its use in Christian literature (especially in the writing of St Paul). Limited to the legal topic as applied within the circle of family, *caritas* belongs to a number of intra-familiar relations; the group of determinations with which this use enriches the meaning of the word fails to find correspondences in its non-legal use. The same remark applies to the case of 'legal' *honestas*, which does not rule out certain forms of *dolus bonus*, and thus contrasts, by its relative character, with the absolute value that the concept carries in the Church Fathers. In sum, as correctly noticed by Antonio Carcaterra (op. cit., p. 153), the famous passage where Seneca (*De ira*, 2,27) compares the respective breadth of the *officia* and of *ius* does not exclusively apply to classical law (as Albertario and Biondi claim it does), but applies as well to the 'Christian' law of Justinian. The same error of perspective is to be found in the beautiful book of G. Nocera, *Ius naturale nella esperienza giuridica romana*, 1962, for whom it is Justinian's egalitarianism which expresses itself in *aequitas, fides, ratio* – terms whose specifically *legal* meaning the author appears not to have perceived (the same statement applies also to *iusta causa*). The same error is also present in M. Kaser, 'Rechtswidrigkeit und Sittenwidrigkeit im klassischen römischen Recht', *Savigny-Zeitschrift für Rechtsgeschichte, Romanistische Abteilung*, pp. 85 ff. For Kaser, the law refers to moral rules of behaviour; whence the 'non-technical' character of the expressions used in this field (as, for instance, and this is extremely questionable indeed, in the case of the *iniusta causa* – the absence of a just cause of a transaction, e.g., gift or sale).

31. Sometimes, law is considered as a technical language (cf. the 'lawyerly jargon'). This is the position expounded in S. Ullmann, *Précis de sémantique française*, 2nd edition, 1959, which speaks of juridical jargon and, as well, by G. Preti, *Linguaggio comune linguaggi scientifici*, p. 90 (quoted after Antonio Carcaterra).

32. Argues against this view: M. Kaser, op. cit., criticised by Carcaterra, op. cit., pp. 178 ff.

33. Cf., in addition to the well-known case of *fundus, ager,* et *possessio,* the definition of *veterator,* in the syntagma, *servus veterator* (*D.* 21.1.65.2).

34. Examples in Carcaterra, *Semantica* . . ., p. 112, with interesting developments on *nudus* (*nuda possessio, nudum factum, nudus consensus*).

35. For instance, those propositions where it is said that *quis* or *quicumque* has brought an action has thereby contracted, or has received in property, etc., always refer these indefinite expressions (which otherwise, or for the non-initiated, can denote any person whatsoever) to a *pater familias,* that is to say to a Roman citizen *sui iuris,* able to be party to the legal acts involved in *commercium.*

36. Cf. on this, the beautiful developments devoted by Marcel Mauss to the autonomy of religious language: 'La prière', in: *Oeuvres,* I, 1968, pp. 377 ff.

37. Antonio Carcaterra, *Semantica* . . ., pp. 11 ff., shows that the reflection on language of the Stoic school, overcoming the Aristotelian dilemma of the natural or conventional origin of words, provided the Roman jurisconsults with the theoretical solution to numerous problems of interpretation. Thus, cases of *ambiguitas* (cf. Chrysippus' theme of the basic ambiguity of language) are resolved with the help of a distinction between énoncé/*enuntiatum* and énonciation/ *enuntiatio,* to be taken up by twentieth-century semanticists, e.g., T. Todorov, 'Problèmes de l'énonciation', in *Langages,* 17, 1970). The jurist Celsus quotes, for instance (*D.* 33.10.7), the opinion of Servius, for whom the terms of a bequest need to be interpreted according to the current meaning of the words used (*ex communi usu nomina exaudiri debere*), but opposes to it that of Tubero, who sees in the *nomina* (debts) a surface on which the *mens dicentis,* 'that which the subject has effectively in mind', is more or less well represented, which he claims needs to be taken into consideration by the interpreter. Rome abounds with writing on semantics, cf. the *'De verborum significatione'* of *Varro, Festus,* Paul the Deacon and, among the jurists, the *'libri regularum'* (*Q. Mucius Scaevola, Neratius, Gaius, Pomponius, Ulpian*), where a vast quantity of definitions can be found. Incidentally, the *Digest* ends with a veritable sum of legal semantics (*D.* 50.16, *De verborum significatione*).

38. Whose hermeneutics was more philosophical than case-oriented, and was inspired by the principles of F. Schleiermacher. Cf. Marini, *Savigny e il metodo della scienza giuridica,* 1966.

39. T. de Mauro (quoted by Carcaterra, *Struttura . . .*, p. 50) does not recognise a specificity to the language of law, or if so, only in the hypothesis of an 'entirely formalistic codification'.
40. On the notion of semantic field, cf. G. Matoré, *La méthode en lexicologie*, 1953; J. Dubois, 'Esquisse d'un dictionnaire structural', in *Etudes de linguistique appliquée* I, 1962 and the introduction to his remarkable *Le vocabulaire politique et social de la France de 1869 à 1872*, 1962; J. Apresjan, 'Analyse distributionnelle des significations et champs sémantiques structurés', in *Langages*, 1, 1966; E. Coseriu, 'Pour une sémantique diachronique structurale', in *Travaux de linguistique et de littérature de l'Université de Strasbourg*, II, 1, 1964. The difficulties of structuring the lexicon into conceptual fields has been emphasised by G. Mounin, who insists upon the non-linguistic starting point of any such proceeding, though recognising the efficacy of this method where it limits itself to certain privileged zones if they are homogenous and isolatable. See his *Clefs pour la sémantiques*, 1972, especially pp. 65 ff., 103 ff. and 130 ff. The notion of '*classeme*', introduced in France by B. Pottier ('Vers une sémantique moderne', in *Travaux de linguistique et de littérature de l'Université de Strasbourg*, II,1, 1964), is related to the componential analysis which strives to show, within the lexemes of a particular semantic field, groups of distinctive features or common semes. There is, thus, no point in mixing up classemes and semantic fields, as does Carcaterra (*Semantica . . .*, p. 62).
41. As reliably proven by M. Villey (*Recherches sur la littérature didactique du droit romain*, 1945), this distinction, which has its origin in rhetoric, is rooted in a prototype of Greek inspiration. Cicero provides us with an echo of it (*De oratore*, I, XLII, 188).
42. Of course it must be understood, as M. Villey (op. cit., p. 38) points out appositely, that the category of actions corresponds to procedural formulas: It is only once the *formulae* have disappeared (even if, incidentally, let us note it, some do survive right into the law of Justinian, in the form of expression-types of substantial rights) that the actions will take the general form of juridical business (transfers, contracts, etc.), as they will do in the didactic treatises of the sixteenth century, here even exclusively. What is noteworthy is that these typical *actiones* do have an effect on these typical legal transactions, whose names at once they adopt (*emptio venditio → actio empti venditi; mandatum → actio mandati*, etc.): They consecrate them. Which incidentally explains why

'*causa*' designates both the lawsuit itself *and* the legal situation that is protected by a legal remedy. The circle of *actiones* in Gaius, of *causae* in Cicero, will thus remain essentially that of legal business considered from the angle of the protection granted by positive law (*actiones* in justice).

43. Carcaterra distinguishes the code of writing, which is that of common Latin, and the code of reading, which is the one of the language of Roman law (*Struttura . . .*, p. 108f.) But in doing so, he mixes up, or so it seems, the result of this proceeding with another, opposite one. Any legal message requires in reality the contributions of two superimposed codes: the common linguistic code, which appears immediately, already on the level of the context, and the legal code which manifests only through the mediation of the legal system in its totality. In fact, the distance between a code of writing and a code of reading corresponds to an optical illusion on the side of the interpreter who, surpassing the proposition's surface in order to get to the deeper legal sense, imagines that the sender of the message was sticking to the sole code required by the superficial structure only. In reality, both in the process of uttering, as in converse process of interpreting, legal language appears as a two-storey pyramid, where the second meaning, the legal meaning, relies on a first, non-legal one; the production of a legal message, as it is the case also of its reception, thus needs to establish two orders of rules which will come into play successively.

44. Cf. the inquiry into the *ordinary meaning* of the terms figuring in the language of law, with as its starting point examples drawn from the canon known as literature (Biondi, Bonfante, etc.).

45. Cf. Ulpian, *D*. 1.6.4: *Nam civium Romanorum* (+S5), *quidam sunt patres familiarum . . ., patres familiarum, alii filii familiarum . . . patres familiarum sunt, qui sunt suae potestatis* (+S6), *sive puberes* (S3), *sive impuberes* (–S3); Ulpian *D*. 50.16.195.2: *pater autem familias appellatur, qui in domo dominium* habet (+S7), *recteque hoc nomine appellatur, quamvis filium non habeat* (–S4). The features *civis romanus* and *sui iuris* are related to the legal function of the classeme *persona* (agent of legal transactions) which comprises the notion of *paterfamilias*.

46. Cf. M. Villey, op. cit., pp. 48 ff.

47. The existence of a legal lexicon *sui generis* brings to light the methodological flaw which taxes any approach of legal meaning operating on the exclusive base of etymology and

of literary occurrences. The thesis of Biondi (op. cit.) can be thus summarised: In the beginning, the terms of law were transparent. The etymology provides us with the key to their natural (!) meaning, which, later on, was superseded by . . . conventional(!) meanings that cast a shadow over the beautiful initial transparency. In order to interpret a legal concept, one needs to go back to find the core of its meaning. It is this attitude, unfortunately quite widespread, which condemns the works of such eminent specialist of Roman law as is P. Bonfante to stay on an approximative level. In dealing with the notion of good faith, Bonfante does not hesitate to write: 'Io consiglio di leggere fuori dei giureconsulti per sentire quello che i giureconsulti romani sentivano veramente nella parola / I would suggest to read *outside of the writing of the jurists*, in order to grasp what the jurists felt in using this or that word.' (loc. cit.)

48. *Semantica . . .*, pp. 83 ff.
49. Cf. Georg Henrik von Wright, *Norm and Action: A Logical Enquiry*, 1963; G. Kalinowski, 'Droit et logique symbolique', *APD* (*Archives de Philosophie de droit*), 1963; 'Le syllogisme d'application du droit', *APD*, 1964; Introduction à la logique juridique, *APD*, 1965.
50. *Semantica . . .*, pp. 51 ff., pp. 95 ff.
51. Example: Paul, *D.* 7.1.1.: *Usus fructus est ius alienis rebus utendi fruendi salva rerum substantia* (usufruct is the right of using of enjoying things owned by another without touching their substance). Carcaterra (*Semantica . . .*, p. 60) suggests that Justinian has integrated this passage with the intention of making of it a legal rule (we would like to add to this that in the mind of the jurisconsult Paul this definition probably had a normative dimension). Its basic structure can be rendered by means of comparison with the action formula that sanctions the *ususfructus*. *Si paret A. Augerio ius esse fundus quo de agitur uti frui . . . : iudex condemna.* (If AA appears to have a usufruct in the land at stake, let the judge condemn [AA's opponent NN]). The search for the deep structure of our statement thus has the effect of displacing it – from the statute of a definition to that of a legal rule:

> *si cui usus fructus est* / if someone has a usufruct (condition, *cas*)
> *ei ius utendi fruendi alienis rebus esto, salva rerum substantia/* then let him use and enjoy without touching the substance (legal consequence, rule).

All Roman legal definitions appear in our eyes to be in need of interpretation according to this characteristic scheme. In this way, the definition that Gaius gives of the species *'res mancipi'* (*mancipi vero res sunt que per mancipationem ad alium transferuntur / res mancipi* are called things that are exchanged by *mancipatio*) reflects in reality only the constative form, within the framework of a didactic exposition, given to the rule according to which the *res mancipi* can be transferred according to the solemn mode of the mancipation. It is legitimate to analyse these definitions as being the result of the transformation of a deep structure, which is imperative, into a superficial structure that is merely constative or indicative.

Four

The Law between Words and Things: Rhetoric and Case Law in Rome

That a rationality reveals itself in law requires no demonstration, common sense offering a broad enough range of evidence. It is equally easy to statistically locate the preponderant ways of legal reasoning. Yet, none of this leads us any further than to the claim that law is the site of one of many manifestations of a currently prevailing general type of rationality. Despite it all, one distinctive feature of law does exist: law is the only discourse that produces the world that it designates. This status reflects itself in what is so strange about legal discourse. In an atmosphere oscillating between Molière and metaphysics, the law presents words in the process of being dissected, and this ever further – until the point where one takes them for things.

Marxist critique, in order to account for the phenomenon, speaks indistinctly of reification and fetishism. It apparently intends to unmask the effectively existing social relations that the law encompasses – yet while doing so, it obfuscates them at the same time, by giving them a formal existence. This type of analysis – that, notably of Michel Miaille[1] – has the immense merit of posing, clearly and without the usual commonplaces, the problem of the law's relation to the thing that it designates. The legal norm is as little the ultimate source of obligation as it is a purely constative model of immanent values. Neither is the jurist the living voice in the service of absolute imperatives, nor (indeed even less) is their role correctly described as that of the judicious gardener of a world featuring good fruit and bad fruit (although, admittedly, countless 'general introductions to law' are introductions to precisely this vision). Law transforms the social world into a language that endows it with a different mode of being, by means of transposing it into a normative register that 'realises' that which is obligatory – much as money, in the moment at which it is exchanged, 'realises' the value of a purchased object.[2] Less easily admitted, on the other hand, is the claim that this type of language has to wait for the commodity form of exchange – and more generally, for the capitalist mode of production – to emerge, in order to impose itself.[3] I do not dispute the existence of a relationship of the sort: abstract value and the abstract subject are, indeed, at the centre of the legal vision. Yet this abstraction emerged on a vastly different terrain than the bourgeois universe. Like it or not, this 'form' is Roman, as is the transposition from which it results. It emerged within a precise mental and cultural context that needs to be understood if one wishes to situate law in its historical setting. Exploring the interval, the qualitative leap, that separates a thought that lacks all the features we recognise as the constituent specifics of law, that is thus pre-legal, from the mode of thinking law that is fundamentally still ours, today; detecting the emergence of the discontinuity that accounts for the advent of an abstract normative language; inventorying the fractures that manifest similar mutations taking place at a variety of levels: these are ways of providing us with a chance to pierce the mystery of the juridical. To limit the analysis to the current mode of production, the self-restraint in which M. Miaille's work excels, just does not do the job. The connection he establishes imposes itself, on closer examination, only once one dispenses with the entire intermediate zone that spans the distance between archaic systems and our own; this parenthesis, though it might be required in view of certain historico-deductive projects, comes at the price of missing the very point that the legal historian must identify as being his essential point.

Contemporary lawyers who look into Justinian's *Digest* find themselves in familiar territory. True, it deals with free men and slaves, land both in Italy and in the provinces, Quiritian and Praetorian property, *actiones* that are 'due' and such that are 'granted'; but in all of this, the lawyer will recognise the same normative-constative discourse that 'reveals' – or indeed 'realises' – that which the relationships between individuals in the city appear to conceal. What the legal practitioner of our days will be struck by when looking into Roman case law – provided he identifies the conceptual oppositions that structure it and the typologies that govern it – is the utter abstraction at work – at work in Rome as much as it is in modern law. There is one identical rationality, indeed, one identical type of speech, whether called legal or jurisprudential, that plays out in the field of law, from classical antiquity to the current world.

At the time in which classical Latin was the language, writers were no longer able to understand the *formulae* of archaic Roman law. In their ears, they had a ridiculous ring. The jurist Gaius made fun of an ancient action to claim damages in which the litigant lost his case because, instead of using the word 'arbor' (tree), he referred to his ransacked vines by referring to them as 'vines'.[4] More generally, all archaisms, except where they were used for stylistic reasons, provoked the indignity of the cultivated public, Cicero included. Even more than the outdated *verba* themselves, what was rejected was the rigidity of the ways in which the tradition used them, and the irrational power of words at large. Yet, it would be insufficient to attribute this to some attempt of 'overcoming formalism'.[5] What the notion of formalism, coined in the context of legal orders that are shaped by a distinction of form and substance, does to a culture where such a separation does not exist, is to anachronistically project a conception that has its origin in a later development. It thereby invites the misunderstanding that this absence is a deficiency, or an undue confusion of opposites. In archaic Roman law, which is essentially ritualistic and oral, the formula is not an added supplement; it is what gives rise to legally binding situations by means of some sort of inherent rule. That the force of law lies in the words that command its enforcement, has never been said more powerfully than by the rule '*Uti lingua nuncupassit, ita ius esto*' ('that which has been said, let it be law'; for current English translations of this phrase of the *Twelve Tables*, see above, Chapter 3, note 24), a *regula iuris* affecting legal acts (*nexum*: loan, *mancipium*: real transfer) in the law of the XII Tables.[6] None of the known archaic formulas can be interpreted otherwise than via the assumed sameness (or 'itselfness') of the thing said; there is no extrinsic reference; rather, the formula confers existence upon its own content alone.[7] Louis Gernet, dealing with Ancient Greece, has demonstrated the interferences from religious factors that have invested pre-law with its efficacy.[8] Yet, there exists a point at which the explanatory power of such interferences stops. This point is to be found in Rome, where some believe they have identified at work what they call a 'secularisation of speech', indeed a 'ritual creation of law'.[9] But formulations like these, albeit suggestive, contribute little to clearing the clouds, even less to bringing to light the effective resources of a mentality that functioned by means of oppositions different from our oppositions. Which oppositions? It might be better to approach the problem backwards, and to try getting hold of the obstacles which prevented a Cicero or a Gaius from looking on these ancient rituals from any standpoint other than that of their own time.

After all, what surprises Gaius is not only the excessive rigidity of the *'legis actiones'*. More decisively, what he refuses to admit is basically the inefficacy of a discourse used outside of its normal designating function. Since vines were, in fact, the matter of debate, to say 'vines' instead of 'trees' was simply to call something by its name: it would be unnatural to reject a word when it applied precisely to the thing signified. Most of the commentators or glossators of the law of the XII Tables start from the same presupposition: language serves to convey a reference to external objects; the search for meanings thus limits itself to that of the referent which corresponds to a particular term. With respect to the magical incantations mentioned (as *malum carmen*) in the legislation of the ten authors committed to writing the law of the Ten Tables, Pliny the Elder asked if the words pronounced in the *incantatio* had any meaning (literally 'amounted to anything': *'valeantne aliquid verba et incantamenta carminum'*).[10] The *occentatio*, a kind of ritual charivari, was rationalised by Festus as an insulting noise intended to damage the reputation of the person targeted.[11] The rule *'uti lingua nuncupassit'*, already quoted, was provided by Cincius with a narrowly literal interpretation, which neglected the inherent power of those formulary words, forestaging, instead, their precision and accuracy, and linking all legal effect they have to the latter, rather than to their dynamism.[12] In the same spirit, Varro translated *nuncupare*, 'to proclaim', by *nominare*, 'to name'.[13] This impoverishment of an initially much richer meaning supposes a purely heteronomous conception of language, itself based on a dichotomy of being and saying. Which in turn explains the anachronistic misinterpretation of Gaius who, commenting on the same decemviral norm, believed he recognised there the contractual principle of the autonomy of the will: if all that is pronounced can be law, then, he thought, this posits the conditions that there are no limits to the will of the parties.[14] The displacement that is enacted, then, is not towards 'reality', but rather towards the will.

All these attitudes are inscribed in one identical state of mind. They denote the emerging of an approach of law as a discourse that is both rational and effective. It is rational, as it serves to communicate that which is, or that which is willed; it is efficient, because this communication is at the same time a 'formal consideration', in other words a sanction supplied with obligatory effect. The step thus leads from a pre-legal type of mentality, in which language was understood (as was gesture) to be a force that is deployed with the goal of obtaining an effective repercussion on the real, and in which thus the function of the symbol transcended the dimension of its meaning, toward a mode of thought enacting, between these two levels, a genuine disjunction. This, at least, is how things tend to appear; for, as we shall see, this provisional separation once enacted, the two planes will meet again in a new space in which it will be up to words to become the new body of 'things legal'. The break between these two states or statuses of juridical discourse, between these two mental organisations of law, takes place right at the centre of the Greco-Roman period. This is what needs to be explained now.

The decisive progress of law since the second century BCE has for a long time been understood by reference to external factors. Among the latter, the economy is obviously in the pole position: the considerable development of contractual and commercial law is effectively inseparable from Rome's position within Mediterranean trade, henceforth central. Also frequently invoked is the thinking of the Greeks; it is true that the triumph of Hellenism takes place in the Rome of the Scipios, an overlay that will be increasingly effectual. Dialecticians and rhetoricians nourished a whole intellectual life which was organised in 'circles'; the teaching they provided was absorbed in the most direct manner by wealthy and intellectually ambitious youth, in the schools or under the schoolmasters active in colonised Greece.

The study of these contacts, however, has been entrusted upon a problematic of 'influences' that has been rather narrowly conceived. Those whose work follows this perspective insist above all upon various examples of 'borrowing'.[15] It is an equally tedious pastime to establish an inventory of the work devoted to the well-worn theme of strict law and equity,[16] to the even more threadbare question of textual interpretation extensive or literal,[17] to any one of the numerous other unjustified rapprochements. For, frankly speaking, these approaches are ways of looking through the small end of the telescope. Apart from the similarities which some specialists are so keen to isolate, what remains to account for is the essential bit: the fact that law in its entirety has been transformed from within; that it has established itself as a discourse and as a system; that it makes claim to be viewed as a science of its own. Law's efforts to become ever more specific – efforts through which it constitutes itself as an autonomous power, and emerges out of 'the social' – cannot be separated, in my view, from a much more compassing reflection on law's language and on the objects of its discourse, with a particular focus on the distance that separates law, within the universe of meanings, from other branches of knowledge. From rhetoric, to start with, that catch-all science that constitutes, in Rome, both a foundational discipline and the most common cultural denominator. And that presents itself, to boot, as a giant venture destined to isolate, words and things, contents of thought and tools for communication (ranging from the linguistic sign to the sphere of vocal or corporeal expression). It is courtesy of its claim of offering a science of discourse as such that rhetoric has been able to give rise to the view, even the (lawyerly) conviction (immediately translated into practice), that law is a science of things.

Even so, rhetoric has not exercised an 'influence on law', nor even provoked a 'reaction against law'. Rather, we should try to understand the social importance of rhetoric as a universal grid of thought, a compendium of common values and recognised mental functions, and, more especially, a social practice – a code that governs all public activity, that is to say: all speech. For in Rome, as well as in Athens, power and social influence were exercised, as we know, through discourse.[18] One only has to read and put into perspective Cicero's *Brutus* and Tacitus' *Dialogue of Orators* in order to understand what was, for the ancients, simply an obvious fact: that the history of public men is a history of orators. Thus, the rise of the goal of liberty, therefore the goal of politics, also sounds the death knell for rhetoric *qua* free speech in a free city: the future it opens is that of the *'belles lettres'*, of those innocent exercises in tropes and figures to which the art of *rhesis* will henceforth boil down.[19] Let us note the primarily eristic function to which this now aesthetic and formal aspect – the study of *verba* – had first of all been subordinated: it used to be a matter of winning the point at stake, of reducing to silence the opponent in an oral confrontation. The oratorical duel, the verbal projection of a fight taking place in a judicial or political arena, was conceived as a fight of two bodies of flesh and blood tearing each other apart on a battleground ending with one of them killing the other.[20] The recurrence of metaphors involving body and war[21] conveys a sense that the debate is a transposed combat and that the symbolic killing of one's adversary is the only recognised form of war or private revenge. Assimilated to a body, discourse can display all its violence, and this – at least to a certain extent – without threatening the civil peace.

Yet, despite the transubstantiation of the orator taking on the metaphorical flesh of discourse, there is nothing fictional about these debates. Power, honour, property is what is normally at stake in them. Many cultures included a rhetoric; the Roman has staged a codified drama resolving conflicts of interest through speech in the presence of a shared audience.

The point here is: that which is at stake in such a dispute, that which will be singled out, is an object, a *res*. The opposition of *res* and *verba* is located at the core of the rhetorical project. It has formed the base of all the divisions and subdivisions of the discipline, from the *Rhetoric for Herennius* to Quintilian's *Oratory Institutions*. Putting aside *actio* and *memoria*, which concern the act of enunciation, and referring instead to 'hysteric ritual' (as R. Barthes called it) – a preference which, incidentally, teaches us more about the Roman human being than many pages of Livy – we find that the work of the orator belongs to three principal operations:

the search for ideas (*inventio*), the articulation of a discourse (*dispositio*), and the fact of putting it in a discursive form (*elocutio*), in which the first concerns the *res*, the last the *verba*, and the second a mixture of the two.[22] The same couple *res/verba* accounts for the essential parts of the discourse: exhibition and argumentation are the abode of the *res*, while the exordium and the peroration serve as an aggrandising foil for the *verba*.[23] Moreover, the three functions of discourse hinge on the preceding distinctions: to instruct (*docere*), which is the proper object of argumentation, belongs to the domain of 'things', whereas to please (*conciliare, placere, delectare*), to touch (*movere*) and to attract the good graces or move the audience, are located toward the *exordium* and the *peroratio*, and are thus a matter of 'words'.[24]

Yet what precisely are these 'things', what is this *materia* that the speaker has at his disposal? We are again confronted with a tripartition, even if its nature differs from previous classifications: instead of divisions that are instrumental or functional, we are dealing with genuine cultural classes. Depending on content, these public discourses belong to the demonstrative, the deliberative or the judicial genre.[25] 'Deliberative' and 'judicial' refer to political speeches and civil or criminal pleas, 'demonstrative' to speeches of praise or blame, *laus* or *vituperatio*, pronounced under various circumstances: funeral eulogies, military eloquence, *damnationes memoriae*, etc. We can see that this *summa divisio* is part of a civic framework which includes three orders of knowledge: courts (specialised judges, or people's courts), where law and justice, *ius* and *aequum*, are pursued through *accusatio* and *defensio*; assemblies; and finally, the senate, where the *suasio* and the *dissuasio* revolve around the useful, understood as the value that is proper to politics.[26] On the other hand, the *honestum* – ethics, in other words – does not have a properly defined place. We can talk about it in all instances where the demonstrative genre, even if it sometimes gives rise to ceremonial speeches, is most often mixed with the judicial and the deliberative, in order to add praise, as well as blame, of a person to specific political and legal arguments.[27] This is why, from the point of view of institutional topography, the realm of ethics is inseparable from the two main functions that, in a city, give rise to speech. For, in the end, all classifications of public discourse boil down to the opposition between deliberations and decision-making processes: *consilium/causa*, or indeed: *res publica/causa*.[28] Strictly speaking, what distinguishes the *causa* is that it deals with the question 'what is equitable' ('*quid aequum sit*');[29] it is in view of this, that it has been 'set up in the law' ('*in iure civili posita*').[30] However, these skills – these human sciences – which the orator will be required to have at his disposal, in no way constitute the object of rhetoric properly speaking. The *res/verba* opposition, which remains fundamental, needs to be understood in the sense that the *res* provides not an end but rather a means, less an object than an instrument. Like *verba*, *res* are used in order to produce convincing arguments, in view of winning a given cause. All rhetoricians since Aristotle agree on this point: judicial discourse does not aim in particular at the truth, but rather at efficacy.[31] In this context, the notion of 'well-adaptedness' (*decorum*) is central at every level of oratory practice: it determines that which, in each circumstance, is appropriate for the orator, to fit, to the case at hand, the arguments, the plan, the words, the style he uses, with no concern other than winning it.[32] This cynical attitude is what has made possible, on reflection, the serenity and the accountant-like cold-bloodedness with which rhetoric makes sure that every idea, every argument, is located in its proper place on the grid. This is what allows these 'things', organised as they are according to the distribution of paradigms, to provide a pool of staple notions – and thus, to fulfil their role as notions that, without ever being discussed between the orators, fuel each debate of their debates with its issues. Justice, or Utility, are among the categories that enable the 'user' of Rhetoric to present their claims.

Thus, even if it is not a science in the sense that it is endowed with a content of its own, rhetoric goes along with a political, legal or ethical material composed of a priori units of discourse. In this sense, it operates a radical disjunction between the order of the word and the order of the world, with discourse, or discursive action, acting as their articulation. It limits itself to the communication of that which exists, or is 'out there'; more exactly (since we are dealing with a discourse of efficacy rather than truth) that which is conventionally recognised as being 'out there' or existing;

hence, it is only in appearance that the action it exercises upon the audience, the reality it tends to produce, resides in the dramaturgy of the *actio* or the spells of the *elocutio*. In fact, these virtues are unessential: in reality, it is in the very heart of *inventio*, where the *res* are arranged to constitute a rational sequence, that the link is formed in which the rhetor imprisons his addressees. That 'sweet *suasio*', Latin sister of *peithô*, is lodged in the argumentation itself.[33] The most astonishing bit here is not that this game, made of lying and of truth-telling, was recognised as such, or that Cicero, for example, a relatively scrupulous mind, was able to outline his own chiaroscuro with good conscience. Let us rather admire the fact that these 'things' were isolated successfully enough, not only to render their exchange possible, but also to shield them from any further curiosity, apart from the interest in their *locus* ('place') – to the point, indeed, of transforming them into a species of intangible cultural items. We will later see how the law, with less cynicism and also with less clairvoyance, will proceed with hypostatising its own objects by placing them in a world of truth.

There exists however quite another sense of *res*, which refers to the subject at stake in a dispute. Litigation supposes that boundaries are defined. These boundaries are traced each time a *quaestio* is formulated, by means of a theory transfer that can be understood conveniently as a form of dialectical labour and that involves a whole legal thinking caught in the act. At the basis of this effort lies the concept of convenience – or of adaptation, if you prefer. That which has been at stake in the discussion above, including the entire issue of argumentation, exists only on the inside of a conflict, and it is this conflict which needs to be situated in its own turn: to subordinate the exercise of *eloquentia* as such, *res* and *verba* together, to the laws of this scheme, we have to identify the type, the model to which it relates. Originally, *res* is all there is: we are confronted with innumerable subjects, subjects of an infinite variety, determined by nothing except by the borders that circumscribe the activities taking place within the space – which as we know is the space of all speech – of politics on the one hand, of the bar on the other.[34] Taken in its initial state, the '*res*' has a '*natura*' of its own,[35] which is to say a set of determinations that are inscribed in it: which is why the arguments, 'entrenched within the thing' (*'in re insiti'*), need to be extracted like a mineral from its matrix.[36] This, however, requires one to rely on 'points of support', solid reference benchmarks. The first of these benchmarks is *controversia*, the controversy itself[37] – which draws between the litigants a closed space in which the subject matter of the dispute is contained. The controversy is not a substance, it is not about content; it is a mere container, an external limit, the one that is projected by the fact of two adversaries facing one another. The 'thing' debated is posited in this common centre, *'res in controversia posita'*.[38] Understood as part and parcel of this setting, the *res* becomes a *causa*. The adversaries, forced to agree on what separates them, are partners of a contract – *negotium, conventio* – which gives rise to a new, purely conventional legal situation, that is to say, to the *causa*, which is defined as an agreement about a disagreement.[39] The *causa* is this 'thing' transformed and placed within the controversy, a 'thing posited in the dispute of the parties and in the controversy'.[40] This is the first step in the process of the conversion into discursive form, by means of a contract, of all the acts of violence to be resolved by the trial.

The second stage takes us from the *causa* to the *quaestio*. Indeed, up to this point, the *causa* still remains too concrete. It must be purged of all determinations – the various circumstances and persons it involves[41] – which occlude what forms its essence: an *infinita quaestio*. A pure problem, in other words.[42] This abstraction results in what every *causa* boils down to: a kind ('genus') of its own.[43] It is in this sense as well that one can speak of a *natura causae*, which is nothing other than the cause's generic content.[44] This is finally, and on a more practical level, also the reason why a good lawyer always needs to master, in addition to the legal *topoi*, an *instrumentum causarum*, or inventory of types of conflict to which he may connect them.[45]

What exactly are these species, these *genera causarum*? The task of establishing them is the proper object of the theory of the *status causarum* or 'patterns of causes', which codifies the dialectical proceedings by means of which a case passes to the abstract level of a *causa* – and by means of which the factual disagreement is converted into juristic concepts or *res incorporales*. It is not a waste of time to have a closer look at these procedures: what one can grasp here is, transposed into temporal figures, the intellectual process that is in use in law. Above all, what this reconstituted logical series makes it possible to discern, is how those things without bodies, which are neither words nor things, and which form the base of legal science in Rome, come into existence.

Attributed to the Greek Hermagoras,[46] the theory of *status* sparked a genuine taxonomic fury. It fascinated the rhetoricians.[47] Generally, they distinguished the questions inherent to a subject (*de re*) from those raised by the interpretation of a document, be it a legal text or a private act (*de scripto*).[48] It so happens that only the latter ones, the purely extrinsic issues, have caught the attention of the Romanists.[49] By far the more important ones are, however, the former, which constitute the *genus rationale* (as opposed to the *quaestiones legales*): through a 'study of its nature' (*naturae contemplatio*),[50] this type of *quaestio* allowed the theoretical problem enclosed within a *causa* to be identified.[51] The *genus rationale* comes in four *species*: the *coniectura*, which raises the debate about the existence of a thing (*an sit?*, whether it is? In criminal trials, this concerns the reality of the facts asserted by the accuser and denied by the accused); the *proprietas*, which resolves the issue of the appellation or legal qualification (*quid sit?* what it is?) – here, what is discussed are not the facts, but only their belonging to. A fact always belongs to an available name: to *this* crime, to *that* contract, to any other legally defined situation); the *qualitas* that, based upon facts recognised and duly qualified, seeks to discover, behind such typicity, a value or a quality peculiar to the action at stake – which if found justifies an atypical solution based in equity (*quale sit?* What type of thing it is? This, incidentally, is the seat of the places of *aequum* and *iustum*, as opposed to *ius*); and finally, *translatio*, a type that is heterogeneous with respect to the others, which displaces and in a way suspends the debate, in favour of preliminary exceptions, regarding especially questions of competence (which is why certain rhetoricians prefer to classify it under the heading of *quaestiones legales*).[52]

The two fundamental questions, from a theoretical point of view, are those of *nomen* and *qualitas*, name and quality. These two 'statuses' have their place between the issues of fact and the extrinsic textual problems, at the very centre of a theory which appeals to the resources of law under law's two manifestations in Rome: law determinate, that is, provided with a *nomen* – or in other words, a heading in the *Edictum perpetuum* – and law lacking such a determination, law that is the object of an open research that relies on no other category than the universal one of *justum*.[53] Must this opposition between the legal and the just be read as that of the named and the unnamed?

Consider the following example of *status definitionis*. Flaminius, a plebeian tribune, is pushed from the speaker's platform by his father, right at the moment when he is in the act of proposing an agrarian law opposed to the will of the Senate.[54] The accusation *de maiestate* (lese-majesty) gives rise to a debate, not about the facts, which are not under dispute, but about their juridical nature. At first, the protagonists are content to affirm, and to deny, that they correspond to the incrimination:

> – *intentio*/accusation: '*maiestatem minuisti, quod tribunum plebis de templo deduxisti*' ('By driving the tribune of the plebs from the sacred space, you have diminished the majesty');

> – *depulsio*/defence: '*non minui maiestatem*' ('I haven't diminished the majesty').

These two contrary propositions lead to a first position of the question:

> *quaestio*: '*maiestatemne minuerit?*' ('Did he diminish the majesty/commit lese-majesty?')

The *intentio* of the accuser, as we can see, is based on a provisional and implicit definition of '*minuere maiestatem*'. The alleged acts are briefly stated and presented in the form of an illustration of the elements constituting the offense: pushing (*deducere*) a magistrate (*tribunum plebis*) performing his duties (*de templo*). The *depulsio* of the accused is, in turn, only a provisional moment of his answer: '*non minui maiestatem*'.

Indeed, the accuser has already given a first proof of his act of accusation: in the ensuing situation, since the facts in themselves are undisputed, the denial presented by his adversary can only be based on a new element. In order for this to happen, the debate must start again in reverse order, enacting some kind of inversion of the burden of proof.

This is why the *quaestio* marks a pause, from which the controversy will enter into a second round. The accused provides a reason (exercise of paternal power over his own son) which is refuted by the other party (a private power, like *patria potestas*, cannot hinder a public power, like the *tribunicia potestas*):

– *ratio*: '*in filium enim quam habebam potestatem, in ea sum usus*' ('The power which I had over my son, I have used it here').

– *rationis infirmatio*: '*at enim, qui patria potestate, hoc est privata quadam, tribuniciam potestatem, hoc est populi potestatem infirmat, minuit maiestatem*' ('But he who thwarts, in the name of some private power such as his fatherly power, the tribunitial power which is the power of the people, diminishes the majesty').

This second exchange gives the definitive formulation of the point submitted to the judge's inquiry: this *iudicatio*, also called *disceptatio*, poses the question, as it were, on a second level. Here, the simple statement of the issue, '*Maiestatemne minuerit?*' ('Has he diminished the majesty?'), is followed, with the new precision that results from a synthesis of *ratio* (ground) and *infirmatio* (refutation), by the more complex *iudicatio*: '*minuatne is maiestatem, qui in tribuniciam potestatem patria potestate utatur?*' ('Is it not the case that he who uses his *patria potestas* against the *potestas* of the *tribunus*, diminishes the majesty?').

The first *quaestio*, relating to the correspondence between the unnamed facts and the crime *de maiestate*, suffices to establish that this *causa* belongs to the *status definitionis*. The *iudicatio*, by incorporating the *ratio*'s supplementary determination, tightens the field of the question and crystallises the juridical type and the *nomen* considered by this ultimate statement: '*in tribuniciam potestatem patria potestate utatur*' ('Fatherly power may be used against tribunitial power'). One thus sees that the topical model of the *nomen* is not applied in a direct and brutal way to the constitutive facts of the *res in iudicium deducta* (the thing to be judged). The comparison which characterises this *status causae* passes, as we have already indicated, through a double process of analysis: decomposition of the referential *nomen* into its semantic units (this decomposition already underlies the *intentio*'s enunciation) and a restructuring of the facts, the *res*, through an articulation proper to the definition considered. However, this restructuring is carried out in two stages, which correspond to the two successive syntheses of the *quaestio* and the *iudicatio*. The second provides the irreducible element that, if necessary, will determine a specific difference between the situation-object of the dispute and the ideal category of *crimen maiestatis*. This is the reason why conflict suddenly re-emerges around the *ratio* and why it is concluded, at the level of the 'point to be decided', with an emphasis on *patria potestas*. Numerous other examples would confirm this model.[55] In all cases, the *nomen* of reference is decomposed into its constitutive semantic units in order to make it correspond, feature for feature, to the essential elements of a *causa* of which it is at once the matrix and the linguistic transposition.[56] It serves, according to a suggestive expression, to *explicare executereque verbum*:[57] to develop the concept and bring out its significant elements.

In the *status qualitatis*, on the contrary, the interpreter has no model to which he can connect the controversy. The disputants focus their debate on a question posed to the judge that derives less from a conceptual logic, based on a set of given premises, than from an open search, which calls for genuine value judgements. More precisely, the argument is based on criteria of equity: '*aequi et iniqui natura quaeritur*'.[58] In the case of criminal trials, for example, the true intent of the accused will be questioned.[59] Whether purely and simply denied (*purgatio*), or excused with reference to a cause of unaccountability (*remotio et relatio criminis*) in case the act was committed either under duress or under provocation – even if it was justified by the greater utility of the achieved purpose (*comparatio*) – the criminal will is here the object of a qualification which, if indirectly, gives rise to legal problems.[60] However, as in the case of *status definitionis*, the final status of the problem results from a kind of resurfacing of the question, the successive steps of the debate marking the dialectical moments leading towards a synthesis.

An example here is provided by the proceedings against consul Opimius, accused of having executed C. Gracchus without a trial. At first glance, the case is based on a direct application of the law: the murder having been perpetrated, the penalty needed to be imposed according to the provisions. But when Opimius claims to have acted legitimately, namely in accordance with the superior principle of the Republic's safety, the *ratio* sends the debate into a second round.[61] We are here in the presence of a case of *comparatio*, thus in the realm of the issue of *qualitas* already referred to.[62] To this argument, which remains outside of the incriminated facts, the accuser opposes a formal negation (*rationis infirmatio*): even if one admits that C. Gracchus was a criminal, could he be executed without judgment?[63] The point to decide (*iudicatio*) arises from this second-order confrontation: 'Could Opimius, in the interest of the Republic, legitimately kill a citizen who imperilled its foundations, before his condemnation?'[64]

As we can see, the mechanism of this type of *causae* is much more complex than the one mentioned above. Here, the law-applying *iudicatio*, instead of automatically ensuing from an examination of the facts is the result of the grafting of a new element onto the factual and legal which has the effect of bringing the dispute back, on a new level. The way out of this debate is found in a problem which, without appealing to existing law, does involve the search for an original solution.

A different example is found in Quintilian.[65] Orestes has killed his mother. The exchange of arguments is not exhausted by the question of whether a rigorous application of the prescribed penalty would have been appropriate. Instead, it begins again with the argument (*ratio*) of Orestes: my act is legitimate, he says, because Clytemnestra killed Agamemnon; and with his accuser's reply (*rationis infirmatio*): despite that, you did not have the right to kill her. The point to be decided on (*iudicatio*) is as follows: did Orestes have the right to kill Clytemnestra, because she murdered her husband?

We can learn from these two examples that the whole debate is centred on the particular quality of an act: the circumstances defined, what remains to be determined is whether the act was committed *recte*; in this manner, since positive law does not admit revenge, the question is whether equity would. Some general notions intervene (*aequum, iustum, ...*), but no specific category. With *proprietas*, the search for a legal solution remained contained in the limits of what has been designated by the *nomen* at stake. Without taking up the endeavour of jurisprudential creation strictly speaking, the interpreter decided or refused to subsume a fact or a concrete situation under a pre-existing schema, itself subject to extensive or restrictive interpretation, depending on the requirements of the case. In dealing with *qualitas*, on the contrary, the process was freer. *Qualitas* operates as a creator of law. *Qualitas* directs to a value judgement, or in other words to a discretionary decision that established, in a single movement, both the solution expected and the justification that supports it.

I have shown elsewhere[66] that the *nomen* and the *qualitas* (under the aspect of the *iustum*), constituted the two poles of legal interpretation in Rome. All the cases brought before the *praetor* – or likewise, before the jurisconsult in asking him for advice – are from either named *causae*, *causae* bearing one of the specific names from civil or praetorian law, and thus corresponding to one of the rubrics of the *Edictum*, or from unnamed causes, generally qualified as *iustae causae*. A corollary: there is no such thing as named situations that also receive the qualification of *iustae*; plus, there is no such thing as *iustae causae* which cover a recognised civil or edictal situation; the latter result from a particular procedure, the *causae cognitio*, which venture to give recognition and sanction to such *casus* as do not fit into any paradigm. Finally and importantly, the concepts that surround the names of named causes are never generic, but always specific: the question is never one of contract and of crime, for example; instead, it is one of sale and of mandate, of theft and of wrongful loss. This set of peculiarities defines what can be called the typicity of Roman law, which only addresses exemplary situations, a priori schemes to which the numberless practical cases coming up need to be reduced. Only those components and elements of a case that boil down to a *nomen* will make it to full legal existence. Roman law was nominalistic to the extent that names are necessary; it was not nominalistic, however, to the extent that these names were essences or *res iuris*. Its analytic reduction proceeded by way of the subject extracting the substance of the object; by way, that is, of eliminating a share of the controversy, for the benefit of another one, which alone is irreducible and central: the *natura* and the *genus causae* manifest the presence, in every and any *res*, of a *quaestio universa* that allowed the extrication of a specific *causa*. This method projected onto the object an artificial structure which is recognised as its real structure. Inscribed in it were, as if in superimposed layers, the successive moments of the investigation, suggesting that knowledge is located at the very heart of being.[67] Initially founded upon a vision that distinguishes between the words and the things (and the *res* and the *verba*) that designate the world, this approach gives rise, in the end, to a world of words that are things, and one of names that were no longer intellectual tools, but rather essences. At the theoretical level that this approach has dialectically reached, the two planes converge, but they can do so only because, at an earlier stage, they had been separated. In this respect, what the rhetorical environment brings to light is a structure of thought that is fundamentally born out of a mutation in the status of speech. Henceforth conceived as exclusively referential, as forsaking the register of a speech that was at once realising what it designates (which is how the juridical, along with the poetic and the religious, had been understood traditionally),[68] discourse, in the absence of external and tangible things, had no other choice but that of discovering its object in itself. And this is how the law could establish itself as, and within, tautology.

This mutation is carried out and accomplished with the notion of an incorporeal thing. The jurisconsult Gaius, living in the second century of our era, divided all *res* into *corporales* and *incorporales*.[69] Under the guise of this *summa divisio* of goods, it is law as a whole that this antithesis brings to light. Indeed, owing to their exteriority, corporeal things are factually given in advance. Law encounters them only where they surface in relation to appropriation and exchange. The *pars rerum* of the *Institutes* (Books II and III, on possession and ownership), deals only with the modalities of transfer, on the one hand, and with obligations, on the other. The empirical object of these laws fades behind the impersonal relations that transform it into property, right of use, debt, etc. Perhaps one could even show that law is based on absence and on waiting: the Roman distinctions drawn between property and possession, between debt and barter, place law in the distance and in the imaginary.[70]

This transubstantiation of the corporeal into the incorporeal is also observed in the formulary procedure which was imposed towards the second century BCE. With written formulas, authority is linked in the form of a synthetic question posed to the judge, an exact replica of the *iudicationes* in the theory of the *status causae*. This question, more precisely, presents itself as a conditional syllogism, shortened by taking away its major premise, while the conclusion is extended by an imperative sanction (*condemnatio*). But at the same time, the passage from the minor premise to the conclusion also corresponds, with respect to the concrete object of dispute, to a transmutation from the state of *corpus* to that of monetary value:

> If it appears that property X here under dispute belongs to Agerius according to quiritary law, and that this item was not returned to him, then we judge and condemn Negidius to pay Agerius as much money as the property is worth . . . (*quanti ea res erit, . . . tantam pecuniam condemnato . . .*).[71]

There are countless such examples. In all of them, monetary estimation transposes the *corpus* (here, a parcel of land) into its value form.[72] A very important text of Gaius underlines this originality of the formulary procedure: in all actions, real or personal, the measures to be taken include a *pecuniaria aestimatio* (*aestimare* = set a price in money); the *corpus*, or *res ipsa*, is alienated as a *res aestimata*, as an abstract value.[73] Like law, money institutes conventional equalities between things – or, rather, a common measure that reduces them to the state of interchangeable entities.

One thought circulates at these several different levels: present everywhere is the corporeal/incorporeal distinction. One of Cicero's rhetorical texts captures well the fundamental character of this antithesis. All the things that can be defined, he says, are divided into two types. Some exist (*res quae sunt*), can be seen and touched (*quae cerni tangive possunt*), and seldom cause difficulty: land, for example, a house, a wall, a gutter, cattle, etc.; the others do not really exist (*non esse*) and cannot be touched or designated (*tangi demonstrarive non possunt*), but are rather the object of a pure intellection (*cerni tamen animo atque intelligi possunt*), such as acquisitive prescription, guardianship, *gens*, agnates, etc. The latter, all deprived of a corporeal substrate (*quorum rerum nullum subest corpus*), are typically the object of debate and must be explained by a definition (*ea saepe in argumentando definitione explicanda sunt*).[74] This dualism is extremely significant. It is also found in a passage from Sextus Empiricus on the Stoic doctrine of the three elements of signification: the signified, the signifier, and the object. The last two, sound and object, are corporeal; the first, the 'sayable' (*lekton*), is an incorporeal entity.[75] However, Cicero (or his model) passes the dividing line between the visible and the invisible through the referents themselves, and not between the signified and the object. The world of law, in particular, is entirely situated on the side of the incorporeal.

The examples that the rhetorician provides should not mislead us in this respect: *agnatio* (kinship) and *gens* are social realities extrinsic to law. Yet, it is generally not to concrete institutions that a Roman jurist would refer in speaking of *res incorporales*. He was concerned with claims and debts, servitude and usufruct, real and personal rights: all impersonal, abstract relations, purified of their social roots and represented as isolated essences. This binary structure served, here, to distinguish the natural and social world, on the one hand, from, on the other hand, the *res iuris*.

At all levels where we encounter it – rhetorical, legal, economical – this abstract thought proceeded by way of transfer, exchange and substitution. The oppositions in which it results – *res/causa, corpus/res aestimata, res corporalis/ res incorporalis* – are symmetric only in appearance: in reality, the second term always derives from the first, of which it is an equivalent, and a universal form. At the level of the rhetorical confrontation, the particular debates were coined in types of *quaestiones infinitae*. In terms of exchange and value, *aestimatio* realises that which is measurable of a *corpus*. Finally, at the level of law, concrete things and relations vanish under notions that are at once names and incorporeal beings. From things to words, the law is not content to pose an equivalence; instead, it operates a kind of mediation that produces, in between the two, a specific world, that of *realia*. In order to pursue this point further, an analysis of jurisprudential epistemology would be required.

It so happens that these codified contents are the object of a science: jurisprudence. Science of the *res iuris* or, according to the more general expression that metaphysically grounds the law: insight in things divine and human, knowledge of the just and the unjust (*divinarum atque humanarum rerum notitia, iusti atque iniusti scientia*).[76] The terminology in use with the jurisconsults – the prudes (*prudentes*) as they were also called – shows that the elaboration of law does not arise from the logic of choices, but from a cognitive effort striving towards the truth. Verbs which denote an opinion – such as *putare* or *existimare* – are far less common in the *Digest* than verbs which denote intuition and vision (*videre, discernere*); they are also less common than locutions that signify conformity to the true (*recte est, verissimum est, verius est, falsum est*, etc.). The structure of the *responsa* confirms this impression. While the purely factual *casus* is written in the past, the solution, generally unmotivated, is written in the present. But this is not a constative present, it is an apodictic present. (In rhetoric, the present tense corresponds to the time of ethical truth, as opposed to the past tense, which is the judicial time of criminal trials of fact, and the future, which is the time of political deliberation.)[77] What are called rules of law are not practical imperatives, but pure definitions: '*regula est, quae rem quae est breviter enarrat*' ('a brief account of what is at stake in a dispute is called a rule').[78] Moreover, the things that the Roman jurist was acquainted with were represented in the framework of a naturalistic vision of law. I do not say, of 'natural law' – this term designated very precisely everything that, in human institutions, bears the mark of belonging to the nature of living beings: marriage, procreation, education of children, etc. Rather, I am referring to a general and diffuse tendency of the Roman jurisconsults, to endow legal concepts with the objectivity of the natural world. Many of these intangible things, the *res iuris*, were assigned a nature: for example, *contractus, servitus, actio* (in the sense of 'formula-type of action') *legatum, possessio*, etc. In most cases, moreover, the invocation of a *natura* is a tautological move destined to found, outside of any argumentation, the appropriateness of a particular legal solution in relation to the institution designated.[79]

A great thinker of our time has compared law to metaphysics.[80] What one finds at work in classical Roman law, certainly is a metaphysics of the object. Judicial decision-making hypostasises its own categories, since it is predicated on the belief that these categories can be beheld in nature. However, this separation – this 'reification' – is in no way coextensive with law, or a primary datum. Neither is it an epiphenomenon of bourgeois thought (although it does provide the foundations of our juridical rationality). In Rome, towards the second and first centuries BCE, this separation can be grasped as part of a profound intellectual mutation, which affected numerous dimensions of thought. Without discounting an economic explanation – and even less the impact of money, a mechanism that is not unrelated to law, and one that reveals a mental transformation[81] present on both sides – we can ask ourselves whether law, as a modality of abstract thought, is not the achieved expression (perhaps indeed, so to speak, the swan song) of the idea of the city. '*Ius civile*': the right, *ius*, is civil before being public or private, because it establishes, between fellow citizens, a common measure that universalises exchange and legality. If the question is how abstraction, norm and mediation emerge, this is the answer. The rest is ideology.

Notes

1. *Une introduction critique au droit*, Paris 1976, pp. 69 ff.
2. M. Miaille, op. cit., pp. 100 ff., who speaks of a fetishism of the norm and the person (pp. 107–8): 'The law names the true problems, and at the same time, it displaces them'.
3. The author specifies that in archaic societies, the system is, in contrast, largely subject to compartmentalisation, and refers to the studies of L. Gernet on the '*prédroit*'. Yet, in between these archaic laws and the capitalist system, an abstract juridical language has formed, one that cannot be ignored, as it is still largely ours.
4. Gaius IV, 11, with a parallel passage: IV, 30.
5. M. Kaser, *Das römische Privatrecht I*, Munich 1954, p. 34; and earlier, von Ihering, *Geist des römischen Rechts auf*

den verschiedenen Stufen seiner Entwicklung (vol. II), 1894, pp. 470 ff.

6. XII Tables VI, 1 (Riccobono, *Fontes*, I, p. 43).
7. This is particularly clear in the formula of the *sacramentum in rem* (Gaius, IV, 16). See, for the most recent contribution, the study of F. Dupont, 'La scène juridique', in: *Communications*, n. 26, 1977, pp. 70ff ; and, generally, L. Gernet, 'Droit et prédroit en Grèce ancienne' et 'Le temps dans les formes archaïques du droit', in *Anthropologie de la Grèce antique*, Paris 1976.
8. 'Droit et prédroit', op. cit.
9. L. Gernet for the first of these formulas; H. Levi-Bruhl for the second one.
10. *Histoire naturelle*, XXVIII, 2, 10–17.
11. Pauli *excerpta*, L. 191.
12. In Festus, L 176 (*id est uti nominarit, locutusve erit, ita ius esto*). The word *nuncupare* is, in the beginning, not legal but probably religious.
13. *De Lingua Latina*, VI, 60 (for Cincius, cf. the preceding note).
14. 3 *ad* l.12, *Tab. Digeste* 2, 14, 48: *in > traditionibus > [mancipationibus] rerum quodcumque pactum sit, id valere manifestissiumum est.*
15. See, for example, F. Senn, 'De l'influence grecque sur le droit romain de la fin de la République', *Atti del congr. int. dir. rom.*, Rome I, 1933; on the same theme and under the same title, B. Kübler, J. Stroux, ibid., and in numerous studies published since. See, lastly, *La Filosofia greca e il diritto romano*, colloque, Acad. nazionale dei lincei, Rome 1976 (interesting contributions, even if it limits itself, generally, to an 'external' and 'comparative' viewpoint).
16. Since J. Stroux, *Summum ius, summa iniuria*, Leipzig 1926.
17. Thus, B. Vonglis, *La lettre et l'esprit de la loi dans la jurisprudence classique et dans la rhétorique*, Paris 1968, et U. Wesel, *Rhetorische Staatslehre und Gesetzesauslegung der römischen Juristen*, Cologne-Munich, 1967.
18. As to Greece, an interpretational framework can be found in the works of J.-P. Vernant (esp. *The Origins of Greek Thought*, Ithaca, Cornell University Press, 1984, pp. 40 and ff.; and Marcel Détienne, *The Masters of Truth in Archaic Greece*, London, Zone Books, 1996, especially pp. 81 ff. on the 'laicisation' of the spoken word in the city). As far as Rome is concerned, we have to admit to a lack of in-depth reflections on the topic – despite the abundance of existing work on specific points.

19. See R. Barthes, 'L'ancienne rhétorique', in *Communications*, vol. 16, 1970, pp. 70 ff., especially pp. 183 ff.).
20. The comparison with armies in fighting order is a frequent one (thus: Cicero, *Brutus*, 222); arguments are the arrows (*hastae*) with which the rhetors are armed, like foot soldiers (Cicero, ibid. 271).
21. Arguments disposed like soldiers on the battleground: *Rhetoric of Herennius*, III, 10, 18; carnal metaphors: Tacitus, *Dial. of orators*, XXI; Quintilian, *Inst. or.*, II, 5, 12; VIII, AP, 10 and ff. The counterpart of this male vigour of an aggressive discourse is offered by examples stressing the feminine aspect of any precious, all-too heavily beautified/embellished discourse: whence the utter importance in this context of the sartorial theme (cf. T. Todorov, *Théories du symbole*, Paris 1977, pp. 73 ff.).
22. Cf. Cicero, *Partitiones oratoriae*, I, 1, 3; Quintilian, *Inst. or.*, III, 5, 7; VIII, AP, 6.
23. Quintilian, VIII, AP, 27.
24. Quintilian, ibid.
25. This division is already expounded on by Aristotle: *Rhet.*, 1358b. 7; cf. Cic. *De inv.*, 1,5,7. It is canonical, part of all rhetoric treatises: *Ad Heren.* I, 2, 2; II, 1, 1; Cic. *De inv.*, loc. cit.; *De orat.*, II, 89, 340; *part. or.*, 20, 70; *Top.* 24, 91. Quintilian, III, 5, 15.
26. Cic. *De inv.*, II, 4, 12; *part. or.*, 28, 100; cf. *Ad Heren.* III, 4, 8.
27. *Ad Heren.* III, 8, 15.
28. Quintilian, III, 4, 8, 67: *consilium/causa*. Along the same lines: Cic., *De orat.* I, 19, 85: '*disputabant contra diserti homines Athenienses, et in re publica causisque versati*' ('certain Athenians well-spoken and trained in legal and public matters, were arguing against' (that is, against the claim that orators need to provide themselves with a philosophical education)). This distinction is coextensive with another one, one that looms large in the Schools, between *suasoriae* and *causae* (injunctions and recommendations vs legal arguments).
29. *De inv.*, loc. cit.; cf. *Ad Heren.*, 28, 98: *eius generis finis est aequitas . . . in quibus causis quid aequius atque aequissimum sit quaeritur. Top.*, 24, 91: *iudici finis est ius, ex quo etiam nomen* (the context of this is a remark on the *genus iudiciale*). On the relationship between judiciary rhetoric and equity, see already Aristotle, *Rhet.*, 1, 3, 5, 6 (the specific goal of rhetoric, the just, distinguishes it, in particular from the art of the Sophists).

30. Cf. *Part or.*, 28, 100. The list of judiciary *causae* (causes) correspond, in the *Topica*, to the common notions on law and equity: *quas ad causas facultas petitur argumentationum ex his . . . aequitatis locis* (the causes at which the power of arguing aims, starting from those notions of equity). See the outline of *aequitas* in *Part. or.* 37, 130. See, equally, *Ad Heren.* II, 13, 19, and ff. This is most significant, also, for the theory of *status* (aspects), specifically in the *genus rationale*, with its interpretation that is built upon law and equity (cf. *infra*).

31. Aristotle, *Rhet.* I, 1, 1355b, *Ad Heren.* III, 7, 13 and ff., with important examples: 'Birth: for praise, one speaks of his ancestors; if he is of illustrious birth, he was equal to them or even superior; if he is of modest birth, he owes everything to his own, not his ancestors' virtues. For blame, if he is of illustrious birth, he was a shame for his ancestors; if he is of modest birth; he was for them a source of dishonour nonetheless, etc.' Ibid., 15. 'Thus, when we praise, we say that an action was just, that another one was courageous (or moderate, or wise); when we blame, we declare this action unjust, this other action out of control, or cowardly, or stupid', and so on.

32. Cf. Cic., *Orat.*, 35–6, 123.

33. This theme already appears in the work of the poet Ennius, who referred to the 'marrow of persuasion' (*Suadaique medulla*, cf. Cic. *Brutus*, 59: Lat. *suada* = Gr. *peithô*). On the theme of deception generally, see Cic., *Brutus*, 82 ff.; besides, there is no secret about the great pride Cicero took in having won the lawsuit of Cluentius despite the latter's cause having been indefensible (see Quintilian, *Inst. orat.*, II, 17, 21, and Rufinianus, in *Rhet. lat. min*, ed. by Halm, p. 42, 13: *se tenebras offudisse iactavit iudicibus Cluentianis*); on the issue of deception in the rhetors and Sophists of Greece (*apatê*), see M. Détienne, op. cit., pp. 105 ff.

34. Cic. *De orat.* I, 12, 52: *certarum rerum forensibus cancellis circumscriptam scientiam.* See also, *Ad Heren.* I, 2, 2; Quintilian, II, 20–2.

35. *Ad Heren.* III, 2, 2; Cic., *De orat.*, III, 30, 120.

36. Cic., *Part. or.*, 1, 5, 6; *De orat.*, II, 34, 147; cf. *Ad Heren.*, 1, 3, 5.

37. Or: *disputatio, contentio, disceptatio.*

38. Cic., *de orat.*, II, 19, 78.

39. *De orat.*, II, 30, 132: *quid faciat causam, id est quo sublato controversia stare non possit* ('that which constitutes the cause, or in other words, that without which the controversy cannot be sustained'); cf., as well, II, 19, 78; III, 28, 109. *Ad Heren.* I, 3,4:

divisio est per quam aperimus quis conveniat, quid in controversia sit ('It is the division that reveals the stake of a controversy'). The *divisio* is the part of the outline which announces the principal points of the demonstration. After the *exordium,* a preamble, of ornamental character, the *divisio* poses the foundations of the dispute. Cf., also, Quintilian, III, 5, 117. *De inv.* I, 22, 31: *quid cum adversariis conveniat et quid in contro-versia relinquatur ostendit* ('it shows that which will be agreed between the adversaries and that which will be left to the dispute to decide upon'), about *partitio,* that is, the *divisio.* Cic., *Fin.,* II, 3: *omnis autem in quaerenda, quae via quadam et ratione habetur, oratio praescribere primum debet, ut quibusdam in formulis ea res agetur, ut inter quos disseritur conveniat, quis sit id de quo disseratur.* This is an interesting text, first because it underscores the contractual nature of the controversy, but also because the use of *praescribere* as the means of express-ing the preliminary agreement supposed by the controversy is analogous to the procedural use of the spoken word (cf. Gaius IV, 131a; 137), and corresponds, as is emphasised by Cicero himself, to the same function as the *praescriptio* of the formula.

40. Cic., *De orat.* II, 19, 78: *'causam appellant rem positam in discep-tatione reorum et controversia . . .'.* Cf. Quintilian, II, 5, 18.

41. *'Hominum innumerabiles personae'* et *'infinita temporum vari-etas'*: Cic. *De orat.,* II, 34, 145 (cf. *De legibus,* II, 47).

42. Cic. *De orat.* I, 31, 138; II, 15, 65; etc. Quintilian, III, 5, 5. *Quaestio universa: De orat.* II, 17, 71 and III, 30, 120.

43. Cf. *Ad Heren.* III, 8, 15: *inventione . . . ad omne causae genus adcommodata; De orat.,* II, 46, 175: *quod autem argumentorum genus cuique causarum generi maxime conveniat . . .; De oratore* 35, 122: *cum tam pauca sunt genera causarum etiam argumento-rum praecepta pauca sunt.* Whence the importance of the dis-tinction between one and the other *genus causae* (cf. *de inv.,* II, 30, 92: *hoc genus causae cum superiore hoc differt, quod . . .).* In the terminology of the orators, the difference between *genus* and *species* is not always sufficiently highlighted: one is often used for the other, except precisely where the whole point is to oppose them one to the other. The same applies to the jurists: Gaius frequently uses *genus* for *species,* and the other way around. On this theme, see U. von Lübtow: *Betrachtungen zum gaianischen Obligationenschema,* Milan, 1951.

44. Thus, in the expression: *in generum causis atque naturis omnia sita esse* (*De orat.,* II, 34, 145); also, arguments refer *'ad causae*

vim ac naturam' (*De orat.* II, 32, 141); *complectare genus naturamque causae'* (*De orat.* II, 34, 145, etc.).

45. *De orat.* II, 34, 146. cf. *Brutus*, 271.
46. Cf. Quintilian, *Inst. or.*, III, 6, 21.
47. See the outline of all these classifications in Quintilian, III, 6.
48. Quintilian III, 6, 56, and ff.
49. Cf. Stroux, Wesel, Vonglis, op. cit.
50. Quintilian III, 6, 86; cf. *Tropiques*, 21, 82: *cognitionis quaestio*.
51. Certain rhetoricians refused to admit text-related questions within the theory of *status causae* (cf. Cic., *Or.*, 34, 121; Quintilian III, 6, 46).
52. Quintilian, and Cicero generally – i.e. except in his first treatise (*De inventione*, I, 8, 10) – belong to those.
53. Cf. *infra* in the text.
54. *De inventione*, II, 17, 52.
55. Examples: trial of C. Iunius Norbanus, accused of *maiestate* (discussion as to rhetorics in Cic., *Part. or.*, 30, 105); trial of C. Rabirius (Cic., *Orator* 29, 103); of Q. Caepio (*Ad Heren.* I, 12, 21); example of *status definitionis* in a case of prevarication: *Part. or.* 36, 124–5. The *Pro Caecina* has its core equally in the question of definition. J. Stroux, *Summum ius Summa iniuria*, op. cit., pp. 55 ff.) refers this trial to an issue of 'interpretation (*status legalis*): equity against the strict sense of the *verba*. See, contra, U. Wesel, *Rhetorische Statuslehre*, op. cit., pp. 31 ff., with decisive arguments as to the belonging to the *status definitionis*. Cicero is, incidentally, quite explicit in *Orator*, 29, 102: *Tota mihi causa pro Caecina de verbis interdicti fuit* (dealing with a prohibition questioned as to its foundation by the adversary, as Caecina has not been evicted from his property, but rather had been stopped from gaining a foothold in it in the first place. Cf., equally, *Top.* IV, 23, about the rule: *'auctoritas fundi biennium est'* ('for land to be called one's own, the delay is two years'). Can this rule be applied to buildings, if *'in lege aedes non appellantur et sunt ceterarum rerum quarum annuust usus'* ('in the law there is no mention of buildings, which figure among the other things, where the delay is one year')? The solution to the problem depends on the definition of the *causa*. A dispute about a building is an analogue to an affair about a rural property, and should be related to the same principles: *'valeat aequitas, quae paribus in causis paria iura desiderat'* ('let equity assign similar rights in similar situations'). It is easy to see that a call for *pares causae* witnesses an effort towards a definition by analogy.

56. Cf. *De inv.* II, 25, 108: *atque in hoc genere causarum* (genre: '*quid vocetur*') *non nulli praecipiunt, ut verbum illud, quod causam facit, breviter uterque definiat*; cf. *De inv.* I, 8, 11: *nominis est controversia, cum de facto convenit et queritur, id quod factum est quo nomine appelletur* (in this type of *causae* some recommend that the two opponents each define the word that stands in for the cause of their dispute). Example: *De inv.* loc. cit.: *quare in eiusmodi generibus definienda est res et verbis et breviter describenda, ut, si quis sacrum ex privato surripuerit, utrum fur an sacrilegus sit iudicandus.* The basic semantic elements: *surripuere* + *sacrum* + *ex privato* are not enough, here, to distinguish the *furtum* from the *sacrilegium*; there is a supplementary seme that is lacking between the two offences, some specific difference that determines, with the *nomen* attributed to the offender, the type of action to be taken against him. On the 'semic' analysis in use with the Romans, see the important works of A. Carcaterra, especially *Semantica degli enunciati normativo-giuridici romani. Interpretatio iuris*, Bari 1972. On these, see Y. P. Thomas, 'La langue du droit romain. Problèmes et méthodes', *Archive de Philosophie du droit* 1974, 103–25 [i.e. Chapter 3 of the present volume, trans. note]; see, also, L. Lantella, *Il lavoro sistematico nel discorso giuridico romano*, Turin, 1975 ; and my review article, Y. P. Thomas, *Revue Historique du Droit*, 1978, 1st section.

57. Cic., *Part.or.*, 36, 161.

58. Cic., *De inv.*, II, 23, 69.

59. *De inv.*, II, 24, 71: *cum ipsum ex se factum probari non potest, aliquo autem fori adiuncto argumento defenditur.* This definition targets, in reality, within the *constitutio iuridicialis*, only the *pars assumptiva*. For reasons of simplicity we are not taking into account the exposition of the *pars absoluta*, which in itself (that is to say within the same *causa*) raises legal problems (*ibid.* I, 11, 15; II, 23, 69). On the topic of 'borrowed' (*assumere*) arguments, situated outside of the sphere of the agent, and on their meaning within an anthropology of the guilty human, cf. Y. P. Thomas, 'Acte, agent, société: sur l'homme coupable dans la pensée juridique romaine', *Archives de Philosophie du droit*, 1977, pp. 75 ff. [trans. note: Chapter 9 in this volume].

60. See the complete outline in Cic., *De inv.*, I, 11,15. For an interpretation, cf. Y. P. Thomas, loc. cit.

61. *Part.or.*, 30, 106: '*iure feci, salutis omnium et conservandae rei publicae causa*'.

62. Cf. *Part.or.*, ibid.: *In his autem causis, ubi aliquid recte factum aut concedendum esse defenditur*/In cases of a defence that something was, or could have been seen, as the right thing to do (= *comparatio*, in *De inv.*, I, 11, 15).

63. Ibid.: *'ne sceleratissimum quidem civem, sine iudicio, iure ullo necare potuisti'.*

64. Ibid.: *'oritur illa disceptatio: 'potueritne recte, salutis reipublicae causa, civem, eversorem civitatis, indemnatum necare?'*

65. Quint. III, 11, 11.

66. Cf. my *'Causa': Sens et fonction d'un concept dans le langage du droit romain* (type-written thesis, Paris 1976, vol. 2, chap. 2, pp. 333 ff., especially pp. 457–79; it offers an encompassing study of the interpretation within the framework of the formulary process).

67. See, on this point, the magisterial analysis of L. Althusser, in his introduction to *Lire le Capital*, I, Paris 1973, although, in truth, Althusser addresses the bourgeois idealism of modern Europe. But this idealism does not entertain illusions about the role allotted to the subject in the process of knowledge: quite to the contrary, the illusion of discovering Being as it is in itself is a component of classical idealism. Althusser's conclusions can thus claim an equal or superior importance for the Aristotelian ontology that underlies the *interpretatio* of the Roman jurisconsults (cf. Y. P. Thomas, op. cit., I, p. 228 ff.; II, pp. 475 ff.).

68. Cf. the studies by L. Gernet and M. Détienne, already quoted.

69. Gaius, IV, 12, and ff.; 13: *Corporales hae quae tangi possunt, velut fundus, homo, vestis, aurum, argentum, et denique aliae res innumerabiles*; 14: *Incorporales que tangi non possunt, qualia sunt ea quae iure consistunt, sicut hereditas, ususfructus, obligationes quoquo modo contractae* ... It is well known that M. Villey has drawn from these texts an interpretation that denies the existence of a notion of subjective right in Rome (a right being a thing, *res*) : cf. his fundamental studies: 'L'idée de droit subjectif et les systèmes juridiques romains', *Revue historique de droit français et étranger* (*R.H.D.*), 1946–47, and 'Gaius et le droit subjectif', in *Leçons d'histoire de la philosophie du droit*, Paris, 1962.

70. See, concerning Greece – and not only Greece – the magisterial interpretation proposed by L. Gernet in his 'Choses visibles et choses invisibles', published again in *Anthropologie* . . ., op. cit., pp. 405 ff.

71. Cf. Lenel, *Edictum perpetuum*, 3rd edition, p. 185 and ff. The interest of this formula – as of many others, for instance,

that of the *actio* of the *lex Aquilia* for the recovery of damages – is that the generic notion *res*, universal term of replacement, is here integrated into the framework of a monetary equivalence. No comparable use of *res* is known in archaic Roman law. Cf. my lecture at the Centre de Philosophie de droit (January 1978): 'Le langage des biens et la perception juridique du monde à Rome' (published as 'Res, chose et patrimoine. Note sur le rapport sujet-objet en droit romain', in *Archives de Philosophie du Droit*, 25, 1980, pp. 413–26).

72. This transformation did not exist in the old 'actions of the law' (*legis actiones*), where the judge condemned to deliver the thing itself ('*res ipsa*'; cf. Gaius, op. cit. n. 74).

73. Gaius, IV, 48: *omnium autem formularum quae condamnationem habent* (in other words, all real and personal *actiones*: excepted are only the *actiones* regarding the status of persons) *ad pecuniariam aestimationem condemnatio concepta est. Itaque et si corpus aliquod petamus* ('*petere*' is said in the context both of real and personal *actiones*, and relates both to real rights and to debts) *veluti fundum, hominem, vestem, aurum argentum, iudex non isam rem condemnat eum com quo actum est, sicut olim fieri solebat, at aestimata re pecuniam eum condemnat.*

74. Cic., *Topica*, V, 27.

75. *Adv. Mathem.* VIII, 11–12. Cf. Todorov, op. cit., p. 17.

76. Ulpian, *1, reg. D.*, 1.1.10.2.

77. The theory of the three times appears in conjunction with the *summa divisio* of three genres. See the texts quoted *supra*, n. 25.

78. Paul, 16 *ad Plautium*; *D.* 50.17.1.

79. Examples in L. Lantella, op. cit., pp. 91 ff. (on the natural consequences of the contracts bona fide, with a critique of the formalist and tautological interpretation of certain specialists of Roman law).

80. C. Levi-Strauss, *Tristes Tropiques*, New York 1961, p. 62: 'A curious fatality hangs over the teaching of law. Sandwiched between theology, with which it had certain intellectual affinities at that time, and journalism, towards which recent reforms have sent it swerving, it seems unable to find firm and objective ground on which to take its stand. The firmer it is, the less objective: and vice versa. Himself a subject for serious study, the jurist is, to me, like an animal trying to explain to a zoologist the workings of a magic lantern'. The ancient and the modern are equally dismissed, in the blur of a discipline characterised by its lack of concepts. But

this discipline, if considered from the outside, can be the object of a scientific study, just as well as any other field of the human sciences: the time lag is substantial – and so are, therefore, the future perspectives.

81. Cf. the great study by L. Gernet, 'La notion mythique de la valeur en Grèce', in *Anthropologie*, op. cit., pp. 93 ff., and Ed. Will, 'De l'aspect éthique des origines grecques de la monnaie', *Revue historique*, 1954, pp. 209–31.

Five

Artifices of Truth in the Medieval
ius commune

As soon as Justinian's *Corpus Iuris* had been received and, from the twelfth to the fourteenth century, broadcast as 'authority' by the universities, from Bologna to Montpellier, from Toulouse to Salamanca, from Orléans to Oxford, the interpreters of law found themselves confronted by a formidable question: how could the properly technical efficiency of Roman law, its ability to fashion the world, the social as well as the natural world, be attuned to the claim to a nature that was intangible, as it was willed and created by God, founded upon an order of salvation, and embodied in institutions that were predicated upon a meaning that was, imperatively, one that it had received as a divine gift? How was one to understand, to interpret and to reconcile, the revelation of Roman law, that was founded upon the quasi-magical presence of 'Rome', gauged upon the actual *sacrality* of the Germanic Roman Empire, and that the living splendour of the texts authored by its jurists showed to be nothing less than a revelation in itself, with the reality of a God who interferes in human matters up to the point of assuming, for the purpose of his edification and salvation, man's bodily nature? How was one to articulate the artifices of a type of institution that was purely and simply political, sustaining itself without help from metaphysics, without reference to nature, a world in the fullest vibrancy of its being, where nature bends under the weight of divine super-nature, of its signs and its *indices*?

The claim that the transmitted texts of the Roman jurists banned *any* reference to nature would be an exaggeration, though. In various passages of the *Digest*, the *Code*, the *Institutes*, it was nature that endowed legal thought with the possibility of offering a solution. Not that this went all the way to elevating nature to the rank of being law's

79

ultimate or paradigmatic reality. Rather, nature was conceived as a tool in the hand of the jurists, in order to provide certain types of legal operations with a rationale, right within the framework of the civil law that they were construing. Ordinarily the reference to nature served as a supplement wherever some legal institution proved deficient, especially in view of another one, to whose model it was supposed to correspond.[1] What was called 'natural', here, was the legal institution recycled by the jurists in order to allow them to forge another institution. Hence, referring to nature was not a means of characterising the relationship between an institution and some pre-institutional reality. In order to understand that the institution of 'filiation', a legal construction in its principle as in its name, was called 'natural', one has to think of adoptive filiation. Faithful to the fiction according to which the son is born from the father, adoptive filiation referred to 'natural' filiation as to its model. Equally, when a slave was freed in such a way that he was endowed with the status, not alone of a free man, but of a man who had been free all the way since his birth, the text of the imperial decision declared: 'as if he were born free'. And it was by reference to this fiction of free birth bestowed upon a slave – by an act of the Emperor, which at once cleans the new state of things to which it gives rise, of any trace of its origin – that the former slave's status as a free man could be qualified as 'natural': the authority of the law allowed the freed slave to lay claim to the image of a free-born, an *ingenuus*,[2] re-integrating him into that 'common birth of all men in their origin',[3] which featured the primitive or natural freedom that had been invested with paradigmatic value.[4] The postulate of a liberty and civil status related to the *concept of naturalness* (*ingenuitas*) was the reverse side of the subterfuge of *bestowing* that same liberty, in the modality of 'as if', on persons who were, precisely, of servile birth. There is no need to multiply the examples. It is in operations of that type, and exclusively in them, that nature and institution or (and it is the same thing) that a first institution and a second institution, could be contra-posed. The context, narrow and precise – and functional – in which the internal pragmatics of Roman law made use of nature, is thus well circumscribed. 'Nature' was the name that the Roman jurists gave to the institutional presupposition of their own artifice, the thoroughly artificial business that was underlying their own interventions, which were essentially acts of deriving what was not in the text from what was in it, of re-using in context B what a text had said in context A.

The medieval schools were thus confronted with the problem of Christianising this 'nature' that the Roman jurists had forged and shaped according to their needs. The formula in charge of this, a formula that has become widespread since the first glossators of the twelfth century, was that of a comparison-assimilation (*aequiparatio*) of nature with God: 'Nature, that is to say God' (*natura id est Deus*).[5] But even having thus verbally 'baptised' Roman *natura*, what still remained was Roman law itself, which had used nature as an artifice in the service of artifice, or as an institution in the service of *the* institution. This, one now had to make interpretable as well. After all, Roman civil law had come up with procedures allowing the forging of gods (*consecratio*), as well as sons (*adoptio*), and to transform life into death (*mors civilis*), or death into life (*restitutio*), and persons into things (*diminutio status*), or things into persons (*personificatio*). Further, remedies allowed space and time to be abolished, by putting presence in the place of absence. In sum, an inexhaustible arsenal of techniques to avoid the obstacles that reality had put in the way of human action over the world – a genuine 'alchemy', as it is formulated in early fourteenth century texts. How, then, to adapt these Roman and juristic practices in order to fit them into a religious universe, in which there was certainly no question of messing around with nature, understood as a divine creation?

The notion that 'natural' (meaning: 'exempted from intervention') was unseated, first of all, courtesy of that potent tool of transforming reality which is known as the 'legal fiction'. Using a legal fiction consisted in first substituting the facts, then travestying them into this fabricated appearance, finally cataloguing the legal consequences that would have applied to what was knowingly falsely asserted. Treating as factual and genuine that which, at the same time, one admits to be false, invoking the counter-factual results of this operation: this summarises the method that allowed the ancient jurists to accomplish their operations of de-qualification and requalification. No subjecting of the actual facts to one's power was conceivable without it. These steps were performed by the Roman lawyers, by means of a complex series of conjunctions that served to establish the inter-exchangeability between two terms (*si, ita . . . uti, ita ut . . . ita, proinde ac si . . .,* etc.). The medieval jurists, in turn, ventured to systematically single out in the Roman *Corpus Juris* these 'words of fiction' (*verba fictionis*).[6] First of all, they attempted to allocate them to classes of fiction, in accordance to those *genera* of being which they found expounded in the *Organon,* a work that, during the Middle Ages, played the role of a fully fledged inventory of taxonomic categories. Hence, one finds Azo (late twelfth century) veneer this whole abounding matter with the categories of Aristotle, and discover that that which the fictions were asking for – that which law was able to give shape to – was Being and Non-being, Quantity and Quality, Relation, Time, Place, etc. Of the 'fiction of Substance', he gives the following examples: law endows with existence he who has none yet, such as to the child-to-be-born;[7] as well as he who no longer has one, such as the citizen who has died for the Fatherland – who according to the *Institutes* is 'alive in glory', and whose father thus benefits from the advantages that the fact of having a son procures for a father, such as to be exempted from guardianship duties.[8] But the law transformed Quantity, as well; it transformed Relation (e.g., by instituting a bond of filiation with he who was a son only by dint of fiction);[9] it transformed Quality; Action (by a fiction of representation); Time (by retroactivity); Place (presence of the absent person, in the case of convictions in absentia; absence of the present person, in the case of the insane).

Medieval taxonomies were perfectly capable of circumscribing the phenomenon brought about by legal fiction: what they were incapable of doing was reining it in. This is why the medieval jurists had, more fundamentally, to come up with a position regarding the capacity of human beings to change the social organisation – indeed, in certain cases, physical nature – by means of using the artificial instruments of institutional proceedings. They had to trace the limits of the enterprise of the juridical denaturation of the world – a task that led them, already, to forging arguments of a sort still used up to this day by lawyers, if unwittingly, when they are dealing with the subject matter of technical denaturation. The

Christianisation of Roman law was fated to take the appearance, first of all, of domesticating a mode of representation of the world in which the things of the world were necessarily instituted by human and political action – including, as Saint Augustine was aware, in the sense that even those 'things divine' (which, for a Christian, had no sense apart from that of a nature wanted and created by God) were, in the words of the Romans themselves, lowered to the rank of human productions and subject to the same regime of fabrication as were, e.g. painting or architecture, both 'instituted by humans' (*hominibus instituta*).[10] For all of this concerned, finally, also a transformation of the relationship between the law and the realm of things. Among the numberless proceedings of institutional construction engineered by lawyerly artificiality and fated to subvert the autonomous work of nature, often enough at the price of contradicting factual evidence, among all those 'artifices' (*artificia*), 'forgeries' (*figmenta*), '*simulacra*', 'fictions' (*fictiones*) which could only irritate, with their unflinching severity, the vision of their own times, the medieval commentators had been busy categorising and classifying Roman law, integrating its lessons into their world – which, needless to say, will naturally emerge upset by that sinister liability.

The law and the fact

Here is a maxim, a *brocardicum*, again from Azo's pen, on D. 4.6.19, a passage dealing with the return home of prisoners of war after the end of war (*postliminium*, or, 'crossing of the border in the opposite direction'). The prisoner is re-established in his rights as soon as he is back to the city. He who was considered as dead and whose rights, therefore, were extinguished, will immediately recover his property, personal status, and the rights that he holds by way of his family, just as if he had never ceased to be free. The time that separates his departure from his return is deleted. Notwithstanding this, the text tells us, the possession he had acquired before being captured, is irrevocably annihilated by the fact that he has been made prisoner, considering that 'possession is first of all a question of fact'. Possession can be consolidated into right, of course, once the time has passed that changes it into ownership, but before the time that is required to make this change happen has passed, there is only fact – a fact that is attached to the presence of the body of the interested party, abolished by its absence, without being restored by a new presence. There is no such thing as 'reconnecting to an earlier possession'; the renewed presence of a possession requires a new 'deal'. This is the meaning of an ancient text that opposes to the fact, its instantaneity and its corporality, the immaterial and long-lasting constructions of the law. Azo refers to the passage at stake under the heading of legal fictions (*figmenta legis*), to illustrate an adage of his, according to which 'in dealing with fact there is no feigning': neither the law nor its interpreters can do anything about the fact that a prisoner of war, deprived by war and captivity of his physical autonomy, has thereby ceased to be able, once back on Roman territory, to possess anything – even if his juridical relationships to things, which are intangible and abstract, remain unaffected by the impossibility of reconnecting to an earlier state. In dealing with that same text (and many comparable ones, almost all of them relating to issues of possession), the Ordinary Gloss, composed by Accursius around 1240, will hold, similarly, that 'one cannot feign in matters of fact in the same way in which one can feign in matters of law'.[11] Thus, according to this first state of the doctrine, the artifices of the law, while perfectly effective in dealing with the law's own postulates, have no purchase upon law-external data. Fictional operations, such as annihilating the time that has passed between the prisoner's capture and his return, have their range of efficacy inside a purely normative order, close to the reality of the world – a reality that is left unchanged on its outside. Commenting on that same passage, Baldus (1327–1400) has recourse to an analogous formula: 'The truth of the fact cannot be changed by the law'.[12] And, dealing with a text from the *Decretals* of Gregory IX, which argues that one can find, exceptionally, canonic equity to admit the possibility of possession in the absence of any real implication of the subject, without any 'corporeal act', he draws the attention of his reader to the doctrine of the old *doctores*, according to whom 'there is no fiction against the facts', given that 'the authority of the laws cannot remove natural truth, nor abolish the absence of a reality underlying the laws'.[13]

This formula was soon applied to limit the legislators' action. As stated in a proclamation of Emperor Justinian, used and re-used during the Middle Ages, both in civil and canon law, in order to provide legislative sovereignty with its foundation, 'the emperor holds all laws in the archives of his breast'.[14] On the other hand, one reads in Cynus (1270–1336) that if the *princeps* is the master of the law, he is not the master of the fact. This is expressed in the claim: 'The *princeps* cannot hold facts in the archives of his breast'.[15] The reference is to a commentary to *D.* 1.5.15, which deals with the following *causa*. The slave Arescusa is freed, conditional upon her having three children. She first gives life to a child, then to triplets. The question is: which one of the children of the second birth is born free, insofar as it is born of a mother already freed by the birth of the third child? Answer: the children of the second birth, even if there are three of them, are necessarily born one after the other. It suffices to have a look at the order in which births take place, for it never happens that more than two children leave the birthing mother's body *uno impetu*, at once. The mother is, hence, freed as soon as appears, in the course of her second birth, the second child. The third-born is born free, being born of a free woman. So much for the Roman *casus*. What complexity do the Middle Ages add to the case, and what is its meaning? Why is the emperor powerless to change this order? He could, if he wished, award freedom to a slave, and therefore, at his discretion, establish in the rights of a free birth, any of Arescusa's children born including those born before the one whose birth frees his mother. Such a decision would imply the fiction that the child born of the slave 'is considered as being of free birth'. However, for a medieval lawyer, a far more essential question was whether the *princeps* can obtain the same result, acting not on questions of legal status, but on facts: can the prince enact a change in the order of births, and assert that the child born as the first, second, or third, is considered as born fourth? The answer of the medieval lawyers was that no one – not even the *princeps* – could determine anything concerning the order of facts. The *princeps* does not carry the facts in his breast, *in pectore suo*, where he carries the law.

The law feigns that the prisoner of war recovers his legal situation from the moment of his return. But the law does so for the purposes of ownership only, not for the purposes of possession. Concerning the law, fiction is perfectly able to abolish time, not so concerning facts. The *princeps*, being entitled to award privileges – as the pope is, to award dispensations – can award rightful birth to a bastard; what he cannot do, is make out of a younger son an elder son. He might enact legislation to the effect that some action has not taken place, if it runs contrary to law, but not to the effect of extinguishing a crime and of enabling a murdered person to be alive. This would require a miracle, which is a thing that belongs to God alone.[16] Hence, there is a certain powerlessness of law, concerning its capacity to change events and things, at least in appearance.

Yet, this restraint imposed on fiction, and repeatedly referred to by the first glossators, indeed frequently alluded to even by Accursius' Great Gloss, is, from the fourteenth century onward, no longer retained as essential. Cino da Pistoia, Baldus, Bartolus, referring to the relevant examples put together systematically by Azo, are all quick to assert that the lawyer or the legislator has no need of an artifice in order to modify the law, but does have to fall back on it when the question is one of modifying the facts. In order to change the norm, it is sufficient to settle an issue differently. To change the facts – whose nature lies outside of the law – requires the artifice of an 'as if'. Reality resists: in order to force it, one needs to subvert it, which imposes the recourse to the mode of the unreal. And this to the point that, in contrast to the initial line of argument, yet starting from the very same presupposition – that law and fact belong to different levels – the jurists now make the discovery that 'the law feigns only about facts' (*circa facta*).[17] Within the limits, admittedly, of a construction that during the Middle Ages never goes beyond the first degree. For the medieval interpretation flattens the juridical artificiality to a single-storey building, in contrast to the complexity resulting from the 'stacking up' proper to the ancient Roman law. The medieval interpretation does not tolerate any 'fiction of a fiction', any more than any 'servitude of a servitude' – a formula coined by a doctor from Toulouse working at the turn of the thirteenth to the fourteenth century, Guillaume de Cuhn. The principle will enter in French law in the form of the adage: '*fiction sur fiction ne vaut*' (there is no such thing as a fiction about a fiction).[18]

The corporeal and the uncorporeal

This power of making, unmaking and changing – or of quasi-making, quasi-unmaking and quasi-changing – the substance and its modalities, remained within the limits of 'nature' and 'truth'. In the glossators of the thirteenth and fourteenth century, we frequently read that this or that interpretation is inoperative because 'impossible in the order of nature' (*impossibile secundum naturam*); or also that the jurists, no matter what they are doing, cannot, in their interpretations, remove nature (*naturam non tollunt*). These maxims are unknown to Roman law. Why is that? As, regarding the means of understanding law, I am a believer in the terrain of practices more than that of doctrine, when it is question of the instruments of problem solving, I will try to explore these principles of interpretation in looking at their use in the relevant branch of case law. Considered in its proper case law, this 'nature' serves to safeguard the intangibility of two orders, the division of the corporeal and the incorporeal – of the physical and the invisible – on the one hand, and, on the other hand, the biological laws governing human reproduction.

The law, *lex* (by which I am referring to the Roman text that the glossators comment on), perfectly allows for the hypothesis of a corporeal handover despite its not having actually taken place, as long as the thing to be handed over does exist. A particular object, one that in fact has not been handed over, *could* have been handed over. Even more explicitly admitted is the fictional handover of a present thing, or, at the price of some additional difficulty, that of an absent thing. Where the object is money, there is no additional difficulty, as money is the single corporeal thing whose absence does not constitute an obstacle to the fiction of its displacement, considering that *pecunia* is gifted with ubiquity and that one can always imagine it existing in some other place than where it is actually located.[19] Otherwise, fiction is not sufficient to allow that an incorporeal thing be transferred as if it were a corporeal thing. It is true that this obstacle, which prevents the transgression of the border between the tangible and the intangible, the visible and the invisible, does not yet feature in Azo, who did accept, dealing with the case of a right of way, the notion of a quasi-handover. It has nonetheless been frequently reasserted later on, from Accursius onward, and fourteenth-century commentators such as Baldus repeated the notion that it constitutes an impassable limitation of that which is 'possible according to nature'.[20] That this is not an empirical, but an ontological limit, is shown by the fact that, as the Great Gloss has it, the basis of the impossibility to hand over an incorporeal thing to another person lies in the indissolubility of spiritual bonds (*gl. D.* 17.2.3, s.v. *in nominibus*). 'Incorporeal things cannot be objects of either possession or handover, and there is no way of feigning that a handover has happened in their case, as fiction is limited to such cases where what is feigned is not impossible according to the nature of things: for instance, he who transfers a debt obligation, cannot separate it from himself. This is so because such a separation would allow the transferee debtor to be even with the transferor, in case the latter, after the cessation, brings in an *actio* . . . Corporeal things are thus more easily lost than incorporeal or spiritual ones, just as it is said of our participation in the sacraments and of the signs of our faith, that they remain attached to our human bones to the point that they cannot be removed.' The formula of the gloss echoes another one on *D.* 15.1.16: 'Debts and actions cannot be separated from their holder any more than the soul from the body.' Body and soul, the physical and the spiritual, the visible and the invisible, the life of the body that is outlasted by the eternity of the invisible: we find here a fundamental division of Christian anthropology, one that the medieval jurists, in their classifications of the fictional operations of the law, and in dealing with its meaning, projected onto the universe of Roman law, which they claimed to contain within the limits of a religious universe.

In Roman law the incorporeal covered legal constructions such as obligations, *servitudines*, inheritance, usucaption, usufruct, guardianship, parentage, in opposition to sensual things the existence of which was ensured by non-legal means. In the scholastic interpretation, this category shifted to a wholly different nature. The incorporeal became the site of the invisible as a present thing – far beyond the institutional things understood as abstractions. A supernature that took hold of the institutions themselves, lending them a reality which subtracted them from certain operations of the artifice. Thus, the incorporeal did not allow of the same treatment as the one that applied to bodies that one moves from one place to the other. One could not ensure by means of legal artifice the visibility of the invisible or the tangibility of the intangible. In contrast, when, from the times of Innocent IV onward, the jurists took up the habit of qualifying communities as 'fictitious persons' (*personae fictae*), either the result of a purely mental representation (*repraesentatae*) or as imaginary,[21] such an operation was conceivable only to the extent that these collective entities did not involve, precisely, the invisible and mystical reality of the substantially incorporeal things. In the jurists' view, they were only 'names' without a referent other than the singular individuals unified under a single vocable: 'The *universitas* is but a collection of several separate bodies, named by one same name.' The jurists stood by the Latin legal tradition, which taught that there are only individual persons.[22] The fiction of incorporation was meant to deal with what is deprived of existence (except perhaps by legal name); to give a body to the incorporeal was beyond its reach. The 'person' could lend itself to all uses law-related and state-related; that there was not the merest trace of a substratum did not pose a problem. The fictitious personality of collectivities in the Middle Ages is, precisely, fictitious, or in other words, a pure artifice. If it is true that the Western tradition has 'substantialised' its legal constructions, let us not forget that it did so not nearly as extensively as is sometimes asserted: political metaphysics has its roots in the work of some contemporary historians, not of the ancient or medieval jurists.

That the genuine 'incorporeal' was permeated with mystery and with presence is, on the other hand, barely subject to doubt. The obstacle that blocked any fiction by means of which it would have been possible to treat the incorporeal as a body, was hard to overcome. The resistance against the idea of accepting a fictional treatment of the incorporeal as corporeal is best illustrated by a thirteenth-century gloss on the passage of the *Institutes* that deals with the 'quasi-continuation', by the son, of his father's property rights (3, 1, 3): 'the text says *"quasi"* [*quasi continuatio*] because, properly speaking, there is "continuation" only with respect to corporeal things, and ownership being incorporeal, it is inappropriate to speak of continuation. But in addition, continuation can take place only where one is dealing with one thing and another, different thing, not with two similar things, as is the case here, considering that, by legal fiction, the father and the son are one single person.' A fictitious continuation (*quasi continuatio*) of the father's ownership passing into that of the son was, hence, impossible insofar as, according to the other Roman fiction quoted by the gloss (*C.J.* 6, 26, 11), which constitutes a classical example of a unifying fiction (*fictio unitiva*),[23] father and son counted as one single and same person. One fiction is at this point replaced by a second, opposite, fiction. The idea of a displacement of an incorporeal thing from one site to another was in itself difficult enough to imagine, but what was totally excluded was the idea of the 'fictitious continuation' of one ownership by another ownership. This was prevented by the impossibility of any transfer from one position to another, when both are welded together in a common fictitious unity, as was precisely the case of the relation of father and son.

Life and death

The second limit to fiction is situated in the biological order of living and mortal bodies. The question that is relentlessly asked, although always in application to highly concrete stakes on the terrain of the fictional technique, is that of the construction of the relationship between law and nature. Where exactly is the limit that separates the law from the things it organises, considering that the way in which law organises things is purely virtual? We touch here the question of the confines within which the law, following the rulebook of fiction, acts to effectively transform the nature of things.

Practice had forged new instruments by means of developing techniques of substitution, of allowing things to stand in for other things: in view of time (retroactivity), objects (real subrogation), persons (personal subrogation and representation), places. Things, but also, and with an incomparably greater impact, lives. The fictions of the law of persons seem especially striking from this point of view. They affect not only actions, procedures, events, in a vast variety of ways, but, doing so, they appear to denature the very elements of human life. The message was not lost on the lawyers of the Middle Ages; it was even the first thing that they had to consider in order to come up with a veritable theory of the limits of fiction. They never omitted to notice that birth and death were displaced only by the action of law. This was so in the case of the fiction that held that unborn children were 'already born', considering them as already present in the human community.[24] If one could postulate that a being that did not yet exist in fact already existed in law, such as the child-to-be-born, then it was also possible to posit that, conversely, a being that still existed in fact, did not any longer exist in law. And indeed, a version of the *lex Cornelia* imposed that a prisoner who died in the power of the enemy, was to be counted as having died prior to his captivity – thus making a dead person out of a living one[25] – in order to ensure the validity of his will. And that the law goes as far as to make a living person out of a dead one is shown by the son who, having died at war, lives on 'in glory', in order not to deprive his father of the benefits he enjoys by virtue of possessing a son.[26] In this manner, the glossators and commentators, found that life and death were a matter which was settled in perfect distance from nature – and this distance was explicitly assumed by the text of the *Corpus Juris*.

And yet, they were keen on keeping that distance within definite limits. It would have looked impossible to them, for instance, to declare of someone alive that he had been conceived by a dead person. This impossibility, which stopped them from antedating the begetter's demise, can be observed in Baldus's way of dealing with the following case (*C.J.* 8, 50, 1). Think of a child conceived in captivity by a father and a mother both prisoners of war, and whose father has died in captivity. Upon his return to Rome, does the son, by dint of a Roman prisoner of war's right of being reinstated to all his rights once he returns to Roman territory (*postliminium*), recover the status which would have been his, had he been conceived – as the rules governing the transmission of citizenship through the father require him to have been – by his father at the time when the latter was a free citizen? Does he have a claim to the same rights that would have been his, had his father engendered him before losing his status as a Roman citizen because of his captivity? In order to admit it, one would have had to extend to his case a fiction that has been elaborated in view of prisoners deceased before rejoining Roman territory, in order to enable their wills to be considered valid. One would have had to feign, in other words, that the father had died before falling into the hands of the enemy, and fictitiously declare that the son was conceived by a father who was still a free citizen. Baldus rejects this claim without ambiguity: 'This fiction cannot be adapted to the case of the child conceived in enemy territory, because it is impossible to imagine that his father, who has died there, has died before his captivity: it is, thus, impossible that this child should enjoy the right of *postliminium* based upon the person of his father and as a successor of his father's rights'. This is not to be understood as a refusal, on Baldus's side, to consider a fiction which let someone die earlier than he factually did. This was a juridical operation of utter banality. The point was that such a fiction entailed the consequence, unacceptable according to Baldus, that, in this case, the son had been conceived by someone who was already dead. This, for the medieval lawyer, was the very example of an absolute natural impossibility. Law can bring forward the father's death, because it is always possible to die at one moment rather than at another; what law cannot do by any such move in time is endorse the fact that a son has been engendered by a dead father. Even if it is permissible for a lawyer to postulate that a dead person lives on 'in glory', this applied only to cases in which nature tolerated that 'he could still be alive today'. If 'three centuries have passed since his death, the fiction cannot feign it'.[27] In addition, where it was an illegitimate act that the law annihilated, by considering it had never happened, such a fiction could not fit criminal law, otherwise one would have abolished murders and resuscitated the dead, a thing that was possible only to God, who acts outside of the constraints of nature.[28]

The jurists of the Middle Ages were used to commenting on texts in which the law's art and ability to modify the

effective conditions of a human birth fully manifested themselves. The award to an individual of a right of claiming to
be born free feigned that the person was born free.[29] Roman
Imperial *rescripta* legitimising natural children provided, as
well, that they 'were conceived in a legitimate marriage'.[30]
From this point of view, Roman adoption was an inexhaustible paradigm: of he who was not a son, a legal act made
a son. Also, while the text of the Roman *Corpus Juris* did
not qualify adoption as 'fictitious', the medieval glossators
did. They were apostles of a conception according to which,
whether a filiation was a truthful one was a matter of flesh
and blood.[31] Even so, while the adopting persons could also
be unmarried, the legal act underlying adoption did involve a
fiction of intra-marital procreation in Roman law. According
to the formula of the *lex* determining *adrogatio* – the archaic
and public Roman mode of adopting – filiation itself was
conceived by building upon the false supposition that the
adopted was born from the adopter 'as legitimately and as
legally as if he or she had been born from the father'.[32] It is
doubtful that the glossators had this text in mind – it is even
improbable that they were aware of it. But the ancient procedure that took place before the people's assembly is equally
confirmed for the adoption before the magistrate, and one
of the texts that mentions this was known to the glossators,
as it figures in the *Digest*. In order to adopt someone as a
grandson, it says, one adopts him 'as if he were born from
the son and his [=the son's] wife'.[33] But it was not this text
that brought about the fact that the medieval reflection on the
relationship between nature and fiction, between artifice and
law, was linked to the adoption issue. This fragment has, in
actual fact, never been commented on. Of capital importance
for the theory was the passage from the *Institutes* that qualifies as a prodigy (*pro monstro*) the strange thing that would
be, for a father, to have a son that would be his father's senior,
for a son to have a father younger than himself. Dealing with
this matter, the Emperor Justinian, following an adage existing since Roman times immemorial, returned to the idea that
'adoption imitates nature'. Starting from this formula, the
medieval glossators and commentators of Roman law developed a general rule, claiming that the 'art' of law in its totality
'imitates nature', that its exercise takes place in its entirety

within the borders defined by nature.[34] In determining the criteria that restrict the hold that the law exercises on nature, no text has been cited more frequently than the passage of the *Institutes* that deals with the age difference between adopter and adopted. Working in a society that practised adoption only minimally, the medieval jurists committed themselves to the task of interpreting the Roman *adrogatio* and *adoptio*: once reoriented according to Christian anthropology, these ancient procedures offered a clear basis for understanding, not adoption in itself – this was, at this moment, no longer that important – but filiation considered in its relation to life and what it implied. Thus, an obsolete institution has offered the starting point of a whole, case-law related, reflection on the power of fiction – that is to say, ultimately, on nature's relationship to law.

Since in nature the father is necessarily older than the son, the begetter born before the begotten, it was considered 'contrary to the truth and impossible in the order of nature' that the adopted be considered as the fictitious son of an adopter younger than himself. This age distance was a limit that the glossators found in the *Institutes* and in the *Digest*. Another equally essential restriction – and one that was even more revealing as to the question of the medieval decline of fiction – consisted in the requirement that the adopter *could* have procreated the adopted. This requirement was radically new with respect to Roman law, which admitted the adoption (and the institution as an heir of a posthumously born legitimate son) by impotent men and eunuchs.[35] The gloss of Accursius that deals with a text in which the *Institutes* discuss the status of those who are excluded from the right of adopting, in order to sanction the crime by which they have made women of themselves by deliberately emasculating themselves,[36] proposes that the word '*castratus*' needs to be interpreted as '*caste natus*' (=born chastely/born chaste), meaning: impotent by birth. It thereby turned upside down the meaning of the text, rearranging it in such a way as to subject the fiction of adoption to the genetic truth. The effect was that the emasculated were now deemed able to adopt: by re-reading them as *caste nati*, the obstacle they had encountered was no longer understood as referring to a mere accident, but as natural.[37] We understand better, in this light, why, according to a commentary of Baldus on the formalities of adoption, the act of adopting required the presence of the two parties, adopting and adopted, since 'adoption, which imitates nature, has the nature of a procreation'.[38] In other words, the bond of fiction is knotted around a bodily presence of the father to the son and of the son to the father, simulated by their simultaneous co-presence at the legal act.

The true and the fake

All these examples of natural impossibility impugning the juridical solution of the issue concern the practice of fiction, which finds itself confined in its exercise as a result. The law does admit that something corporeal is displaced by fiction, but there is no such thing as a possession without corporeal action, nor is there any corporeal transfer of an incorporeal thing. The law does admit that a citizen has died before he died, but it refuses to accept that a living person is begotten by a dead one. It admits that a dead person is alive, but it cannot ensure that a living person stay alive beyond the confines allotted to a human being. It can make a free-born person out of a slave, but it cannot invert the order of succession between the later born and the earlier born. It does admit of fictional filiation, considering that A could always have been born a son of B, but it cannot make a father of someone who has been impotent since birth, or make of him who is older by birth the son of someone younger. What emerges in these cases, preventing the virtual transformation of real into institutional from doing its work, is a natural impossibility; the medieval jurists will cast this in phrases like 'truth prevails over fiction', or 'the authority of laws cannot abolish nature'. What appears quite precisely in their case-related dispositions are the contours of Christian anthropology, wherever it is projected onto a re-used passage of Roman law. In classical Roman law, the boundary that cannot be transgressed is that which separates the tangible and the intangible, the visible and the invisible, the material and the immaterial; this boundary was barely perceptible any longer already in Justinian's *Corpus Juris,* upon which the glossators depended. Other notable sites of divergence include the order of the living, of generation, defined (in direct opposition to the ancient Roman law) as a specific, individual filiation, thus in purely bodily terms, as an incarnation. Medieval civil science, notwithstanding its contributions to the unfolding and the refinement of Roman techniques of legal fiction (the fiction of perfect representation, for instance, was devised by medieval jurists), has at the same time made every possible effort to contain it within the limits imposed by 'nature' and 'truth' – limits unknown to ancient Roman law.

From the thirteenth century onward, the jurists will say, on the one hand, that the law acts against (or 'makes', or feigns) against the truth.[39] This means, first, that the law specifically qualifies its own objects, but most of all, that the interpreter and the legislator suppose the facts to be other than what they were, either in view of their existence or in view of their modalities: 'Where obstacles cannot be eliminated in truth, they are eliminated by means of fiction' (*quod non potest tolli vere, tollitur per fictionem*). Seen from that angle, the law never stops taking the false for the true (*falsitas pro veritate accepta*), a formula leading to the paradox – noted by Alciatus – of the 'fake truth' of the law (*veritas falsa*). Yet, the jurists also claim that, conversely, every interpretation, every fiction, remains subject to the truth: 'Truth prevails over fiction' (*veritas fictioni praevalet*).[40] The hermeneutic injunctions abound that impose the effectively impossible as a limit on the fictional operations of the law: 'One cannot change the truth of the fact', 'fiction holds only where truth can hold', etc. What does this mean? One simply has to admit that there are now two registers, two layers of truth, or better still, a hierarchy of two zones of truths. Ordinarily, the law acts against the facts and necessarily disturbs natural reality. Yet, occasionally, the law's manipulations of reality encounter a truth that is equally unsurmountable to the interpreter and the legislator: the 'natural truth' strictly delimits the sphere where legislation unfolds; 'the authority of laws cannot abolish natural truth' (Baldus, on c. 9 X 2, 14). What is referred to under the name of 'truth' are, essentially, the intangibility of the border between the corporeal and the incorporeal, and the law of the reproduction of bodies. The hijacking of truth operates only within the limits of what is physically possible, and discounts miracles.[41] This is, for the medieval interpreters of the Roman law, in the final analysis, the concrete figure of the interdictions beyond which the fake truth of law no longer operates.

Yet, within these limits, the law acts fully, free from any conformity to the true. The wide field dedicated to fiction, thus, expands further. That the proceeding travestied the facts, declaring them different from what they were, and drew from this very adulteration, from this false supposition, the legal consequences that were attached to this feigned truth, just as if it were the 'true' truth – nothing was new about any of this. But what the glossators did, is make of this reversal of the ordinary relationship to the truth a definitional feature of absolute necessity: the fiction absolutely required the certainty of its falseness. 'Fiction is an interpretation that is contrary to the truth', as Azo reported;[42] or, according to a later formula of Baldus, fiction 'consists in taking the false for the true' (*on C.J.* 9, 2, 7); but none of these was sufficient; the fake, the denaturation it imposed, were required to be definitively ensured. An elaborate definition of Cino da Pistoia, relentlessly recopied by later fourteenth and fifteenth century jurists, encompasses a good century of canonic and civil doctrine on the matter: 'Fiction takes for true that which with certainty is contrary to truth' (*on C.J.* 4, 19, 16).[43] A single doubt that one could have about the reality of the fact designated by this sentence, a single suspicion of a distance, not between words and their meanings (this displacement of meaning would barely ensure anything beyond the normal language and legal qualification), but between that which declares itself and that which exists, between that which is said and that which is, would leave in place a passage, even a tenuous or improbable one, linking the words to the reality of things. Such a merely relative interval and its mere manipulation would fall into the competence of presumption, not of fiction.

Presumptions, even irrebuttable presumptions, do not absolutely forgo any bond to the substrate of reality referred to in their statement. That everyone is presumed to know the law only supposes that at least one person knows it. Another maxim, which claims that a judgment always includes the presumption of its truth, means, in the most pessimistic hypothesis, that it could so happen that the judgment is true. The law repudiates the doubt wherever it must come up with a decision irrespective of any doubt that might exist: the demand of coming up with a decision suspends the demand of truth, after having subjected itself to it provisionally. What the presumption decrees is that no doubt is admitted. Therefore, a presumption is based, as is underlined by the jurists of the Middle Ages, not on the certainty of its being false – which would transform it into a fiction – but on the lack of certainty whether it is true or not: '*super incertum praesumitur*'.[44] In such a way that the simple uncertainty, carried by the presumption in regard of its correspondence to the true, is still enough to authorise the notion that it is ultimately based on the true: '*praesumptio fundatur super vero*'.[45]

The scholastics were perfectly aware of the difference between fiction and irrebuttable presumption – not a thing that can always be claimed when speaking of current theory or doctrine.[46] This difference is not gradual. It is a difference of nature. Even though their effects are the same in practical terms, insofar as the supposition used by legislator or judge as starting point refuses to admit the proof of the contrary, a presumption enacts a conjecture that is not impossible; a fiction, on the other hand, an alteration of the truth, certain in all cases, irrespective of circumstances. This difference is ontological. There are two statements of the truth; starting from the one, there is no way that would, imperceptibly, bring you to the other one. The distance between the statement of a presumption and the absolute blatancy of the lie by means of which one feigns the truth might be only infinitesimal: it would not go away. Between these two manipulations of the true and the false, the first subscribes to the vagaries of the common opinion, while the second assumes a radical decision, rebellious to the order of being and not-being. The presumption integrates the imperfection of human knowledge, by allowing the law to veneer, with an appearance of certainty, something that is both probable and prevented from being forever subject to debate. The fiction, though it leads in certain cases to empirically comparable results, proceeds from a resolutely inverse position. Rather than content itself with putting an end to the inquiry of what is true, it repudiates this inquiry from the outset. The fiction is, hence, a negation of the manifestly true. It infringes the very nature of things and its order, so as to give rise to a different one: it 'feigns that which it claims to be a valid right, and it does so by referring to a fact the opposite of which it declares' (*ius certum de aliquo facto fingit statuando in oppositum*).[47]

* * *

With the Roman fiction, the glossators and the commentators were placed in the presence of a mystery. The element most radically foreign to common sense was offered, not by legal thought, but by legal technique, by law's manner of proceeding, i.e. by 'the art of the law' (*ars iuris*). What is most puzzling about these aspects of technique is that they also seem to be foreign to today's lawyers, who content themselves with putting them into action, without being prepared to make the step of taking them on board, be it factually or ideologically. What most attracts the attention here is law's strange power of transforming the order of things, of remodelling it, as well as its power of controlling the real, a power that it acquires by means of ostensibly breaking with the real. Roman law recognises this power as a prerogative of the jurisconsults and of legislation, which is one of the fundamental features of Western legal culture over the very long term. In this view, the *fictio* is without precedent or comparison in the legal orders that precede the emergence of civil law in Rome in the fifth and the fourth century BCE. Yet, it appears, in its full originality, in all its freshness if I dare put it in this way, only courtesy of the contrast that the Christian interpretation of this same civil law has put into place – courtesy, in other words, of the interpretive effort of the scholastics to limit, and to keep within the boundaries of their own intangible reality, the distance from nature that the civil law had taken the liberty of vindicating. These limits and boundaries are, as we know, a core topic of contemporary political debate. But that debate would gain a lot from some more precise knowledge of the bedrock that maintains our juridical culture, the most ancient strata of which have fallen into oblivion.

Notes

1. Cf. Yan Thomas, '*Imago naturae*. Note sur l'institutionnalité de la nature à Rome', in *Théologie et droit dans la science*

politique de l'Etat moderne. Actes de la table ronde organisée par l'Ecole Française de Rome les 12 à 14 novembre 1987, Rome, Ecole Française de Rome, 1992, pp. 201–27.

2. *Imago ingenuitatis*, talking about freedmen, cf. *C.J.*, 9.21.21; Papinian, *Vatican Fragments*, 226.

3. We are here dealing with the 'restitution in one's birth-right' (*restitutio in natalibus*); cf. Marcianus, *D.* 40.11.2: in that status in which, originally, all humans are at birth . . . let him (i.e. the slave who is just being freed) be considered as if he had been born free' (*natalibus . . . in quibus initio omnes homines fuerunt . . . perinde habetur atque si ingenuus natus esset*).

4. *D.* 41.1.7 *pr.*: 'they recover their primitive liberty'. *D.* 1.1.4; *D.* 1.5.4; *D.* 12.6.64, 1; *D.* 50.17.32: 'natural liberty'.

5. On this *adagium*, already known from the sum of Placentinus, *Summa Institutionum*, 1, 2, *de iure nat. gent. pr.*), see the hyper-critical study of De Fasso, 'Dio e la natura presso dei decretisti ed i glossatori', in *Diritto ecclesiastico*, 67, 1, 1956. On the canonistic sources, see Walter Ullmann, *Medieval Papalism: The Political Theories of the Medieval Canonists*, London (Methuen) 1949, 40; Ugo Galazzini, 'Natura, id est Deus', 3 *Studia Gratiana* (1955); Ennio Cortese, *La norma giuridica. Spunti teorici nel diritto comune classico*, Rome (Giuffrè) 1962, vol. 1, pp. 45 ff.; Brian Tierney, '*Natura id est Deus*: A Case of Juristic Pantheism?' in id., *Church Law and Constitutional Thought in the Middle Age*, London, Variorum reprint, 1979.

6. Cf. Bartolus, in *D.* 41.3.15, n. 5.

7. Cf. Azo, *in lib.* 1 *cod., inc. materia ad Cod.*, n. 10: '*circa substantiam . . . esse, quod non est interpretantur ex eo, quod futurum speratur, ut est de eo qui est un utero . . .*'.

8. Cf. Azo, loc. cit.; *gloss Inst.* 1.25.1 *pr.* and *D.* 27.1.18; Bartolus, on *D.* 41.3.15, n. 28b.

9. Cf. Azo, loc. cit., n. 12: '*Circa relationem ut cum fingunt eum filium esse, qui non est.*'

10. Cf. Augustin, *De Civ. Dei*, 6.5.3. Equally, 4, ch. 1, about the unintelligibility, for a Christian, of this relationship between the divine and the human. Varro, in the commentary about the senate that he had addressed at Pompey, had already expounded on the dichotomy between divine and human laws and procedures (cf. Aulus Gellius, 14, 7, 9). See also, for Varro's plan, A. G. Conderni, Preface to Books 1 and 2 of the *Antiquitates Rerum Divinarum*, Bologna 1967: volume vii ff., and B. Cardauns in his own edition, published in Wiesbaden, 1976.

11. Accursius, esp. gloss on *D*. 4.8.21; *D*. 4.8.19; and *D*. 41.2.23 *pr*. In the later history of the gloss, this formula is no longer found.
12. Baldus, on *D*. 4.6.19: 'The law does not enact fictions about the fact itself, understood as such, separately from the law . . . because the truth of the fact cannot be changed' (*super facto mero et abstracto a iure ius non fingit . . ., quia veritas facti non potest mutari*).
13. *Ad tres priores libros Decretalium*, on c. 9 of book II, Ch. 14, *de dolo et contumacia*: '*authoritas legum non potest veritatem naturalem tollere et ab absentia realitatis suae eradicare*'.
14. On the adage '*iura in scrinio pectoris suo*' and its pontifical or imperial applications, see F. Gillman, '*Romanus pontifex iura omnia in scrinio pectoris sui censetur habere*' (*Archiv für katholisches Kirchenrecht*, 92, 1902); A. Steinwenter, *Nomos empsychos. Zur Geschichte einer politischen Theorie*, Vienna 1946, pp. 256 ff.; Gaines Post, 'Two Notes on Nationalism in the Middle Ages', *Traditio*, 9 (1953), pp. 281–320.
15. Cino da Pistoia, *On the Codex*, 1.14.5: '*Princeps non potest habere facta in scrinio pectoris sui*'.
16. Cf. Dinus, *On the Codex*, 1.14.5; and Cino da Pistoia, same passage.
17. All this teaching is recapped by Bartolus, on *D*. 4.6.20: 'the fiction feigns everywhere and at all times dealing with questions of fact, rarely or never about questions of law' (*fictio universaliter fingitur super his que sunt facti. Raro vel numquam super his, quae sont iuris*); and especially, on *D*. 41.1.15, which is a fully fledged systematic treatise on *fictio iuris*. Thus, n. 1, *in fine*: 'the law feigns against the fact' (*ius fingit contra factum*); n. 22: 'the law cannot change reality, except through fiction' (*lex non potest facere veritatem mutari, nisi per fictionem*); n. 29: 'suppose that the law wants to make of a son under the *potestas* of his father a son *sui iuris*, of an illegitimate son a legitimate one, of a slave a freeman. Can it? Of course, only not thanks to fiction; rather, the law can do so following pure truth, given that the son will be *sui iuris*, or legitimate, or that the slave will be free . . . In contrast, when we are dealing not with law but with fact, one cannot, speaking truthfully, ensure that the facts (are different from what they are): where equity requires it, one must therefore fall back to fiction'; n. 39: 'one cannot really make sure that a child, once it is born, does not exist, but one can assure that it is considered thus, and this fictionally . . . But insofar as questions of pure law are concerned, is fiction

necessary? . . . Where law lawfully removes other law, it is true that it removes it effectively, or according to the truth'. Also, he says, *On the Codex*, 1.14.5, n. 15: 'One does not draw on fiction where something can be done: . . . for instance, contracts can, insofar as they are a matter of law, genuinely be disposed of by means of legislation, wherever, depriving them of any legal significance, they have been concluded in violation of the law: they are thereby, from a legal vantage point, genuinely neutralised and invalid; yet, from a fact-related vantage point, they are fictively considered as having never existed, given that they cannot be viewed as not having existed in truth.'

18. The difficulty of the double fiction is not referred to before the medieval scholastics. See the discussion of the *doctores*, in the *Great Gloss*, on *D*. 45.3.2,18 and the hyper-artificialist position taken by a Hugolinus on *D*. 49.15.12,2, which has been criticised by most of the *doctores*; the contrary opinions of Jacobus de Ardizone, Andreas de Isernia, Dinus, Raymundus of Penyafort, Odofredus, are recapped by Bartolus, on *D*. 41.3.15, n. 17 f., in the context of *plenius fictionem legis accipi*. Guillaume de Cuhn (citing *D*. 2.14.58: '*fictio non recipit fictionem, sicut servitus servitutem*') looms large in this refusal of the double fiction. He is repeatedly quoted, together with Pierre de Belleperche, by Cino, *On Codex* 5.11.1, by Baldus, on the same passage, and on *D*. 23.3.69 ('*duae fictiones non possunt concurrere*'), as well as by Bartolus, on *D*. 41.3.15, n. 69 ('*fictio fictionis esse non potest, sicut nec servitus servitudinis*'). See also: Cino, *On the Codex*, 8.50.1 and on *D*. 50.12.2 ('*duae fictiones non possunt concurrere circa idem*'); *Consilium* 130, n. 2 ('*fictio non generat fictionem*'): Oldradus da Ponte, *consilium 79, in princ.* ('*duo specialia non possunt concurrere circa idem*'); Baldus, on *D*. 23.3.69; on *C.J.* 1.2.1, n. 74 ('*fictio non trahitur ad id., nisi quod directe agitur*'); and on the *Decretals* of Gregory IX, *c.*2, X, 2,10 ('*fictio . . . non potest expediri per aliam fictionem*'); Bartolus, on *D*. 1.1.9, n. 62, s.v.; Alexander of Imola, *Consilium* 130, etc.

19. The corporeal transferral of absent *pecunia*, which Azo allowed, was a much-debated problem during the first half of the thirteenth century, especially by Jacobus Balduini and Odofredus. This discussion starts again, half a century later, courtesy of Cino, on *D*. 12.1.5, who takes up Azo's view. Yet, consider also Bartolus, who says, on *D*. 45.2.9: 'It is naturally impossible that one identical sum of money should reach several persons at once.'

20. Azo, *in quatuor lib. Cod. de actionibus empti et venditi*, n. 9, dealing with the sale of a right of way: 'Incorporeals cannot be objects to a handover; but they do appear to be objects of a quasi-handover' (*'sed quasi tradi videntur'*). Accursius, on *D*. 17.2.3. Baldus notes of this same text: 'Fiction takes place only where truth can take place' (*'ibi demum locum habet fictio, ubi est possibile, quod habet locum veritas'*).

21. (a) 'Fictitious person': Innocent IV, *Apparatus c.* 57 X 2, 20; Bartolus on *D.* 45.3.26. Constant references to the legal fiction in matters of crediting communities with personality one finds in: Bartolus, on *D*. 48.19.16, 10; Baldus, on *c.* 3 X 2, 19; Francesco Zabarella, on *c.* 30 X 5, 3, n. 6; Paulus de Castro, on *D*. 46.1.22; cf. as well, at the very end of the scholastic tradition, Nicolaus Losaeus, *Tractatus de iure universitatum*, Venice, 1601: fol. 19r. Equally, the idea of fiction is well expressed through that of representation (*pace* Hasso Hoffmann, *Repräsentation: Studien zur Wort- und Begriffsgeschichte*, Berlin, Duncker & Humblot, 1990, 2nd edition, pp. 116 ff.);

(b) 'representative person': Jean Monchy, *Apparatus* on *c.* 6, VI, 5,11 (Bibl. Vat. Lat. 1392); Jacques de Révigny, on *D*. 3.4.7.2; Pierre de Belleperche, on *C.J.* 1.3.31 (on whom depends Cinus, *ad.loc.*: cf. R. Feenstra, 'L'histoire des fondations. A propos de quelques études récentes', *Tijdschrift voor Rechtsgeschiedenis*, 24, 1956: pp. 432 ff.); Johannes Andreae, on *c.* 16, VI, 3,4 (*'non vera sed repraesentata'*); Bartolus, *D.* 2.1.1; *D*. 41.2.1.22, n. 3; *D*. 45.3.26. The link between representation and fiction appears well in the association *repraesentata et ficta*: Bartolus, *D.* 45.3.26; Bartholomaeus Salicetus, *C.J.* 9.30.1; Petrus de Ancharano, *c.* 16 VI.3.4; Johannes ab Imola, *D*. 46.1.22, n. 1–3; Panormitanus, *c. 48* X, 1, 6 and *c. 30* X, 5, 3 (*'corpus fictum et repraesentatum'*); this link is overlooked by S. Panizo Orallo, *Persona juridica y ficción. Estudio de la obra di Sinibaldo de Fieschi (Inocencio IV)*, Pamplona, Eunsa, 1975, pp. 141 ff., and by H. Hoffmann, op. cit.;

(c) 'representative and imaginary person', a phrase coined by John XXII, in his decretal on the friars minor: *Extrav. Joh. XXII, c.5,* 14 (*'non vera, sed repraesentata et imaginaria'*).

22. Bassianus, Azo, Hugolinus, *in nomine Patris . . . principium omnium rerum*, on the heading *quod cuiusque universitatis nomine* (*D*. 3.4); Accursius, on *D*. 3.4.7.1: '*the* universitas *is nothing but the singular individuals which are there assembled'*. Bartolus, on *D*. 48.19.16.10. See also, for the fifteenth century, Bartholomaeus Salicetus, on *C.J.* 9.30.1.

23. Cf. Baldus, on *D.* 23.2.57: 'one feigns that two days constitute a single one; that fathers and sons constitute a single body; that husband and wife are one single flesh'.

24. Iulianus, *D.* 1.5.26: *'pro iam natis'*; Celsus, *D.* 38.16.7; Ulpian, *D.* 38.16.3.9: *'perinde atque si in rebus humanis esset'*; Paul, *D.* 1.5.7, and *D.* 50.16.231.

25. This being the positive formulation of the *fictio legis Corneliae* in numerous passages of the Digest, e.g., Ulpian, *D.* 28.3.6.1; *D.* 35.2.1; *D.* 38.16.1, *pr.*; Paul *D.* 49.15.18.

26. *Institutes* I, 25 pr.: *'in perpetuum per gloriam vivere intelleguntur'*. On the nature of this fiction: *Azo, in lib. 1 cod. incip. materia ad Cod.*, n. 10; Accursius, *gl. ad loc.*; on *D.* 27.1.18; Bartolus, on *D.* 41.3.15, n. 28b.

27. Cf. Bartolus, on *D.* 41.3.15, n. 28b.

28. The question of whether the annihilation of acts that were contrary to the law applies to criminal, as well as to civil law, had been asked from early times onward, and was answered in the negative. The argument from natural impossibility is adopted, especially, by Cino da Pistoia, on *D.* 33.16.1, n. 12–13, and on *C.J.* 1.14.5, as well as by Baldus, on *C.J.* 4.28.7.

29. Cf. Marcianus, *D.* 40.11.2: *'atque si ingenuus natus esset'* ('as if born free').

30. Marcus Aurelius and Lucius Verus, *D.* 23.2.57.1: *'perinde atque si legitimi concepti fuissent'* (just as if they had been conceived as legitimate children). As to the legitimisation as *fictio*, see, e.g., Baldus, on *C.J.* 6.8.1, n. 3. This terminology, proper to the imperial chancery, needs to be looked at from the same point of view as the writs awarding army veterans, where one sees (unbeknownst, however, to the medieval jurists, since the documentation is here based upon epigraphy), that children born out of a union with an unattached woman are submitted to the power of the father 'as if they had been born from the marriage of two Roman citizens' (*ac si ex duobos civibus romanis nati*).

31. Cf. Franck Roumy, *L'adoption dans le droit savant du XIIe au XVII siècle*, Paris, LGDJ, 1998.

32. Aulus Gellius 5,19,9.

33. Neratius, *D.* 1.7.44: *'quasi ex filio suo et ex matre familias eius natus esset'*. The other text is *Epitome Gai* 2,3,3: 'Before the magistrate, the adopter feigns that the adopted is born from him'.

34. On fiction as an 'imitation of nature', see Ernst Kantorowicz, 'The Sovereignty of the Artist', in *The King's Two Bodies:*

A Study in Mediaeval Political Theology, Princeton, Princeton University Press, 1957.

35. Cf. Gaius 1,103; Modestinus *D.* 1.7.40.3; Ulpian 8, 6; *Epitome Gai* 1,5,3; *Inst.* 1.11.9. I devote a chapter to this question in a collective volume that I am preparing together with J. Andreau and Ph. Moreau, dealing with Roman adoption [trans. and eds note: we have not been able to trace this publication].

36. *Inst.* 1.11.9, with the following comparison: 'Those castrated cannot adopt . . . , not any more than women'; cf. on this the paraphrase of Theophilos and the Novella 26 (Byzantine Emperor Leo the philosopher, ninth–tenth century). The latter reconsiders this prohibition, and awards the right of adopting both to those castrated and to women.

37. Ordinary gloss on *Inst.* 1.11, see below, s.v. *sed et illud*: 'a natural obstacle is more powerful than an accidental one'.

38. Baldus, on *C.J.* 8.47.11.

39. Cf. Azo, *Brocardica, rubr.19*: '*interpretatur contra veritatem*'; Cino, *on C.J.* 4.19.16: 'Fiction consists in taking for truth something which is certainly contrary to truth'; a formula taken up by Bartolus, on *D.* 41.3.15, n. 21, on *D.* 1.1.9, and on *D.* 48.19.16.10; Albericus de Rosate on *C.J.* 4.19.16, n. 5; and *Dictionarium iuris*, s.v.: *fictio*: 'fiction is contrary to truth'; Baldus, on *D.* 2.14.40.1 ('fiction is always contrary to truth'), on *D.* 9.2.7 ('fiction must be contrary to truth'), and on *C.J.* 7.62.2; Antonius de Butrio, on *c.* 27 X 1,1, n. 3, and on *c.* 13 X 1,11, n. 20: 'fiction is built upon the fake'; etc. The entire doctrine would be systematically reconceived in the sixteenth century, especially by Cujas, *Opera omnia*, IV, 785 B; 1261; VII, 363 C, 375 E (quoted after the Naples, 1722 ed.).

40. Cf. *gl. D.* 28.2.23 and 29, and Bartolus, on eod. loc.

41. On the relationship between legal fictions and miracles, see, e.g., Accursius, on *D.* 28.2.9 *pr.* dealing with the possibility, for an impotent and invalid old man, to designate as his heir a posthumous son (a case law issue rather close to that of the adoption by an impotent or an emasculated adopter): 'It has already happened that God gives children to those who did not expect children any more'. Dinus, on *C.* 1.14.5: 'By subjecting acts contrary to law to a fiction of inexistence, one cannot delete a crime: Only God can resuscitate the dead.'

42. Cf. Azon, *Brocardica*, rubr. 19, dealing with *figmenta legis*.

43. '*In re certa contrariae veritatis pro veritate assumptio*', a formula taken up especially by Bartolus, on *D.* 41.3.15, n. 21.

44. Great Gloss, on *C.J.* 5.13.13a.

45. Ioannes Andreae, on *c.* 13 X 1, 11.
46. See the contributions collected by Chaïm Perelman and Paul Foriers (eds.), *Les présomptions et les fictions en droit*, Brussels, E. Bruylant, 1974.
47. Panormitanus, on *c.* 30, n. 1 X 4, 1.

Six

The Subject of Right, the Person, Nature: Remarks on the Current Criticism of the Legal Subject

The question of the subject of rights has turned into an openly polemical topic. The adversaries of modernity today direct their critique toward a very old legal construction, making it bear the burden of all the evils attributed to the hypertrophy of the subject. On all sides, among jurists and legal theorists, among certain philosophers as well, not to mention diverse currents of psychoanalysis, critics have multiplied their attacks against the omnipotence that the law is accused of attributing, by referring to the modern category of the legal subject, to the individual as master of self and nature.

A new, reactive or rather reactionary ideology has emerged, which denounces, variously, 'technique', the individual and the market. This ideology has a history of its own. It often refers to Heidegger and, in France, it makes use of Jacques Ellul's critique of 'technique', alongside Michel Villey's critique of modern subjective rights. There is no question of going into the details of the history of these controversies, which are purely doctrinal and fairly well known to boot. It makes more sense to pay heed to the legal debate itself, by surveying it on the terrain of case law, where arguments are made in the service of decision-making and constrained by the imperative of their practical effects. I will content myself with presenting, here, some of the contemporary legal questions that have given rise to the controversy over the supposedly modern idea of the subject of right as well as that of its corollary, the right of the subject. After this, I will attempt to show to what point and by which means, this subject – legally armed to master and transform itself and the world, and set to realise its mastery in the technical as well as in the political sphere – is inscribed in the text of our oldest legal tradition. It is far more deeply inscribed in it than we tend to believe, and, in particular, than the detractors of the so-called modern natural right believe.

The anti-modernist critique

The most heated debates among civil law scholars today are located in novel fields – fields that are made accessible by new techniques and by the expansion of the powers of inter-vention held by the subject over nature and over itself (con-sidering that it is after all itself a work of nature). The first techniques targeted by such critics are those that transform the very conditions of the production and reproduction of life: biotechnologies. Whole sections of the law of persons and the law of filiation are believed to be directly affected or threatened by biotechnologies – especially in contexts where its techniques are solicited and supported (as is very widely the case) by an evolution that is increasingly indistin-guishable from that of the market. What many are concerned about is that a number of general legal principles appear to be subject to a direct challenge: first, the principle of the non-marketability of persons, and, expanding on this, by way of the civil law categories of the inalienable and of that which is '*extra commercium*', the inalienability of the human body;[1] secondly, the principle of filiation, in itself a simple extension of that of persons; thirdly, a still wider circle surrounding the irreducible core of that which is outlawed, the inalienability of gender, publicly inscribed in the civil state and thus, by consequence, constituted within the political universe. Far beyond this limit, entire areas of social institutions that, tradi-tionally, had fallen outside the purview of law, are now being taken up by jurists. Some with the sense of urgency that they must fight, using the weapons of law, against the dangers that these life technologies pose to life – life, understood not in the biological sense but in the sense of human, law-based life, life built upon social organisation.[2] To these new challenges that recent advances in biotechnology and genetic engineer-ing pose to the order of human life, some authors respond by affirming principles that, or so they claim, have always had the force of law – for example, with respect to cloning, the principle of the necessarily sexual character, in law, of human reproduction, or the principle of the necessary genetic singularity, in law, of human subjects.[3] Some jurists, in order to ban certain market practices, discover what they believe to be new principles, such as the principle of human dignity, which cannot be disposed of, either by third parties or by the subject itself.[4] What is overlooked here is the fact that, as a legal category, dignity is very ancient indeed, derived from the inalienability of certain politico-administrative institutions (e.g. the dignity of office, the dignity of the crown), which escape the power of decision with which these (always provisional) titles endow their holders. Equally overlooked is the fact that, if one wishes this category to carry the slightest practical significance, the part of inviolability that everyone possesses simply by virtue of belonging to humankind, needs to be defined. That is to say, one needs to draw a line that separates, within each subject, its non-alienable dignity, which arises from its common belonging; and its individual dignity, which is part and parcel of its liberty, and which the subject is, thus, entitled to dispose of. In other words, one would do well to consider the difficulties – the dangers, even – that lurk in the fact of conferring on this nature and this dignity the seal of juridical sanction, before wielding law against technology and the market and in the name of nature or human dignity. To be able to operate, the law requires rigorous specifications around which there is a chance of reaching a consensus – made up of narrow, reliable specifications, not of the type of vague allusions that are always favoured by ideologues. As we are dealing here with human nature, and as nature is now back in fashion, it is worth being reminded that the political experience of nature, from the Middle Ages to the tyrannies of our times, demonstrates the extraordinary dangers that such a reference contains – via the corollary figure of a counter-nature, as it was invoked by those who elaborated, in the West, the most terrifying constructions of absolutism, such as the Inquisition, torture and extorted confession.[5]

Yet, none of these really constitute the core of the matter. The core of the matter is that a number of jurists have used this debate as a pretext to settle scores with the category of the legal subject as a subject of rights – a category that is, or so they allege, at present distorted, by a distortion that has its virtual roots in the very constitution. Increasingly, we are told that the new modes of appropriating nature – starting with the human nature of each subject – correspond to a new and properly demiurgic conception of the legal subject. According to this argument, technical possibilities are fulfilling the omnipotence of the desire for mastery, and this very fulfilment, borrowing the traditional instrument of subjective rights, would empower a being whose every desire, every fantasy even, now has access to the public stage. Such would seem to be the new legal subject: a subject of an unlimited desire imposed as a legitimate request; a subject capable of satisfying its appetites by virtue of a legal capacity that has been imprudently introduced by modern legal science.[6]

From the point of view that concerns us, what is decisive here is the issue of industrial patents. A patent, as everyone knows, is a title deed in relation to technical knowledge. It protects the inventor, in the way that ownership protects the exclusive possessor of a material thing, whether that thing be man-made or whether it already exists in nature – even if some natural things, such as air, the sea, space, etc., are inappropriable for the reason of being held in common. These are things without subject; or, where a subject is named as its master, it can only be a collective: a state, or humanity as a whole, erected as a subject of right,[7] as we find in the case of treaties over Antarctica, over the seabed, or about outer space. The patent specifically lays claim to something that did not already exist in nature. It protests the novelty of an inventive activity which existed neither in the prior state of the art nor a fortiori in nature. There are things in the physical universe that are traditionally inappropriable, being a matter of undivided ownership; the construction goes back to Roman law (cf. the complementary categories of *res nullius* and *res communes*). In the technological universe, very much the same applies: that which already existed for everyone – natural laws are an example, but so are natural products – is not appropriable and cannot be protected by a patent, even if the discovery of its existence is of recent date. Even so, as shown by M.-A. Hermitte, industrial logic, the logic of the market, has ultimately commodified nature itself.[8]

The first step was to patent seeds and plant varieties, whether created or simply discovered (according to a statute from 1957). The second step concerned living organisms,[9] first bacteria, living micro-organisms created in the lab (US Supreme Court, *Chakrabarty* case, 1980), then transgenic animals, multicellular living organisms whose genetic heritage had been modified (Myc mouse, 1988, patent granted in Europe to the oncogenic mouse, 1992). The third and final stage concerns human nature itself.[10] Carrying the promise of huge profits, the discovery of an extremely rare cell, taken from the spleen of an American patient, ended up as a patent in 1984. What was at stake in the Californian proceedings was not the principle of the patentability of human cells, but the sharing of profits between the Sandoz laboratories, which had 'farmed' it, and Mr Moore, the patient, who, as the owner of his body and its cells, was thus also the holder of a right to the economic exploitation of himself.[11]

Other examples seem to lend even more support to the diagnosis of a disintegration of the limits without which, or so we are told, there can be no validly instituted subject. For instance, the impact of biotechnology on filiation and the status of persons. This is a sensitive area – it is here that the critique of the subject of rights, and of the modernity from which it is thought to spring, becomes most radical.[12] Aside from biotechnology's irruption on the legal scene, the 1975 French abortion law already indicates what it is that may have led our contemporaries to confuse subjective right and the validation of the subject's desire. Some commentators – and by now, the idea has spread to the public – claim that this law recognises a woman's subjective right over her own body, a right in whose name she is authorised to terminate the life she bears. I am referring here, neither to the controversy over the legal status of the unborn child (which a French law from 1994 defines as an embryo and as a foetus without naming the stages of its development), nor to the problem of its designation as a human being, a living person, a potential human subject, etc., which needs to be determined in more detail. The only question at stake is that of the recognition of maternal rights.[13] Whenever one encounters this matter being analysed in terms of a subjective right that a woman exercises over her own body, the spirit of polemics prevails over all legal reasoning. The law simply exempts a woman from prosecution when she successfully requests the termination of her pregnancy under certain conditions. This immunity has nothing to do with a subjective right. If it were a subjective right, it would be the corollary of an obligation – specifically the obligation of the medical practitioner to always comply with the woman's request.[14] This is precisely not the case here. A woman who interrupts her pregnancy does not exercise a private individual right, even less a right over her own body. All she does is send a request to the state, a request that is sanctioned on the advice of a doctor. The model of a subjective right is here fallacious in that it serves to suggest that the legislator has allowed the subject's desire and the individual's egoistic advantages to triumph – just as if there was an obvious and immediate affinity between the construction of the juridical subject and the psychological reality of the subject of desire. Such an analysis is not objective; it is only polemical.

Unfortunately, the outrage over subjective rights obscures many dangers beyond those mistakenly attributed to the legal validation of desire. No heed is paid to a wholly different development that rather concerns biopolitics: here, what is at stake is the contemporary displacement of the limits within which life is no longer protected. In the past, to be sacrificed was reserved for those human beings who were under the sway of a power holder: the father's power of life and death over his children, the monarch's power over his subjects, the sacrifice of life requested by the love of one's country. Today, it is the organic weakness of certain human beings – the fragility of those situated on the boundaries of life – that makes them naturally sacrificeable. On the one hand, embryos before birth; on the other, the moribund after brain death, understood as a veritable living reservoir of organs, since progress in transplant techniques has led to a new definition of death as brain-death. What makes these current transformations intelligible is not the regime of the legal subject. A study that looks at opening access to them would have to look at the relationship between power and life. Such a study could attempt to grasp the human stakes of biopolitics only if conducted over a long period; to take into account its recent manifestations alone would make no sense.

The objections against the social practice of medically assisted procreation should equally be kept apart from an analysis of the legal subject. Contrary to what is so often argued, this practice does not rely on a model of private subjective right. Parents who want a child have no claim against any party. They turn to the state, which deals with the requests and, through its public bodies, defines conditions for fertilisation, pregnancy and birth. Yet, the desire for a child, interpreted as a subjective right, has been taken up, as a theme, by psychoanalysts with insufficient knowledge of law, or lawyers with insufficient knowledge of psychoanalysis. In view of the partisans of the institution, one could add to this that the French statute of July 1994, far from giving in to the subject's desire, establishes a mode of non-biological filiation: a mode of filiation that takes up, in a way, the ancient system that instituted a legal presumption as the base of paternity. This presumption is now understood as an irrefutable presumption – in opposition to a recent development that tended to reduce filiation to biological truth. Indeed, according to the statute of 1994, the donor's identity cannot be searched for. A man who has accepted the insemination of his wife or partner has thereby renounced any action to contest paternity.[15]

More delicate is the question of transsexuals. Their request for a change of civil status is recognised by various European instruments, following Sweden in 1972. Sometimes the legislator goes as far as to allow them to marry. In France, until very recently, trial judges would admit an adjustment of the civil status of transsexuals as part of the medical protocol, wherever expert assessments had established the prevalence of psychological sex over the person's physiological sex at birth. The *Cour de cassation*, however, has declared such requests inadmissible, considering that a person's status cannot be subject to their dispositive power. The court's reasoning was based on the idea that a person cannot dispose of what it has been endowed with from outside: one's filiation and sexual identity.[16] Such an endowment, inscribed in the body, is inseparable from the inalienable status of the legal subject.[17] By virtue of the same principle of the inviolable character of filiation, it had become possible to condemn and legally prohibit the hiring of a uterus, which is to say the practice of surrogate mothers. First of all, when the rented uterus carries the egg of the contracting party – an egg fertilised by a spermatozoon of their husband or partner, or even by the spermatozoon of a third donor – this practice dissociates two maternities, genetic and gestational; but, more fundamentally still, it makes filiation contractual, since the person who had been legally recognised as the mother until then, and who carried the child and gave birth to it, commits herself to renounce her maternity of the unborn child in exchange for money. If such an operation is approved, as is the case in the United States, then a contract would have the effect of abolishing a legally instituted filiation, without allowing it to leave a trace.[18]

Effectively, what the transsexual subject requests to see forever erased – except possibly from the memory and subjective experience of others, which no one can control through legal means – is precisely the origin of their filiation, that is: the trace carried in the civil registry. This is also the solution found by the decisions of the European Court of Human Rights, which upholds the right of every subject to itself determine its own bodily shape, plus the right to receive the public assurance that the intimate conviction one has of one's own identity will be recognised – at least (and this is a significant qualification) where one's appearance renders it credible to others.[19] It cannot be denied that the Europeans are on course to upset that which constitutes the juridical presupposition of identity and its foundations (or of that which the law has accepted as such), or in other words, of the classical institution of the subject. More precisely, genealogical and sexual identity, even historical and corporal identity, both anterior and external to the construction of the subject that has been grafted onto it, and that absorbs this construction by ratifying it as its own – this identity is now freely accessible to the subject. Its right to dispose over itself appears to have eradicated 'identity' to such an extent that it authorises a change not only of body, sex and name, but even the reassessment of the historical event of a gendered birth. Not only does this imply a transformation of nature, but in addition, the change seems to be combined – through the operations of the law – with a negation of history. For here is what transsexuals have obtained before the Strasbourg Court: that a male person x, born the son of y and z, is a female person, born daughter of the same, or vice versa. In 1992, the Court of Cassation had to align itself with this tendency of case law, which gives right to individual self-realisation.[20] It is true that the decision was based on the theory of the subject's outward appearance, and not on the theory that the subject holds a right to see ratified what is its own subjective conviction: which, one might conclude, justifies the court's claim that its decision avoids reducing the law's role to that of the therapeutic treatment of a fantasy (although certain dissenting opinions at the Court of Strasbourg, including that of Judge Martens, opposed the argument).[21]

Yet, even here, the problem is not that of the subject as such. It is exclusively that of the object of the rights conferred on individuals legally constituted as subjects, or, in other words, as points of imputation for the obligations and rights that are recognised by the legal order. We must, once again, be on our guard against imagining anything like a natural connection between the juridical endowment of this or that subject or person as defined in terms of law, and the subjective experience of one or the other existing individual; we must resist the propensity (of common sense) to mix up these two registers, and heed instead the division between them, even if it is disguised behind the fact that one identical word, one identical demand, appears on both levels. Nothing obfuscates the understanding of law more than the fact of confusing these two levels. That the identity claimed by the transsexual corresponds to their intimate desire, to their fantasy even, is one thing; the right that the law authorises them to lay claim to, is another, wholly different thing. All the latter can amount to is a recognised, that is to say, a valid cause of action within a given legal order. Far from boiling down to any subjective determinations, it always operates only within a given legal structure, and only insofar as it is universal and abstract. Law forces every person to formulate its demand in impersonal terms; this is why it can in no way be confused with the desire of the rights holder. If it has become possible to validate the desire to change sex, this is because the law has been reformulated to include the right to respect for private life.[22] (One belongs to one sex: whether this fact has no relevance beyond private life – not that the claim would look sustainable to me in the current state of the law – is not a question I am concerned with in this context.) However, the question has changed status by way of this qualification. It is no longer placed outside of the zone of desire. The law refuses to ascribe relevance to purely subjective motives. It limits itself to admitting generalisable entitlements and causes that are supposedly 'common to all', without reference to subjectivity. It is the effect of the separating institution – law and its organisation – to give rise, both to a desire and to a right; but doing so it keeps both apart. Thus, to claim that allowing a request of identity based upon the right of respect for private life would be equivalent to letting oneself be guided by desire, is absurd; just as absurd as it would be to claim that by admitting a property owner's desire to enforce his property right, one would let oneself be guided by desire. Also, our psycho-jurists, concerned as they are with the 'constitutive limits' of what they call the 'logical structure' of the subject, have still to explain why the right to extend one's possessions and bequests infinitely, without restriction as to value or duration, and hence to deprive the world of an ever-increasing share of its value, to the detriment of others, is any less a fantasy of omnipotence than the right accorded to transsexuals to change their own body and identity.

The subjectification of nature

To the all-powerful desire of mastering nature that characterises the new legal subject in the world of technology and the market, many jurists, American, German or French, respond curiously in a manner that, far from deconstructing the juridical category of the subject, only further affirms and expands it. These lawyers propose nothing less than to institute nature itself as a legal subject. In 1972, an American jurist launched the basic idea: *Rights for Natural Objects*.[23] In the case at hand, an environmental conservation group had to define, before the Supreme Court, their interest in taking legal action. The California Court of Appeal having already concluded that no personal injury had taken place, they based their claim on a subjective right. Following this, were conceived 'crimes against the ecosystem' on the model of crimes against humanity.[24] Even a 'biological surveillance' has been postulated, to be exercised by guardians representing the rights of ecological-interest areas such as biotopes, the latter being created as legal subjects. All these subjects were unable to exercise their rights themselves, yet capable of enjoying them passively, thanks to the mechanism of representation.[25]

Let us pass over the scenography of personification, which in itself solves nothing, since it boils down to a question of techniques of representation. The question that remains is whether nature is better protected when personified and represented by legally instituted organs than when it is abandoned to the status of a thing, especially if it is a thing protected by a particular status, itself of legal standing. Legal techniques offer numerous answers to this question, of varied ideological significance. To personify natural places, or even certain natural species, is to institute rivals to the human subject (it is difficult to interpret the meaning of the proposals inspired by deep ecology otherwise). It manifests the refusal to endorse that man is at the centre of the universe. It also manifests the refusal to accept the principle that Dominique Bourg presented under the aptly chosen name of *practical anthropocentrism*: namely that, whatever our thoughts and discourses, the values that we declare to protect exist only through the very act by which we declare them to be such values.[26] Wherever nature is instituted as a subject, this is so thanks to the very act of this institution, which is a human act. In short, man is as much at the centre of the fiction that nature is a subject, as at that of the opposite fiction that nature is an object. Between these two fictions, the difference is ideological.

To realise that the debate on personification has virtually obscured any alternative solution is a striking experience. Nature's objectification might have provided safer ground for building protection regimes, looking at western anthropology. One should not forget that, just a short time ago, persons were considered inalienable and protected against appropriation insofar as they were, precisely, considered as things. The French *Code Civil* allows commercial exchange only of 'things that are in commerce', excluding those that are not. The person was legally protected, not as a non-thing, but as a thing outside of commerce. Under the category of 'things outside of commerce', French case law notably includes: rights of the person; collectives of customers in commerce;

the human body.[27] In order to guarantee their status to the persons or elements of the person that were outside the market circuit, it was necessary to 'make things' of them; it was precisely by means of this detour that they could be treated as non-commodities. Indeed, this step – which today is subject to universal rejection – is the one that is by far the most adequate and the most conformable to the permanent structures of juridical culture. The *Code Civil* itself here only pursues the immemorial tradition of the *ius commune*, in which the topic of being exempted from market-related dispositive powers had its exclusive seat in the law of things. The only non-transferable things were 'things outside of our estate', *extra nostrum patrimonium* or, according to another way of saying it, 'things of which there is no commerce', *res quarum commercium non est*. Note that, what the notion of 'commerce', as it is used here, aimed at, is a reference not so much to market activity as simply to such legal operations that transfer a 'thing' from one estate to another, whether gratis or for a fee.

To subtract things from the market and keep them under a protected status, there is no need to dress them up as persons. Incidentally, any attempt to do so would be simply unsuccessful in obtaining the effect that, today, certain lawyers expect from it. The stratagem of personification – of investing entities with legal personality, a stratagem that can already be observed in the way in which the classical Roman law of estates dealt with still unsettled inheritances, as well as in the medieval treatment of specific human communities – has not, traditionally, been linked to a venture of preserving or 'sanctuarising' things or people, or of transferring them into precincts of inalienability; all it did is provide a tactic of imputation that made it possible to ascribe obligations and rights even where the identity of those holding them was unclear. Personification, for example, allowed the situation of an inheritance pending its acceptance to be dealt with – estates needed, after all, to be spared the fate of floating in the void between a deceased bequeather and a still inexistent heir. In order to achieve this, the inheritance was interpreted as being a person itself – a solution that dates back to the beginning of the second century of our era. In a community, the question arose as to whether common goods remained undivided between inhabitants, or whether they belonged to the community itself, considered as a third party instituted above the individual persons. This was a much-debated question in the Middle Ages. It was, as one can imagine, the site of political and economic interests that were formidably concrete. Mind, as well, that the arrangement was not motivated by a concern to upgrade the entities under consideration to autonomous substances, or to guarantee their inviolability by inferring it from their effective existence; there were other instruments, relating to the monopoly of legitimate violence, which were amply sufficient for this purpose. The personification of communities was a purely technical device, one that obeyed only the constraints of the imputation of obligations and rights: in order to depart from a state of undecided ownership relations between the members of the same community, it was necessary to identify the community itself as a person. That this was a legal artifice was, incidentally, a fact that was evident to everyone. The law produces mechanisms that require some kind of qualification in order to insert them into the existing legal fabric. Hence, one made use of the traditional legal category of person in order to find solutions to newly emerging legal problems.

The goal that was served by personification was not to protect something. It was the imputation of rights. For the purpose of protecting, Roman law allowed recourse to commercial transactions. This exchange had the function of transporting things from one status to another one, without the need to introduce any anthropomorphism. A good that one wished to shield by an interdiction, precluding it from being alienated, was transferred from the domain of its original owner to that of another subject, alienating it for instance to the advantage either of the gods, by making of them 'sacred things', or to the city, by making of them 'public things'; this provided them with sufficient legal stability, as both gods and cities were considered to be everlasting. The status that one forged in this way for the benefit of certain types of goods was related either to civil religion or to public law; a legal status, it was in any case grounded on a procedure of transferring ownership. *Essentially* 'sacred' or *essentially* 'public' the things at stake had never been, and there is a lesson from antiquity to be found here for the attention of those who believe they can allow nature to escape from the procedures of human qualification that are imposed by the properly occidental form of law. What was needed in order for something to be sacred, was a consecration; what was needed in order for something to be public, was a political decision of appropriation: it was not the nature of the things at stake that was decisive, but the formally correct decision taken on their behalf. It is true that, later on, in the Middle Ages, the category of the sacred, initially a legal category, will be profoundly reshaped in the crucible of Christian anthropology. But this prevented the category of the sacred neither from serving institutional uses – derived from consecration – nor from being associated with the regime of the 'public things', a field in which, in novel configurations, it contributed to the rise of particular statutes.[28] Those 'things', finally, that today we hesitate to call 'things' considering that they belong to nature, and that some would like to assimilate to persons in order to better protect them, were invested with a singular legal condition: that of 'things common to all humans', which precluded them from being appropriated by anyone in particular. Mind that this category presupposes a legal construction, no less than all the others – which, in this case, turns out to be no less than the unity of the human race.[29]

Such were, all the way from Rome to modern Europe, on the basis of a Latin legality reformulated in the crucible of Christianity, the major lines of a regime that acknowledged that certain 'things' came complete with a certain status of inalienability. These, as well as certain categories of persons, were protected by imputing to them a status of inalienability; yet, to this end, it was necessary to objectify them, i.e. to make things of them. The common proposition that 'the person is inviolable and sacred' has in all probability no other meaning apart from this: in a culture that defines itself as secular, it boils down to saying that a person cannot be any person's thing, except its own. The fundamental juridical structure, over the very *longue durée*, all the way to the *Code Civil*, distinguishes between things and persons and, among things, between those that may belong to private persons, and those that may not. Yet all these things, no matter whether religious or public, were treated as a matter of personal inclination. 'Things produced by nature' did not escape this dispositive.

This is even one of the major hypotheses through which, starting from ancient Roman law, the universality of the notion of man acquired a very precise institutional meaning: nature, from that moment on, has become a thing of humanity. But this structure also compels us to objectify that which, of a person, belongs to others, and that which belongs, on the contrary, to itself. Two regimes are conceivable, and there is no third one. Either the person *is objectified* through their affiliation with some other instance, for example in view of the claim that it belongs to God, or to the state. This was the traditional regime of the untouchable character of the body and the life of military recruits, including, with the ban on suicide, for the military recruit himself.[30] Or the person *objectifies itself*. This transforms the relation to oneself into a relation between a person and a thing. The latter can be found in the liberal regime of the body which only belongs to the subject itself, but also of work, which is a ramification of the body, one which the subject makes available to others via contract. The conservative legal ideology observable today, especially among French authors, should draw the necessary conclusions from this. When for instance, following recent case law from the *Conseil d'État*, the advent of human dignity, a new legal concept, located beyond the sphere of disposition of the subject itself (with the effect that the subject is located outside of commerce)[31] is greeted with satisfaction, it should be noted that, once it is no longer up to the subject of such a dignity to define itself and to use it as she or he sees fit, what becomes necessary, in exchange, is that some third agency, be it a legislator or its interpreter, objectifies this very dignity and defines, if necessary also in opposition to the person involved, that part of the person which is not subject to its own power of disposition (such as: specific uses of one's body, specific uses of one's dignity, etc.). It is, then, ineluctably, up to this authority (even if the only guarantee it offers is its own self-proclaimed assertion to hold the decisive third position) to sovereignly dispose over the disposition that persons have over themselves – in the way in which it had been done by churches, monarchs, patriotic states, i.e. by asking of everyone a sacrifice when it comes to how to deal with one's own person.[32]

This detour allows us to better understand the meaning of certain displacements within our contemporary culture.

Objects move from one juridical place to another – as for instance, when it is proposed to replace an item's status by moving it from the case 'object' to the case 'subject'. By way of such displacements, that is, in the manner of simple referential shifts (rather than by the invention of new concepts), the map of law is recomposed and new questions are formulated. Yet, if, today, lawyers act under the freedom, the duty even, of suggesting new institutional arrangements to supply with meaning and form the ruptures introduced in our culture by the expansion of technology and the market, and, in order to improve their grasp, of integrating them within the older dogmatic storehouse, they must not nourish illusions about the terrain on which they are acting. This is, however, what they do when they hastily introduce, in the name of law, proposals that fail to correspond to any technical-legal requirement. Legal history makes it possible to appreciate, from a point of view that introduces a certain anthropological distance into the heart of our own culture, how difficult it is to draw upon the arsenal provided by the juridical tradition as long as no sufficient mastery of its slow development is available. We are dealing, under such conditions, less with viable interpretative constructions than with some ephemeral ideological varnish. In this sense, the *subjectification of nature* is the symptom of a crisis, if not of the legal subject, then at the very least of the understanding that we have of it. All too often, we are mixing up two completely different things, namely the real or natural subject on the one hand, and the artificial, instituted, subject on the other. And it is in the real or natural subject, the human subject in short, that we tend to locate excess – that we tend to find hubris, outrageousness, and a demiurgic appetite for subjecting the world to a law one wishes to make. Yet, at the same time, through a movement which is in no way the necessary consequence of the first, the same excesses are attributed to the artificial subject, to the abstraction of the legal subject, which is to say (or so it is sometimes believed), to legal modernity. More concretely, in order to restrict the subject's field of action, not only does one impose prohibitions upon it, but one enlists other subjects to institute them for this task. One multiplies subjects until finally mistaking them for the world of nature – just as if the legal subject, assuming its human incapacity of exercising control over its desires, could find its defining limitation only in a rival legal subject. Yet, it should be clear that the legal subject qua legal subject, the legal subject in itself, is not the concrete subject of any desire whatsoever: it is an institution, an artefact, and no more than that. What is being confused here – and all lawyers are familiar with the difficulty – are legal constructs and psychological or social realities. In the past, even in the recent past, it was not uncommon to encounter arguments according to which, for example, the desire for possession is the basis of the right to property, sexual instinct is the basis of marriage, jealousy is the basis of the monogamous family, and the genitor's love of his progeny is the basis for paternal power. As soon as we leave these truisms behind, we can say that they boil down to a confusion of psychological facts and institutional elaborations. Abetted by a certain common sense, this confusion of nature and law has been based in an ambient culture, in which the entire issue of rights was ultimately suspended over nature, and which has never ceased to be dominant (least so in France, where the general theory of law is far less developed than in other Western nations). Today, the antimodern criticism unleashed against the institutional subject proceeds in the same way, reducing the institutional construction of the individual – in its abstract legal form as person or legal subject (which is, as we shall see presently, a very old construct) – to a contingent reality: that of the 'subject-king' (with an expression that is today fashionable), suggesting that the subject is either diabolic or demonised to the point of bending technology, and even law, according to its desires and fantasies. Those who, mixing those registers, pass, pursuant to circumstances, from the real to the constructed, or from the juridical to the psychological (and social); they are also those who are most inclined to find further uses of this instrument by extending it beyond its human substrate. Who can be sure, after all, whether categories that have proven ill-conceived and dangerous when applied to humans, will not be able to provide help to pelicans or to trees?

The artefact of the person

From a humanist and a political point of view one can certainly be taken aback by this extraordinary extension of the commodity sphere, which ends up incorporating the very subjects of exchange, insofar as the body of the subject is itself part of the subject, and insofar as the organic body is of a fundamentally different nature from those supplements of the body that we find, for example, in physical effort and work – the status of which, as is well known, is that of a commodity since the law of ancient Rome, well before the analyses of liberal economists. Equally comprehensible is the disquiet about the establishment of a system in charge of the circulation of goods and resources, as this leaves, at least in the first analysis, virtually no place for that static point, for that unchangeable immovable of which Maurice Godelier, in his beautiful book on gift and exchange, claims that it is an anthropological universal.[33] In the Western legal tradition, this fixed anchoring has a name. It is named: 'not subject to exchange', or 'inalienability'.

The legal subject, however, was constructed well before this extension of its domain; first of all, these new objects of its mastery do not affect, as far as I can see, the classical form of this institutional arrangement. It is indeed impossible, except by way of an undue psychologisation of these juridical constructions, to transubstantiate the legal subject into the subject of a desire – a desire whose demand could be called a claim, and whose satisfaction could be called a subjective right. All too often, the adepts of intellectual history, and there are sometimes even jurists to be found among them, identify a legal form in the idea of a subject that precedes everything and that is autonomous and almighty. This form appeared, for some in the seventeenth century with Descartes, for others, in the fourteenth, with nominalism.

But things are not that simple. It is true that the use of the composite expression *subiectum iuris* to refer to the equivalent of what was traditionally designated as the 'person' had barely been in use before the seventeenth century. It is equally true that the expression 'legal subject', where it is taken in this sense, undergoes in modern authors who are writing on natural law a process of inversion with respect to its traditional uses. In scholasticism, and even among the humanist lawyers of the sixteenth century, the expression *subiectum iuris* mostly refers straightforwardly to the sphere of what is at stake in a debate: to a controversy, or even, simply, to a legal concept. In the seventeenth century, on the contrary, we are confronted by a 'subject' that refers, not to something, but to someone – a someone who freely deploys their will and unilaterally realises their autonomy through the appropriation of external things, according to one or both of the two modalities of subjective right: the right *in rem* (possession, property), the right *ad personam* (contract, obligation). In addition, still in the seventeenth and eighteenth centuries, those rights of which the subject is the fulcrum are thought of as coming first, leaving only the second place to an objective norm, which only confirms them. Subjective rights are not the counterpart of legislation, or the result of their accreditation by the legal order. Rather, as we know, the political fiction of the social contract serves to create the image of a synthesis between the purely subjective sphere of a priori existing rights, and the existence of the norms of statute law, which were imposed a posteriori.

Yet, the subjective right taken in this sense is an artefact – and not one of the law, but rather one of some more recent legal ideology. Let us note to begin with, that 'legal subject' has a purely doctrinal meaning and has never replaced the word 'person'; it is 'person' which remains the only technical term that is both recognised by the *Code Civil*, and known to civil lawyers (note that I am not referring here to the genre 'general introduction to law', whose exercises are largely ornamental). 'Person', on the other hand, is a technical artefact, the history of which remains entirely to be written, except for the usual and much-repeated commonplaces about the topics of the mask, the role, the actor, all of which serve as common proofs that the legal person is a double of the real subject. It is well known that what was called *persona* in archaic and classical Latin is not the actor, but the role and the mask – in other words, both the sign that represents and the action that is represented. Hence, the expressions specific to theatrical language: 'to take a role' (*personam sustinere*), 'to assume a role' (*personam gerere*), even 'to assume someone's role' (*personae vicem gerere*). All of these expressions are, and have been since very early on, a part of legal language. In law, as in dramatic art, this or that actor or concrete subject, holds, assumes, or takes the place of, a person, yet it does so without reducing himself to the person. The subject is double: it is both itself, and the function that the law imposes upon it; the subject is also called a person – the person of the father in relation to a family, the person of a slave, the person of a citizen, etc. – precisely to the extent to which it is, as a subject, invested with such a function. This being said, institutional practices are not limited to metaphorically reproducing the theatrical category of the person. Things are relatively simple as long as we are talking about theatrical art. *Personam gerit*, one endorses a person: this designates an actor wearing a mask, playing a role, representing a person. The reduplication produces both the contact and the contiguity between the representative (the actor) and the represented (the person). Yet, these two subjects, one real, the other fictitious, are both, and to the same extent, individuals: the 'person' is an individual, the actor embodying it, as well. Nothing in common with what happens in law. The operations of law are infinitely more complex. In Roman law, one identical concrete individual can single-handedly assume several different persons, and several concrete individuals can be 'supported' by one single person. In law, the person is an abstract function, a container in which all contents fit.

To better explain this, it makes sense to look at some examples from case law related to estates and their succession. It is through dealing with the estate that this conceptual construct finds its full development. Suppose two masters, A and B. Each of them is the owner of a patrimonial estate. Each of them also owns a slave: slave (a) and slave (b). These slaves manage the property of their masters, contract in their name, make binding agreements between their masters and third parties and receive commitment from third parties, all according to the mechanism of perfect representation as developed by the law of the Roman family. But they also own a common slave (a'/b'). What happens if the common slave (a'/b') makes a verbal promise to (b), slave of B? In what capacity does the actor (a'/b'), split as he is between two domestic spheres, between two properties and two statuses, pronounce the formula that makes the contract? Does he do so as the slave (a') of master A that he does not share with his contractual partner, slave (b)? Or, does he do so as the slave (b') of master B, whom he does share with his partner (b)? In the latter case, the master should not be obliged by the promise made by one of his slaves to another: no person, indeed, can contract with himself. To break down the question into its basic legal terms, one needs to distinguish in the one who made the promise, two persons, (a'/b'): in him are conjoined the 'person of the slave of A' and the 'person of the slave of B'. As 'person of the slave of A', his promise made to slave (b) commits his master A to B: as the enunciator and the addressee of the promise do not belong to the same master, they constitute two distinct subjects. As 'person of the slave of B', however, he cannot commit, by the promise made to the same slave (b), his master to himself: the addressee and the enunciator of the promise belong to the same *dominus* and therefore constitute a single subject. Through this complex construction, case law establishes a safe solution, which can be stated as follows: a promise made by the shared slave to the slave of one of the two joint owners, commits that one of his two masters who is not at the same time the beneficiary of this promise, i.e. only that one of the two masters who does not possess the addressee in his estate. The slave promises, but his single promising act is made under two titles – one of the two titles, between which the slave is split, needs to be external to his act of promising. When he promises to (b), the slave (a'/ b') acts as A's slave and has no other role to play; as B's slave, he cannot have any role.[34]

The law, in order to compose 'persons', effectuates a genuine dissociation of subjects and bodies. The slave co-owned in joint ownership by two masters, part of two estates, pronounces a single promise. Yet he is in two different positions, in that of the first master, that which makes him commit the first master, in that of the second master, that which does not make him commit the second master. What nature unites in one body, one mouth, one voice, the law separates into two distinct legal formulas and two irreducible persons. Consider the next case. Here, conversely, several subjects are gathered in a single person. A testator institutes his son and his grandson as heirs on one side, and his friend on the other. How should one interpret the testator's intention? Did he want to divide his inheritance into three equal parts, intended respectively for his son, his grandson and his friend? Or did he wish to divide it into two halves, one for his two descendants and the other for his friend? According to the text, which notes the rule that sons have no autonomy as to an estate, since 'father and son are one person', it is the second solution that prevails.

The unity of the 'person' does not refer, first of all, to that of a physical or psychological subject. It principally, originally at any rate, indicates the unity of an estate. This unity forms part of an administrative intervention. What one called a *persona* referred, in Roman law, to the legal subject holding an estate, as well as to the agents (sons, slaves) that it included; the latter were therefore entitled to act legally in its name. The criterion of consistency resided in the goods at stake, or rather in what was their legal implication, the fact that several goods were reduced to a single point of imputation. The law recognised as many persons as there are estates, rather than as many as there are individuals. Whence the possibility for a single subject to contain several persons, or for a single person to contain several subjects. One identical individual, if divided between two estates, constituted two persons, just as did the slave of two masters. Several individuals acting under the name of the same estate were conversely considered as forming one single person. The slaves of one single master constituted, in this sense, one person. In this sense, too, the legal adage that 'a father and his son are one and the same person' was not mystical: it was purely juridical. In the same way, even where a property was provisionally without a master, for example at the time of a succession, they still constituted one person in their unity. According to a saying repeated from the eleventh century onward: 'the estate takes the place of a person'. We have, here, the first medieval case of personification, destined to have a great future throughout the Middle Ages and beyond.

For the medieval jurists, on the other hand, the circle of the person is coextensive with the concrete human subject. How can one otherwise understand the fact that, whenever the commentators of the *Corpus iuris civilis* want to account for Roman solutions in which there figures a single individual constituted by two persons, such as the shared slave, this proposition is so strange to them that they have to translate it into a formula that places the emphasis, on the contrary, on the necessary adequation of the person and the individual. Baldus and Bartolus explain that, in such conditions, 'the common slave *represents* his two masters'. The text[35] shows that, while classical antiquity, in order to express the juridical unity formed by the slave with his master, would include two personal entities in a single subject, the medieval commentary will, on the contrary, underscore the irreducible singularity of the personal entities, even where they are conflated with the subjects themselves. This is why, in order to account for the legal identity of the two on the legal level, the medieval commentary resorts to the category of representation. It makes of representation an instrument that allows the two persons to be connected. Rather than the two being inseparable from each other, one of them acts on the other's behalf; this way one secures the quasi-presence of the other without letting the other appear as contained in the one. This is how representation saves the principle of the unicity of the person. Everything looks as if, in the legal interaction between humans, in medieval times it had become virtually impossible to imagine other persons otherwise than as concrete, carnally human persons.

This is why the medieval jurists, dealing with the Roman maxim 'the estate takes up the office of the person of the deceased', modified the meaning of the *office of a person* in a way that avoided personifying the world of objects. Likewise, in antiquity, the estate was understood, according to an immemorial formula, as a *universitas* of goods; and yet, in addition to thus personifying the property of which it was composed, it at once also provisionally substituted itself for the deceased, considering that the accomplishment of its function (*fungitur*) consisted in replacing the dead person in his role, in his 'person' (*vice personae*), as the master of the goods involved. To consider property as actually being the person of the deceased posed no problem in Roman law, just as little as to integrate the slave into the person of the master, or to identify the son with the person of the father: the unit of the person was abstract and, therefore, extensible. In the Middle Ages, on the other hand, this formula was replaced with one that posed fewer problems from the point of view of the individuality of persons; the estate hence-forth *represented* the person of the deceased. It was thanks to *representation* that the glossators and the commentators, from Accursius to Jacques de Révigny, from John of Imola to Bartolus, managed to abstain from unifying under the common label of the person such heterogeneous contents as things and people. It was equally thanks to *representation* that they tried, now moving in the opposite direction, to forge a link between elements which they thought to be naturally disjointed. Thus, no amalgamation between the dead and his estate: their unity is achieved by the sole fiction that an absent person is replaced by a different, yet present person. It is the permutation between absence and presence that assures the functional solidarity of two poles, rigorously kept at distance from each another.

In the same manner, the medieval jurists, while agreeing to recognise that several individuals can constitute a single person (a case that came up with the emerging of the moral personality of religious or political communities), did also hasten to note that the validity of any such effect is owed to fiction. It is well known that the idea of a fictitious person was first formulated by Pope Innocent IV in the thirteenth century. Legal historians have not paid enough attention to the linguistic route that was taken in order to achieve this end. The great canonist pope limited himself to move from one word to another by changing one single letter. *Fungor* ('to act as') – the verb used by Roman legal texts to confer the role of the deceased provisionally upon an estate – is transformed into *fingor* ('to act as if'). He employs this alteration regularly. This means that the matter is no longer one of estates that substitute themselves for their defunct owners; rather, *one does as if* it happened that way. Hence, function is converted into fiction. Hence, as well, goods (or any other support) do not assume 'the person': they simulate it. To the medieval jurist construing his oppositions, of what is 'true' and what 'fictitious', of what is 'true' and what 'representative', the moral personality is the foremost topic. The 'representative' combines with the 'fictitious' to point to the genuinely arti-ficial nature of any social unit endowed with proper legal individuality. Pope Innocent IV and others in his wake still note that religious or political communities 'are names given by law, not names of persons'. In doing so, they counterpose the appellation of legal abstractions to the designation of singular beings. Thus, the person properly speaking, the 'true person', could be considered to be regularly and naturally an individual, in opposition to the Roman tradition where the relevance of such a legal qualification was less narrowly related to the reality of its substrate.

A *persona* is initially a double – a double whose complex constitution can be principally understood through case law in the fields of property and inheritance. But the idea of a double is also contained in the *subjectum iuris*, which designates the subject as support of a right. In this case, the double, instituted by the legal order itself, can certainly embody sets of persons or things; however, starting from the Middle Ages, it is generally held in this case that this double is false or fictitious, or indeed, that it is only juridical – which amounts to pretty much the same thing. Yet it remains a double wherever the unity considered is that of the physical person: the one thing that is straightforwardly excluded, is to have the person coincide with the natural individual to which it pertains. This autonomy being, as we have seen, most evident in Roman law, it nonetheless persists in medieval law, where, in a context suffused with theology, the 'true person' still retains its nature as a legal unity – i.e. as a person – irrespective of whether it now recovers the empirical individual.[36] The autonomy of the person has been preserved intact, as it were, including by modern law (even if the latter has, at the same time, invented the category of the 'physical person'). The artifice of the construction is pushed to the point of keeping the body entirely outside of the person's definition – a regime that, in France, lasts until the change introduced by recent legislation (1994) into article 16 of the *Code Civil*. Notwithstanding this, many jurists, with prominent legal theorist Jean Carbonnier among them, still write that the person, or the legal subject, is none other than the human individual itself in its natural reality.[37] Now, this naturalistic view of things is contradicted, it seems to me, by everything that we are taught by the Western legal tradition. Moreover, and at the same time, it reveals the reason why, today, there is the feeling that a new legal subject has appeared, a subject whose unlimited desires are validated as claims held against nature, indeed even against oneself. It is this psychological and social subject to which, or so one supposes, the law lends its form.

In reality, the very idea of a subjective right turns out, as soon as one analyses the stakes, to be a source of misapprehension. It suggests that the law conceives of a legal subject that exists by nature – regardless of the fact (amply demonstrated by Kelsen) that all there is is a set of norms that impose duties upon the individuals governed by a given legal order. Since every subjective right is the corollary of a legal duty, these duties point to subjective rights as to their counterpart.[38] The person subject to rights and duties is not the concrete human being with its physical and psychic characteristics, but an abstraction rooted in the legal order, a point of personalised imputation of the legal rules governing the human being. It is of course true that, in general, the person has as its substrate a single individual; yet, it can also have several individuals as its substrate, as shown by the example of what is known as a moral person. And it may have none at all, as proven by the legal theory of absence, which assumes that a dead person, in its quality as a subject to rights, might be considered as being alive. Equally deprived of an individual substratum is, hypothetically speaking, the strange case of the subject to which recent American and, now, French case law have awarded a right not to be born, and have granted damages and interests for the harm of being born in an abnormal state (actions for *wrongful life*). Here, the subjective right is retroactively attached to a fixed moment, either before conception, or at an embryonic stage in the subject's life.[39]

Even so, the unity of the *physical* 'person' appears assured of a long future, despite the current transformations of the legal conception of the body and despite the idea of a unity of a bodily substrate underlying the person, today fading to give place to an organicity of a less-and-less individualised kind. The two French statutes (*lois*) of 29 July 1994, one relating to respect for the human body, the other to the donation and use of products and elements of the human body, are still determined by the traditional category of the person, even though these laws enact a dismemberment of the body's representation, which is here fragmented into elements destined to pass from one subject to another through free exchange.[40] This legislation marks the first time that the body enters the categories of French civil law – that the body is allowed a place in a context traditionally reserved for persons (thus: abstractions). Moreover, the substitution of the body for the person is not limited, in these curious texts, to conferring a legal value to the bodily substrate of the person. Rather, it is the very identity of this substrate that is virtually undone. In fact, the legislator, referring to a person, stops short of postulating the existence of a homogeneous organism, defined according to common sense by the affinity and complementarity of its constituents – by their unity, their autonomy. Rather, these laws refer to organs, tissues, products of the body, embryos, blood, as well as to operations that are performed upon these various elements. It is as if the body, which used to be a person's body and was protected only as such, revealed itself as having been only a temporary arrangement of transitory elements, an organisation that now is no longer able to exist otherwise than in motion, forcing us to modify our concepts of the natural, as well as of the artefact. What surfaces here, oddly enmeshed in the traditional scholastic notion of the person, is a new bodily nature made of temporary associations of portfolios whose constituents, being transportable from one set to the other, have not necessarily originated in the bodies of which they form part. Understood as bodily entities, human beings, at least when observed from the vantage point of autonomy and will, might thus appear as some form of collective office-holders, who can be required or presumed to provide each of the bodily elements of which they are composed with the ability to make their own free decisions. A new bodily type of social bond seems to emerge here, which unites subjects defined as candidates to delivering or receiving body transplants amongst themselves. And yet, equally strikingly, the old categories of civil law end up expanding their regime, in terms of both meaning and norm, all the way down to these disjointed bodies. For in a certain way, the unifying projection of the person upholds its regime even in dealing with this disjointed organic material, whose non-lucrative circulation is assured by the law. This is a regime that is based upon the inviolability of the body and the consent of the person, that vindicates the person's protection against interference, that defines the person by its subtraction from the world of objects, and that remains, in short, as classical as it gets. For, all appearances to the contrary, it does maintain the classical figure of the person as a thing *extra commercium*.

The law understood as a technology for the substitution of the natural with the social

Even qualified as 'physical' – a word that only tends to further obfuscate the analysis – the person always remains no less an artefact. It is an artefact insofar as it institutes a singular human being as an abstract and universal juridical entity. Such an artefact is necessary, incidentally, since apart from it nothing else would allow the law to generalise and universalise its own propositions. The law is thereby enabled to address its commandments to units that are equal among themselves, and to impute to these units the conducts prescribed by its commandments. The norms of law rest upon comparable entities, rather than upon irreducibly singular 'beings'. Like language, law is an instrument of abstraction and, in this sense, of equality. Now, the existence of a Promethean subject, keen to exercise an ever more demanding mastery over nature, can be observed on anthropological, industrial, technical and psychic premises; where it is not equally easy to observe it, is law. Legal categories are, so to speak, in themselves neutral and empty of meaning. They are containers, forms, forged long ago, and offered to all possible uses. Any type of content can be reduced to one juridical form or another. This signifies that all modes of social organisation can be signified through one single language and inscribed in the same rationality set-up. And this is indeed what is observed both in the *longue durée* of European law, in which Roman juridical forms have constantly been superimposed on new historical contents, and in the contemporary economic and political space, where divergent traditions and rationalities end up fitting themselves to the mould of Western legal forms.

The most difficult question is that of the ratio underlying, in our history, the relationship that unites the modern model of techno-science to what one might call the technical spirit at work in law. The Latin sources often define law as an *ars*, a word that the Greek versions of Justinian's compilation mostly translate as *technè* – a fact that allows me to express, in passing, some scepticism as to the relevance of the opposition of the Ancients and the Moderns, and of the law of the Ancients and the law of the Moderns. This all-too famous, all-too eternal opposition suffices to account for the distance between Aristotle and Descartes, not however for the striking continuity between Roman law and modern European law (via its medieval reformulations). This opposition ignores the fact that the juridical fabric that spreads, through textbook cases and rhetorical topics, from the European civil law tradition (*ius commune*) into administrative law as much as civil law, incorporates, especially from the sixteenth century onward, increasing shares of theological and political arguments (even if it is equally true that the theology and politics from which these were borrowed, had themselves been shaped, over a long time, by the mould of the law). It ignores the constructions that characterise the institutions forged under the reference to the *Corpus Juris Civilis*, which are based on institutional invariance. Contemporary debates focusing on the legal subject all too often overlook the artificialist tradition of Western legal science, and base themselves instead upon the distinction between classical natural law and modern natural law, between the law of the nature of things and the law of the subject and its power (of minor relevance in my view), nearly unaware of the fact that Roman law itself, viewed by some as the paradigm of classical natural right, had entered history by absorbing and reconstructing the reference to nature, transforming nature into a supplementary instrument of civil law.

If contemporary lawyers had any access to the inventories of ancient case law, including that of medieval scholasticism, they would have to recognise that certain properly stunning inventions of contemporary case law are predicated upon a number of equally stunning constructions of the – civil and, thus, common – tradition of European law. Obviously, there is, for me, no denying that law has a history. Neither will I dispute the singularities of its history in the age of technology and the market. Notwithstanding this, my aim is to define the timescale in which it becomes possible to understand the constructions of contemporary law, and especially the anthropology that they channel. And from this point of view, the opposition between the Ancients and the Moderns, though it provides the common yardstick for the reflection on subjective rights, proves irrelevant. First, because this opposition is a product of the ideology of liberalism and carries no meaning outside its realm. But above all, because in matters of law, it was precisely the 'Ancients' (first the Roman jurists, then, after the absorption of Roman law by Christianism, the jurists of the Middle Ages) who developed and constructed precisely that which is attributed to the 'Moderns': the legal subject understood as a support for a power-to-act; nature, as the object to which this power applies; finally, the denaturation of the world as a technical means of this action. We are dealing with a question of technique: the technique at hand was institutional before it became industrial. Yet, a technique (*ars*, in Latin) it was all the same, as it aimed at efficiency, at logics, and at building operational models able to conform to the goals to be achieved, while leaving the issue of truth in suspense.

One does not have to search far in order to find practices and institutions subjected to the same critique as those levelled today against the expansion of subjective rights into new domains – except perhaps if one is lazy enough to grant that these institutions, validated by the fact of having been around for a long time, are more 'natural' than others. New types of domination generate new types of fear, while well-known ones tend to leave people unimpressed. Do we give due consideration to the question of what is implied in the ancient regime of paternal power, which consisted in concentrating autonomy on the one side, and heteronomy on the other side? Whenever we criticise the figure of the 'subject-king', do we pay due regard to the question of what is and what is not included in the right of property? Where is today the merest critical reflection about why the right over the finished product is held, not by the party who made it, but by the party who commissioned it? Other questions should address the modalities that determine the possession of things too distant to move from one hand to another otherwise than by passing through those of delegates, sub-delegates and other representatives. Equally questionable, the right of succession and the unilateral entitlement that it imposes. Ditto for the question of the subjective rights in speculative investment. And for the question of the extent to which the law opens the gates wide to those who accumulate capital without limit, and correlatively excludes others from the possession of goods or resources: Why is this absence of rules not a violation of the limits that should preside over the power of the subject? Why are, instead, the rights that the subject exercises over its body or even its status, considered as a violation? And why should these rights be disparaged in the name of a human dignity defined by some third instance, or indeed in the name of a 'structure of the subject' which is steadfastly correlated to institutions that favour power over freedom, and invariably prefer genealogically determined fate to autonomy? And why is it that the issue of prohibitions and limits takes the apocalyptic turn that is familiar today in the arguments of our anti-modern lawyers, as soon as the discussion revolves around the subject and its closure?

A group of substantive issues raised with particular gravity prevents us today from appreciating the extreme plasticity of the law with regard to the supposed 'natural values' which some today believe they can save through legal means. To speak truthfully, these natural values are no more legal than they are, for example, industrial, or technical. From its most ancient and scholastic days onwards, law has never ceased to be an (increasingly absolutist) enterprise in the service of mastering nature and empowering the autonomy of the subject. But these two dimensions of law are, as a matter of fact, intimately linked. For example, when a text of third-century jurist Ulpian, endlessly commented on by later Roman lawyers from the twelfth to the eighteenth century, proclaims that natural law encompasses both men and animals, because sexual reproduction is common to both, he hastens to add that only the first, not the second, know marriage and filiation. He adds to this a collection of presumptions and fictions that cannot be found in nature – from the presumption that the husband of the mother is the father all the way to the presumption that an unmarried adopter is a father (just as if he were the husband of a woman who does not exist). It is on the base of such artifices that the law has constantly forged subjects, that subjects have forged themselves.

One admittedly extreme example will clarify what I mean by a technical operation of the law on nature. Roman adoption radically denies three fundamental rules that, according to an anthropological suggestion,[41] are necessarily at work in the universal order obeyed by human reproduction. There are only two sexes, and their meeting is necessary for the act of procreation. Not so according to Roman adoption which, on the contrary, requires only one sex and does not demand even a fictitious meeting of the two sexes: in order to adopt, it is necessary and sufficient that one is a fully capable male citizen. An order of succession of births within the same generation classifies individuals as elder and younger in such a way that parallel lines of descent are derived from the individuals thus classified. Roman adoption makes it possible to reverse this order, since the adoptive parent can make of the younger son an elder son. Finally, procreation leads to a succession of generations whose order cannot be reversed (that of the parents precedes that of the children). Roman adoption, on the other hand, can subvert this order, since a *pater familias* can emancipate his son and then re-adopt him in such a way as to make of him the father of his own brother. The latter thereby slips to the lower generation. He may even adopt his grandson at the level of a son, making him the brother of his own father, who now finds himself in the same generation as his son.[42]

Those jurists who pretend, in the name of the law, to stop or to set limits upon the 'infernal machine' of technique, forget that law is a technique of its own kind, and indeed one of denaturation. The jurists of the Middle Ages sometimes spoke of their own legal constructs as being 'chimeras', calling those who elaborate them 'alchemists'. The 'person' that is constituted by a corporation, a city, a state, offers the example of a chimera. Chimera, because here a being is created that does not exist in nature. But this chimera is reinforced by the fiction of representation, resulting in the fact that, through the organ empowered to act in its name and for it, it is the artificial person that acts as if it were really present. Thus, since this 'person' is both artificial and represented, it can both act, and not be responsible for its actions. In short, it can kill (one can kill in its name) without committing a crime – we find here the first legal basis for the power of states to kill, and their criminal irresponsibility. All of medieval legal theory is also linked to the chimerical fiction of the 'fullness of power' (*plenitudo potestatis*) which enables the legislator, just like God, to bring into existence what does not exist and deprive of existence that which does. Indeed, he can also change the substance as its qualities: time (retroactivity), place (representation: when an absence changes into presence), relation (power to change filiation).[43] It is the same for juridical acts, by which individuals, by means of laws, perform the same operations and the same miracles as states.

There is, from the vantage point of the Western transformation of nature, much to be learned from Roman law and from the Roman legal tradition. Its laboratory prefigured and institutionally shaped what science and technology realise today. We see that, from this vantage point – not a self-evident one, I do admit – the analysis of institutions takes quite a different turn from that which, I fear, is misguided and mistaken in embracing as its watchword the notion of a 'limit'. The 'limit' has become the password of conservative and fundamentalist lawyers, eager to pass on their values in the name of the law. They do so without caring sufficiently for historical accuracy as to the question of the relationship that the law itself has constructed by means of values. Have we only as much as asked the question of the empire exercised by institutions, an unlimited empire? Have we come to terms with the advancement of the juridical mode of social organisation, barely less staggering than those of technology and the market? And would it not be about time, especially, to stop interpreting the 'limit' in the sense of the final blow that the law is supposed to level against anything that threatens the pursuit of the human order? Understanding it rather as that which protects and defines the law *itself*, throughout its successive historical trajectories, as the effective *limes* that the empire of law traces ever further into the management of human affairs? Enabling us to think of the limit in the guise of a dividing line, a road-map endowing the institutions with an ever-provisional form and unstable figure? A notion which would imply a reappraisal of the very question of interdiction – and thereby open the door to an undertaking of a wholly different type.

Notes

1. M.-A. Hermitte, 'Le corps hors du commerce, hors du marché', *Archives de philosophie du droit*, 1988, pp. 323–46; J.-C. Galloux: 'Réflexion sur la catégorie des choses hors du commerce: l'exemples des éléments et des produits du corps humain en droit français', *Les cahiers de droit*, vol. 30, n. 4, 1989, pp. 1011–32; I. Couturier, 'Remarques sur quelques choses hors du commerce', *Les Petites Affiches*, 6 September 1993, n. 107, pp. 7–12; 13 September 1993, n. 110, pp. 7–14; B. Oppetit, 'Droit de commerce et valeurs non marchandes', *Mélanges P. Lalive*, 1993, pp. 309–19.

2. On this concept of organised life, in contradistinction to a purely animal life, or *'vie nue'*, see G. Agamben, *Homo sacer*, Stanford University Press, 1998. The opposition of *bios* and *zoê* endows the Greek language, on this point, with the value of a paradigm. On the other hand, the expression 'instituting life' (*vitam instituere*), pretendedly Roman and frequently used by P. Legendre to refer to the European discourse as a site of foundation and law-making, has strictly no echo in Latin, even less in Roman law: there is no text that would confirm this formula.

3. See the excellent critical study by M. Iacub, 'Faut-il interdire le clônage humain?', *La Mazarine*, n. 2, September 1997.

4. B. Edelman, 'Le concept juridique d'humanité', in *Le droit, la médecine, et l'être humain*, 1966, pp. 245–69; 'La dignité de la personne humaine, un concept nouveau', *Dalloz*, 1997, pp. 185 ff.

5. On the political and especially procedural effects of the reference to nature and to natural law in the Western tradition since the Middle Ages, see the fundamental study of Jacques Chiffoleau, *'Contra naturam.* Pour une approche casuistique et procédurale de la nature médiévale', *Micrologus*, n. 4, 1996, pp. 265–312.

6. See, for instance, B. Edelman, 'Nature et sujet de droit', *Droits*, n. 1, 1985, pp. 125–42; 'Sujet de droit et techno-science', *Archives de philosophie de droit*, 1989, 34, pp. 165–79.

7. M. Chemillier-Gendreau, 'L'humanité peut-elle être un sujet international?', *Actes*, 1989, n. 76–8, pp. 14–18; A. Bekkouche, 'La récupération du concept de patrimoine commun de l'humanité par les pays industriels', *Revue belge de droit international*, 20, 1987, pp. 124–37; M.-A. Hermitte, 'La convention sur la diversité biologique', *Annuaire français de droit international*, 38, 1992, p. 182.

8. M.-A. Hermitte, 'Histoires juridiques extravagantes: le droit de la reproduction végétale', in B. Edelman et M.-A.Hermitte (ed.), *L'homme, la nature et le droit*, Paris 1988.

9. J.-C. Galloux, 'La brevetabilité du vivant. Historique juridique', *Dossiers et brevets*, n. 2, pp. 1 ff; M.-A. Hermitte, 'L'animal à l'épreuve du brevet', dans *Natures, sciences, sociétés*, n. 4, 1994; B. Edelman, Le droit et le vivant', *La recherche*, n. 212, 1989, pp. 966 ff.; 'Vers une approche juridique du vivant', *Dalloz*, 1980, pp. 329 ff.

10. F. Bellivier, *Le patrimoine génétique humain:* étude juridique, thesis, Paris 1997.

11. *Moore* v. *Regents of California*: California Supreme Court, 9 July 1990. On this case, see F. Bellivier, op. cit., pp. 136 ff.; B. Edelman, 'L'homme aux cellules d'or', *Dalloz*, 1989, chronique, pp. 225–30; G. Dworkin and I. Kennedy, 'Human Tissue: Rights in the Body and its Parts', *Medical Law Review* I, 1993, pp. 291 ff.

12. Examples: L'Homme, la nature et le droit, op. cit.; J.-L. Baudouin and C. Labrusse-Riou, *Produire l'homme: de quel droit? Etudes juridiques et éthiques des procréations artificielles*, Paris 1987; B. Edelman (ed.), *Le droit, la médecine et l'être humain*, Paris 1996.

13. As opposed to other European legal orders, such as the English one for example.

14. See D. Thouvenin, 'Le droit aussi a ses limites', dans J. Testart (ed.), *Le Magazin des enfants*, Paris, 1990.

15. Law of 29 July 1994 'relative au respect du corps humain', art. 10 = *Code civil*, art. 311, 19–20.

16. Cass. Civ., 31 March 1987, chronique, p. 446; see S. Gobert, *Jurisclasseur périodique*, 1988, 3361, and 1990, 3475.

17. See D. Salas, *Sujet de chair et sujet de droit: la justice face au transsexualisme*, Paris 1994.

18. Cass. 1° Civ., 13 December 1990, *Dalloz*, 1990, chronique, p. 273, Rapport Massip et Cass., 3 May 1991.

19. C.E.S.D.H., arrêt B/ France, Strasbourg, 25 March 1992, Série A, n. 231 C.

20. See the decisions of the French *Cour de Cassation*; Cass. plenière, 11 December 1992, Bull. inf. *Cour de Cassation*, n°360, 1 February 1993, concl. Jéol.

21. C.E.S.H.D., Gosey c/ Grande-Bretagne, Strasbourg, 27 September 1990, Série A, 184; see the analysis of this decision and of the dissident opinion of Judge Martens, in D. Salas, *Sujet de chair et sujet de droit*, op. cit., pp. 82 ff.

22. Cf. n. 20 above.

23. Ch. Stone, 'Should Trees have Standing? Toward Legal Rights for Natural Objects', *Southern California Law Review*, 1972, pp. 450–501.
24. S. Rowe, 'Crimes against Ecosphere', in A. Bradley and S. Duguid, *Environmental Ethics*, Simon Fraser University, Burnaby, 1988, vol. 2, pp. 89–102.
25. M.-A. Hermitte, 'Le concept de diversité biologique et la création d'un statut de la nature' (1987), also in *L'homme, la nature et le droit*, op. cit.
26. D. Bourg, *L'Homme artifice*, Paris, 1996. With regard to other attempts to protect nature without resorting to personification, see F. Ost, *La nature hors la loi: L'écologie à l'épreuve du droit*, Paris, 1995.
27. *Code Civil*, art. 1128. With regard to the legal protection of the body categorised among 'things', and regarding the advantages that, in view of governing one's relations to one's own body, would arise under the conditions of a commerce-based society, from the fact of legally qualifying the body as property, see the important considerations of J.-P. Baud, *L'Affaire de la main volée. Une histoire juridique du corps*, Paris 1993. In positive law, the matter has been given a new shape since the promulgation, in 1994, of a statute dealing with the respect owed to the human body: the body, now considered constitutive to the person is, as such, declared inviolable and incalculable (Law 29 July 1994, art. 3= *Code civil*, art. 16, al. 1, 5, 6, 7).
28. See, for instance, E. Kantorowicz, 'Christus-Fiscus', in *Mourir pour la patrie*, Paris (1984), pp. 66–73.
29. See *D.* 1.8.2–5; 41.1.1–6; 41.2.1.
30. See M. Iacub, *Le Corps de la personne. Enquête juridique*, thesis, E.H.E.S.S. (Ecole des Hautes Etudes en Sciences Sociales), Paris 1993.
31. See, for instance, B. Edelman, 'La dignité de la personne humaine, un concept nouveau', op. cit.
32. On the dangers that threaten the attempt to make the dignity of persons a question of public order, and on the interpretational proceedings that are at work in the misappropriation of the notion, see the article, commenting on the Judgment of the Assemblée du Conseil d'Etat, 7 October 1995 (commune de Morsang-sur-Orge), O. Cayla, 'Le coup d'Etat de droit?', *Le débat* 1998, vol. 100 (same issue as the present article), pp. 108–33.
33. M. Godelier, *L'énigme du don*, Paris, 1996.
34. Salvius Julianus, *D.* 45.3.1.4: 'The common slave holds the

person of two slaves (*communis servus duorum servorum personam sustinet*). If my own slave promises to a slave who is common to both you and me, everything happens as if, in this single verbal formula, the two promises had been pronounced separately, one to the person of my slave, the other one to the person of yours.'

35. Translator's note: For the passage in the *Digest*, cf. the preceding note.

36. As to the theological construction, see A. Boureau, 'Droit et théologie au XIIIe siècle', *Annales E.S.C.*, 1992, pp. 1113–25.

37. J. Carbonnier, *Droit civil*, I, iie partie, 'Les personnes'.

38. Cf. H. Kelsen, *Pure Theory of Law*, Berkeley, 1967, pp. 125 ff.; *General Theory of Law and the State*, Cambridge (Mass.), 1946, pp. 75 ff.; *General Theory of Norms*, Oxford 1991, pp. 136 ff.

39. The highest French jurisdiction, the *Cour de Cassation*, has equally acknowledged, in 1996 that a child had a legitimate compensatory claim against the medical establishment due to whose fault the termination of its mother's pregnancy has not been carried out. See, F. Bellivier, *Le Patrimoine génétique humain*, op. cit. vol. II, pp. 423 ff. See also [translator's note], Yan Thomas, *Du droit de ne pas naître. À propos de l'affaire Perruche*, Paris, Gallimard, 2002 (co-authored with O. Cayla).

40. The best commentary on these laws, and the one from which I take my inspiration, is M. Iacub: *De l'éthique à la responsabilité juridique des médecins. Bioéthique et écologie, l'élaboration d'un nouveau statut pour le corps humain*, pp. 52 ff.

41. Fr. Héritier, *l'Exercice de la parenté*, Paris, 1981.

42. Salvius Julianus, *D.* 37.4.13.3; 37.6.3.6; Ulpian, *D.* 37.8.1.9; 37.4.3.3 and 4.

43. For examples, see Y. Thomas, '*Fictio legis*. L'empire de la fiction romaine et ses limites médiévales', in *Droits*, n. 21, 1995, pp. 17–73.

Seven

Vitae Necisque Potestas: *The Father, the State, Death*

I.

The power over life and death, *vitae necisque potestas*, bestowed upon Roman fathers, is a peculiar prerogative. The mode in which this right to put to death is expressed is both hypothetical and absolute. It thereby excludes any comparison with provisions of criminal law, where the capital punishment is subject to a condition, encapsulated in a sentence starting with a *si* (if) or in a relative clause. The catalogue of penal provisions introduces punishments that may be specified or not, but which are invariably formulated as the consequence of some delinquency. In the case of *vitae necisque potestas*, on the contrary, death is categorically prescribed, abstractly and without context. It is not formulated as the sanction of a fault. What is declared here, in the guise of a reference to death, is a power of which death is not a means. It is, rather, all there is: giving death is the content of a relation linking the agent of a *potestas* to its object. For instance, in the procedure of *adrogatio*, a form of adoption, the high priest submits to the vote of the *curiae* a law by whose disposition the legal bond is intended to emerge between the adopter and the adopted. As we read in Aulus Gellius, 5, 19, 9, confirming 'that Lucius Valerius is the son of Lucius Titius, as perfectly legally as if he were born from the father of this family and his legitimate wife, and that the latter wields over him the right of life and death, just as every father over his son'. Fatherly power is defined by its legal foundation and its content. The foundation is, here, supposed to be acquired thanks to the fiction that the adopted is to be seen as if born within a marriage between a Roman citizen (*paterfamilias*) and his legitimate spouse (*materfamilias*). The substance is reduced to the *vitae necisque potestas endo filio* (= over a son). A legal provision, stemming from the time of the Roman kings and invoked by Papinian, is conceived identically: *cum patri lex regia dederit in filium vitae necisque potestatem* (*Coll.*, 4, 8, 1). The same applies when the Codex of Theodosius refers to a right of the father, of which it is not clear whether it is conceived in the present or in the past tense: *ut patribus, quibus ut vitae in liberos necisque potestas permissa est* (fathers have received a power over their children's life or death) (*C.Th.*, 4, 8, 6 *pr.* = C.J., 8, 46, 10, a.323).

On the contrary, the Greek authors refer to an arbitrary power; that death is its only criterion is not something that strikes them. According to Dionysius of Halicarnassus, the power that Romulus has given to the father over his son is a full power, held for one's lifetime; the right of killing is only one among other examples. Other rights include prison, lashes, penal servitude in the fields, the selling of the son – which he quotes at the end, so as to underline that it is the worst (2, 26, 4; 2, 27, 1). If Flavius Josephus and Dio Cassius content themselves with the word *exousia* in order to explain that a Roman had every right over his son, Dion of Prusa takes over the same catalogue as Dionysius almost in its entirety, in a context in which Roman law is designated under the universal and pluralist figure of 'numerous peoples having excellent laws', but where the originality of a norm that has provoked the surprise of the Greeks, from Polybius to Dio Cassius, is nonetheless easily recognised. Dion of Prusa, thus, lists the powers of a *paterfamilias*: the right to shackle one's sons, to sell them, but also, far more terrible, 'to have them killed without either judgment or accusation'.[1] We shall come back later to the theme of the *indemnati* sons, which is central to the debate on the peculiar privilege of Roman fathers. But only Dion of Prusa – or some other rhetors, like Calpurnius Flaccus – go as far as to promote this negation of a rationale in such a way as to make of it an element of the definition of a right – a right that is, incidentally and on the contrary, understood in perfectly positive terms by the juristic tradition. And let us not forget that, in Rome, the modality according to which the *potestas* characterises itself, is never represented by anything like a list of legal capacities. Instead, it is represented by that which forms the *ultimate* attribute of the *potestas*, which contains all other elements. In this view, the right of giving death is a definition of power.

On the other hand, it is striking that when Cicero tries to characterise the right to coercive power of the superior magistrates, he links it to the hypothesis of insubordination or fault.[2] There is no absolute definition of *imperium*. Only the axes of the *lictor* symbolise, outside of the city, a power of death that, at this point, appears to share the substance of the *imperium*, to the point that the *lictores* immediately precede the magistrate, without there being anyone allowed to interpose himself between them and him, with the sole exception of the magistrate's own infant son.[3] This is doubtless also the reason why, whenever there was a vacancy of power, and until the first *interrex* is appointed, the location where the *fasces* are removed into storage was a site consecrated to Libitina, entitled divinity of burials, as well as, according to an inscription from Puzzuoli, of capital punishments.[4] However, what is said symbolically about the *imperium*, is said explicitly about the *patria potestas*, and most of all, it is said absolutely. There exists to this power neither condition nor limit.

The very modality upon which this power is confided bars any confusion, frequent as it is nonetheless, with the punishment of the married woman. The law of Romulus knows of two causes authorising a husband to kill his wife: adultery and wine consumption (Denys, 2, 25, 6). Cato the Censor, wrote: 'If you have caught your wife in the act of adultery, you can kill her with impunity without any form of trial' (in Gellius, 10, 23, 5). There are disputes on whether this sanction needed to be related to a 'domestic jurisdiction', or to a *vitae necisque potestas* of the husband as the holder of the *manus* over the wife. Yet, while it is certain that the *vitae necisque potestas* presents the case of an essentially circumscribed power, there can be no question that the husband wields unlimited power over his wife's life and death. The *lex Iulia de adulteriis* adopts this stance: the father's recognised right to kill his daughter *in flagrante delicto* with her lover can only be exercised in his own house or in that of his son-in-law; above all, it is limited to sanctioning a flagrant crime. Taking as an absolute that which is relative, putting under one single category the general right of taking the son's life, with the right to kill one's wife or daughter, if caught in adultery, is thus the wrong way to go.

It is true that a *responsum* of Papinian appears to bring together these two capacities (*Coll.* 4, 4, 8, 1). The person seeking the celebrated jurist's advice wished to inflict death, as punishment on his adulterous daughter, not heeding the *lex Iulia* which regulated the modalities of a legitimate ire by declaring that it is appropriate only within precise boundaries in time and space. It provided that, if caught in the act under the father's roof or that of his son-in-law, the lovers are to be struck on the spot, 'in one single impetus' (*D.* 48.5.24.4; *Coll.* 4, 2, 3; 4, 9, 1).[5] In the case at hand, the father seeking advice evidently missed the deadline allowed for his wrath, as he suggested to the jurist that, since the time of Roman kingship, the law spelled out the father's right over life and death, authorising him also, by extension, to kill his daughter: '*ut potestas fieret etiam filiam occidendi*'. But Papinian dodges the question. He keeps silent about the *lex regia* about which he is interrogated, and he disguises his reply in a commentary about the *lex de adulteriis*: 'This law does not seem to have been about endowing someone with a right that he would not have had otherwise. It did not state a right to kill one's daughter, it stated that the daughter could be killed at the same moment as her accomplice, in order to make sure that the father, being the person who kills the adulterer, appears as inspired by a superior sense of justice, if, in addition, he kills the daughter as well.' There is little doubt that the jurist's devious response to his correspondent was understood by the latter in the sense that he could proceed with impunity in the way that he had in mind. But by avoiding the audacious move of crossing the intangible boundary between the merely conditional power over daughters, and the primordial right held over sons as it was given to the Romans by Romulus, the jurist's evasive reply makes clear that the *lex regia* was still understood, in the period of the Severan Emperors, as a law formulated exclusively in view of sons.

The point is not to show that a husband in Rome had no right to kill his wife, even less that a father had no right to kill his daughter. They acted this way, every now and then, without their act being qualified as a homicide. But when they did, they did so without invoking the authorisation of

the *vitae necisque potestas* over women, which no text recognised. The single exception to this rule only confirms it.
Caesar draws attention to the outlandish character of family
law among the Gauls. Spouses put in common equal contributions, to be inherited in their totality by the surviving
spouse, together with the interest of the total capital (*Bell.
Gall.* [*B.G.*] 6, 19, 1–2); indeed, 'husbands have a right over
the life and death of their wives, as of their children' (*B.G.* 6,
19, 3). In the same way in which, among the Gauls, the community of property is a particularity of their dowry regime,
unknown to that of the Romans, to have a right over life and
death of one's wife and one's children is for Caesar an oddity,
indeed a monstrosity. Caesar goes as far as saying that,
among the Gauls, women, if their husbands die in doubtful
circumstances, are subjected to torture just as are slaves (*ib.*).
In short, the Gauls reserve for their women the same treatment as the Romans do for their sons and their slaves: they
had a power of death over their women; they even subjected
them to a *quaestio*.

Dealing with slaves, everyone knows that a Roman master
wielded a limitless right over their body. But how was this
ability legally conceived? Strange as this might appear, there
is no legal principle governing the subject. The *Digest* does, of
course, refer to numerous examples where the owner or even
the simple possessor of a slave – such as the usufructuary
– has reportedly inflicted corporal punishments, including
death, upon a slave.[6] But none of these fragments includes
the analysis of a right. The latter seems conceived, ultimately,
only by means of referring to its excesses.

One text exists that does seem to invalidate this conclusion.
Gaius writes: *dominis in servos vitae necisque potestatem esse*
(masters have a power over life and death of their servants).
It is difficult to escape the impression that, here, a power is
indeed qualified as a right. But a few paragraphs later (*I*, 55),
Gaius's *Institutes* seems to keep silent over the content of the
patria potestas: 'Are under our power the free descendants
that we have engendered in a legitimate marriage': the legal
foundations are thereby clarified; 'There are practically no
other men who have over their sons (*in filios*) a power such as
ours (*talem potestatem*)': here, the *potestas* is characterised only
by its superlative character. The two passages must be set

against each other. In dealing respectively with their slaves, *servi*, on the one hand, and with their children, *liberi*, on the other hand, they illustrate the common condition of those who are not under their own right but *alieni iuris*, whom one holds, thus, in one's power (*I*, 52). It would seem that, for Gaius, if a master holds power of life and death over his slaves, a father does not do so over his sons. And effectively, certain scholars do not hesitate to refer to this silence in order to imagine a whole process first of gradual obsolescence, then of abrogation, a process in which they persist in finding confirmation in practice, while the question one would need to ask is how to conceive it in law.[7] Nonetheless, the superlative (with the hint to a merely relative connection that it contains), by means of which this power is singularised by Gaius's *Institutes*, should have sufficed to induce some surprise about the contradiction to which we are led by this reading of the text. Indeed, how are we to both understand that there are no other nations where the fathers hold a comparable power over their sons, and suppose, at the same time, that the power over life and death – mentioned in later texts as well – is unknown to the Romans, or has disappeared? We have, then, to forgo the flat antithesis between *servi* and *liberi*, between those who, being slaves, are not in their own power, as opposed to those who are, and place them in a context that makes it all both legible and meaningful. To be precise, the choreography of oppositions mobilises here the main split in Roman society, which, continuing the issue of personal status, draws a line between the entirety of the *gentes*, on one side, and the *cives Romani*, on the other. Gaius writes that slaves are subjected to a right of death among all nations alike, '*apud omnes per-aeque gentes*' (*I*, 52); regarding the *liberi* procreated within just marriages – meaning sons, as he clarifies a bit further – he writes that the eminent power that weighs in on them, is a privilege of the Romans, a right belonging to the Romans, a *ius proprium Romanorum* (*I*, 55). The right over slaves is part of the *ius gentium*, and thus belongs to 'what natural reason commonly establishes among humankind' (*I*, 1). The *potestas* over slaves is, thus, foreign to civil law. The fact that one holds bare ownership as conferred by the law of the *quirites* does not mean that one holds a *potestas* over slaves. The latter factually belongs to anyone holding a possession that is protected only by the *praetor* (who is not a source of rights: *I*, 54). And dealing with personal relationships and with the master's repressive faculty in particular, the *Digest* confirms that physical abuses and brutality against slaves, which the jurists always agreed to abide by, were typically exercised by the simple usufructuary. The slave is an object of civil property, this is perfectly true: to the realm of law he belongs as a thing under the category of *dominium ex iure quiritium*. Yet, when we look at the power of the master, *dominus*, we are no longer within the range of this right. What Gaius – who incidentally is the only author to describe it in this manner – calls here *vitae necisque potestas*, has no more in common with a *ius* than did the capital power that the Gauls held over their wives, and which had caused Caesar's bewilderment. As such, the expression which Gaius uses here points to something that lies perfectly beyond its context. He uses it to introduce the words *talem . . . potestatem*, which concerns the sons (*I*, 55). In this we find its real juridical relevance.

When Gaius endows the paternal power of the Romans with a superlative determination, he does not content himself with opposing, to the finite space of the *ius proprium Romanorum*, the undifferentiated mass of all those other nations, where one can kill one's slave (as one can in Rome as well). It is clear now that the contrast functions only because Gaius knows, and with him his readership, that Roman citizens wield over their sons the *vitae necisque potestas*, and that they are the only ones to wield it. The Emperor Hadrian knew it as well, and expounded it in an *edictum* (*I*, 55; *D*. 1.6.3). This exclusiveness did not mean, by the way, that one was unaware of the social practices of other nations: the Galatians, Gaius writes, think that they hold their children *in potestate* (*I*, 55). This *credere*, this 'thinking' of the Galatians, is not some legend to which Gaius, the author of the *Institutes*, refuses all credit. If he uses the formulation, 'they think', this is only because, as they were not Romans, their praxis was foreign to the fact of having a *ius*. Unlike Caesar, Gaius does not make himself an observer of foreign customs: sometimes he does refer to them, but when this happens, it is in order to draw the sharp distinctions of a jurist. Only the Romans have a right over the life and death of their sons, and this is so because, in Rome, to kill one's son is not an issue ruled by legal thinking.

Dion of Prusa, in an erudite dialogue, engages in a game of law and fact in the manner of a lawyer. The lines are blurred to the point of no longer knowing who is free and who is a slave: in the case at hand, the blurring is such that it causes the reader no longer to know who is a slave and who a son.[8] Amongst the 'nations that have excellent laws, the fathers have a right to do to their sons that which, everywhere, one has a right to do to one's slaves: to chain them, to sell them, and to kill them. And yet, even here, these children are absolutely not slaves of their fathers, as they are their sons' (XV, 20). There is no way of crediting Dion with social critique, which, according to some, would witness a moral crisis of paternal power.[9] The rhetorical universe of Dion of Prusa is universalist, and Roman law is doubtlessly an integral part of it. Like the jurists, the orators cultivate aporias and focus on the inconsistencies of the law. An extraordinarily high number of controversies, in Seneca, Quintilian or the Pseudo-Quintilian, elaborate upon the themes of conflicts where the status of the son oscillates between the freedom of the citizen and his subjection that is *in potestate*.[10] Various texts of the *Digest* suggest that the jurists found some kind of pleasure in knotting and unknotting such problems. They were no doubt present and, indeed, they were frequent. How to proceed in order to keep my *nepos* (grandson) in my power, subtracting him in advance from the future power of my son?[11] How to proceed in order to transfer my grandson from one filiation to another, say for instance: from the father of the child to his uncle on the father's side (*patruus*)?[12] How to legally organise the management of the political offices and honours of the sons of a family when – as it is almost always the case – they impact on the estates and the rights of others?[13] Can a son who holds a political office coerce his father?[14] Can he free his slave?[15] Can he make himself, before his own tribunal, an adoptive son – can he pass to another father? Can he emancipate himself and become *sui iuris* by his own intervention?[16] Case law is, here, brought to a sophistication of exercises-in-style that push the virtualities of law into their most extreme consequences. When Dion of Prusa feigns belief – or rather, has his interlocutor, as staged in one of his dialogues, feign belief – that a son can appear to be a slave, or a slave, a son, and that, therefore, one is not necessarily that which one seems to be, he finally says nothing other than what is found, earnestly expounded, in Gaius's textbook, where the difference between killing one's slave and one's son boils down to the notion that the first case is factual reality among all nations, while in the second case we are dealing with a right, and this in Rome alone.

It is incidentally not killing that is at stake, but the ability to put to death, through which, and through which alone, *patria potestas* defines itself. Where the right is obtained or realised, the expression of *vitae necisque potestas* is: *in filium*; where we are dealing with its subsisting presence as a norm, it is: *in filio*. In the formula of the *lex curiata* of adoption, the passage from the accusative to the ablative case appears to manifest the distinction between the *potestas* that the legal act conjures up over the actual person of the adopted by transforming its condition, and, on the other hand, the latent condition that abstractly defines the status of being a son: *'ut ei (L. Titio) vitae necisque in eum (L. Valerium) potestas siet, uti patri endo filio est*; so that Titius holds over Valerius (in the accusative) the *potestas* that a father holds over a son (in the ablative; Aulus Gellius, 5, 19, 9). Equally, in the *rogatio* that preceded the vote of the *lex adoptionis* of Clodius: *'auctorne es, ut in te P. Fonteius vitae necisque potestatem habeat ut in filio?* (Do you agree that P.F. holds *vitae necisque potestas* over you as over his son?)' (Cic., *De domo*, 77). The change of status indicated by the accusative, as opposed to the ablative, is a necessary nuance to the formula of adoption: it is the unique context where the law over life and death marks the transfer of a citizen, from the category of those having right over themselves (*sui*) to those who have not (*alieni iuris*). Hence the need to legitimise this alteration by means of recalling the permanent status of sons: *ut in filio*. We find *'potestas in eo'* among the statutory formulations; indeed, it is in the ablative case that it belongs to the language of the XII Tables (V, 7a).

Incidentally, *vitae necisque potestas* defines itself frequently in the absolute, referring simply to the power of fathers. With regard to him who is subject to this power, there is silence; what is said is only: *'cum patris potestas talis est, ut habeat vitae et necis potestatem* (as the father's power is such that he has power over life and death)'. It is, one could say, a right embodied in its holder, and which does not seem to have an object to which it would apply. Again and again, the orators use the formula without even mentioning the son: '*patre quo . . . vitae mortisque arbitrium datum est*' (Sen. *Contr.*, 2, 3, 11); '*nobis arbitrium vitae necisque commissum*' (Quint., *Decl. maiores*, 19, 2, p. 340, ed. Lehnert). '*Nobis*', as '*patribus*', refer, in the *Codex Theodosianus* (4, 8, 6 *pr.*), to the virtual totality of the fathers: it is the collective that gives its name to the institution.

For the formula of adoption (*adrogatio*), as already mentioned, the content of the *patria potestas* consumed itself in the power over life and death. This applies no less to Gaius, who does not define it otherwise. The incapacities, which result from it, with respect to disposing of an estate, are abundantly developed: the personal relationship limits itself to this prerogative of sovereignty. To refer to it as to some attribute of sovereignty is also a mere approximation. It leads one to think that power is composed of distinct elements, and indeed, it tends to suggest that the Roman law proceeds, in the way in which the Greeks do, by breaking it down into an enumeration of transgressions. In law, *vitae necisque potestas* designates the personal juridical relationship between father and son, and nothing else. Authors writing on rhetoric have perfectly understood this, rejecting in its name any confusion between the right of the father, on the one hand, and the natural obligations of any older parent on the mother's side, on the other hand[17] – thereby also disowning the absurd notion that the father and the mother were given equal rights.[18] In Christian times, Lactantius will not find the slightest difficulty locating in God a right that Seneca had already displaced to the Emperor: '*solus pater vocandus est qui habet vitae ac necis veram ac perpetuam potestatem*' (*Inst. div.*, 4, 4, 11). The *patria potestas* is, in this case, eternal, no longer ascribed to a mortal human. Yet, it has not changed its nature.

How to interpret *vita nexque*? The simplest way would be to deconstruct the phrase into *vita* and *nex*, as Seneca, by the way, commits himself to do in speaking of the 'gift of the gods to give and to take life' ('*munus deorum dandi auferendique vitam*': Clem., 1, 21, 2). But what is a 'right to give life'? Some have thought here of the *ius liberos tollendi*, the father's right of letting his son accede to social existence by recognising him as being his son. The *ius vitae*, in this view, would equal a waiver of his right of abandoning his child.[19] Others had imagined that the right to life was a right, held by the father, to absolve his son. The father of Horatius, deeming his son not guilty, had thus used a 'right to life', a right which Rome, in this instance, had incidentally refused to endorse. This is why, it was argued, the *ius necis* alone had survived, designated by a phrase emptied of half of its meaning, but which did conserve the remembrance of an abrogated provision.[20] Yet, hypotheses of the sort are unnecessarily complicated. They are also open to two objections. It is by looking into them that we shall try to restore the unity of the concept.

In the language of law, the particle *que* is seldom disjunctive. It unites the two elements that it combines in one identical notion. *Familia pecuniaque* designates the totality of the estate, admittedly considered under two complementary aspects, but understood as a whole. To translate it as 'all the servants plus the wealth',[21] is a mistake, and one that is even less acceptable for the fact that it risks favouring the misunderstanding that what a citizen declares to the censor every fifth year, is on the one hand his *familia*, and on the other hand his belongings – whereas, according to the very terms of the Heraclean Tablets, what he did was give an overall estimation of his *ratio pecuniae*, meaning: his assets, deducting his debts. Also, when the law of the XII Tables says: '*cum nexum faciet mancipiumque, uti lingua nuncupassit, ita ius esto*', it would be wrong to make of *nexum* and *mancipium* two separate contracts, one of a loan, one of a *mancipium*. There is only one single act by which the debtor commits himself to the creditor, articulated in two successive moments: he first undergoes symbolical attachment to the creditor (*nexus*) by means of a lump that is knotted around him; he then manifests his submission when the creditor takes his hand (*manum capere*), in order to perform some sort of handshake, of the sort also known in the rites of old-Germanic law. *Nexum mancipiumque* is, then, the solemn contract regarding a loan, accompanied by its specific clauses where necessary (*uti lingua nuncupassit*).[22] For further examples, the asyndeton *pacta conventa* is not the accumulation of two distinct juridical acts, but simply the convention, the consensual contract.[23] Neither is the legitimising formula that one finds in the *leges* of the Republic, *siremps lex ius causaque esto atque si . . .*,[24] compatible with a dissociation; and the same is true of the clause *ius ratumque*:[25] these are expressions of legal validity, seen under multiple facets, but with unifying effect. *Vita nexque* needs to be understood in the same way: what this pair of nouns does not do is disassociate life and death, which need to be understood as constituting a unity. Even so, we are not dealing with a philosophical truism: the formula is a technical one, carrying a precise meaning. The dismemberment of this right in different species is even less admissible given that the two terms *vita* and *nex* do not respond to each other, do not echo each other in one common register of opposition. *Vita* is generic; but *nex* does not mean 'death', as in the opposite of life. Rather, it designates killing without bloodshed: 'One says that he who has been killed without bloodshed (*sine vulnere*), for instance by poisoning or by hunger (Fest. p. 158 L; cf. equally 190 L: *sine ictu*) has, properly speaking, been given to death (*neci datus*)'. These words of the great antiquary are confirmed by penal law. *Necare*, in the law of the XII Tables, is used in connection with burning alive (*Tab.* 8, 10) and hanging (8, 9; 8, 24b). According to one tradition, the domestic punishment of the woman guilty of having drunk wine is the withholding of food, *inedia* (Pliny, *Nat. Hist.*, 14, 89). In a commentary to the edict '*de agnoscendi et alendis liberis*', there are two modes of killing (*necare*) of a new-born: by strangulation or suffocation (*praefocare*); and by privation of food (*alimonia denegare*): also, it is precisely *necare* that the XII Tables use in order to refer to the killing of the child carrying a malformation.[26] Thus, in its technical sense, *nex* does not refer to death generally, but to death given without bloodshed. *Ius necis* cannot be put on the same level as *ius vitae*. Yet it does imply *vita*, which is the corollary of *nex*. One has, then, to start from *nex* in order to understand what *vita nexque* is supposed to refer to. We are not confronted by two separate faculties, each of which has its own background; we are confronted by one identical right. The power of killing includes that of letting live.

II.

Let us take a break, for a moment, from *nex* and from the difficulties raised by this word, and in particular, that which consists in discerning in one modality of its exercise, a right that contains the entirety of the *patria potestas*, in absolute terms. Meanwhile, we have clarified that it fails to partake of one common category of objects of domestic jurisdiction (supposing that such a concept has ever existed in Rome). It fails, except perhaps on a merely factual level, i.e. outside of the law's rule, to feature any commonality with the killing of a slave or a woman: it is the sons upon which it lays claim, and far from presupposing the legal unity of the *domus*, it establishes between them and their fathers a relationship that resists being reduced to any other one, and that escapes any domestic jurisdiction. What is this inimitable link for which the Roman law has no other technical expression apart from death? How does one proceed in order to understand what it is about? Is there any known origin, any known norm upon which we might found it?

The question we ask might seem strange to a historian of social practices, and in this case even more to a historian of family behaviours. What is important to us is not so much to know what use the Roman fathers made of their right, but what was the Roman conception of it. Supposing that one finds it relevant, by the way, it is doubtful whether the curiosity which one nourishes concerning these facts will ever be satisfied, looking at the sources. What certain and contemporary evidence could we invoke? Seneca remembers Tricho, a Roman knight, pierced through and through by the stiletto knives of an angry crowd on the very Forum, after he had whipped his son to death (Sen., *Clem.*, 1, 15, 1). A *rescriptum* of Hadrian mentions the suicide of a murderous father (*D.* 48.21.3) – belated regrets that make one think of an episode in a fable of Phaedrus (*Fab.*, 3, 10). The same emperor banishes to an island (*deportatio in insulam*) a father who has savagely killed his son on a hunting expedition (*D.* 48.9.5). Not enough to constitute a file, even if one added to it two earlier examples, contained in Orosius, a Christian author fond of pagan turpitudes: in 221 BCE the censor M. Fabius Buteo is said to have executed his son under the false pretext that he had committed a theft (*Or.*, 4, 13, 17–18); in the year 104, consular Q. Fabius Maximus Eburnus was accused before the *comicia* of having had his son killed in the countryside by slaves (5, 16, 8). This story became an *exemplum*, archived by Valerius and repeated in oratorial mooting exercises (*V.M.*, 7, 1, 13;

Ps.-Quint. *Decl maiores*, 3, 17, p. 55 ed. Lehnert). More interesting from the vantage point of family relations are the suspicions concerning an Oppianicus or a Catilina, that they had eliminated their sons from a first marriage in order to eliminate an obstacle in entering a second one (Cic., *Cluent.*, 27–28; Sall., *Cat.*, 15, 2). Even if we have to qualify all we receive as malevolent gossip, what is sure is that we are dealing here with a type of conflict in which the stepmother is the central person, and which, in Rome as much as in Greece – and generally in societies that authorise remarriages and late remarriages in particular – mobilises tensions on all levels: estate-related, due to the now divided inheritance;[27] sexual, as the normal relationship between the ages is doubly transgressed: the mother is too far from her husband, but too close to her stepson, in such a way that adultery, either as obsession or as reality, becomes an activator of the discord between *noverca* and *privignus*[28] and the site of a rivalry between father and son.[29] None of these is among our topics here. The disorder introduced by the stepmother is a matter for a study of second marriages: in order to convince oneself, suffice it to read the passage that Tacitus (*Annales* 12, 1–2), devotes to the deliberation of the advisers of Claudius, after Messalina has been killed, about the choice of a new spouse. The ominous go-between that is the *noverca* can, on occasion, subvert the relationship of father and son, but without defining it: the *ius vitae necisque* is a primordial right, a fact that puts it immediately on another level. It is surprising, in this light, to see that its use, every time it is exceptionally confirmed by the sources, has always been subject to disapproval. We need to come back to this contradiction between a right that is formally declared, and yet at the same time sacrilegious. If the *ius vitae necisque* is able single-handedly to characterise paternal power in Rome, then it clearly was not a reality of everyday life, but much rather something that belongs to the order of a pure concept. This invites us to delve into the representations to which it has given rise.

The track we have to follow here is a political one. It leads us toward constitutional law. In the *exempla* that the annalists give of them, a punishment inflicted by the father is, in their interpretation, always an extraordinary event for Rome. By giving free rein to his anger, the father makes the step of committing the state along with himself. By putting his son to death, by sacrificing that rebellious citizen, be he an office-holder lacking in discipline or a seditious political author-ity, the father imperiously manifests a power that, going far beyond the limits of his *domus*, is a genuine prerogative of public law. His act has a normative dimension: it founds the right of other fathers to imitate his example.

The *pater imperiosus* (cf. Livy, 7, 4, 3) combines, first of all, the two qualities of father and magistrate. He lets the law of Rome triumph over his son, delivering him to the *lictores*, on the Forum, as with Brutus, or in the military camp with Postumius Tubertus in 426 and with Manlius Torquatus in 340. In this case, the son is beheaded with an axe, *securi per-cussio*, according to the consular mode of capital punishment. We are here very far from *nex*, and, one is tempted to think, in a register that is wholly different from that of *patria potestas*. And, indeed, the argument has repeatedly been advanced, that the execution of the sons of Brutus, Postumius and Manlius should be considered as unrelated to the paternal right over life and death. Mommsen has correctly observed that the *imperium* was sufficient to legitimise these rigours, and that cases of this sort fall within the exclusive compe-tence of the *coercitio* of the superior magistrate.[30] No one since has quoted them as examples of domestic jurisdiction – the generic designation under which, erroneously, the *ius vitae necisque* happens to be discussed.[31] Indeed, if one takes the episode of Brutus, one sees that the paternity of the consul, far from founding a right to capital coercion, can rather appear as an obstacle placed in his way by nature in order to test his sense of duty: How will a father behave, if he embod-ies power? Will he be able to be a consul – and nothing else? The sentimental aspect of the theme is, however, very soon exhausted: the nature of the father is juridical in nature, and in this respect opposed to that of the maternal uncle, intimately beset with the tendency to give the floor to the voice of the blood. If Brutus, remaining impassive, lets his own sons be executed, his colleague, Collatinus, tries to spare his sister's sons. The narrative of Dionysius of Halicarnassus coincides with that of Plutarch: the father's attitude represents the law, when that of the *avunculus* (uncle on the mother's side) remains subject to a narrow solidarity between parents.[32]

In Rome, as well as in the Greek city, the fact of opposing what belongs to the public entity versus what belongs to blood ties, in order to have the first take precedence over the second, has the rank of a *topos*.[33] But what is particular, in Rome, is that the dilemma is so often, so regularly, decided by the fathers in favour of the public law, that there seems to be a genuine political function attached to these narratives.[34] On this basis, one cannot limit oneself to saying that the capital punishment of the sons of Brutus is in the exercise of his *imperium*, rather than of his *patria potestas*. One has to account for the fact that the legal titles have been confused. The union of both qualities is remarkable in itself. The beheading of some of the traitors is reserved to their father, that of others to their *avunculus*: a distribution that is even more singular if one considers the principle of the alternating exercise of the *fasces* according to which only one of the two consuls commands the *lictores*.[35] The narrative of the first capital execution cumulates public coercion with the *pater*'s right to give death. For the episode to make sense we have to presume that the two powers are complementary aspects of one common representation.

In Livy, the scene is reduced to the onlooking father's face. For the people, the spectacle is not in the beheading, but in its reflection, as it can be read in Brutus's features. Everything is concentrated within the *pater* and in the expression of his face (*voltusque et os eius*), because it is *inter publicae poenae ministerium*, in the moment in which he fulfils his office of public punishment, that he acts '*eminente animo patrio*', with the superior resolution of a father (Livy 2, 5, 8). One has often understood this animus as love,[36] whereas nothing in the context indicates it, and the narratives of Dionysius of Halicarnassus and of Plutarch, where the same feature is underscored, speak only of anger and severity.[37] The image of the father who, informed of his son's death, imperturbably accomplishes the mission that Rome has entrusted to him is a widespread commonplace.[38] Whether he holds a public office or not, a father bears his son's death with courage.[39] This virtue characterises a father to the point that, where it manifests in a mother, this is so because she has a manly soul.[40] It is tempting to confront these *topoi* with a norm that defines the father by the death which he has the right to give, which is not the same as giving in to the temptation of taking these norms – and even less these commonplaces or these examples – for reality or indeed (an even less acceptable concession to facility) for some sort of psychological fact. We should be looking exclusively at rights, and at the episodes in which it pleased the Romans to see them loom large in their history. Brutus' *animus patrius* includes nothing sentimental. If there is suffering, it is left behind – Brutus is, after all, a father. What is designated is, then, a function. This is why I would translate *animus patrius* as 'his essence of being a father', as a reference to the 'paternal principle' that he embodies. This principle is, in some way, a correlative of the *patrium ius*, the fatherly right, the one that will be claimed by Horatius-the-father, when he claims, before the Roman assembly, to be the only one capable of upbraiding his son, '*in filium animadvertere*' (Livy 1, 26, 9). That all the interest of this scene is, thus, displaced from the Forum as the site in which lives are being taken, to the face of Brutus in which the *animus patrius* becomes visible, is a striking fact from a literary point of view. But it is also juridically relevant. A bond is established between the *vitae necisque potestas* and the *imperium*. One single face embodies two powers, the exercise of which offers the same terrifying spectacle in the eyes of the people of Rome.

Brutus and Manlius Torquatus are always quoted together, sometimes along with other names to which we will return.[41] These two father-magistrates embody such a fundamental value of the state that when Anchises, in the *Aeneid*, guides his son through the *fata* that are promised to his posterity, he opens the list of republican and consular achievements with Brutus' deed, closely followed – after the mention of the Decii and the Drusi – by the exploits of Torquatus, another Roman statesman who ordered his son's life to be taken by the axe.[42] There are two paternal and consular executions that flank this reminder of the two modalities of heroism: the *devotio* of the Decii Mures, father and son;[43] and the victory over the Carthaginians, in the person of Livius Salinator, victorious over Hasdrubal and Metaurus, who, fittingly, is part of the same *gens* as Livia – the other Drusus being a close parent.[44] The conjunction of a *devotio* and the sacrifice of a son both belong to the range of annalistic themes: Publius Decius Mus and Titus Manlius Torquatus are both heroes in 340. But, while in Livy's narrative (VIII, chapters 7 to 10) the paternal sanction precedes the *devotio*, letting the two exploits appear in juxtaposition, Virgil reorders the sequences in such a way that the imperious paternity includes all other cases in point, plus the supplement after Torquatus, namely Camillus who is the crowning example of this whole aggregate of fundamental virtues of the Republican state (v. 824: *aspice Torquatum et referentem signa Camillum*).

The inclusion of deeds involving civic and bellicose virtue in a representation of power where the *imperium* is cumulated with the *patria potestas*, definitely carries a meaning. This, it seems to us, follows from a passage of Polybius – a passage from which it is appropriate to draw a parallel to the verses of Virgil. I am referring to the funeral eulogy. The speaker, determined to edify his co-citizens, makes us think of the glory of all the dead whose images are exposed:

> Thus, while the reputation that is attached to the worth of these heroes constantly renews itself and the sublime deeds of these benefactors are granted immortal greatness, their fame extends to the masses of the people and passes over toward posterity. Most of all, the young generation (*hoi neoi*) are spurred to endure everything the service of the state requires them to put up with, in order for them to deserve the glory that accompanies the value of heroes (6, 54, 2–3).

But which are the examples that the Greek Polybius uses to illustrate this glory, the *eukleia* necessarily present 'in the best of men', *tois agathois tōn andrōn*? One is the gift of one's life in single combat (Horatius Cocles is quoted in ch. 55); the other one is one's own death, embraced in advance: 'numerous are those who have chosen a death that was sure in advance, be it in times of war in order to save others, be it in times of peace in order to assure the defence of the state' (54, 4). The voluntary death to which a citizen commits himself makes one irresistibly think of the *devotio*. As to war, one thinks immediately of the *devotiones* of the *Decii Mures*; as to peace – even if the opposition is rather one of *domi*/at home vs *militiae*/on a military campaign – the purpose of the sacrifice is not to assure, as one French translator of Polybius has it, the defence of the political community, but much more its stability, its safety (*tēs tōn koinōn pragmatōn asphaleias*): hence, how can one not think of the *devotio* of Marcus Curtius, who was charged, according to the very words of the soothsayers, with the protection of the permanence, the *perennitas* of the state: '*Si rem publicam perpetuam esse vellent*' (Livy, 7, 6, 3).[45] The proximity of the two formulas is beyond dispute. In his funeral eulogy, Polybius evokes *devotio*, just as does Virgil in the underworld, in both of its two forms, for the victory of the Roman armies, and for the survival of the state. Moreover (*kai mēn*), he adds this: 'Men in office have put to death their own sons, contrary to any custom, any law, by mere preference for the interest of the fatherland over that of natural bonds in the narrow sense' (54, 5). It is telling that this practice has been judged by a Greek as a case of genuine transgression of *ethos* and *nomos*: and that he had considered *parà phusin* (against nature) a bond that is, in Rome, of exclusively juridical essence.[46] But what is even more telling than the *topos* of paternal and consular punishment, is that it appears as associated, in the context of the *laudatio funebris*, with the same type of exploits that Virgil places in the *Aeneid* precisely in the middle between the two names that are its first and foremost illustrations: Brutus and Torquatus. The phrase *kai mēn* in Polybius even has a value of inclusion: it announces the pledge that that which precedes (the fact that one sacrifices one's life, in Rome, either in single combat or by means of the rite of the *devotio*) is implied in that which will follow (the fact that magistrates pronounce capital punishment for their sons). In both cases, and by an equivalent process of inclusion, the virtue of the citizen and the warrior is eminently among the potentialities of a city whose office-holders can be fathers killing their sons. The association of these ideas is confirmed, around 150 BCE at the latest, in a traditional context; it is restaged by Virgil in a story that is paradigmatic for Rome, frozen as it is in its timeless values. Its constitutive elements, the *exempla*, belong to an annalistic archive that is of far more ancient origin. They are successfully called to attention by a republican statesman in 63, in the Senate, with the purpose of having the Senators take a vote and decide the death of the plotters. Cato had no need to recall any example from 'our ancestors' (*apud maiores nostros*), apart from that of Manlius Torquatus (Sallust, *Cat.*, 52, 30).

Under the Empire, the young orators learned, in the schools, of two reasons that can be given to justify a homicide: with respect to the adulterous daughter and her lover, 'you have killed the adulterers, because the law authorises you to do so' (Quint., *Inst. Or.*, 5, 10, 39); with respect to sons, 'I had the right to do so, as a father, as a magistrate' (ibid., 40). Killing one's daughter is one thing: it is the sanction of an offence according to the modalities of the *lex Iulia*. Death meted out to a son is the matter of a permanent right of a father, *a fortiori* if he is magistrate: it is the manifestation of power in its purest state.

When he proceeds to illustrate the *vitae necisque potestas* that Romulus has endowed upon Roman fathers, or rather this unlimited prerogative of the father over the son (*hapasan . . . exousian patri kath' huiou*) which presents itself as a list of distinct rights including, among others, that of putting him to death, Dionysius of Halicarnassus alludes to the numerous *imperatores* (in the sense of holders of *imperium*) including Manlius Torquatus, who had their courageous but undisciplined sons executed (2, 26, 6). This *coercitio* of the magistrate is for him included in this right, as the *severitas* of Manlius is used by way of example. After this he will treat the question of the sale of a son (27, 1). The same applies to book VIII with the episode of Spurius Cassius killed by his father, who, in this specific case, held only the *patria potestas* without the *imperium*. Dionysius adheres to this tradition only by reason of other deeds, where the *pater* unites both qualities (VIII, 79). In short, for him, the two powers are not only cumulated, as in the *topos 'quia pater, quia magistratus'*; they are intimately blended. This is no longer about a double support in law, a re-enforced legitimation. Rather, the registers of the *ius patrium* and of the *imperium* are indistinguishably entangled. Is Dionysius wrong to interpret the tradition in this way? Is he the only one to imagine that the category of fathers (*pateres*) implies other functions, involving the public imposition of death?

Of the capital judgment in 486 BCE of Spurius Cassius, the demagogic consul, we have two principal versions, both of which are reported by Livy and Dionysius. One is the judgment of a *quaestor* dealing with a count of *perduellio*,[47] instructed before the people, followed by an execution enforced by a father, *domi* [at home].[48] The older Pliny, whose source is Calpurnius Piso, reports only the paternal punishment,[49] which is also the case of Valerius Maximus who adds the detail of a board of parents and friends, summoned by Cassius father in his house, before proceeding with the execution, itself preceded by the flogging of the condemned – the latter detail being imported from Livy.[50] Finally, according to Cicero, the people resolved to condemn the consul, after his father has spoken out against him before the assembly: *'cum pater in culpa esse comperisse se dixisset'* (*Rep.*, 2, 60). Mommsen thought that this version was the oldest, as he supposed that the two others only served to solve, in different ways, an *aporia* of law, which was that the *peculium* of someone who was *alieni iuris* cannot be confiscated by the state (*Römische Forschungen*, II, 177). However, one detail escaped Mommsen: the text upon which he relies, precisely in order to imagine this first, albeit juridically impossible tradition, neither speaks of a *peculium* nor of a consecration of what had been owned by Spurius Cassius. All that Cicero says about the accused is that his father contributed to his death sentence. The two other versions do not imply a difficulty; they are, hence, not a late invention to get over the contradictions of the first. Where one finds the question of *perduellio*, there the house of Spurius Cassius is destroyed, but no mention is made of his father;[51] where, on the contrary, the characterisation that is suggested is that of a domestic execution, there the City of Rome does not seize any goods, and effectively it is Cassius's father who makes a donation to Ceres from his own fortune.[52] Dionysius shows well the extent to which we are dealing with an alternative at this point: there is no way to believe, he says, that Spurius has been condemned by his father, and at the same time, that his fortune has been confiscated by the state; hence, as he follows the tradition that involves the statue of bronze publicly consecrated to Ceres, he ascribes the responsibility for the death sentence to the popular jurisdiction.[53]

On the other hand, Livy, Pliny, Valerius Maximus, all claim that the private fortune of Cassius was sacrificed by Cassius's father. But this private fortune uniquely serves to build a statue, which carries the inscription '*Ex Cassia familia datum*'.[54] Yet whether Calpurnius Piso, upon whose report this tradition rests, had qualified as *peculium* the resources that were used to allow the erection of the *simulacrum*, remains doubtful. In republican times, the *peculium* is a servile institution, there is no mention of the *peculium* of sons. The first *peculia* of children in a father's power – that we know of – are those of Iulia and Tiberius.[55] Let us therefore leave aside the *peculium*, understood as it is when used by authors that are contemporaneous with this institution, and let us focus instead on the statue that is given to the state and dedicated to Ceres by a father who has just put to death his consul son. This tradition is the more trustworthy also for the reason that the person of Spurius Cassius is associated, in the Annals of Piso, with another statue, that was built in front of his house – which since has become the site of an *aedes Telluris* – and which represented himself: the censors, we are told, had it torn down.[56] One would not be able to tell whether the two traditions have been contaminated, whether the legend of the *statua* destroyed by the tyrant has given rise to an opposite story of a *signum* commemorating his fall, or whether the trajectory is just the other way round. What is important, however, is that a father, having executed, in his house, a consul who has just forfeited his charge, and this under the accusation of claiming royal powers (*affectatio regni*), has offered a monument commemorating this sacrifice, a sort of atonement (*piaculum*) dedicated to Ceres, whom his son had particularly offended.[57]

Dionysius of Halicarnassus had at his disposal an annalistic tradition permitting him to think that the *patria potestas* in Rome was experienced as a public office; this authorised him to put on the same level *ius vitae necisque* and the examples of Brutus, of Cassius, and of Manlius Torquatus.

That both cases, that of a magistrate who kills his son, that of a father who kills his magistrate son, were treated alike, equally seems to result from a – distorted – account of the story of the tribune Flaminius, chased from the *rostra* upon his father's instigation. Speaking of the law of Romulus, he mentions those fathers who did not hesitate to kill their sons, even when the latter were already committed to dealing with public matters, and were counted among the highest magistrates (II, 26, 4). Here is what he says:

II, 26, 5: In virtue of this law, highly regarded personalities, siding with the people and therefore sustained by great popular reputation, who delivered discourses directed against the Senate, have been pushed away from the speaker's platform by their fathers, to be subjected to the punishment imposed by their fathers' whim. And, while they were dragged through the Forum, no one amongst those present, consul, tribune, not even the crowd itself that they had flattered, and that was full of the certainty that no power was superior to theirs, proved able to prevent their fate.

In this narrative about magistrates interrupted by their fathers while addressing the people with a demagogic discourse, wrested from the tribune while being lambasted by diatribes under the eyes of a dumbfounded crowd, without anyone who would have dared to intervene in their favour, one recognises without difficulty the *exemplum* of the tribune of 232 BCE, namely C. Flaminius, who, proposing an agrarian law against the Senate's will, resisted all oppositions and all threats, except that of his father, who snatched him in the lawful mode, stopping his movement by seizing him (*manus iniectio*), using the *patria potestas* as a means of interposing a political veto. The narrative of Valerius Maximus (5, 4, 5) shows that, with the exception of one detail – that of the *timōria* (chastisement) that he imposes upon his son – Dionysius perfectly reproduces one of the circulating traditions about Flaminius:

A similarly considerable effect the paternal authority had on Gaius Flaminius. The tribune of the plebs had posted, against the Senate and resisting its opposition, a legislative proposal about a per capita distribution of the *ager Gallicus*. There were threats to stop him pursuing his project, but he did not give in to these threats, moving forward with utter determination. He was not even dissuaded when he was told that, if he persisted, one would march against him with an army drafted for the occasion. He already expounded his law from the *rostra*, the speaker's platform: his father seized him – *manus iniectio* – and, in a matter of moments, he stepped down the *rostra*, broken by a private *imperium*, without even a single voice of protestation being heard from the assembly that he left, or a single attempt of holding him back.

We will not buy into the theme of the *privatum imperium*, which is of late origin. Yet, it does belong to the democratic invention of a trial *de maiestate* launched against Flaminius's father, for having violated the *potestas populi*, under the pretext of his *privata potestas*, by seizing his tribune son. This scholarly controversy is communicated to us in Cicero, *De inventione*. However, this fable cannot go further back than the first law *de maiestate*, that of Saturninus, in 103 or in 101.[58] The paternal *potestas* is here qualified as *privata* – with a polemical purpose, and one that is limited to the narrow context at hand. *Privatus* generally means 'not invested with a public office'. Note that the meaning of *'privatus'* is itself privative: this word simply refers to a function or a charge one fails to possess. One never uses 'private' as an absolute qualification; indeed, there is never question of a power supposed to be private in its nature.[59] Least of all could the *patria potestas* be characterised in these terms; it is an entire and undivided power by definition. The father is invested with it; apart from this, there is no other lexical determination it would contain. When, at about the same time at which the false trial against the father of Flaminius was invented, Quintus Mucius Scaevola defined the paradoxical legal situation in which the magistrate was posed if he happened to be a family son, what he did not say was that the latter holds, be it only provisionally, anything like a public power that is superior to his father's private power. All that he wanted to suggest is the notion that, in order to enable a family son, incapable by definition, of dealing with the estate-related functions of his office, there was no way around accepting the fiction according to which a son, if he is a magistrate, needs to be assimilated to a father: *loco patris familias habetur.*[60] The law, in Rome, considers a family son who possesses a public office as a quasi-father, in the same way as it considers as quasi-free the slave who is in charge of his own private fortune, or as a quasi-citizen the stranger whose belongings deserve protection if he happens to be the victim of a theft: the legal fiction settles everything on the factual level, but doing so it conserves the core, as well as its appearance. The trial against the father of Flaminius is a school case (*Inv.*, II, 17, 52): 'Gaius Flaminius, plebeian tribune, proposed to the people an agrarian law, proceeding seditiously, against the Senate's opposition and the unanimous will of the aristocrats. He held an assembly of the *plebs*, but his father made him climb down from the speakers' tribune – before being accused of crime against the majesty.'

Given that one has invented a trial against a father who showed himself disrespectful of the rights of the magistracy, one could also have spiced it up and added that Flaminius also killed his tribune son. Dionysius of Halicarnassus echoes this rhetorical variant, when he shows the son dragged through the Forum to be led to the punishment reserved for him by his father. There is proof that this version circulated in the schools, as well. We read in the Pseudo-Quintilian (VI, 14, p. 124, ed. Lehnert): '*hoc nomen* (i.e. *pater*) *omni lege maius est. tribunos deducimus, candidatos ferimus, ius nobis vitae necisque concessum est.* (This name (i.e. the name 'father') is stronger than any law. We are granted the right over life and death, thus we can chase tribunes and kill candidates)'. The paternal right over life and death is such that it subjects a tribune of the people to unmitigated powers, including that of putting to death a son who presents himself to an election for high office. Dionysius invents nothing, he only reproduces an authentically Roman *topos*. In that sense, he is not wrong to find – as he does – in his eighth book, quoting the examples of Spurius Cassius and the sons of Brutus, some affinity, under the heading of *ius vitae necisque*, between the cases of Flaminius and Torquatus, although for us they point in opposite directions.

Dio Cassius also presents a similar comparison. Writing about the advocates of Catilina he says that a large number of them have been killed by their fathers, some of which were *idiōtai, homines privati*, while some other were *hypatoi*, consuls (37, 36, 4). This is, of course, once again a commonplace not a piece of factual information. In order to complete the antithesis and fine-tune the symmetry, one would need to add to these consul fathers who, like Brutus, have proceeded to subject their sons to capital punishment, the fathers not holding any public office, *idiōtai* or *homines privati*, who have inflicted capital execution upon their political office-holding sons, such as Spurius Cassius and Flaminius. But, precisely, there are two versions that circulated about the death of a Fulvius, apprehended and executed by his father on the path to join Catilina. According to Sallust (*Catilina's War*, 39, 5) and Valerius Maximus (5, 8, 5), A. Fulvius (father) is a *vir senatorii ordinis* (that he is not a consul but a senator makes no difference to the value of the example; he still embodies a state function). According to Dio Cassius, on the other hand, it is Fulvius (son) who is a *bouleutēs*, holder of a public *officium*, whereas his father, who kills him, is an *idiōtēs* (loc. cit.). We find, then, once again associated, though of course not within one single source, but rather in two diverging traditions, which however make sense only if one confronts them with each other, two precisely complementary and interlocking relationships. In order for Dio's formula: *oukh hoti hupatoi alla kai idiōtai* (these included not only office-holders; there were also men without office amongst them) to make sense, we have to not forget about this. We need to read this formula backwards, as it were, in order to correctly interpret it, in such a way that it says something like: if you can move mountains, you can move molehills. In other words, one of the two constellations, the one in which a father puts to death his senator or magistrate son, makes clear that its conclusion applies, a fortiori, also to the other one, where a senator or magistrate father kills his son.

Using a norm as our starting point, and in order to clarify its meaning, we had to commit ourselves to the representation given to it by what is known as *exempla* literature. All episodes related to the *ius vitae necisque* involve only fathers and sons: they thereby confirm that which is proclaimed by the legal formularies. Either this power over life and death is enriched by adding to it an *imperium* held by the father, in such a way that it redoubles its weight over the son; or on the contrary, the *potestas*, as it is, deprived of any consular extension, confronts a subversive magistrate, tribune, or senator. One tends to judge these cases useless and paradoxical, and correctly so, if one reasons in terms of pure legal logic. A consul has the same coercive right against a citizen who is not his son; a father has the same power over a son who is not a magistrate. Even so, these remarks show precisely what is at stake in these *exempla*. Far from exhausting all the inherent virtualities of the norm, far also from illustrating its domain of normal application, they devise borderline cases, they draw the extreme limits of the field of sovereignty within which death is called upon: at the upper limit, the exaggerated, hyperbolic sovereignty of he who cumulates *patria potestas* and *imperium*; at the lower limit, the residual and irreducible sovereignty of the *pater*, to whose rigours even a magistrate can be subjected.

A whole chapter on the political content of the *patria potestas* in Rome should be opened at this point: there is no way to interpret *vitae necisque potestas* other than as a paternal right, one that is public and private to the same extent, and that transcends the divisions of modern juridical thinking. Let us stick to one brief observation, destined only to suggest the setting in which we conceive our subject. Initially, the problem is a juridical one. A *pater familias* is not only the chief of a house, a *domus*. He is also invested with a state function in that he represents his son in all matters concerning the *census* – given that an *alieni iuris*, someone who does not hold a right over himself, has no estate to declare to the *censor*. He also lets him have what is necessary in order to apply for and conduct any public *officia*, in such a way that the *voluntas patris* is required in all cases of the sort.[61] This type of public law-governed relationship gives rise, under the Empire, to a whole regulation of public functions, when the *honores* (responsibilities) deteriorate into *munera* (commissions): the liability of a family son is limited to the allowance (*peculium*) that the state forces his father to provide him with; beyond the *peculium*, the father's liability is predicated upon the condition that he has given his consent to his son's taking a public office.[62] Thus, the father/son relationship is a singular one, being both domestic and political, private and public. If one fails to consider these elementary juridical structures, the risk is that one takes Rome for Athens, and that one believes that all citizens are equal before the law. Roman public law has, apart from fathers, that is to say apart from those who are *sui iuris*, no other subjects endowed with fully exercised rights. Other citizens, that is to say sons, have no access to public life other than courtesy of a member of that first group (*voluntas patris, peculium*). These institutions did stretch out into the field of political and moral aspects[63] involving the moral figure of the father in the tradition, the paternal metaphors of power, etc., a field that is admittedly slightly better known, whose legal roots are, however, generally ignored. All these cultural features become meaningful only if one keeps in mind that a legal subject, a legally capable individual, is, in Rome, necessarily a *paterfamilias*, never mind his age, or the reality of his condition. Nothing stops a person who has no children, or has not yet reached puberty, from being a *paterfamilias*;[64] conversely, a mature man, a father or, indeed, the forebear of a numerous family himself, counts as a minor as long as his father lives. This normative specificity incidentally reduces the relevance of any questions that one might ask about youth and old age in the Roman world: this is not a criterion to which the major division as to personal status attaches any importance. The *summa divisio*, for citizens, is between fathers and sons. Hence the extraordinary vitality of the case law dedicated to the relationship of fathers and sons, to the excesses of the power of one group, to the limits of the obedience of the other group. When can one refuse to obey one's father? In other words: *An in omnia patri parendum sit*? (Whether one has to obey one's father in everything?)[65] Whence also, on a symbolic level, the immense scope of the quarrels over etiquette – precedence – between a father and his magistrate son, which takes us back to certain constellations illustrating the *ius vitae necisque*: can a father remain seated on his horse in the presence of his consul son?[66] In such circumstances, which of the two will be the first to descend?[67] Does the one have the right to sit down in the presence of the other? In public? In private?[68]

The *patria potestas* is defined by the law as a power over life and death. If one thinks in terms of law rather than fact, each example mobilises a norm that comprises the totality of citizens. A passage in Florus – who, as he often does, presents us with a rhetorical commonplace – says that Brutus, in killing his sons, adopted the people of Rome in their place. What is certain is that this *topos* can be, and ought to be, taken in a first, obvious, sense: Brutus, preferring the state over his own sons, sacrifices his sons to the state. But if one admits that the words *publicus parens* and *adoptare populum* retain their proper value, and thus their strong sense, the text also means that the power that Brutus has exercised over his sons reveals itself as being, in its essence, for the people he has adopted, the power of a consul wielding the *imperium*. The theme of death unfolds on two registers, moving from one to the other. What is decisive is that the parent–child metaphor has been possible:

> As to Brutus, it is by paying the price: the ruin of his family, and a parricide, that he has succeeded in obtaining the favour of his fellow citizens. Indeed, having discovered that his sons plotted for the return of the kings . . ., he had them dragged to the Forum, then, in the middle of the assembly, beaten with rods, and beheaded with the axe, in such a way that it appeared manifest that the father of the fatherland has adopted the people and chosen it as his family, in place of his sons. (Florus, I, 3, 5)

III.

Women are no more subject to the *vitae necisque potestas* than slaves. As daughters in the power of a father, as wives *in manu* (literally held in one's hand) they largely escape the empire of a law whose mode of expression is death. All the relevant texts point in that direction. Notwithstanding this, the dogma of a unity of the right of capital coercion within the *domus* is, universally and without the slightest expression of a doubt, repeated by scholars.[69] Indeed, we are forced to realise that textual evidence is an inadequate means of also defeating the other preconception, on which the first depends: the notion that, at least at an early stage, the *domus* forms a juridical unity.

There is, therefore, a necessity to interrogate the base of that 'domestic justice' which is said to extend to women, wives and daughters, subjecting them, together with sons, to a penal law within the family – a penal law, however, that the law keeps silent about, concerning females. Quite wrongly, and yet with surprising unanimity, a large number of specialists of Roman law and Roman legal history mix up, by putting them under one identical heading, repressive procedures that have common aspects on the sociological level, but that the law treats as unrelated. Incidentally, even considering only the level of practices, there is a group of texts which, on closer examination, reveal some highly significant differences between judging a daughter or a wife, and judging a son – texts that one tends to read from what appears to be a slightly exaggerated distance. These differences concern the composition of the family *consilium* that assists the *pater* in finding his verdict. Where the *consilium* is dealing with a woman, only close parents, *cognati*, *propinqui*, participate in the deliberation; while, on the contrary, when dealing with a son, the list of participants includes friends, senators, the senate in its entirety, even the Emperor.[70] In itself, this distribution shows that, if it is kinship that limits the moral horizon and the penal commitment of a daughter, the social space in which the sons have to respond for their offences, is a far larger one. Dealing with a son, the circle with which the *pater* environs himself in his own house tends to be ultimately coextensive with that of the city. But this is not even the viewpoint that we would need to choose in order to understand an opposition that we intend to grasp at its root, which is the norm: the power exercised over daughters and wives is, generically, not subject to a requirement of legal authorisation. There is a formally recognised law, referred to by the curiate law, that invests a *pater* with the right – absolute, abstract, primordial – over life and death over a *sui iuris*, according to the legal formula '*uti patri endo filio est*'. Nothing of the sort is to be found concerning the domestic punishment of women. It attaches itself to the order of customs (*mores*).

The repression of the *adulterium*, a married woman's sexual *commercium* with someone other than her husband, was regularly left to families to deal with. The guilty wife was judged by her husband and her relatives, whenever there was a need to establish the evidence (when caught *in flagrante delicto*, she was instantly killed). The 'judgment' which Dionysius addresses, the marital *condemnatio* that Cato the Elder opposes to the 'right to kill without judgment', show that the domestic procedure corresponds to a regime of offences that did not necessarily suppose that she was caught in the act.[71] The custom that underlies this judgmental practice, and to which both 'Romulus's law' and Cato in his discourse *De dote* refer, was, in the time preceding Augustus's *lex Iulia de adulteriis*, omnipresent enough for the sources not to report even a single trial because of adultery brought against a woman. On the other hand, we are informed that comitial procedures about *stuprum* (rape) are brought by the officers of the City (*aediles*). In three cases, the accused are men;[72] in two, they are matrons.[73] These, we have to suppose, were widows and *sui iuris*. The first case of an adulterous woman subjected to a head of accusation is attested under Augustus, directly triggered, no doubt, by the *lex Iulia*. This explains why this law, only qualified as *de adulteriis*, deals, for the time to come, with the criminal prosecution of *adulterium*, as well as *stuprum*.[74] From now onward, *adulterium* was subject to public condemnation and prosecution, just as *stuprum* had already been. Now, as with men, a woman *alieni iuris* will be dealt with for her sexual offences by state tribunals.

In 17, Tiberius authorised, by way of a Senate decision, that Appuleia Varilla be judged for adultery and condemned for it by her next of kin, *a propinquis suis* (Tac., *Ann.*, 2, 50, 3). Since female adultery is now governed by law, in order to authorise a return to family jurisdiction over women – that *mos maiorum* (Suet., *Tib.*, 35), *exemplum maiorum* (Tac., *Ann.*, 2, 50, 3), or *priscum institutum* (Tac., *Ann.*, 2, 50, 3) – an explicit concession has become necessary. The legal void underlying 'domestic jurisdiction' had been filled: for any family eager to judge, the city is required to allow it to judge in its place. It is the administration that actively delegates and officially displaces its competence to the family. It has not been sufficiently noted that it was only in proceedings against women that either the magistrate in charge of instructing criminal trials or the Senate proceeded to provide such admissions for family judgment by proxy. Thus, in the tumultuous affair around the Bacchanalia in 186 BCE, those who had only initiated themselves to the rites were arrested; capital punishments were pronounced against those guilty of *stuprum*, against murderers, false witnesses, kidnappers, counterfeiters of testaments: 'One killed more than one imprisoned. Those who found themselves in one or the other situation were numerous. Condemned women were handed over to their parents, relatives, or those holding them in their *manus*, to be punished by them in private; where there was no one who had the right to execute the punishment, public officers inflicted it upon them' (Livy, 39, 18, 5–6). Each word of Livy's narrative has its importance: *Damnare* (condemn), *tradere* (handing over), *idoneus exactor* (enforcer). Women are first condemned by an extraordinary commission created by the Senate; they are then handed over to their parents, or their husband, to one of those qualified as *idoneus exactor* (this term being a technical expression, designating those who, by custom, hold a repressive power over women, wherever the city has not stepped in).[75] In 154 BCE, Publicia and Licinia, guilty of having poisoned their consul husbands, were put to death upon a decision of their family, Livy, 48, *cognatorum decreto necatae sunt* (have been *necatae*, i.e., killed without bloodshed), following a decision of their relatives; Val. Max., 6, 3, 8, *propinquorum decreto strangulatae sunt* (have been strangled by a decree of their kinship). But this domestic capital punishment was triggered by an official criminal instruction. Earlier, what was instituted was an extraordinary, *praetor*-presided *quaestio*, as also confirmed in numerous other cases of poisoning (*Periochae*, 48: *de veneficiis quaesitum ... causa cognita, cum praetori praedes vades dedissent*; Val. Max., eod. loc.: *non enim putaverunt ... longum publicae quaestionis tempus exspectandum*). The domestic sentence had to be a matter of a genuine delegation, considering that the relatives had to provide real as well as personal securities (*Periochae*, 48: *de veneficiis quaesitum ... causa cognita, cum praetori praedes vates dedissent*). In the case of Apuleia Varilla, it is the Senate who, on Tiberius's request, restores a prerogative that the *lex Iulia* had erased. In 57, the prevailing of this traditional procedure is still confirmed. Pomponia Graecina is handed over to her husband's judgment, '*mariti iudicio permissa*' (Tacitus, *Ann.*, 13, 32). However, that 'the domestic jurisdiction has never existed, because the state has conceded it', is not what this text proves.[76] The appropriate reasoning is, on the contrary: such a prerogative is granted, because the public tribunal has eliminated its raison d'être. The indecent acts of which Pomponia doubtlessly stood accused, as every time in Rome when it is a woman who is at stake (cf. *de capite famaque conjugis cognovit*), fell under the *lex Iulia de adulteriis*. The *permissio* of the Senate renewed the '*priscum institutum*', the age-old institution, the custom for a husband to judge and to acquit his wife in the presence of a family council (*propinquis coram*) in a field – that of sexuality – in which public law had abrogated it. Thus, the file is coherent. The events that compose it present the common feature of treating the family and the city as two alternative realms, whenever a woman is at issue: each of them excludes the other. Had the fathers, the husbands been invested, at any time, with a genuine right, a formally recognised *ius* over their daughters and their wives, the state would simply have had to relinquish the prosecution in order to divest itself, thereby allowing the resurgence of the earlier, more fundamental principle that had been momentarily suspended.

There is never a question of delegation when it is a son who is judged. No doubt, the paternal right over life and death, upon which the *patria potestas* is built, does not constitute a dispensation from the customary obligation of holding a *consilium*, the composition of which incidentally exceeds the limits of the *domus*. Nonetheless, this authorisation founds, in the sphere ruled by public criminal law, a power that does not have to be explicitly renewed on a permanent basis. Spurius Cassius is put to death for *affectatio regni* just after having been relieved of his charge. A. Fulvius slays his conspirator son, Lucius Gellius Publicola, after 70, and Lucius Tarius Rufus, after 16 BCE, judge their sons for *parricidium*, the public crime par excellence (Val. Max. 5, 9, 1; Seneca, *clem.*, 1, 15, 2). Quintus Fulvius, at an unknown date, proceeds in the same way when he implores the aid of the Senate to search for his son, who, having been arrested, is later absolved (Val. Max. 5, 9, 3). The annalist tradition conveyed the image of the fathers being holders of the ultimate punishment. That Flaminius, after interrupting him, also dragged his tribune son across the Forum in order to put him to death in his house, is not necessarily the invention of an overflowing fantasy. Collective behaviours occasionally show that these annalistic motives were not pure intellectual constructions: they translate the perception of norms well. In 48 BCE, the magistrates bullied the tribune M. Caelius Rufus, because he had come up with the idea of systematically receiving the calls of debtors pursued by their creditors. When he was attacked and his seat broken by the consul Isauricus, all he did to respond to this was to invite his attacker to a Curulean seat. Such a seat being made of tightly taut straps, the invitation was an insolent metonymy reminding the consul, and his laughing public, of the consul's father's whip: the consul had had to suffer it so often. If the *lorae* (straps) provoke laughter and are instantly associated with whipping, this is because, in Rome, there is nothing more amusing than imagining a magistrate being beaten by his father.[77]

The legal system depicted by these examples is based on such a degree of homogeneous evidence that the single exception that one can find only confirms it – the exception on its own would be almost sufficient to single-handedly reconstruct the system. In 140 BCE, M. Manlius Torquatus, whose *gens* had distinguished itself for a long time by its intransigent conception of *patria potestas* and *imperium*, required from the senate that his son be handed over to him. Indeed, the praetor Silanus, returning from his province, had been accused *de repetundis* (of extortions) by the Macedonians, who had sent their envoys to Rome.[78] Their demand was, according to the *epitomator* (the author of an abridged version of Livy), related to a request for delegation of a trial to be conducted (*Ep.* 54: *ut sibi cognitio mandaretur*). According to Valerius Maximus, all Manlius wanted to obtain from the senators was 'that they abstain from taking any decision about this matter before he has himself examined the issue of the Macedonians and of his son' (5, 8, 3). However, these two narratives, in addition to that of Cicero (*fin.*, 1, 7, 24) agree in attributing the initiation of the trial to the father of the accused. *Domi causa cognita* (after examinations taking place in his house) (*Ep.* 54), the latter repudiates his son. At this point, let us leave aside the significance of what the *Periochae* – another abridged text of Livy – call the *abdicatio*, which, according to the definition of Cicero and, later, Valerius Maximus, is more precisely a prohibition of ever again letting your father catch sight of you (Cic., eod. loc.: *et in conspectum suum venire vetuit*; Val. Max.: *e conspectu meo abire jubeo*). A son's rejection by his father is a measure that instantly provokes the suicide of the cursed – Silanus hangs himself (Ep. 54: *cum suspendio vitam finisset*; Val. Max.: *suspendioque se proxima nocte consumpsit*). Equally, in 101, when a messenger tells the son of Aemilius Scaurus, who has fled the Cimbri, that he is henceforth precluded from ever again meeting his father, whom he has disgraced (*conspectum degenerati patris vitaturum*, Val. Max., 5, 8, 4), he turns against himself the sword that he had been unable to wield against the enemy.[79] But, for us, the salient point is that normally – the corrupt behaviour of a magistrate being a matter subject to a permanent *quaestio* in the Senate since 149 BCE – a father should have asked the Senate to authorise him to condemn his son, when what was at issue was a public offence. There is no doubt that the *patres* had the choice as to whether or not to divest themselves of their right of judging Silanus. However, if our juridical reconstruction is correct, they should have abstained from giving to Manlius an explicit permission to judge. It would have been sufficient, in principle, if this severe father had taken the initiative, while the high assembly, for its part, had stayed the proceedings, as we are informed that they did in the case of Spurius Cassius, and as is shown still in 63 BCE by the anecdote of A. Fulvius. However, the texts say unquestionably that it is the opposite that happened: Manlius presents an urgent request, which is granted (Ep. 54: *petit impetravitque*; Val. Max.: *summo deinde . . . amplissimi ordinis consensu cognitione suscepta*). Cicero, writing that Manlius 'commanded' that the matter be pleaded before him (eod. loc..: *causam apud se dicere iuberet*), reduces the events to the result to which they give rise, but this short-cut offers no counterweight against the in-depth narratives describing a genuine procedure, comparable in all aspects to the delegation of judging a woman. Indeed, in this particular case, such a delegation was necessary. This, however, is only because Silanus, having been given into adoption at an earlier date, had in the meantime been freed from Manlius's paternal right.[80] M. Torquatus was, in other words, no longer the *paterfamilias* of that unworthy son – even if, impersonating the values of his *gens*, he continued to reproduce all the attitudes of a *paterfamilias*.

Patria potestas and *vitae necisque potestas* are established as an abstract and permanent empowerment. The city can place an obstacle before it, of course; and in fact, it does not refrain from prosecuting sons. The father, in this case, speaks up for his *patrium ius*, manifests his *probatio*, and claims to speak for his son, to take the role of an *advocatus filii*. But as soon as the public jurisdiction ceases to interfere, the father's primordial and latent right resumes, for all intents and purposes, without requiring any delegation. Whereas the condemnation or the execution of a woman 'in private' is a purely domestic matter.

It is founded by no law. That of sons authorises itself by reference to a power that is a priori recognised to fathers and inscribed in a continuity – less that of the city than that of the paternal order to which the Curiate law refers, because it is constituted outside of it. This right belongs to fathers as a matter of principle – each of whom, having been a son, has been under the power of a father. Exceptionally, the city suspends this linear arrangement, in according a right over life and death over someone who had the title of *paterfamilias*, thus disadvantaging him by declaring him a son. This induces a crack in the order of regularly transmitted rights, introducing – through the rite of investiture – a discontinuity in the chain of inherited powers. Without this procedural incident we would not know that the right to mete out death is all there is of the *patria potestas*, and that, represented in this way, the paternal power is only over sons – or, in other words, that it has no other subjects, apart from sons.

IV.

How is such a right to be conceived within the city? The annalistic tradition resolved this question in its own way, by cumulating *patria potestas* and *imperium*, or by allowing fathers not holding a public office a power of control over their magistrate sons. But there is in Republican law a major principle that is not subjected to this power: this is the interdiction, possibly already formulated by the law of the XII Tables, of executing a citizen without judgment, of killing a *civis indemnatus*.[81] The orators of the Empire openly debate this contradiction, as they generally do (and as it is their custom to do), both in terms of natural and of political law, in dealing with the inconsistencies that always risk resulting from the principle of paternal power. This resolution of contraries is pushed a long way, in fact quite far into the realms of the absurd, as can be best seen in Calpurnius Flaccus. The right of the father is here explained as a legally based transgression of the law; one kills one's son, no longer in virtue of one's *patria potestas*, but because of a law authorising the putting to death of citizens who have not been condemned: *lege indemnatorum interficiendum* (Decl. 4; 24; 45; 46). The theme must have been widespread, as one finds an echo of it in Dion of Prusa. Let us remember that, in his paradoxical and erudite dialogue, the son was said to be juridically not a slave, even if his father held the right of taking his life 'without judgment, and without any count of accusation'. Consider two illustrations of this paradox. In the *declamatio* 24, a father hands his son over to the executioner, because he wants to have him killed in accordance with the law authorising killing without judgment (*lege indemnatorum interficiendum pater filium carnifici tradidit*). The son insists on being killed at his father's hands (*ille vult manu patris interfici*). The controversy is not a sentimental but a juridical one. Can one make of the executioner, whose *officium* is the execution of public judgments, the instrument of a right that presupposes the erasure of the tribunal? Is it not contrary to the *ratio iuris* to use his services against a person who has not been presented to a judge (. . . *ut adhibeatur in eum carnifex, in quem non fuit iudex*)? Now, take the symmetrically opposed case of a criminal, condemned through public procedure, though held captive by his father '*in carcere privato*'. The son demands the public prison (*ille petit ut in publico carcere servetur*). The point of law is the following: can a publicly condemned man be returned to fatherly punishment? Is it possible to use one's paternal right against someone who is publicly condemned ('*adversus damnatum iure patris uti*')? How can respect for the law be reconciled with a law that legitimises the arbitrary? What is to be made of the fact that the city claims jurisdiction over the punishment of *damnati* against fathers who hold a right over their life and death that is independent of any condemnation pronounced against them (*lex indemnatorum interficiendum*)? The laws demand things that are impossible (*leges impossibilia desiderant*), as is noted elsewhere by Calpurnius Flaccus (*Decl.* 45). These aporias are developed in the realm of the imaginary by the *rhetores*, just as they are resolved in the *exempla* of the annalist tradition. But they have their origin in the law. Cicero paid for having put to death the partisans of Catilina without judgment, by being sent into exile; it remains an open question, on the other hand, whether Fulvius or any of those named by Dio Cassius for having taken the lives of their sons to prevent them from joining Catilina, have ever been pestered for killing them. And if there are good reasons to think that the trial brought against the father of the tribune Flaminius is a fake, or that the accusation of violating the majesty of the tribune is a fictitious one, this is owing to the notion (coined on this occasion) of an 'excessive use' of the *vitae necisque potestas*.

Of all these antinomies, the one that weighs most heavily is still that which results from the very designation of such a right: *ius necis*. In Rome, the capital coercion held by the magistrate in charge of the *imperium* involves bloodshed. Decapitation, preceded by *verberatio* (lashes), is its ordinary mode.[82] *Nex* is the opposite of slaying with an axe (*securi percussio*). It is defined – one will remember – as putting to death without bloodshed. But the latter is the unique form of capital execution that is applied to women. Within the domain of the *domus*, women are put to death either by the denial of sustenance (*inedia*), or by strangulation and suffocation.[83] Women also die of strangulation or hunger in public prisons.[84] This form of execution is so closely linked to the status of a woman that, in order to be subjected to it, she must have lost her virginity. Before strangling the daughter of Seianus, the hangman rapes her (Tac., *Ann.*, 6, 5, 9). Not out of sadism, but in order for the norms to be respected: we read in Suetonius that, in the prisons of Tiberius, *immaturae puellae* were first violated by the executioner, in virtue of the immemorial rule according to which it was impious to strangle a virgin (*quia more tradito nefas virgines strangulari*: Tib., 61, 5).[85] The death without bloodshed of women is always the price to be paid for their impurity. The vestal who dies buried alive, dies at once of suffocation and of hunger, because she is both par excellence indecent and par excellence woman. Her death combines the two forms of the feminine death penalty, because her crime is the gravest in the order of the sexual. Apart from this, the penal norms which are specifically foreseen for women only consider adultery and indecency (in the law known as the 'law of Romulus', and in the *lex Iulia de adulteriis*): for other offences it is sufficient that they have been committed by a woman in order to associate them, by contamination, to impudicity; this is shown by the tradition that assimilates with adultery the drinking of wine, or the theft of keys, as well as by the commonplace, used especially by Cato, according to which an *empoisonneuse* is necessarily indecent (Quintilian, *Inst. or.*, 5, 11, 39; *Rhet. Her.*, 4, 6, 23; Sen.,

Contr., 7, 6, and 7, 3, 6). All the trials of homicidal women that we know of are trials of poisoning, while all the accused that we know of died by strangling.[86] Daughters put to death by their father suffered this fate by reason of impurity, and the texts that mention their death speak only of *nex*.[87]

This, then, is a first register: to it belong virtually all men under the power of a father, in view of the *vitae necisque potestas* weighing over them. A second register is that of the newborn. The jurist Paul considers two ways of putting a newborn to death, once the father no longer has the right to recognise it as his, and had thus no longer a right to kill (*necare*) it: either by suffocation (*praefocare*), or by privation of food (*alimonia denegare*).[88] In his polemic against the pagans, Minucius Felix mentions the abhorrent custom that consisted in exposing children to wild animals – the reproach is hyperbolic – or strangling them: *procreatos filios . . . adstrangulatos* (*Oct.* 30, 2). For girls, the only mode of recognising them seems to have been the fact of *alere*, of feeding them.[89] For boys, the ritual of 'lifting them up' from the floor (*tollere filium*) has the symbolic finality of introducing them under their father's *potestas*.[90] But at the very moment that they are entering the world of the law, they at once enter a space in which looms over them, irrevocably linked to their essence of being sons, a right of death, the very name of which, *nex*, associates them with a mode of existence that is neither civic, nor masculine.

The *ius necis* is not the right of exposing, which is known under the name of *ius exponendi*. Moreover, to expose a child is an act, while the power of imposing *nex* is understood as virtual and unrelated to an event. Roman law itself represents the essential privation of men and citizens ruled by a *pater* by means of a metonymy: it mentions the death of women and of newborn infants, their killing through hunger and through suffocation.[91] Yet, we are dealing here with *vita nexque*, life and (bloodless) killing. Life, in its general designation, is the necessary counterpart of a right embodied in a looming threat. *Ius vitae necisque*, there is just this single juridical occurrence in Roman law of *vita*, but, considering that '*que*' is not disjunctive, life plays the role of a mere corollary.[92]

The father's *vitae necisque potestas* is not a fact of social history. In reality, the cruelty of fathers, where it is reported and confirmed, is also condemned. To kill one's son is almost always sacrilegious, except where a father embodies the state, or where the state is badly represented by a son. Apart from that, the anecdotes that are, here and there, reported by the sources, are of no help in understanding the meaning of this right, except in showing us the extent to which it remains, in itself, as a right, immune from doubt, despite the total lack of favour attached to its exercise. Certain scholars have read too much into a constitution of Hadrian, where the emperor shows himself agitated about the fact that a father has slaughtered his son 'like a robber would do, rather than according to paternal law' (*latronis magis quam patrio iure*: D. 48.9.5). This text only suffices to show, precisely, that the *ius patrium* is not disputed. The son had been savagely killed during a hunting expedition: a bloody and ferocious death, at once a marginal anecdote, nothing in common with *nex*. But let us remember, before Hadrian, the rage of the crowd against the knight Tricho, riddled with numerous dagger wounds in the core of the Forum, because he has beaten his son to death: this cruel father received the same punishment as the tyrant Vitellius a little later, also slashed by pointed poniards. Even earlier, in 103 BCE, Q. Fabius Maximus was condemned, probably by the *comitia*, and had to flee into exile, because, having relegated his son to the countryside (after having him judged for indecency, it is true), he staged his assassination by his slaves. If one really wishes to write the history of these collective sentiments, one would extend one's viewpoint to include the annalistic domain. In 340, Manlius Torquatus, back in Rome after defeating the population of Latium, beheaded his unruly son, and was welcomed by the elderly who went to meet him, but the young generation 'turned away from him as from someone abhorrent' (*iuventutem . . . adversatam exsecratamque*: Livy 8, 12, 1; Val. Max. 8, 9, 1).

What was intended in this study, was to gain an understanding not of the practices but of a category, *patria potestas*, and of the systematic implications that its operations draw within Roman law. The relationship between fathers and sons, while it reveals a tight interlocking between the family and the state (which one supposed radically separated, in the image of the classical Athenian model), also shows the normative irreducibility between masculine and feminine, distinguishing their roles within the *domus,* and giving short shrift to their generally supposed unity under one homogenous power. Finally – but this conclusion is a truism – either power is all there is, or it is nothing at all: the citizen who, subjected to the power of a father, waits to become a *paterfamilias* one day in the future, is nothing for the time being.

The historiography oscillates. Most writers focus, either on the origin of a right, traces of which still subsist today by anachronism; or else on that same right's final destination, the harbinger signs of which they strive to unearth. Accordingly, one either refers back to a primitive state which is still free of any admixture of what constitutes a city, or one tells the story of an erratic prerogative wasting away in slow decay. This second wing is, needless to say, a complement of the first. The stages upon which the specialists take a stand in order to describe the decline of this inconceivable right (inconceivable if one takes it as a reality, and if one translates *necis potestas* as paternal cruelty), are located in a stretch of time that starts with the law of the XII Tables and ends with a constitution of the year 323 of our era. From this date onward, almost everyone agrees that, when Constantine, writing about *patria potestas,* says: *ut patribus quibus ius vitae in liberos necisque potestas permissa est (Cod. Theod.,* 4, 8, 6, *pr.*), the words *'permissa est'* need to be understood in the past tense, as 'it was permitted' rather than as 'a permission has been given'.[93] It is sometimes conceded that one needs to wait until 374, by which date the murder of an infant is sanctioned by the death penalty (*C. Th.* 9, 14, 1 = *C.J.* 9, 16, 7).[94] But it is generally assumed that the historical lifespan of the *vitae necisque potestas* ends much earlier. A constitution of 318 includes the murder of descendants in the masculine line under the category of *parricidium*: is this not evidence that *vitae necisque potestas* is abolished?[95] Even earlier, Hadrian, pronouncing the *deportatio in insulam* (deportation to an island) against an assassin father (*D.* 48.9.5), or renouncing the confiscation of goods when the father, out of regret, has taken his own life (*D.* 48.21.3), is said to have already abolished that inhuman prerogative.[96] After all, one knows well enough, surely, the concern for *pietas paterna* shown by the Antonine Emperors.[97] Indeed, what if the rule, recorded in the *Digest* (48.8.2), according to which a son cannot be put to death *inauditus* (i.e. without being given the opportunity to be heard), turned out to be the same as the one that we see Gaius of Autun – a writer of the fifth century CE – attribute to the founding fathers of the Roman republic, the law-giving commission of the *decemviri*, namely that before going to the extreme of putting his son to death, the father – or someone, at least – has to convince himself of the presence of a *iusta causa*: would that not be proof that the *vitae necisque potestas* has, at this point, only been a survival, a relic right from the start, that is, since as early as the mid-fifth century BCE?[98]

One does not abolish a privilege by means of controlling its application. Nonetheless, there is a moment at which what used to be a present norm has become a past norm. It is probable that this point of inflection is reached when the compilers of Justinian take hold of the constitution of 323 and introduce a modification of the present tense to the past tense, which in addition they underline by the adverb 'once' (*olim*): *ius vitae in liberos necisque potestas olim erat permissa* (C.J. 8, 46, 10).

Notes

1. 15, 20: '*Epheitai gar autois apokteinai, mēte krinantas, mēte holōs aitiasmenous.*' Many thanks to Marie-Henriette Quet for having allowed me to use her translation of Dion's *Dialogues on slavery*. The dialogue I am referring to here and later is the fifteenth.

2. *Leg.*, 3, 3, 6: '*Iusta imperia sunto, isque cives modeste ac sine recusatione parento. Magistratus nec oboedientem et noxium civem multa vinculis verberibusve cohercetur . . .*' Pomponius, *D.* 1.2.2.16, does not define *imperium*, but only the limits of the *coercitio*.

3. Valerius Maximus, 2, 2, 4: '*Maiores hunc morem retinuerunt, ne quis se inter consulem et proximum lictorem, quamvis officii causa una progrederetur, interponeret. Filio dumtaxat et ei puero ante patrem consulem ambulandi ius erat.*'

4. Asconius, *In Milionianam*, p. 33, Clark. Inscriptions of Puzzuoli, published by L. Bove, in *Labeo*, 1967, pp. 22 ff.

5. Paul, *coll.* 4, 2, 3: '*Ut is pater eum adulterum sine fraude occidat, ita ut filiam in continenti occidat*'; 4, 2, 4: '*. . . qui adulterum deprehensum occiderit, et in continenti filiam*'; Papinian, *Coll.* 4, 9, 1: '*Si pater qui adulterum occidit et filiae suae pepercit, quaero quid adversus eum sit statuendum? Respondit: Sine dubio iste pater homicida est* (If in killing his daughter's lover the father

spares his daughter, I ask how to judge him. The answer is: this father is no doubt a homicide)'. The text clarifies the one here discussed; the father has first chosen to spare his daughter, only to change his mind later on. A difficult case, as there is no provision to be found for it in the formulation of the *lex Iulia*; also, Papinian struggles to find an answer to it, in *Coll.* 4, 4, 8, 1.

6. Cf. *D.* 6.1.17, *pr.* (Iulianus); 9.2.12 (Paul); 4.3.7.4 (Ulpian); 45.1.23 (Pomponius); 46.3.95.1 (Papinian); on the excessive chastising of the beneficial owner (*usufructuary*): *D.* 7.1.66; 7.1.15.3; 7.1.17.1; 7.1.23.01.

7. A. Watson, *Rome of the XII Tables: Persons and Property*, p. 48; A. M. Rabello, *Effetti personali della patria potestas*, I, 1979, p. 181.

8. Dion, discourse XV, the theme of which is formulated: '*estin, ō ariste, eidenai hostis doulos ē hostis eleutheros* (What needs to be known is who is servant, and who is free)'. Among its themes, we find problems of filiation, of the possession of status, of the sources of the servile condition from the viewpoint of natural law (with a long treatise on captivity), of acquisitive prescription, etc. The passage dealing with the comparison of the status of a son and that of a slave is on pp. 18–20.

9. See V. Scarano Ussani, *Valori e storia nella cultura giuridica fra Nerone ed Adriano*, chapter I, section 4, where this passage of Dion is discussed, but also commingled with fragments from the *Digest* referring to the *rationes* of past institutions.

10. These themes are particularly discussed in mooting exercises dealing with the theme of unjust *abdicatio*. Very often the conflict of duties – and of laws – construes an opposition between the obedience to the father on the one hand and civic loyalty on the other hand (for instance, with respect to the obligation to alimony with respect to close relations. Sen., *Contr.* I, 1; Quint., *Decl.*, 330; on the refusal of matricide, Quint., *Decl.*, 300; Sen., *Contr.*, 1, 4; Calp. 31; or fratricide: Sen., *Contr.* 7, 1; on the dilemma between state and father: Quint., *Decl.*, 378, and Aulus Gellius, 2, 7, 11, who echoes these mooting debates when he quotes treason and matricide as cases of legitimate refusal to obey.

11. *D.* 1.7.28; cf., also, 27.10.16.2.

12. *D.* 1.7.15.1.

13. Numerous texts in *D.* 50.1: *ad municipalem et de incolis*; and 2: *de decurionibus et filiis eorum*.

14. *D.* 36.1.13.5.

15. *D.* 1.14.1.
16. *D.* 1.14.2.
17. Sen., *Contr.*, 9, 5, 7: '*Habet sua iura natura, et hoc inter avem patremque interest, quod avo suos servare licet, patri et occidere* (Nature has got its laws, and the grandfather differs from the father in that he can be in charge of his offspring, but the father can also kill)'. The reference is to a maternal grandfather, *maternus avus*, who, in the case at hand, kidnaps his third grandson after the two preceding ones have been poisoned by their stepmother.
18. Ps.-Quint., *Decl. Maior.*, 19, 15 (p. 340 ed. Lehnert): '*iam vero quid impudentius, quid indignius quam, cum sibi de liberis credunt licere tantundem, et aequum ius patris ac matris esse contendunt, quasi nesciant nobis arbitrium vitae necisque commissum?*'
19. A. Albanese, 'Note sull'evoluzione storica del 'ius vitae et necis', *Scritti Beato Contardo Ferrini*, vol. III, 1948, pp. 343 ff.
20. C. Longo, *Diritto di famiglia*, 1946, p. 93; R. Yaron, *T. R.*, 1962, pp. 250ff; Rabello, op. cit., p. 32, n. 26.
21. See the French translation by G. de Plinval, Cic., *Leg. III*, 7, Belles Lettres.
22. A. Magdelain, 'L'acte *per aes et libram* et l'*Auctoritas*', in *RIDA*, 1981, pp. 129 ff.
23. In the *edictum* of the *praetor*, §10, *pacta conventa . . . servabo* is a recognition of a consensual contract. See the fundamental study of A. Magdelain, *Le consensualisme dans l'édit du préteur*, 1968.
24. *Lex Rubria*, c. 2, 21–2; *lex civ. Narbonensis* c. 20–5; *lex Quinctia de Aquaed.* c. 25; Valerius Probus, *lit. sing in iure civili . . .* n. 3.
25. On *ius ratumque*, cf. Y. Thomas, *RHD*, 1977, pp. 194 ff.
26. See, respectively, *D.* 25.3.4 and Cic., *Leg.*, 3, 8, 19 = Tab IV, I: *cito necatus tamquam ex XII tabulis insignis ad deformitatem puer*, cf. Seneca, *de ira*, 1, 15, 2: *mergere*, burying alive or drowning.
27. On this aspect, see M. Humbert, *Le remariage à Rome, étude d'histoire juridique et sociale*, 1972, pp. 195 ff.; Juvenal, *Sat.*, 6, v. 626 ff. perfectly summarises the estate-related stakes of the hatred of stepmothers.
28. See O. Bouvier and Ph. Moreau, *Phinée, ou la marâtre aveuglante*, in *Rev. Belge Phil. Hist.*, 1983, 61, fasc. 1., for the theme in Greek mythology. The text by Sallust, quoted above, clearly illustrates the difficulties resulting from the insufficient distance of *noverca* and *privignus*, who are of the same generation. On this theme, see for instance Seneca, *Contr.* 7, 1, 5; Ps-Quint. 1, 2; Calp. Flaccus, 4, 22.

29. On this aspect, in Latin Rhetoric, cf. Y. Thomas, 'Paura dei padri, violenza dei figli: immagine retoriche e norme di diritto', in *Paura dei Padri*, Rome 1983.
30. *Römisches Strafrecht*, I, 22.
31. Except by E. Sachers, *R.E.*, 22, 1, s.v. *patria potestas*, c. 1086, who, however, fails to explain this inclusion, unjustifiably in his case, as he confuses *ius vitae necisque* and domestic jurisdiction (which extends to the totality of those who are *alieni iuris*).
32. In Livy, 2, 5 ff., two consuls preside over the capital punishment: but Tarquinius Collatinus, the maternal uncle of the Aquilii, who had already had to go into exile from Rome because of his kinship, has been replaced by P. Valerius. In Denys, on the contrary, the opposition is very clear between the consular rigour of the father (5, 8) and the extreme weakness of the other consul taking the side of his nephews: they throw themselves at his feet, try to draw him to their side and to plead to Brutus the excuse of their youth and folly (5, 9). After the ensuing disagreement of the consuls, the people are summoned. Brutus suggests dismissing a public office-holder who has given the advantage to blood ties over the loyalty owed to the Roman republic (5, 10): After this, Collatinus has to exile himself (5, 11). This is the same opposition between behaviours that we find in Plutarch's narrative (*Public.*, 6, 3f./7, 1–6). J. Gagé, 'Les traditions des Papirii et quelques-unes des origines de l'"equitatus' romain et latin', in *RHD*, 1955, pp. 20 ff. (followed by J. P. Néraudau, *La jeunesse à Rome*, 1969, p. 169) directs all his attention to the relationship, related by the maternal uncle, between the *Vitellii* and the sons of Brutus; we are told that, in this solidarity that persists in the margin of the *gentes*, are revealed the vestiges of an old companionship, of course in conflict with the values of the collective discipline of republican Rome as embodied by Brutus. But this is to forget another *avunculus*, the consul Collatinus: the maternal uncle of the Aquilii, without participating in the conspiracy, demonstrates a weak stance in relation to them. It is therefore better to give up the idea of considering those elements of the narrative which can authorize a sociological reconstitution only at the price of letting other elements go unconsidered. One then sees that the maternal uncle is either a plotter, who draws his nephews with him, or an indulgent consul unable to make up his mind to punish them. The relevant opposition is that between *avunculus* and *pater*. The first can barely

embody anything apart from the voice of the blood ties; the other lets the law triumph. In the tradition, that same role is also that of the *patruus*, who is something like a double of the father in the order of severity. Cf. Cic. *pro Caelio* II, 25; Horatius, *Sat.*, 1, 6, v. 131; 2, 3, v. 88; Persius, *Sat.* 1, v. 11; Sueton, *Claudius*, 9 (Caligula, who is outraged about the fact that one sends him, in order to compliment him, his *patruus* Claudius, as if he were a child), etc.

33. For Greece, see S. C. Humphreys, '*Oikos* e *Polis*,' in *Riv. Stor. Italiana*, 91, 1979, pp. 545–63: N. Loraux, *L'invention d'Athènes: Histoire de l'oraison funèbre dans la cité classique*, 1981, pp. 24 ff. For Rome, this type of question is mostly studied according to evolutionist schemes, rather than in terms of a conflict of values (cf., however, recently C. Gallini, *Protesta e integrazione nella Roma antica*, 1970, as to the conflict between institutions, individualism and family status during the Bacchanalia). The narratives of Livy and Denys diverge as to the conjuration of the sons of Brutus: in Livy, the danger represented by maternal kinship is virtual, and in time it is brought under control: in Denys it is allowed to realise itself, under the generous gaze of the uncle-consul. But overall the meaning of the episode remains the same. See also the examples compiled by Valerius Maximus (3, 7, 3 ff.; 6, 2, 3; 6, 1, 12).

34. This is so even in cases where, a son holding a public office, his father imposes upon him the respect for the duties of his magistracy, exhorting him that he has to treat his father like a simple citizen. This gives all its sense to the episode of Q. Fabius Maximus, who has challenged his son's capacity to be a consul, waiting until he helps him to descend from his horse: Claudius Quadrigarius, VI, fr. 57 Pet. = Gell. 2, 2, 13. The father subjects himself to the command of the first *lictor* and congratulates his son for having given precedence to the *imperium populi romani*. In Livy, 24, 44, 10, he shouts: '*experiri volui, fili, satin scires consulem te esse* (I wanted to test, son, whether you are sufficiently aware that you are consul)'; equally Val. Max., 2, 2, 4, and Plut., *Fabius*, 24. What one generally retains from this episode is that a father must obey his public office-holding son. But this is an insufficient analysis. Far more remarkable is the fact that these exemplary fathers function as controllers of whether their sons have the force to impose civic discipline upon them. They constitute, in some way, a warranty of the credit that one might confer on a family son having made it to the consular office. They

proceed by imposing a trial upon them. In this light, a father who descends from his horse before his consul son has done so, or who follows him on his triumphal chariot (as an e.g., Fabius Rullianus, 291: Livy, *Per.*, 11; Plut. *Fab.* 24, 3; Val. Max. 5, 7, 1 cf. 4, 1, 5; Eutropius, 2, 9, 3; Orosius 3, 22, 6–9; Suidas 2 1401 B), does not act that way because this is the conduct required of him by law: on the contrary, he is an incarnation of the law, and this to the point of testing it upon his son. The superior importance of the public office exists for the sons only because their fathers make sure that they exercise it in line with what they expect from them. Being responsible 'patrimonially' – in other words, as estate owners (cf. Y. Thomas, *MEFRA*, 1982, pp. 561 ff.) – the fathers are also responsible in moral terms. They will also come up with sanctions where necessary; one father will have his son placed at the head of a *provincia* he has chosen for him (Livy, 4, 45, 8: Q. Servilius imposes upon his son, a military tribune with consular power, the – inglorious – charge of the Roman city, a choice which the son, like all other contenders for the office, would have preferred to avoid: 'My son will consent to take the command of the City'/*Filius meus extra sortem Urbi praeerit*). Another father addresses a gathering of the *comitia* asking them not to elect his son for the office of consul (Val. Max., 4, 5, 1; it is true that this Q. Fabius Maximus is the one who had already refused three consulates for himself: in 299 (Livy, 10, 9, 10); in 298 (10, 13, 5–5) and in 296 (10, 5, 8)): but even if one considers that this is an error in Valerius or in his source, one has to admit that it is telling). Fathers also vouch for their sons: Fabius Maximus Gurges has suffered an inglorious defeat and, in 292, the Senate strips him of his command. On this, his father steps in, taking over the operations under his son's nominal command, whose triumphal chariot he then follows (Denys, 17, 4, 6; Livy, *Per.*, 11; Dion, *fr.* 36, 30–1; Val. Max. 4, 1, 5 and 5, 7, 1; Plut., *Fab.*, 24, 3). If the father was deceased, the family counsel could represent him where necessary: this is how the son of Scipio Africanus was prevented from taking up an office, a *praetura*, of which his family judged him unworthy, on which occasion they also stripped him of a ring with an engraved portrait of Africanus, and barred him from taking the Curule seat (*id egerunt, ne aut sellam ponere aut ius dicere auderet, insuperque a manu eius anulum, in quo caput Africani sculptum erat, detraxerunt*, Valerius Maximus, 3, 5, 1: Incidentally, Valerius here mixes up Gn. Scipio, elected thanks to his father's secretary, Cicereius, – cf. Val. Max. 4, 5, 3 – with L. Scipio, erased from the senatorial album in 141: cf. Broughton, *RM*, 1, p. 406, n. 2).

35. Mommsen, *Römisches Staatsrecht*, Vol. 1 (Engl. ed., Cambridge University Press, 2010).

36. Cf. the French translation by G. Baillet (ed.), *Les Belles Lettres*: 'Meantime, one had to see the father, his features, his physiognomy, where fatherly love breaks through his function as an avenger'. That of J. J. Dubochet (1839) says: 'One saw fatherly feelings loom'. Or that of E. Lassarre, 1947: 'The fatherly soul appeared . . .' The philological commentaries focus on these sentimental aspects. Already in A. Drakenborch we find the elements of the debate thus summarised: *animus* was taken to mean, either, that: '*affectum paternum erupisse*' (that the fatherly affect turbulently manifested itself), or on the contrary, that the '*studium in patriam omnes affectus in tam duro ministerio superasse* (that the love for the fatherland proved stronger than all affects in this cruel duty)'; for this second interpretation, which he found more convincing, he referred to Virgil, 6, 824: *Vincet amor patriae* (*Titi Livii Historiarum libri*, reed; Leipzig, 1820, II, p. 46). See also S. Alschefski, Berlin, 1841, 1, p. 96 n. 12 ('the feeling of the father'). Weissenberg also insists on the notion that 'Brutus has not shown any sign of emotion' (Berlin, 1875, II, p. 13). To the extent to which we are down to speaking in terms of emotion, we are effectively limited here to emotions of a negative kind: *exuit patrem, ut consulem ageret* (he left behind the father, in order for the consul to act) (Val. Max., 5, 8, 1). But are we dealing with emotion alone? (Cf. Ogilvie, A *Commentary*, p. 246: Brutus displayed no emotion). Indisputably, the significance of this scene is not limited to a sentimental debate that subjectively agitates a *pater*. At stake are the institutions, a right is being inaugurated and manifests itself, functions – fatherly and consular functions – are mobilised: the image of an individual, suffering or overcoming his suffering, is surely not the best point of departure for drawing lessons from this *exemplum*.

37. Plut., *Publicola*, 6, 4: *orgēs kai barutētos*. That an interpretation of the text has to go beyond the simple question of the personal sentiments of Brutus, is also manifested by a passage in which his act is explicitly assimilated to the founding of a *politeia*: 'Because the Romans are convinced that the deed accomplished by Romulus in founding Rome was not as great as that of Brutus in creating and instituting the

Republic': *tēn ktisin tēs politeias kai katastasin*. See also Denys, 5, 8, 6. The context shows unambiguously that it is the capital punishment of the traitors that assures the foundation of the state.

38. Cf. the consecration of the temple of Jupiter Capitolinus by the consul Horatius Pulvillus, during which he receives the news that his son has lost his life. Livy 2, 8, 7–8; Servius, *Aen.*, 6, 8; 11, 2; Val. Max., 5, 10, 1; Plut., *Valerius*, 14, 6–8. The first testimony of this *exemplum* is in Cicero, *dom.* 139. Also, the *responsa*-giving by Manlius in his *atrium*, where he fails to interrupt the session when his son has just taken his life (Val. Max, 5, 8, 3); Tiberius returning to his affairs immediately after the burial of Drusus (Suet., *Tib.*, 52, 1).

39. One quotes in particular the older Cato (Cic., *Cato maior* 15, 68, 84; *ad fam.* 4, 6, 1; *Tusc.* 3, 70; *Laelius*, 9; Plut., *Cat.*, 24) and Q. Fabius Maximus (Cic., 2 *Verr.* 2, 5, 25; *Fam.* 4, 6, 1; *Tusc.* 3, 70; *de nat. deor.* 3, 80). Other *exempla* are: Val. Max., 5, 10: '*de parentibus qui obitum liberorum forti animo tuleront* (On parents having shown fortitude in enduring the death of their children)'. This was a *topos* of the *consolatio* (cf. *cons. ad. Marciam*, 12, 4–15, with numerous examples). The response of third-century Emperor Decius to the death of his son matches this exemplary tradition (Aur. Victor, 29, 5: '*Patrem autem, cum perculsi milites ad solandum imperatorem multa praefarentur, strenue dixisse detrimentum unius militis parum videri sibi* (As the soldiers, shattered, tried to beat about the bush in letting the emperor know about his son's death, he told them stoutly that the loss of one soldier was in his eyes a minor thing)', cf. Jord. *Get.*, 18). In the *Aeneid*, the behaviour of Evander and that of Mezentius feature opposite responses: the first controls his suffering; the second allows it full expression. Cf. G. Thome, 'Gestalt und Funktion des Mezentius bei Vergil – mit einem Ausblick auf die Schlussszene der Aeneis', Frankfurt, *Berner Europäische Hochschulschriften, 15. Serie, Philol. und literar. Kl.*, vol. 14, pp. 106 ff. One recognises in these *topoi* of this lament of the death, the tragic opposition between the courage of the elderly and the distress of the young father, responsible for his son's death (see, H. Strehlein, *Die Totenklage des Vaters um den Sohn in der sophokleischen und euripideischen Tragödie*, Diss., München, 1958). There exist interesting continuities in contemporary Mediterranean cultures, especially in the folklore of the toreros: cf. B. Pellegrin, 'Sacrifice du fils et mort du père', in *Etudes corses*, 1979, pp. 227 ff.). Further

pieces could be added to a rich documentation that would deserve a special study. Let us draw attention to the text of Denys about the death in single combat of the two Horatii. He describes, here, Horatius offering sacrifices to the *dii manes* – souls of the dead – of his ancestors, inviting his family to a funeral banquet, where he said that he gave less importance to his personal woe than to the public benefits for the fatherland' (3, 21, 9). Other fathers, Denys continues, acted in the same way, 'offering sacrifices, weaving crowns, celebrating triumphs, immediately following the loss of a son, all to the advancement of the city'.

This theme of the son's death, understood as a source of glory for the father, needs to be related to the opposite case of the son who, dishonoured on the battlefield, finds himself disowned and takes his own life; cf. Val. Max., 5, 8, 4.: M. Aemilius Scaurus, after his son has run away from the Cimbri in 101 BCE, 'had sent after his son to let him know that he would have preferred to see his bones after his death on the battleground rather than himself after his ignominious escape, which would have spared him the character of a degenerate father, upon receipt of which message the young man felt that he was under the duty of using his sword with more strength against himself than against the enemy; *filio suo misit qui diceret libentius se in acie eius interfecti ossibus occursurum quam ipsum tam deformis fugae reum visurum: itaque conspectum denegerati patris vitaturum . . . quo nuntio accepto iuvenis coactus est fortius aversus semet ipsum gladio uti quam adversus hostes usus fuerat*').

40. Cf. Seneca, *Cons. ad Helviam*, 16, 5: '*Non potes itaque ad obtinendum dolorem muliebre nomen praetendere, ex quo te virtutes tuae seduxerunt; tantum debes a feminarum lacrimis abesse quantum vitiis* (You cannot thus claim that you are suffering because you are a woman . . . you cannot have female tears any more than female vices)'. Seneca quotes the example of Cornelia, mother of the Gracchi, who was fond even of her sons' funerals: '*magno aestimavit gracchorum funera*'. She behaves like a man; the glory of her dead sons has become her own glory. In the same way, he also quotes Rutilia, who followed into exile her son Aurelius Cotta, but did not shed tears at his funeral (7). And Seneca concludes: *Cum his te numerari feminis volo* – i.e. with these women whose virtues have placed outside of their sex (*ex quo . . . virtutes . . . seduxerunt*).

41. Denys 8, 79: Brutus and Manlius Torquatus, considered in relation to Spurius Cassius; 2, 26, 4 ff.: Manlius Torquatus

and the tribune Flaminius: Val. Max., 5, 8, 1–3: Brutus, Spurius Cassius, Manlius Torquatus; Plut., *Parall.*, 10–12: Brutus, Manlius Torquatus.
42. *Aeneid*, 6, v. 817 ff.:

> *Vis et Tarquinios reges animamque superbam*
> *ultoris Bruti, facisque videre receptos?*
> *Consulis imperium hic primus saevasque securis*
> *accipiet, natusque pater nova bella moventis*
> *ad poenam pulchra pro libertate vocabit.*
> *Infelix! Utcumque ferent ea facta minores:*
> *vincet amor patriae laudumque immensa cupido*
> *Quin Decios Drusosque procul saevomque securi*
> *aspice Torquatum et referentem signa Camillum.*

> (tr. H. R. Fairclough, 1916–18:
> Would you also see the Tarquin kings,
> the proud spirit of Brutus the Avenger, and the fasces regained?
> He first shall receive a consul's power and the cruel axes,
> and when his sons would stir up revolt,
> the father will hale them to execution in fair freedom's name,
> unhappy man, however later ages will extol that deed;
> yet shall a patriot's love prevail and unquenched thirst for fame.
> Now behold over there the Decii and the Drusi,
> Torquatus of the cruel axe, and Camillus bringing the standards home).

On book VI and its confrontation with the historical mythology that sustains the Augustan ideology, cf. A. Degrassi, 'Virgilio ed il foro di Augusto', in *Epigraphica* 7, 1945, pp. 88 ff. (dealing with the unity of conception between the disposition of the statues on the Forum of Augustus, and the history magnified by Virgil). On the historical vision of Book VI, we have been able to consult: M. von Albrecht, 'Vergil's Geschichtsauffassung, in der "Heldenschau"', in *Wiener Studien, Zeitschrift f. klass Philologie und Patristik*, 80, 1967, pp. 156 ff.; H. Altevogt, 'Vergil. Exemplarische Behandlung der Römerschau in Aen. VI', in *Interpretationen lateinischer Schulautoren mit didaktischen Vorbemerkungen*, H. Krefeld, ed. Frankfurt 1968, pp. 83 ff.; J. P. Brisson, 'Temps historique et temps mythique dans l'Enéide', in *Vergiliana. recherches sur*

Virgile, H. Bardon and R. Verdière (ed.), Leiden 1971, pp. 56
ff. Contrary to this author, we precisely do not think that the
disorder in which the crowd of republican heroes between
the expulsion of the Tarquinian kings and the funeral eulogy
of Marcellus is depicted, is intentional. Incidentally, the list
of foundational heroes does not start with v. 824, but with
v. 819); v. 819–25 constitute a foundational and indivisible
unit: we then pass to the civil wars (826–36), the wars of
the second century (837–43), the Second Punic War (843–6):
each of these parts possesses an indisputable unity. But the
inaugural group of lines 818–25 summarise the founding
virtues of Rome: to place a *caesura* at line 824 interrupts this
structure.

43. Cf. Servius, *Aen.*: loc. cit. 'Or rather, consider the Decii.
Two of them, father and son, known by the name of Mures,
made sacrifice of themselves for the Republic, one in the
war against the Galli, the other in that against the Samnites;
*Quinimmo Decios respice. Hi duo fuerunt, qui Mures dicti sunt:
pater et filius. Horum alter se bello Gallico, alter Samnitico vovit
pro republica cum terra et Manes universum bello exercitum
perdere.'*

44. Servius, loc. cit.: *Drususque procul et hi duo fuerunt. Horum
prior vicit Asdrubalem, Alter est filius Liviae, uxoris Augusti*
(acc. to G. Thilo, H. Hagen, Teubner); (*Alter est filius Iuliae
sororis*, acc. to H.A. Lion, Göttingen). P. Grimal, (*REA*, 1954,
p. 48) notes that, if M. Livius Drusus is specified by his
name, that of his colleague T. Claudius Nero, the second
winner of the battle of the Metaurus, is absent. Comment:
'Unsurprisingly so, as, unfortunately, that name would have
made one think of the other Claudius Nero, from whom the
Prince has abducted Livia, in circumstances not pleasant
enough to be invoked.'

45. On the *devotio* of M. Curtius, see Livy, 7, 6, 1–6; Denys, 14, 11,
1–5; Varro, L., 5, 1, 148; Val. Max., 5, 6, 2; Pliny, *N.H.*, 15, 78.
Concerning the meaning of the rite of the *devotio*, a reference
to other modalities of burying in Rome offers a source. Cf. A.
Fraschetti, 'Le sepolture rituale del Foro Boario', in *Le délit
religieux*, Rome 1981, pp. 47 ff. The different modes under
which bodies are delivered to the subterranean gods participate in common features of meaning: it is legitimate to
establish a relationship between them. The rite and the religious conceptions that it mobilises can be used for various
functions (as one identical formula will serve different uses
in law). Between the exorcism of a defilement (the *devotio*

in favour of a victory), and the sacrifice carried out for the permanence of the state, the ends, served by one single rite, give it the status of a supportive operation, an abstract act. Hence the importance of the formulation of its cause: '*Si rem publicam perpetuam esse vellent*'; This makes one think, in effect, of the *nuncupatio* grafting itself upon formal legal acts in the law of the XII Tables (*uti lingua nuncupassit, ita ius esto . . .*).

46. Cf. *D.* 1.6.4: *patres familiarum sunt, qui sunt suae potestatis sive puberes sive impuberes. D.* 50.16.195.2: *pater autem familias appellatur, qui in domo dominium habet, recteque hoc nomine appellatur, quamvis filium non habeat: non enim solam personam eius sed et ius demonstramus.*

47. Trials before the comitial assemblies are quaestorian trials, according to Cic., *Republic*, II, 60 (*De occupando regno molientem . . . quaestor accusavit*); Livy 2, 41, 11: *a quaestoribus Caesone Fabio et L. Valerio diem dictam perduellionis, damnatumque populi iudicio . . .*; Denys, 8, 77, 1, also speaks of a trial before the people, triggered by Caeso Fabius and Valerius Publicola. In Livy 10, 38, 3, we are dealing with an accusation of *affectatio regni*.

48. Livy, 2, 41, 10–12, and Denys, 8, 77–9. Diodorus, 12, 37, 7 has no details about the procedure through which Sp. Cassius was put to death. On the episode of Spurius Cassius, see the fundamental study by Mommsen, in *Römische Forschungen*, II, 1907, pp. 9 ff. Münzer, Cassius, *RE*, III, 2, c. 1749 ff; Ogilvie, *A Commentary*, pp. 337 ff.; H. le Bonniec, *Le culte de Cérès à Rome*, 1958, pp. 233 ff. (on the statue dedicated to Ceres courtesy of a donation by Cassius); E. Gaba, 'Dionigi d'Alicarnasso sur processo di Spurio Cassio', in *La storia del diritto nel quadro delle scienze storiche . . . Atti del primo congresso internazionale della Soc. Italiana di storia del Diritto*, Florence 1966, pp. 143 ff. (largely, a restatement of what Mommsen had said about the Gracchian and post-Gracchian aspects of this episode); A. W. Lintott, 'The Tradition of Violence in the Annals, Sp. Maelius, Sp. Cassius, Manlius Capitolinus', in *Historia* 1970, pp. 18 ff. (these three trials are put together as cases of a 'private reaction', that they are said to witness; the procedural specificity of each of them disappears behind their common context: specifically violence). D. Capanelli, 'Appunti sulla "rogatio agraria" di Spurio Cassio', in *Legge e società nella repubblica romana*, (ed.) F. Serrao, 1981, deals with the sources as if they were contemporaneous with the events: we return to a pre-mommsenian stage. P. Botteri,

'Padri pubblici, padri privati', dans *La paura dei padri*, Rome, 1983.

49. *Hist. Nat.* 34, 15: *Romae simulacrum ex aere factum Cereri primum reperio et peculio Sp. Cassi, quem adfectantem pater ipsius interemit.* On Pliny's source, cf. 34, 30: *L. Piso prodidit . . . M. Aemilio C. Popilio iterum cos. a censoribus P. Cornelio Scipione M. Popilio statuas circa forum eorum qui magistratum gesserant sublatas omnis praeter eas quae populi aut senatus sententia statuae essent, eam vero quam apud aedem Telluris statuisset sibi Sp. Cassius, qui regnum adfectaverat, etiam conflatam a censoribus.* Paragraph 15 evokes Spurius Cassius and his fate only on the occasion of the statue dedicated to Ceres. It is thus clear, as had already been well perceived by Mommsen, that the source is the same – and that one cannot trace back to Pison, at the latest, the domestic version of the death of Cassius.

50. Val. Max. 5, 8, 2: *Cassius filum . . . postquam illam potestatem deposuit, adhibito propinquorum et amicorum consilio, affectati regni crimine domi damnavit: verberibusque affectum necari iussit, ac peculium eius Cereri consecravit.* Cf. Livy, 2, 41, 10: *sunt qui patrem auctorem eius supplicii ferant: eum, causa domi cognita, verberasse ac necasse peculiumque filii Cereri consecravisse et inscriptum: 'Ex Cassia familia datum'.*

51. Livy, 2, 41, 11; Denys, 8, 77, 1; 78, 5; 79, 1; 10, 38, 3.

52. Livy, 2, 41, 10; Pliny, N.H., 34, 15; Val. Max., 5, 8, 2.

53. 8, 79, 3. Denys speaks of statues the inscription on which indicated their origin: this corresponds with the words '*Ex familia Cassia datum*' of Livy (see H. Le Bonniec, op. cit., p. 234).

54. Livy, 2, 41, 10; *signum*; Pliny, 34, 15: *simulacrum*.

55. *MEFRA*, 1982, pp. 547 ff. If the tradition mentioning the inscription '*Ex familia Cassia datum*' is to be believed – and there are no reasons for doubting this – the choice even of the word *familia* proves that the statue has not been offered by the *peculium* of Cassius, but the estate of the *gens Cassia* – courtesy of the fortune belonging to Spurius's father.

56. Pliny, N.H., 34, 30, quoted above, n. 49.

57. H. Le Bonniec, op. cit., p. 233, on the possibility of common features between this consecration and the formula of execration (Livy, 3, 55, 7), the sacrilege having, in both cases, consisted in impairing the liberty of the people.

58. One cannot believe in the qualification *de maiestate* given to trials before the *lex Apuleia*, which dates back to one of the two tribunates of Saturninus. It is true that Suetonius makes

of the *multae inrogatio* of 246 against Claudia, the sister of P. Claudius Pulcher, a *iudicium maiestatis* (Tib., 2): but Ateius Capito, in his book *de iudiciis publicis* (ap. Gell., 10, 6, 3–4) fails to qualify Claudia's offence, in such a way that one needs to attribute an anachronism to Suetonius. The case of L. Quinctius Flaminius, who in 193 beheaded a prisoner from Gaul to amuse his mistress at dinner, is equally qualified as *crimen maiestatis* in a scholarly mooting exercise (Sen. 9, 2 *pr.*): but our other sources only say that Flaminius was excluded from the Senate by Cato the censor (Livy, 39, 42–3; Plut., *Flam.* 18 and *Cato maior*, 17; Cic. *Cat.* 42; Val. Max. 293 and 4, 5, 1). These are, with those of the tribune Flaminius, the only examples of an accusation *de maiestate* preceding the law of Saturninus: they do not have any juridical value, and the efforts of R. A. Bauman to prove that in Rome it was an existing *crimen maiestatis* that was codified by Saturninus (*The crimen maiestatis of the Roman Republic and Augustan Principate*, Johannesburg 1967, pp. 23 ff.) are expended in vain. The trial of the tribune Flaminius's father is reported in *de inv.* 2, 17, 52. Valerius Maximus, whose sources are annalistic, does not speak of it. O. Botteri, op. cit., makes of it a Gracchian theme. I would rather tend to situate this forged document in the years 100 to 90 BCE.

59. The evidence that we have perused shows that *privata potestas* is used in this single context only. Valerius Maximus, telling the anecdote of Fabius Maximus descending from his horse before his consul son, has the father say: '*publica instituta privata pietate potiora iudico*/In my judgement, public institutions take precedence over private piety' (2, 2, 4). So, first, it fails to qualify a power. But this antithesis is rhetorical as well. Quadrigarius, in Aulus Gellius, limits himself to speaking of *imperium*. There is no question of anything else. '*Fabius imperio paret et filium collaudavit, cum imperium, quod populi esset, retineret* (F. obeys the imperium and lauds his son for keeping the imperium to the people, to whom it belongs)' (2, 2, 13). In the discussion that comes up around Taurus regarding the precedence between magistrate sons and fathers (Aulus Gellius, 2, 2), the categories of public and private do not amount to a symmetric opposition, as they qualify on the one hand, a space and functions, '*in publicis locis atque muneribus*', and on the other hand, interests and life, '*extra rempublicam in domestica re atque vita . . .*' (2, 2, 9): not part of these determinations are the essence and nature of the power, be it of the father, or of the magistrate son.

Vitae Necisque Potestas

When a magistrate son is associated with a *pater privatus* (eod. loc.), *privatus* does not characterise the entirety of the *patria potestas*, but only the fact, for the father, of not possessing a public office (cf., further down, in connection with Fulvius and the conjuration of Catilina, the fathers who, whether consuls or *homines privati*, meted out death to their sons).

60. Pomponius, 16 *ad Q. Mucium, D.* 1.6.9.
61. Which provides the institutional context of an anecdote reported by Suetonius (Vesp. 4, 3): '*Convictus quoque dicitur ducenta sestertia expressisse iuveni, cui latum clavum adversus patris voluntatem impetrarat, eoque nomine graviter increpitus* (He is also said to have been convicted of extorting a large amount of money from some fashion victim in exchange for procuring him, against his father's word, a distinctive band worn only by senators, an action for which he was severely reprimanded)'. On the other hand, a list of cases of obedience to one's father, given by Aulus Gellius (2, 7, 18), silences any discussion.
62. *MEFRA*, 1982, 2, pp. 567 ff.
63. Cf. R. Önnerfors, *Vaterporträts in der römischen Poesie unter besonderer Berücksichtigung von Horaz, Statius und Ausonius*, Stockholm, 1974. A Wlosok, 'Vater und Vatervorstellungen in der römischen Kultur', in *Das Vaterbild im Abendland*, H. Tellenbach (ed.) 1978, pp. 18 ff. (very general); R. Lesueur, 'Latinus ou la paternité manquée (*Enéide* VII–XII)', in *REL*, 1979, pp. 231 ff. The figure of Aeneas, the model of filial *pietas*, has given rise to an abundant bibliography (collected by W. Suerbaum, 'Hundert Jahre Vergil-Forschung: Aeneis', in *ANRW*, II, 31, 1, 1980, pp. 144 ff., on Aeneas; pp. 169 ff. (*virtutes* v. *pietas*). Another pole of the philological-literary study is the title *pater patriae*: see, as for the last example, A. Alföldi, *Der Vater des Vaterlandes im römischen Denken*, 1971, renewing and enlarging his earlier published work from the *Museum Helveticum*.
64. *D.* 1.6.4; 50.16.195.2.
65. The theme is treated very early in the schools (to say nothing about Latin comedy, where the person of the son is frequently disobedient, but we will stick here to the juridical and rhetorical order); cf. Seneca, *cont.*, 2, 1, 20: *Silo Pompeius . . . coepit a vetere et explosa quaestione, an in omnia patri parendo sit*; equally, 1, 4, 5; 1, 4, 9; 1, 6, 8, etc. Numerous controversies also deal with the case: *nolentem abdicat* (he who does not want to obey, is disinherited). The chapter of Aulus Gellius

already quoted (2, 7: *de officio erga patres liberorum; deque ea re ex philosophiae libris, in quibus scriptum quaesitumque an omnibus patris iussis obsequendum sit*) shows that a theoretical literature was devoted to this subject. But most of the treatments are of a scholarly topic. That young orators had been formed in dealing with this type of subjects is not without importance: the causes of familial nature were those of which they had most experience – and these causes are by far best represented in the declamations that have come down to us. Of course, these are *fictae causae* (Pliny, *ep.*, 2, 3, 5): but the *disputationes* that are grafted onto these fictive hypotheses cannot be understood outside of the family statutes of Roman law. The *De beneficiis* also contains a long passage devoted to the justifications and the limits of the *patria potestas* (III, 11 and 29 ff.). It ends with a *prosopopeia* of the son who being subjected to the fatherly *imperium*, nonetheless competes with his father in generosity (3, 38, 2): '*Parentibus meis parui, cessi imperio eorum, sive aecum sive inicum ac durum fuit, obsequentem submissumque me praebui: ad hoc unum contumax fui, ne beneficiis vincerer* (I obeyed my parents and subjected myself to their *imperium*, no matter how just or unjust or hard it was; only in one point was I intransigent: not to be defeated by them on the level of mutual generosity)'. The reciprocal largesse between father and son constitutes another scholarly *topos*. This motive casts light on the ambiguity of the son's legal status, in the hypothesis where the son has done the father a favour or saved his life and is nonetheless expelled out of sheer ingratitude (Seneca, *contr.*, 3, 4: *servatus a filio abdicat*/the son obeys, the father disinherits him; Quint. 256: *qui tres filios habebat, duos per furorem abdicat; a tertio sanatus abdicat eum*/a man, in rage, cuts out two sons; nursed back to health by the third he repudiates him as well), or because he refuses to obey an unjust order (Seneca, *contr.*, 1, 6; 4, 6): one then discusses the nature of the obligation created by having received one's life through one's father: is the resulting debt to one's father extinguishable? Can one reverse the direction and obligate one's father? Are there cases in which favours done by the son force the father not to reveal himself as inequitable in his commands? But the scholarly debate here also remains dependent on a deeply Roman tradition, conveyed by the annalists: that of the *pietas* shown for a cruelly unjust father, against whose orders the son never rebels (cf. the history of the young Manlius who, regardless of the abuse that he suffers from his father, threatens death

Vitae Necisque Potestas

to the tribune Pomponius to force him to drop an accusation against his father: Livy, 7, 5; Seneca, *Ben.*, 3, 27; Val. Max. 5, 4, 3). The *corpus* of rhetoric is thus irreplaceable for what the rhetors contribute to the study of the law-founded imaginary: it cannot be used as a facsimile of positive law, and it is the great weakness of the book of P. Lanfranchi (*Il diritto romano nei retori romani*, 1938) not to have understood this. The study of the orators still continues to be flatly positivist; one tries to find 'facts' and nothing else.

66. Cf. the episode involving Q. Fabius Maximus.
67. *Obviam alicui ire*/to bid someone welcome, *occurrere alicui venienti*/to greet the person calling, are marks of respect and statutory distance: a son goes to meet his father, a wife to meet her husband (cf. Cic., *Fam.*, 14, 5, 1). Hadrian thus shows his deference to his brother in law (S.H.A., *vita adriani*, 8). Hence the importance of that which Aulus Gellius (2, 2, 13) contributes to the relevant case law. *Ei consuli pater proconsul obviam in equo vehens venit*: the proconsul father comes to greet his consul son, remaining seated on his horse.
68. Aulus Gellius, 2, 2, 5 ff.
69. Thus, Geib, *Geschichte des römischen Criminalprozesses*, 1842, pp. 82 ff.; Voigt, 'Über die "leges Regiae"', in *Abhandlungen der philologisch-historischen Classe der Königlichen Sächsischen Gesellschaft der Wissenschaft*, VII, 6, pp. 580 ff.; Mommsen, *Problems of Roman Criminal Law* (Engl. tr. 2012), vol I; Liebenam, *RE*, IV, col. 915 ff. (s.v. '*consilium*'); M. Kaser, *ZSS*, 1938, p. 62; 71; E. Volterra, *RISG*, 1948, pp. 113 ff. (dealing with Denys, 2, 25, on the 'domestic jurisdiction' over the adulterous woman, a text which that author believes to be an error, because of the *ius vitae necisque*, which according to him applies to wives just as it does to sons); W. Kunkel, *Kleine Schriften*, 1974, pp. 177 ff., considers the *consilium domesticum* in all cases (whether we are dealing with sons, wives or even freedmen) as a moderating measure to which the *mores* have subjected the absolute paternal right over life and death: in this sense, his thesis agrees with that of E. Volterra, despite appearances to the contrary; see also E. Polay, in St. Volterra; A. Balducci, 'Intorno al "iudicium domesticum"', in *Arch. Giur.*, 1976, pp. 69 ff.; E. Sachers, *RE*, 22, 1, s.v. *potestas patria*, col. 1084 ff. (1087); G. Wesener, *RE*, suppl., IX col. 373 ff., *s.v. iudicium domesticum*. The contributions quoted are chosen among those holding the most explicit positions: yet, the entire body of specialists in Roman law does not allow any exception from this dogma.

70. See, on a related topic: 'La division des sexes en droit romain', in G. Duby-M. Perrot (ed.), *Histoire des femmes en Occident*, tome 1, *L'Antiquité*, dir. P. Schmitt Pantel, Paris, Plon, 1991, pp. 103–68.

71. Cf. Denys, 2, 25, 6, to be read in parallel with Cato, *ap. Gellium*, 10, 23, 4: '*Vir, inquit, cum divortium fecit, mulieri iudex pro censore . . .; multitatur, si vinum bibit; si cum alieno viro probri quid fecit, condemnatur* (the man who has divorced his wife judges her like a censor; if she has drunk wine, she is punished; if she has done wrong with another, she is condemned).' *Multitare, condemnare* (to punish, to condemn) suppose a domestic procedure (which does not lead to death, as in the 'law of Romulus', but to a penalty and probably to a judgment of *infamia*: the comparison with the office of the *censor*, which we have already encountered in dealing with sons (*probatio, nota . . .*), is thus explained. We find a vestige of this metaphorically censorial regime in *D.* 48.5.27 *pr.: uxorem a marito probatam . . .* But the immediate execution that follows the offence if caught in the act is in opposition to all of this: '*in adulterio uxorem tuam si prehendisses, sine iudicio impune necares*' (Cato, eod. loc., 5); this *ius occidendi* (cf. Aulus Gellius, eod. loc.: *De iure autem occidendi ita scriptum . . .;* Cato writes *nex*, but Aulus Gellius, no doubt erroneously, thinking of the terms of the *lex Iulia*, renders it as '*occidere*') remains present in the *lex Iulia*, to the benefit of the father, as we have seen, but also of the husband, in case of *iustus furor* (E. Cantarella, *Adulterio, omicidio legittimo e causa d'onore in dir. romano*, in *St. Scherillo*, 1, 1972, pp. 243 ff.).

72. Livy, 8, 22, 2; Val Max., 6, 1 7; 6, 1, 8.

73. Livy, 10, 31, 9: *Q. Fabius Gurges consulis filius aliquot matronas ad populum stupri damnatas pecunia multavit* (QFG, the son of the consul, condemned before the people some matrons for sexual offence, imposing fines on them) (cf. Mommsen, *Roman Public Law*, vol. IV, p. 187, n.2, on Q. Gurges as a municipal officer, an *aedile*); T.L. 25, 2, 9: *L. Villius Tappulus and M. Fundanius Fundulus aediles plebei aliquot matronas apud populum probri accusarunt, quasdam ex eis damnatas in exilium agerunt* (LVT and MFF, aediles, accused some matrons before the people, and sent some of them into exile). In Aelius Capito (*ap. Gellium*, 4, 14), the Curulian aedile A. Hostilius Mancinus condemns the sex worker (*meretrix*) Manilia only for having thrown stones at him, at night, from her attic (*quod e tabulato eius noctu lapide ictus esset*).

74. Cf. *D.* 48.5.6.1. *Adulterare,* 'to corrupt, alter, defile' can only apply to a man as a subject (see Thesaurus, s.v.): but only the married woman can be guilty of *adulterium* (Cato, *ap. Gell.,* 10, 23, 5). The man who defiles a woman commits a *stuprum*; likewise, a non-married woman, a widow, or a virgin *sui iuris,* commits a *stuprum* (the matrons dragged before the people's court, are necessarily *sui iuris*; cf. the precedent note:); Ph. Moreau, *Clodiana religio,* 1982, p. 24, n. 30, makes the following important remark: Clodius's offence is qualified as *stuprum* in the sources of Republican times, while it is as *adulterium* in imperial sources. The reason is simple: the *lex Iulia de adulteriis* subjects the adulteress to a regime of public accusation, even subjecting her to a painful *quaestio.* The married woman is, henceforth, subject to the same penal and public regime to which only men, matrons and virgins *sui iuris* used to be subject. The opposition *stuprum/ adulterium,* the reason for which was statutory, undergoes an alteration of meaning: adultery now becomes an object that is indifferently masculine and feminine. However, Papinian, who notes this confusion, still maintains the remembrance of the ancient system: *sed proprie adulterium in nupta committitur . . .: stuprum vero in virginem viduamque committitur* (adultery properly speaking is committed with a married woman; *stuprum* with a virgin or a widow) (*D.* 48.5.6.1). If one returns the proposition and considers the passage from the passive agent to the guilty subject, one has to say that *adulterium,* in the narrow sense, was committed by married women and a matter of domestic jurisdiction (Cato, *ap. Gell.,* 10, 23, 3 ff., as well as the 'law of Romulus'), while the *stuprum* of widows and of virgins *sui iuris,* was a matter of the comitial trial of the *ediles.*

75. See, for purposes of comparison: *idoneus accusator,* in *D.* 48.5.16.6, dealing with the age required to lay a charge of adultery: the law here presupposes a social convention (for which, in order to judge a person's sexual conduct, there is a requirement to have attained sexual maturity oneself); and especially: *idoneior,* in *D.* 43.9.3.12, in connection with the choice of those among whom the *praetor* will choose him who has standing to bring in an action *de homine libero exhibendo,* by which a parent or a relative is authorised to demand that some free person, unjustly constrained by others, be presented to him. The criteria of the choice are *coniunctio, fides, dignitas*; the law here depends on social rules and on moralities that lie outside its scope; equally, as to Livy's (39,

18, 6) *idoneus exactor*: the woman is executed only by those who, according to the *mos maiorum*, the ancestral custom, hold the right to do so.

76. E. Volterra, *RISG*, 1948, p. 119 f.
77. Quintilian, *Inst. or.*, 6, 3, 25 (cf. Dion Cassius, 42, 23, 3).
78. Livy, *Per.*, 54; Cic. *De finibus*, 1, 7, 24; Val. Max. 5, 18, 3.
79. Cf. *supra*. n. 39. One would need to re-examine, in this perspective, the entire topic of *abdicatio*, of immense rhetorical richness, and which has never been effectively treated – this despite the study of R. Düll, *ZSS*, 1943, who assimilates the procedure to a domestic form of relegation (a softened form of banishment); B. M. Levick, in *Historia*, 1972, limits his inquiry to the *abdicatio* of Agrippa Postumus. The aspects involved in what is imposed by *abdicatio* are complex: physical distance (Suet., *Aug.*, 65; Tib., 15, 2, Pliny, *Hist Nat.*, 7, 150), personal disowning, the symbol of which is the deprivation of the *conspectus patris*. Many further sources need to be added to those quoted: Val. Max. 7, 1, 5 (relative to the son of Q. Fabius Maximus); Seneca, *Clem.*, 1, 15, 7 (relative to the son of Tarius Rufus, who has to withdraw from the sight of his parents *a parentis oculis summoveri*); Sidonius Apollinaris, *Ep.* 4, 23, 3: letter of intercession addressed to Proculus about his *abdicatus* son (between 470 and 477 CE): 'What a happy day, what a joy for you, for him, would reconciliation bring', '*cum paternis pedibus affusus, ex illo ore laeso, ore terribili, dum convicium expectat, osculum exceperit!*'; Cassiodorus, *Hist. Eccl.*, 6, 44, about the emperor Julian, who commits the error of inviting, to a banquet, a Christian father and his non-believing son, who has been expelled from his father's house (*expulit sua domu et coram omnibus abdicavit*: 6, 44, 6): a reconciliation turns out to be impossible, and the narrative of Cassiodorus dwells on the emperor's 'face', turned again and again from the one to the other (6, 44, 9: *Tum ille rursus mansuetudinis induens vultum; et declinans ab eo vultum adulescenti dixit . . .*); this mediation of the imperial gaze manifests the physical distance between father and son, the son remaining banned from his father's gaze. This personal aspect of the *abdicatio* is not necessarily echoed by estate-related effects: the *exheredatio*, to which corresponds, in its estate-related dimensions, the *apokēruxis* of Greek law, is a specific act. The *abdicatio* remains a personal privation, an act of disavowal, symbolically equivalent to an execution (whence the theme of the suicide of the *abdicatus*, an important topic in the schools: Sen., *Contr.*, 7, 3; Quint., *Decl.*,

281; 377; Ps-.Quint., *Decl. min.*, 17; see also Quint., *Decl.*, 372, p. 411, Ritter: *abdicare potui, occidere potui.*) Nonetheless, the *exheredatio* itself also has an effect not just on succession law: it also supposes a moral judgement symbolically equalling a disavowal: cf. Val. Max., 7, 7, 2; 7, 7, 8; 9, 1, 2; Cic., *Pro Roscio Amerino*, 19, 53; *de domo*, 49 (*exheredatio=improbatio*); Sen., *Clem.*, 1, 1, 1 (*exheredatio* followed by death: compare with *D.* 28.2.11: *nec obstat, quod licet eos exheredare, quos et occidere* [*licebat*]).

80. Cic., *Fin.*, 1, 7, 24: *illam severitatem in eo filio . . . quem in adoptionem D. Silano emancipaverat . . .* On D. Iunius Silanus, the adopter, and on D. Iunius Silanus (Manlianus), the adopted, see Münzer, RE, X, 1, col. 1088, n. 160, and 1089, n. 161.
81. *Tab.*, 9, 6 = Salvianus, *de gubern. Dei*, 8, 5.
82. Mommsen, *Problems of Roman Criminal Law* [Engl. tr. 2012], vol. III, pp. 252 ff. E. Levy, *Die Kapitalstrafe*, 1931. K. Latte, Todesstrafe, in *RE*, Suppl. VII, col. 1015.
83. Pliny, *N.H.*, 14, 89; Tertullian, *Apol.*, 6, regarding *inedia*; Livy, *Per.*, 48 = Val. Max. 6, 3, 8, regarding strangulation. Fausta, immersed in a bathtub filled with boiling water by pious Constantine, suffers death by pulmonary congestion (Zosimus, II, 29). See generally Cato (*ap. Gellium*, 10, 23, 5): *impune necares.* On strangulation in Greece and on the symbolic relationship of this method of execution with the female status, see the very innovative study of Nicole Loraux, in this volume.
84. Pliny, *N.H.*, 7, 121, and Val. Max., 5, 4, 7, only example of a death in public prison (apart from Seianus's daughter, Tac., *Ann.*, 6, 5, 9). More generally, Suet., *Tib.*, 61, 5 (see below).
85. Mommsen, *Problems of Roman Criminal Law* [Engl. tr. 2012], vol. I, p. 87, n. 2, notes that the revolting manner in which Seianus's daughter was executed has no juridical explanation, and can only be explained as the strict application of the rule mentioned by Pomponius, *D.* 21.1.23.2: '*Pomponius ait neque impuberem neque furiosum capitalem fraudem videri admisisse*' (in a context where *fraus* has the meaning of *poena*). But Suetonius's text, which has escaped the otherwise vigilant attention of Mommsen, proves that the rape of this young virgin was necessary to avoid that her death belong to *nefas*.
86. Confirmed *quaestiones veneficii* (cases of poisoning) : in 331 BCE (Livy, 8, 18, 3 ff. = Val. Max. 2, 5, 3); in 184 (Liv., 39, 5–7); in 180 (Liv., 40, 37, 4); in 179 (Liv., 40, 44, 6: the only case where it is not pointed out that the accused were women); in 154 (*Per.*, 48; Val. Max. 6, 3, 8). In Val. Max., 8, 1, *ambust.*,

1, a girl kills her mother by beating her with a stick. Death by beating is also, according to the tradition, the mode in which, in Romulus's times, Egnatius kills his wife, surprised while drinking wine (Val. Max., 6, 3, 9: *fusti percussam interemit*; cf. Servius, *Aen.*, 1, 37: *occisa est a marito*; Plut. *Romulus*, 22). But this is not a regular mode of feminine violence, nor of executing women; the rage of Egnatius shows a *furor* that only Romulus tolerates, and the matricide committed against a woman guilty of poisoning reveals an uncontrolled vengeance, a *commotio*. In principle, whipping is excluded for women: contrary to her accomplice, the incestuous vestal is not subjected to this punishment (against Denys, 9, 40, who contradicts the detailed description given in 2, 67, and the totality of the historic documentation). Women are condemned by their family, and strangled: Val. Max., 6, 3, 8: . . . *propinquorum decreto strangulatae sunt*. See also Val. Max. 5, 4, 7, where the strangulation is apparently accompanied by *inedia* as, waiting to be put to death, the pious daughter breastfeeds her mother. Horace, *Sat.*, II, 3: where a husband kills his wife by means of a string. Tac., *Ann.*, 6, 5, 9; Sueton, *Tib.*, 61.

87. Val. Max., 6, 1, 3: The Roman knight Pontius Aufidianus kills (*necare*) his daughter, deflowered by her *pedagogos* Fannius Saturninus; 6, 1, 6: P. Attilius Philiscus kills (*interire*) his daughter, guilty of *stuprum*. Augustus considers whether he should kill (*necare*) his indecent daughter Julia (Sueton, *Tib.*, 65, 3, *etiam de necanda deliberavit*). Agrippina, daughter in law of Tiberius, is, after the death of Germanicus, exiled to the island of Pandateria: after having endured repeated violence, she refuses all food and dies by *inedia*; informed of her death, Tiberius boasts of having avoided strangling her with a lace, then giving her over to public obloquy: '*imputavit etiam, quod non laqueo strangulatam in Gemoniam abiecerit . . .*' (Suet., *Tib.*, 53, 4–5). Let us remember once again (above, n. 71) that, when Cato the Elder writes '*necare*' in the context of the punishment for adultery, Aulus Gellius transcribes: *occidere*, thinking of the *ius occidendi* of the *lex Iulia*, where the death prescribed is swift and violent.

88. *D.* 25.3.4. This passage belongs to the wake of the *Senatus Consultum Plantianum*, a bill relative to the filiation of children who are to be born of a woman who had been divorced. When the former husband, upon having been told by the mother of her pregnancy, has abstained from recognising the infant, he loses every right over it: as one can conclude

from the passage of Paul, this means above all that he can no longer expose the child or put it to death; the complement of this dispossession is that the infant can no longer be left without food (*D.* 25.3.1.14–15): the child is thus allowed to live, in opposition to its progenitor.

89. Suet., *Claudius*, 27, 3, writing about the emperor's daughter left, naked, at the door of her mother, despite her having already received her first feed, *natam alique coeptam*: the crime committed by Claudius consisted precisely in exposing a girl, once nourished. It is never said about a girl that she is *suscepta, sublata*, etc.; Cf., also, Suet., *Aug.*, 65, 4; *Calig.*, 25, 7.

90. Only sons are 'taken up' (*suscepti, sublati*): the expression *tollere liberos*, when it is not used in the generic sense of 'having children', always refers to the rite of the father recognising the newborn male, placed on the floor, by raising him up. *Alere*, feeding, is said, about a newborn male, only in the context of the law imposing upon his genitor the obligation to keep him alive (cf. above, n. 86): it is, for males, not a mode of recognition.

91. *Necare* is used, in the XII Tables, for the fate of the infant subject to malformation (4,1). The same verb is used to refer to the domestic execution of Spurius Cassius: *verberasse et necasse*. Cf. Val. Max. 5, 8, 2: ... *necari iussit*. Drusus and Nero, grandsons of Tiberius by adoption, also die in accordance with the specific modalities of *nex*. Drusus dies of *inedia*, in the prisons of Tiberius's palace, abandoned to eat the padding of his mattress (Suet., *Tib.*, 54, 2; Tac., *Ann.* 6, 23, 2); Nero is relegated to the island Pontia, and takes his own life after the executioner shows him the lace with which he will be strangled and the hook that will serve to drag his body (*cum ei carnifex . . . laqueus et uncos ostentaret*: *Tib.* 54, 2). In Martial, *ep.*, 4, 70, a father hands his son a piece of lace to hang himself. Pausanias (107b, 28, 4) describes a painting of Polygnotus in Delphi; the *Nekuia*, presenting the ritual of the invocation of the dead, on the half of the wall of the meeting- and discussion-hall *Lesché*, where, above the river Acheron, a father strangles a son, who behaved unjustly against him. In contrast, this reminds Pausanias of an *exemplum*, very common in the Roman world, of filial piety, also the *sujet* of the poem *The Etna*, which tells us of a son who carries his father and mother on his shoulders, saving them from the volcano's flames.

92. In the *Digest*, *vita* is either the biological fact of life or the mode in which a life is lived: it is not by any means a concept

of law (see *Voc. iur., s.v., vita*). The only expression that could make us think of any specific legal sense is *societas vitae*, twice used to speak of a marriage. But the expression is only a metaphor serving to justify that an action for theft is impossible between spouses. It was invented by Cassius Nerva, then taken up by Paul (*D.* 25.2.1) and by Tryphoninus (*D.* 32.1.52), in the context of the *actio* for purloined objects (*actio rerum amotarum*).

93. *Permissa est* is understood as dealing with the past: A. Albanese, *Scritti* Beato Ferrini, III, pp. 343 ff.; M. Kaser, *Iura*, 1951, pp. 167 ff.; *Römisches Privatrecht*, II, 143, n.14; p. 204, n.12; B. Biondi, *Il diritto romano cristiano*, III, 1954, pp. 13 ff. And yet, the same constitution, in the Code of Justinian, is modified: *olim permissum erat*; an insistence upon the past which shows the Justinian did not understand *permissa est* as do our contemporaries (with the exception of R. Sargenti, *Il diritto privato nella legislazione di Constantino*, 1974, p. 7).

94. *Si quis necandi infantis piaculum adgressus adgressave* (*erit capitale istud malum*) (C. Theod.); (*Sciat se capitali supplicio esse puniendum* (C.J.)). The formula *piaculum adgressus est*, 'has committed the abominable atrocity', refers to the practice, condemned by another constitution of the same year 374 (C. Theod. 8, 51, 2 *pr.*; cf. *supra*, n. 37), of letting a newborn die of hunger or exposing it: this is the meaning of *infantem necare*. But this prohibition of putting an infant to death does not amount, *pace* E. Sachers (RE. XXII, 1, col. 1089), to an abolition of the *vitae necisque potestas*.

95. C. Theod., 9, 15, 1 = *Si quis in parentis aut filii aut omnino affectionis eius, que nuncupatione parricidii continetur, fata properaverit* . . . (= the culleus or penalty of the sac). See the last contribution on this text, R. Martini, 'Sulla costituzione di Costantino sul tema di parricidio', in, *Att. II. congr. int. Acad. Rom. Constantiniana*, 1976, pp. 106 ff. The murder of the son is surely assimilated to a *parricidium*, and completes the list of extensions to the primordial notion of parricide (cf. Y. Thomas, *MEFRA*, 1981, pp. 648 ff.), that had already been delivered by the *lex Pompeia*. But around 103 BCE already, Q. Fabius has been condemned *'de parricidio'* for having killed his son. Let us distinguish, therefore, what the Romans were experts in not confusing: on the one hand, a father has over his son a right of life and death; on the other hand, he can nonetheless be qualified as a parricide if he kills him. Our logic of facts and common sense is not that of

Roman law, which defines powers in such a way that their essence is absolutely not modified by practices or norms that make their exercise impossible.

96. On *D.* 48.9.5, see the erroneous interpretation of F. Casavola, 'Potere e persone tra Adriano e Antonino', in *Giuristi Adrianei*, op. cit., pp. 205–6. 'A prince who, in his edict, recognised that the raison d'être of paternal power was the benefit that sons could draw from it, obviously could not allow that the father continued to exercise the supreme right of putting to death his own descendants': the author comments, in far too simple a manner, on a text that distinguishes very clearly between the substance of the right and the modalities of its exercise (cf. above); *D.* 48.21.3: *videri autem et patrem, qui sibi manus intulisset, quod diceretur filium suum occidisse, magis dolore filii emissi mortem sibi irrogasse et ideo bona eius non esse publicanda divus Hadrianus rescripsit* (to bring together with Phaedrus, Fab. 3, 10). E. Volterra, 'Sulla confisca dei beni dei suicidi', in *Riv. Stor. dir. Ital.*, 6, 1933, p. 397; F. Casavola, op. cit., p. 207; and A. Wacke, 'Der Selbstmord im röm. Recht. . .', *ZSS*, 1980, p. 58 and n. 145, all think that this text implies a capital accusation against the father who is a murderer of his son. Yet, suicide, in criminal jurisprudence, is considered a confession (cf. *D.* 48.23.3, *pr.*): one does not quite understand how someone who is guilty and who confesses his crime should have been able to spare his heirs the confiscation of his property. It is therefore probable that the father, under prosecution for another capital crime, has killed himself after having killed his son: his suicide has not been the confession of the crime he was accused of, but the final stage of a disorder that was itself deemed to be sufficient as a punishment (cf. *D.* 48.9.9.2: *sufficere furore ipso eum puniri*). On the *publicatio bonorum* and the suicide, see P. Veyne, *Latomus*, 1981, pp. 230 ff.

97. On *patria potestas* as a modality of *pietas*, see M. Roberti, 'Patria potestas and paterna pietas', in *St. Albertoni*, I, 1933, pp. 259 ff.; and J. Gaudemet, 'La vie familiale au Bas-Empire', in *Romanitas*, 5, 1962 = *Etudes de droit romain*, III, 1979, pp. 73 ff. for the Christian era.

98. Cf. A. Albanese, 'Note sull'evoluzione storica del ius vitae et necis', op. cit.; A. Watson, *Rome of the XII Tables*, p. 43; A. M. Rabello, *Effetti personali della patria potestas*, op. cit., pp. 89 ff.

Eight

On Parricide:
Political Interdiction and the Institution
of the Subject

The Romans constantly spoke of parricide, and accused each other of it with surprising ease. Qualifying an adversary as 'parricide' was an everyday insult and part of the panoply of commonplace invectives. But on the other hand, parricide was for the Romans also the most unimaginable of all crimes. Textual sources provide us with a simple formula. Like incest, and in close relation to it, parricide was marked as a crime to which one refused to give credence. One rejected the possibility that this unbelievable crime (*scelus incredibile*) could really happen. It was inconceivable that it happened – not even as a misdeed.

There is a delusion lurking in this formula, to which we should be careful not to succumb. It is the temptation to invest them – armed, who knows, with a few references to Freud's work – with a meaning that is not really at work in it. Let us steer clear of this temptation to seize upon it in order to feed our familiar penchants for dramatising and for pathos. Let us, moreover, avoid the trance to which thinking frequently abandons itself when it supposes that it is engaged in communication with some fundamental principle or other. A number of detours deserve to be tried. They might enable us to get rid of all too far-reaching and vague impressions, offering in exchange the bits and pieces with which the labour of erudition can help us gain an insight in questions of fact. In order to do so, we need to successfully extract them from the past in which they are buried. They could prove capable of allowing us to limit the desire of interpretative omnipotence which always tends to haunt the interpreter.

I. The 'unbelievable crime'

The theme of the 'unbelievable crime' belongs first of all to the rhetoric proper to the courtroom of the *praetor*. It has its location among the arguments that an orator can employ in a criminal trial. The commonplace notions of the judiciary are nothing more than simple drawers in which one finds, tucked away according to an order adapted to the capacities of memory, an entire arsenal of means of accommodating the largest number of legal causes. Notions belonging to the category of two-term syntagmas (such as 'unbelievable crime') run to the hundreds, offering a profusion of suitable labels for arguments. The accusation, or the defence, only needs to pluck them from the inventory in order to compose their own discourse, a discourse that is never definitive but rather a case-by-case collage of elements that are ready to serve any case at hand. This is also the nature of the common topos of *credibile* and *incredibile*. In other words, is it plausible to assume that the accused has committed the deed? 'A man's fortune, his nature, his way of life, his pursuits and actions, the events he has experienced, his speeches, his usual habit of mind or body: the question is, does all of this, taken together, render the crime of which he has been accused, plausible or implausible? If one decides that the inquiry should be made in this way, the next question is whether it is possible that it has been performed; performed, that is, by anyone at all?' (Cicero, *De inventione* 2, 13, 44–5). In an oration pronounced in 63 BCE in defence of Roscius of Ameria, accused of having killed his father, Cicero applies to the letter the argumentative precepts concerning 'place'. In order to show the implausibility of a parricide in such circumstances, the orator invokes the precedent of a widely known case, on which, some years earlier, a judgment had been issued in Sicily. One morning, two brothers were found sleeping, in the repose of the righteous. Their room was attached to that of their father. The father lay with his throat cut. The Caelii brothers' lawyers pleaded that it was absolutely implausible that after such a crime the two parricides could be found asleep: the fact that they were, prevented any belief that they had committed the crime. The argument stood, and the brothers were acquitted (Cicero, *pro Roscio Amerino* 23, 64; Bobbio Scholiast, p. 432,

Orelli). The trial passed into posterity; it is part of Valerius Maximus's collection of exemplary cases (8, 1, 13).

Augustus, invited to sit on a domestic tribunal in order to consider the case of a son suspected of having attempted to murder his father, dissuaded the accused from confessing to the impossible, by turning his question this way: 'Certainly, you have not killed your father?' (Suetonius, *Augustus*, 33). Here it is the Emperor himself who uses the commonplace of the impossible crime. In the schools of rhetoric, on the other hand, apprentice orators would embellish this theme by anchoring their argument in the matricide of Orestes. This is an *exemplum* that illustrates the torments of a conscience preyed on by the Furies. It demonstrates, above all, that the crime was considered conceivable only if the killer was bound to obey the most extraordinary imperatives, such as vengeance for one's father's death, or the commandment of an oracle (Quintilian, *Institutiones Oratoriae*, 5, 10, 19 and 7, 2, 31). Only insanity, both as cause and consequence of the crime, was reason enough to allow that this universally shared incredulity could give way to the notion that, in the case at hand, a manifest murder has been committed. 'Only an extreme outbreak of rage combined with insanity', a lawyer explained, 'could render the murder of a father or mother as much as plausible' (Cicero, *pro Roscio*, 23, 66). We even see the deranged accuse themselves of the 'unbelievable' and plead that their deed was due only to their madness, while a confession of this unmistakable, irrefutably tangible and present *crimen* would have proven insufficient. A young man, accused of parricide, had been acquitted by half the voices of the jury: roaming through the city, he shouted, in his madness: 'It is I, father, who killed you'. The local magistrate had him put to death immediately without any other form of trial, on account of the fact that, although his confession was made in a state of mental affliction and, thus, offered no ground to put any faith in his words, his madness on the contrary constituted a confession in its own right, because 'tradition tells us that those who had committed such a crime were hounded by the Furies and wandered delirious throughout the world' (Pseudo-Quintilian, *Declamationes*, 314).

The theme of *scelus incredibile* is, first of all, linked to the intuition that the legislator has committed a devastating imprudence by making of parricide a punishable offence: that of giving rise to the notion that parricide is something that is altogether possible. The topos of the *unbelievable* presents itself in such a way that the law appears, rather than as its mere symptom, as the very cause of the evil. The Romans inherited this legal pessimism from a well-attested tradition in certain Platonism-inspired currents. Outlined by Plato, this position was, via Aristotle, taken up by Posidonius, who notably inspired Seneca's ninetieth letter. The reign of the law, introduced by the founding act of the first legislator, has put an end to the golden age in which omniscient, clairvoyant and sage monarchs were the shepherds of a transparent society that spontaneously observed nature's commandments. That everyone was transparent to the others, as much as to himself, was at once a psychological and social condition: it was a state in which the appetites lay dormant, or had retreated to what was their just and reasonable abode; yet it was at the same time the result of political direction addressed directly to the soul, in an immediate communication of the herdsman's age-old wisdom to that present in each of the animals of his flock. It was between this state of grace and the law that the appetite for domination emerged. It degraded the monarch into a tyrant and, above all, it degraded communicative transparency into barriers of threat and prohibitions. Acquainted by the law with the evil of the deed, the relevant appetites set themselves free immediately and universally.

From this general theme derives the theme of the unfortunate legislator who first instituted a punishment for parricide, thereby providing parricide with indisputable plausibility. It led people to compare the wisdom of a Solon, or a Romulus, both staunch sceptics as to the possibility of such a crime, to the foolishness of certain Romans, who, at some remote moment in the past – and one about which, in the tradition, reigned supreme obscurity – had first endowed parricide with the image of a misdeed, by exhibiting the horror of its punishment. No one up to that point had encountered or seen such a misdeed, even admitting that everyone had carried it inside themselves. As long as it was beyond thought to ratify law's claim that law's directives required their effective enforcement, the crime of parricide was a matter of blissful ignorance. This was followed by its fall into the domain of the unbelievable. Indeed, the one generally shared feeling was the conviction that any effective case of parricide that had happened, had only happened courtesy of the law. Endowing it with a name, it had first provided it with visibility. The first offence was not the crime committed by someone who perpetrated a parricide; it was the lapse of a legislator who had been audacious enough to break the silence.

It is thus from *inside* the law that this disorder first irrupted into the world, no matter whether this happened through abusive legislation or through a murder perpetrated by sons against their fathers. Here is what Seneca taught the young emperor Nero, his disciple: the more you exaggerate a crime's punishment, the more you make it likely that it will be perpetrated. And he reminded Nero of the evils of the time just before his own: that of Claudius, during the fifteen years of whose rule more parricides had been sewn alive in a sack and thrown into the Tiber than in all the preceding centuries combined. In the past, sons did not yet dare to transgress the ultimate interdiction, and this was so true that this crime remained *crimen sine lege*, a crime without a law. Yet what is a 'crime without a law'? It is a crime *ultra audaciam positum*, a crime that was beyond the limits of audacity, an 'unbelievable crime', *scelus incredibile*, which, for this reason, ought to remain unseen at all costs. The rise of parricides started with the famed law against parricide. It was their punishment that provided parricides with the publicity of their offence ('*et illis facinus poena monstravit*', Seneca, *De clementia*, 1, 23, 1).

What is striking is the near-complete obscurity that covers the history of this crime. An impossible crime calls for an equally impossible history, to sustain the impossibility of the law itself. All the way up to some *lex Pompeia* dating from either 70 or 52 BCE, the strategy of the tradition consists in studiously confusing the issues and in trying to offer proof after proof that it knows nothing. Let me add that the *lex Pompeia* itself would have remained unknown to us, were it not for the citations of the jurisconsults that are compiled in the *Digest*: among contemporaries there is silence. There is nothing in Cicero, through whom we know of so many laws, starting with Sulla's law on murder; there is nothing in Plutarch's biography of Pompeius; nothing in any Latin or Greek author whatsoever. Later legislators, when dealing with parricide, continue to refer either to the vague notion of 'ancestral custom', *mos maiorum*, feigning to have forgotten that one historical *lex* at least truly exists – that of Pompeius – or to some other *lex*, which they were not able to identify or date. Before the *lex Pompeia* as much as after it, tradition refrains from admitting that any legislator had ever resolved to define and name this crime, just as it refrains from recognising that this crime could ever have been committed. Let us begin with the traditions that concern the crime, before envisioning those which, even more obscure, dealt with its law.

The Romans knew very well the year of the first murder, the year of the first treason, of the first rape, of the first incest, the first adultery, the first divorce. Only the date of the first parricide remains uncertain and subject to huge discrepancies. That its date of appearance on the theatre of moral squalor was quite a late one is about the only thing that was generally accepted. According to Plutarch (*Life of Romulus* 22, 4), the first Roman to kill his father would have been L. Hostilius, a short time after Hannibal's war, that is to say after 201, but a very long time after the foundation of Rome by Romulus! Livy ignores this event and postpones the first fatal example until 101: that year, a certain Malleolus was thrown into the Tiber for having killed his mother (*Ep. Liv.* 68 and Orosius 5, 16, 23). As this affair offered the occasion to debate the equivalence between matricide and patricide (*Rhetorica ad Herennium* 1, 23 and Cic., *de inventione* 2, 148–149), one might have thought that the precedent only consists here in the first extension of the punishment of parricide to the murder of one's mother. Between these two dates, the biography of Tiberius Gracchus mentions the punishment of Caius Vitellius, locked in a chest with snakes and thrown into the Tiber in 132 (Plutarch, *Tib. Grach.*, 20, 5). This punishment precisely corresponds to that reserved for those unfortunates who killed their father or mother: they were to be sewn into a leather sack, with snakes and possibly other animals, such as roosters or monkeys (Juvenal, *Satire* 8, v.213; *Sententiae Hadriani* 16, *Corpus Gloss. Lat.* III, 390; Modestinus, *D.* 48.9.9 pr.; Constantine, *Code Justinien* 9, 8, 1). Yet the text says nothing about the crime of Vitellius. And this uncertainty is even greater considering that, that very same year, the dead bodies of Tiberius Gracchus and his partisans were also thrown into the Tiber.

This is more or less all that can be said about its origins: it is surreptitiously that parricide makes its entry in Rome. Let us also note that, in the chronicles, mentions of parricide take the form of reports of odd signs: in the priestly records, parricides are always indicated among the year's inexplicable and highly significant happenings (*prodigia*). The crime of Lucius Hostius (after 201) figures in the list of those exceptional events of the year that created a need for expiation (*procurationes prodigiorum*). In particular, in 207 and in 200, the birth of several hermaphrodites is mentioned. They were, upon consultation of the *aruspices*, eliminated by drowning (Livy, 27, 37, 5 and 31, 2, 8). Again, in 132, the date at which Vitellius was drowned in the company of a serpent, an androgyne is thrown into the river, *in flumen deiectus* (Julius Obsequens, 27a). And, once more, it is as one of the memorable happenings of this particular year that Malleolus's matricide is indicated by the abridger of Livy, *Ep.* 68. His report of the events of the year 101 reads as follows: 'Publicius Malleolus, after having killed his mother, was the first to be sewn into a sack and thrown into the sea. The shields of Mars trembled, just before the Cimbrian War had reached its end'. Over the course of the following years, from 98 to 95, further androgynes were ritually drowned (Julius Obsequens, 47, 48, 50).

Thus, the years 200, 133 and, last but not least, 100 BCE, witness constellations of monstrous births, which by all evidence are assimilated with parricides. In such configurations, the person of the parricide appears indeed as a *monstrum* himself: a disorder of nature, an oddity that the city was liable to remove from its body. But the androgynes and the parricides were not alone in this respect. Those with two heads, four feet, or two penises, were in the same category. All of them were eliminated in the same manner (Julius Obsequens, 12; 25). The most elaborate of all these chimeric associations, where animal mingles with human, where members and organs multiply, where the sexes double or where any other form of perplexity is triggered, and where, finally, sons feature as an instrument in the death of their father or mother, remains the one mentioned for the year 83 BCE: a woman gives birth to a snake. The *aruspices* have it thrown into the river, where it starts to swim upstream. Considering that the atonement imposed by the rite of procuration evokes *two* monstrosities, one by nature: the serpent born from a woman's womb (which, in Greek tragedy, is in itself a symbol of matricide), one by crime: the same serpent follows the parricides thrown into the Tiber, the confusion here comes to a head.

The history of the attempt against one's father's life seems thus to commence by accident, as it were, and simultaneously with the arrival of monsters in the world, reported from the second century BCE onward. And yet it is never presented as a primordial story. The founder of Rome was the murderer of his brother – but, in order to see a Roman murder his father, we must wait close to six centuries! As for the first *lex* against parricide, neither the Roman authors inquiring into ancient times, nor the chroniclers made a secret of the fact that they knew practically nothing of it. The only certainty on the subject was that one could not impute it to the founder of Rome. Plutarch says that Romulus has not prohibited a crime that he was incapable of imagining. It is true that such a claim confronted a major obstacle: for Romulus himself employed, in order to designate simple homicide, the word *patroktonia*, a Greek term with the literal meaning of 'parricide'. In other words, according to the tradition, Romulus knew the word. But he ignored the thing: he failed to impose any penalty on *patroktonia* understood in the sense of the murder of one's own father (*Life of Romulus,* 22). Plutarch's remark makes one think immediately of a note from a scholar working in the time of the end of the Republic, Verrius Flaccus, about the law of Numa against murder: the word *paricidas*, this antiquarian tells us, does not have, here, the sense of parricide which is now familiar and current: it referred to the murder of a free man (Festus, p. 247, Lindsay: 'One calls a parricide, not the one who killed his father, but the one who killed any person who has not been condemned'). In short, this orthodox tradition tells us that Romulus and Numa called *parricidium/patroktonia* ordinary murder, and *paricidas-parricida/patroktonos* an ordinary murderer, and that their laws did not aim at parricide properly speaking, at parricide as the Romans (with the remarkable exception of their first kings) ordinarily understood the term, i.e. as patricide, the murder of one's father. For the murder of one's own father or mother, no specific punishment was envisioned.

This enigma is among those that have led historians of archaic Rome to spilling the largest amount of ink. More than any other matter, it has called upon the imagination of those specialising in origins. But their efforts have proven less than useful, in my opinion. Simply, such a paradox stands no chance of being untangled either through its etymology (which remains totally unknown), or through its history (which is impervious to research for lack of documentation). It is much better to simply take it for what it is: a paradox supplemented by a denial, or better, a denial that takes the form of a paradox. Romulus dubs homicide 'parricide', while at the same time refusing to make a law that might have been taken as evidence to the effect that he was able to imagine that parricide might actually exist. He thus achieves the tour de force of emptying the word of its inadmissible sense: he takes the mere shell of the signifier, using it as a label to designate something else, something that has nothing improbable about it, namely murder – the murder of any person, rather than only of the father. This is the fortunate operation which is attributed to Romulus. If we follow Plutarch, it resulted in the fact that the crime remained unknown in Rome for nearly ten centuries – the time that precedes the crime of Lucius Hostius. Little can be learnt from all this as to the archaic history of parricide and murder. What it does enlighten us about, on the other hand, is the extraordinary power of repression triggered by the theme of the *scelus incredibile*. At its origin, 'parricide' was not parricide. At its origin was Romulus's knowledge that parricide did not exist.

The first mention that a law about patricide has been applied is that of Malleolus's matricide in 101. The penalty consists in tying the culprit in a sack before plunging him into either the Tiber or the sea. Livy does not mention a first act of legislation strictly speaking. He is content to signal that Malleolus was the first to suffer the penalty of the sack (*Periochae* 68: 'He was the first to be sewn into a sack and thrown into the sea'. Or, the same, Orosius 5, 16, 23: 'He was tied in a sack and thrown into the sea: the crime and its expiation were thus brought about by the Romans at the same time'). On the other hand, the author of the *Rhetoric for Herennius*, who was a contemporary of the issue at stake, does have some more details to give to this law. Here is what he says: 'One who has been judged for having killed his father or mother will have their head placed in a hood, before being bound and taken in a chariot to the river'. But is what we are dealing with here truly the matter of a *lex*, a legal pre-scription? Should one not rather think, as has already been suggested, of a decree by the *aruspices*, consulted about the mode of atonement (*procuratio*) for a prodigy?[1] Above all, were the terms of this response effectively formulated for the first time in 101? Was this not, much rather, the outcome of a recycling of an older prescription, and a first time only to see it applied to a matricide case?

In my opinion, the last reconstruction is far the most likely. First of all, the rhetorical tradition tells us that the entire interpretative debate here bears on the possibility of applying to the murder of one's mother the penalty that was imposed for the murder of one's father: the referent of the word *parens*, which properly speaking designated, espe-cially in legal language, the father or the male forebear in the masculine line, was on this occasion extended to the mother. *Rhetoric to Herennius* I, 13, 23: 'He who has been judged to have killed their father (*parens*) will have their head, etc. Malleolus was judged for having killed his mother'; simi-larly, Quintilian, *Institutiones oratoriae*, VII, 8, 6: 'One who has killed their father (*pater*) will be sewn in a sack: Malleolus has been judged for killing his mother'; finally, since the abridger of Livy reports that Malleolus was not the first to have been thrown into the sea or the river, but that he was the first to have suffered this punishment as a matricide (*Periochae* 68: 'He was the first, after having killed his mother, to be thrown into the sea'). One must suppose that matricide was hence-forth qualified as parricide by extension: it is the father that the notion is first tied to and it is with respect to the father that the interdict was principally formulated. We may say that the rest comes in addition and by analogy.

A note by Festus dealing with the nuptial rite, incidentally alludes to a 'law about the father', *lex parensta,* where, in the same criminal context, father and mother are associated in the same way. The text is mutilated. All that remains is this: 'Aelius and Cincius said that one designates marriage by the name of *nuptiae* because one covers the head of the spouse with a veil, a gesture that the ancients called "to veil", *obnubere;* in the same way, the law . . . of the father (*lex parensta*) . . . prescribes to cover, which is to say to "veil" (*obvolvere*), the head of one who has killed his father or his mother' (Festus, p. 174, Lindsay). The fact of associating the nuptial rite, in which one covers the head of the married with an orange coloured (*flammeus*) veil, and the penal rite, where one seals the head of the parricide in a leather hood (*folliculum*), is here borrowed from Cincius (about whom we know nothing) and from Lucius Aelius Stilo, whose teaching was continued by that of Cicero and Varro. This text does not furnish any clue that would permit us to situate this 'law about the father' before the first application that has been attested, on the occasion of Malleolus's matricide in 101 BCE; but neither does it invalidate the plausible hypothesis of the previous tradition, fixed somewhere in the course of the second century. Above all, the specifically masculine value of *parens* is here extended from the murder of the father to the murder of the mother, following the same method as with Malleolus's crime. Hence, everything looks as if no indication is to be found that would enable us to decide which was there first, whether it was a decree of the *aruspices* or, on the contrary, a 'law', or whether it was the 'law of the year 101' or some other, earlier *lex*. The tradition makes itself visible only indirectly, in the form of a later extension – or indeed of a contemporary extension, if we follow the author of the *Rhetoric for Herennius* – of some more ancient legislation, but how much more ancient we do not know.

Sometimes, the Romans attributed the punishment of parricide to ancient custom, the *mos maiorum*: we find this in Cicero's defence of Roscius and, even later, during the Empire, in a jurist like Modestinus (*Digest* 48.9.9). More often, however, the measure was qualified as a 'law' (*lex*). It was designated as such, as we have seen, by the *Rhetoric to Herennius* and by Festus. By Valerius Maximus, as well, when he says that death by immersion, applied first to the sacrilegious, was extended 'much later, by means of a legal provision' to extend to parricides (I, 1, 13). Seneca attributes the cause of the first crimes to this 'law', described as both 'legendary and unascertained': 'With this law, parricides started to happen' (*De clementia*, 1, 23, 1). In his anti-pagan polemic, the Christian Orosius adopted the formula in order to charge the Romans with inventing the crime as well as its punishment at the same time (5, 16, 23). Hadrian, as well, who in turn was very much in favour of this ancient form of execution, without adding anything more precise, traces it back to 'a particular law' (*Hadriani Sententiae*, 16); and it is undoubtedly by availing himself of this 'law' that he ruled that the decurions of the cities, despite the privileged status they enjoyed as members of a public body, be condemned to death by sack if they killed their father (*D.* 48.9.9; 48.19.15).

The tradition locates the origin of the prohibition of parricide thus either in custom or in a law – an unidentified law without author and date. A law that is assumed to stem from the time after Romulus, indeed a merely recent law, a law mostly considered deplorable, a law 'about the father' which was probably extended to the murder of the mother only in 101 BCE, an unidentified law without author and date. In dealing with this particular matter, everything that the Romans knew of their history was filtered through one theme, itself traditional to the point of banality: that of the danger lurking in laws. Mind that this theme remained otherwise unused in Rome. It appears in the context of parricide alone. But here, it supplies the topos that conditions, from Cicero to Seneca, from Seneca to Plutarch, from Plutarch to Orosius, all the information that we have, about a crime that boils down to one single essential feature: that of having its origin in an appalling legal recklessness.

II. Autonomy and heteronomy in civil law: the prohibition of parricide and the institution of the subject.

One thing that we do know with certainty, on the other hand, is the obsessional fear haunting Roman fathers. Sons are a danger to fathers: this is a theme that recurs with a persistence bordering on obsession.[2] This worry that harasses the father is a theme we find told and retold in a thousand forms in the laws, in the poets, in the orators. Now this theme has its roots in the very structure of the legal personality in Roman civil law. A son had to await his father's death in order to get access to juridical autonomy and to take up the status of full legal capacity, a status that the language of civil law designates suggestively with a reflexive form: that of being *sui iuris*, that is – of being 'by one's own right'. Let us take a moment to examine this notion of autonomy.

In order to understand parricide in Rome, one must consider the autonomy of the subject, which is to say the very structure of a person's legal status. The Roman law of persons and goods delayed the moment for a son to acquire legal capacity until that of his father's death. Paternal power gave the father lifelong exclusive rights over his property. In an extremely concise formula, Roman law tells us that the son, in order to have a lawful claim to his father's estate, must find himself 'under [his father's] power at the time of his father's death', i.e. *in potestate morientis* (Gaius, *Institutes*, III, 2). It adds that, in order to lawfully succeed his father, the son must be under his father's power 'at the moment in which the father is in the process of dying', *moriente eo* (Iulianus, *D.* 38.16.6). The present participle is essential. With a surprising degree of concision, the jurist formulates the rule that the *'heres suus'* – literally: *'his* heir' – is required to have been alive simultaneously with his now deceased father, but above all, that the son, at the moment of the father's demise, must have been *suus* – *'his'*. The decisive point here is duration. The law seeks to dodge the transition by imposing a junction which has the purpose of smoothing the passage between successive generations into one single duration. Any interruption would give rise to a time not covered by a legal relationship, to a waste or no-man's-time during which no tie of belonging can be identified, a time during which, in other words, the tie of the son's belonging to the dying father would be dissolved, and, with it, the quality of *suus*. In order to succeed the deceased, the law demands of the living that they be subjected to the right (*ius*) of the dead until that very ultimate moment at which the transmission takes place. The ascendant's paternal power incorporates the descendant in such a way that, until the instant of his father's death, the descendant remains a person *alieni iuris,* a person deprived of his proper property rights and proper legal capacity. Up to this point in time the son thus belongs to another's rule. It is true that, already, this other is almost himself. For father and son are, with respect to their legal status, effectively one: 'father and son constitute the same person', *pater et filius eadem persona* (*Code of Justinian* 6, 26, 11). One single trajectory merges he who holds the power, with he who is subject to it. In this way, the successor does not take the place of another: he turns out to be this other. A text by the jurisconsult Paul, around the year 220 CE, makes it possible to get some clarity about the stakes:

> Looking at heirs who are *sui* ('under *his* power'), there is no succession, meaning that ownership continues. The sons were already owners in their father's lifetime, or at least now they are considered as having been. Whence the epithet of a 'family son' (*filius familias*), formed after that of a 'family father' (*pater familias*). The only difference between them lies in the fact of procreating and of being procreated. This is also why, after the father's death, the sons are not considered to have inherited the father's estate as his successors; rather, they are considered to acquire the right to freely manage their own goods. (*D.* 28.2.11).

What we have here is an image of an identity endlessly reprogramming itself: the same, perpetuating itself within the same.

Considering this construction that goes back to Roman civil law, of a subject that becomes fully a legal subject only by the death of their father, one gets a better grasp of what defines the murder of the father in Rome, its originality and its unmistakable specificity. One's father's death functions as an irreplaceable condition; as long as it is not fulfilled, there is no way of being a legal subject in the full sense. It would be futile to project this Roman specificity into the contemporary legal universe, tantamount to negating history and liberty, through which humans are steadily in the process of redefining themselves. Quite simply, these structures have been subject to change since. The Roman law is, in my understanding, unique in that it permits a legal analysis that is internal to the relation that *unites* paternal power and parricide, power and the crime of majesty perpetrated against power, heteronomy and the conquest of autonomy by violent means. Only in Rome is it true to say that parricide was a crime against civil law as such, in its entirety. Parricide disturbed the natural order of death upon which legitimate transmission was suspended. In rebellion against his father and, beyond that, against the civil order, the parricide accelerated the moment at which he was going to be 'under the power of him who was in the process of deceasing'. This 'power', the parricide seized on his own initiative, without waiting to be seized by it, without waiting to be invested in his turn at the moment foreseen by the destinies, as law's internal processes demanded. In a law from 318 CE, Emperor Constantine defined parricide as an act through which one 'hastens destinies', *fata properare* (*Code*, 9, 17). Seen from the viewpoint of civil law, parricide was indeed an act of self-appointment and self-creation. By murdering his father, the parricide granted himself the status of *suus heres* – the status of '*his* [meaning: the dying father's] heir' – and, thereby, that of being *sui iuris*, a subject of its own right. Yet, it was by virtue of his act alone that he became *sui iuris*; he did not receive this status as an effect of the law. He precipitates the obtainment of this effect of the law, *acting as if it was he who had the power of doing so, rather than either his father, or destiny.*

This material does offer a fitting point of departure from which to reflect on the relation between heteronomy and subjectivity in the Western legal tradition. The subject, let us not ask whether it is a cause or an effect, or whether it is autonomous or confronted by the reality of a world that surpasses it. Rather, we will pose the question of how its autonomy has been constructed in law. And we shall see that there is a genuine Roman institution of the subject, which is an institution of the legal subject: something that we situate, as far as possible from the so-called modern idea of the subject as such, as an absolute within nature.

Let us start from the notion, today widely accepted, that the distinctive feature of communitarian systems is the lack of a distinction between the civil and the political. This is foreign to the scholarly – originally Roman – legal construction of the subject's autonomy. The Roman model from which the institutions of the European *ius commune* took their departure is remarkable and unique in terms of the normative regimes exterior to it, in that the subject is here defined a priori as a universal and abstract being, posed in the absolute of its own existence. The development of contract, the antithesis of subject and object, the reification of nature, the abstraction of exchange value from the link of personal obligation: all of these go back to the mould of the autonomy of the subject according to Roman law. In the *longue durée* – to cast it in the words that an economic or social historian would use – one finds above all the explosive institution of the subject according to Roman law.

And yet, the subject that features in the European *ius commune*, remarkably autonomous as it is, cannot be comprehended otherwise than through the heteronomy that founds it. Once again, this is not about the position of the subject in the world in general, or whatever other vague or pointless generalities that there might be. The heteronomy construed by law pertains to a different order. What we should pay heed to is the properly Roman modalities of this construction (just as, in the Middle Ages, we need to consider the properly Christian modes). The autonomy of the subject in Roman law is expressed, from very early on, with the assistance of the reflexive possessive pronoun *suus*: to every citizen a status is attributed, defined as *the state of one who falls only within his own legal sphere: 'sui iuris'* – literally, '*by his own right*'. Yet, as we have seen, this absolute subject is construed in a relation of absolute alienation. I would suggest this: the state of legal autonomy, the status of being *sui iuris*, necessarily follows a state of submission to another's right (*alieni iuris*). There is no such thing as a *sui iuris* subject who has not, at some earlier moment, fallen into another power. This is as much the case for emancipated slaves and slaves liberated by their master, as it is for subjects born free, men or women who leave their paternal power, either through emancipation, i.e. an artificial procedure, or through the death of one's father, i.e. owing to a natural event. There is no autonomy of the subject, no *sui*-juridicity – to risk a fitting formula – that has its origins elsewhere than in a state of *alieni*-juridicity. Everyone begins his career within the legal dependence of another. And this other is neither the world in general, nor whatever being in ontological terms, nor god. It is a product of institution. And it exists in law as master, *dominus*, or as father, *pater*.

This other subject is the father. The father also draws his autonomy from the same base of alienation, and so on, infinitely, in an ascending line. Mind that, in practical terms, this analysis is no more than a paraphrase of Roman law, which as we have seen, provides that every subject *sui iuris* becomes such only at the moment of their father's death, when they cease to be *alieni iuris*. Subjective reflexivity, the subject's effective turn towards itself, is not originally grasped in the field of contract, as the constructions of legal philosophers naïvely assume. It needs to be grasped in the sphere of an estate that moves from one hand to another.

Yet, that which 'belongs properly' to the legal subject, in the sense that the language of law reflects in the reflexive possessive adjective *suus*, is one thing. The city, the constitution of a permanent 'public thing', the reference to an illustrious 'Roman Name' is another, wholly different thing. The Roman *political* entity positions itself essentially outside of the 'proper' and its internal space. It is exterior to it in two senses. First, it appears as a sum of primary elements, rather than as a totality broken down into primary units. The abstract *civitas* is built upon the reference to the concrete *civis* – just the opposite of the Greek political model, where the city, *polis*, logically precedes the *politēs, the* citizen.[3] Secondly, the Romans chose *not* to credit the totality – by metaphor, by fiction, in short: by institution – with a subjective identity. In Rome, the collective entity is devoid of moral personality. No instituted personality, as will be required by the state, can be seen at work before the start of the medieval subjectification of the collective body. In this perspective, the legal history of modern subjectivity is a blend of the interiority of the individual subject with the fictive interiority of the collective subject. The two subjectivities march in step. Roman law itself, on the other hand, regardless of the fact that it has equipped modern constructions with their entire vocabulary (*corpus, universitas, persona*), does not recognise this analogic identification of the whole with the individual element of the whole.[4]

To speak of a distinction between these two levels of institutional organisation, the individual level and the political level, does not imply, however, the notion of a conflict between them. The sphere of '*sui*-juridicity' proper to every subject is nested within the sphere of the city. The difficulty can be unfolded – solved, perhaps – by sticking to the notion that it is the citizen who constitutes the subject, who features as the subject's irreducible legal self. Roman law does not counter-pose the subject on the one hand to the city on the other; rather, it posits the citizen-subject. The city appears as the abstract concept of this citizen-based subjectivity: it derives from the citizen, both from an etymological and a legal point of view. In the same manner in which *civis* is prior to *civitas*, rather than *civitas* to *civis*, the *ius civile* is not the law of the city, it is not even the law whose domain of validity is the city, it is the law of the citizen, *civis*. The citizen comes first.[5] The Romans thought of the law of politics by reference to the civil law, not the other way round.[6]

We find it more and more difficult to understand how to figure out what would be a full autonomy that is not upheld by some effective overarching structure and that nonetheless exerts an ascendancy powerful enough to provide it with its foundation. We conceive of the sphere of the legal subject, which is the field of deployment both of the power one holds over one's things proper, and that of the obligations that bind persons to other persons, not as of a certain level within the juridical edifice of autonomy, but as of a thing-in-itself. The autonomy of the legal subject strikes us as being not of the rank of an institutional provision, but of the very same substance as the subject itself. Nurtured as we are by the dualism that has characterised European legal culture since the seventeenth and eighteenth centuries, we struggle regarding how to assess things differently. For what we have ever since accustomed ourselves to is based, on the one hand, on positing the subject in the absolute terms of its relation to itself (that the relation to oneself is absolute, has, incidentally, been prepared early in another field: the theology of the immediate relation to God, derived from Saint Paul and Saint Augustine), and, on the other hand, on confronting it to the state, another absolute subject, that is exterior to it. In order to escape this irreducible confrontation, we have been trying to conceal it behind a sophism – which, since then, has become integrated into the 'general theory of law'. In order to imagine a possible articulation of the autonomy of the subject with the law of politics, we are ready to admit this alternative: either a law that recognises the subject's autonomy, or one that declares it. The alternative is then between: autonomy prior to law, and law prior to autonomy. In the words of one of the most ruminated commonplaces of modern legal literature, what we have is either an inventory of what pre-exists the law, or a declaration of what the law institutes. But this endless balancing act begs a crucial question. The difficulty that escapes the grasp of this game of equivocations is, if one puts it into the jurists' distinctions of their subject matter, not a 'formal' but a well-nigh 'substantive' distinction. In short, if we limit ourselves to the – elementary – opposition between subjective rights and objective law, we can say we still do not know how to articulate *at their base* the two moments that are so difficult for us to reconcile, wherever they appear, concretely, in institutions: the subject on the one side, the law on the other.

To pose this question and to circumscribe some of the *topoi* where it could be solved is the sole purpose of these reflections. I will approach it through the study of mechanisms and legal operations located where one would least expect to find them: in the field of paternal power, and especially, of the institutions that it commands – such as the organisation of what happens at the death of an owner (i.e. succession), such as the ban on parricide. What does the father's power have to do, after all, with the study of the relation between subjective autonomy and civil law, with the link that, being neither formal nor external nor synthetic, but constitutive and substantial, associates the autonomy of the subject, the *sui iuris* autonomy of the citizen, with the law of the city (considering that the city is but an expression, and an extension, of the citizenship carried by each citizen in its quality of a support of the *civil law*)?

We need to start once again from the *sui*-juridicity that the subject acquires when it passes from the status of son to that of father – when the subject, by becoming *pater*, fully emancipates itself as a subject – and the status as a citizen that, inseparably, goes with it. This transfer needs to be outlined rigorously in its terminology and its concepts. Some of these concepts defy any logic, any logic based on the principle of non-contradiction at the least: to begin with, what should one make of the notion that the subject is fully itself courtesy of another subject's mediation, that it needs to conquer its autonomy in a state of utter heteronomy? *Patria potestas* is an external power, a power exercised over sons. Yet, at the same time, it is an internal power, a power that one exercises over oneself and one's *sui* (those 'of one's own'), a power that entails that the subject wielding it is emancipated from any legal dependency in relation to another. What is important, to get an appropriate idea of this power and to correctly understand its juridical nature and that of the institutions of subjective autonomy that, both personally and really (i.e. in the law of obligations, and in the law of property), derive from it, is that one should not imagine *patria potestas* as a power that is in the hand of *someone* – of this or that father in particular. It must be taken in a radically different way: as the power of *the father in general*. The father's power is not the power of a particular subject, it is that of a spokesperson par excellence of the subject, the power of the provider of the paternal function. Let us give full weight to the issue of how to correctly understand *patria potestas*. It is not called *paterna potestas* – which would instantiate a mode of suffixation that refers to the singular person of some empirical father. It is called *patria potestas* according to the mode of suffixation connected to a function.[7] *Patria potestas, patrium ius* – these refer to the paternal position taken abstractly. Any legal subject's power is defined, in Roman law, as a power that attaches to the role of *the* father *in general*.

It was in reference to this sense of the word 'father' that the crime of parricide was considered 'unbelievable'. The very structure of the civil order hinged upon this crime. However, the same rationale that relegated parricide to the realm of things that were 'beyond belief', also instituted its possibility, made of it something that was to be expected regularly, permanently.

One mooting exercise for law students expands on the following theme: a father pleads the defence of his three sons who have tried to murder him. This was, he argues, because I have been all-too avaricious in managing my estate (Quintilian, *Institutiones oratoriae* IV, 2, 72f.). Another one stages an accusation of parricide brought against a son who, blamed for being spendthrift, says to his father 'don't worry: you won't have a further occasion to rebuke me!' (*Ib.*, V, 10, 47). These are chosen from a wealth of school examples, epitomising themes that were imposed for defence speeches.

However, scandal stories of the type were in no way limited to the well-protected zones of lawyerly education. Cicero, in order to argue that Roscius has not killed his father, felt the need to refer to the fact that his client has been neither sent off to some distant countryside, nor disinherited. Public rumour accused a famous writer, heir of an important estate, of precipitating his father's death (*Invectives against Sallust*, 14). And we also know of a senator who ended up instituting as his heir a son who had tried to kill him (Valerius Maximus, V, 9, 3). Parricide is regularly mentioned in connection with expenses and debts: it is associated to the *locus de divitiis*, in other words: it belongs to money-related matters (Juvenal, *Satire* XIV, 250 ff.). The civil law ends up by putting a stop to the deep-rooted fear it provokes, by stopping credit grantors from loaning money to the sons of estate-owning fathers, thus depriving them of the possibility of using the estate to pay their loans, with interest, at the death of the debtor's father. This provision – inspired by a criminal case from the 70s of the first century BCE, as it is openly mentioned in the text – prevents money lenders from placing the lives of fathers at risk of being killed by their sons who are impatient to enjoy their wealth. Here is the disposition, together with the account of its motives:

> To the many factors that led him to perpetrate his crimes, and that had their roots in his nature, Macedo added his debts. It often happens that money lenders give credit in situations where repayment is, to say the least, uncertain, thus providing vicious penchants with the trigger that makes the deed happen. This is why it has been decreed that the action of a creditor for the reimbursement of a debt will be rejected, if the debt arises from a loan made to the son of an estate-holding father, and this even if the action is only submitted after the father's death. Let those whose money-lending commerce has given rise to such a regrettable example take in the lesson that no good debt can be obtained by lending to a son who desires his father's death. (*D.* 14.6.1)

Parricide is doubtlessly the form of criminality that is most referred to in the sources. A banality anchored in language, as it has already been suggested? Maybe yes, except that the matter is not about language alone. Anyone looking attentively at the evidence offered by the available documentation can only be struck by the motive of the murder of the father and its tragic presence in Roman society. For contingent reasons owed to what we have in matters of reliable documents of the period, we can say that this is the case with Roman society from the second century BCE to the second century AD. In various contributions to the political function of the father, I have put together the principal elements of a list of such documents which turned out to be abundant far beyond what had been expected.[8] To name only a few out of a large number of points:

(1) Cicero had, either to plead or to judge, four parricide cases in the course of his career (*ad Quintum fratrem* I, 2, 5; *pro Roscio*; *de inventione* II, 58; Plutarch, *Cicero* 26, 7). He was also himself accused, in an edict published by Antonius, of plotting against his father's life, as well as that of his paternal uncle (*Philippics*, III, 7, 17).

(2) Following Pompeius's law on parricide, the number of those convicted was so high that Caesar felt the need, in addition, to come up with a special legal provision which dispossessed of half of their fortune those exiles who contrived to remove their property out of harm's way (Suetonius, *Caesar*, 42, 5).

(3) Suetonius, talking about the first period of the Principate, reports that one of Claudius's foremost pastimes was to attend the spectacular execution of parricides: the account clearly assumes that, during the fourteen years of his reign, the emperor had numerous occasions of thus diverting himself (this squares perfectly with Seneca's observations to Nero, as quoted above).

(4) The civil wars in Rome were accompanied by genuine explosions of cases of parricide. In the conspiracy of Catilina, in 63 BCE, the project of the ringleaders implied that sons were to kill their wealthy fathers and take possession of their fortunes, before taking up arms and joining the ranks of the conspirators (Sallust, *Catilina*, 63).

(5) During the last period of the Republic, in times of civil war, the establishment of official lists of personalities condemned to death (*proscriptiones*), including the fact of putting

a bounty on the heads of political opponents, provided, in a general way, conditions that were extremely effective in breaking up the solidarities based upon duty or respect, and in increasing domestic murders: sons, slaves and freed slaves were often in the vanguard of those staging violent settlements of accounts, betraying and denouncing their fathers, masters, or managers, having them put to death, and enriching themselves on their spoils (e.g. Appian, *Bellum Civile* IV, 3, 13 and 3, 18; Dio Cassius, 47, 6).

(6) Under the Empire, judiciary parricide – the accusation against one's father in a criminal court – was a full-fledged method in the fight against conspiracies. Tiberius very openly encouraged sons to accuse their fathers in order for them to be put to death (Dio Cassius, 57, 19, 1b = *Excerpta Vaticana*, 6, p. 199, ed. A. Mai; Tacitus, *Annals*, 4, 29, 2; Suetonius, *Tiberius*, 61, 5). This practice of denouncing one's parents in the service of the emperor and the state revealed itself very early as an endemic threat, directly linked to the defence of empire and majesty (Suetonius, *vita Lucani*; Pliny, *Panegyricus*, 42). The practice was even explicitly recommended by criminal law, which accompanied the call for such murderous informer services with substantial economic and fiscal advantages: as was the case of any successful accuser, the son who denounced his father received the spoils of the condemned. It was, at the same time, a technique for preventing the loss of one's father's estate through confiscation, as the punishment of state criminals extended in part to their descendants.

III. Inviolability – of power, of the father

The Roman political tradition equally and contradictorily exalts the father and the city. There were frequent cases of conflict between these two opposing allegiances: to disobey one's father so as not to rebel against the commandments of the city; or, alternatively, to violate public law with one's father's backing. Examples of such antinomies are myriad in the writing of the annalists. And yet, in their reports of exemplary cases, most of the fathers who confronted their sons, held the role of magistrates as well, a fact that neutralised the conflictual aspect; the paternal and the state function were merged in one single person, in such a way that the two orders of subordination found themselves in some manner compounded in one. This is the reason why, in Roman history, one so frequently finds father-magistrates putting to death their insubordinate sons, and never the reverse: the orthodox convictions of the historians preferred harmony to the conflict of norms. Yet, in imperial times, when the majesty of the emperors was successful at pushing their power to an absolute apex (known, precisely, under the name 'majesty'), the safeguards embodied in traditional case law lost a large share of their relevance. The very hypothesis of a conflict between two groups of interests became unthinkable. Faced with the emperor, fathers and sons were almost equals and it was no longer imaginable to consider a conflict between contradicting allegiances. Obeying one's father was subject to a prior subordination to the orders given by the *princeps*, as the son's subjection to the father presupposed the father's subjection to the sovereign. A genuine hierarchical subordination prevails over the dependencies that one sees emerge from the first decades of the Principate – when the Romans had to take an oath that they would place their fidelity to the prince over and against everything else, including close friends and family. Paternal law is, henceforth, very clearly subordinated to patriotic love, in other words to the exclusive love of the Prince, according to an equivalence which was well established from the first decades of the Empire. One of the most authentic versions of this imperial political construction is owed to the pen of the jurist Marcellus, who, in the second century CE, writes:

> Our ancestors did not remotely consider that a person who in his lifetime had contrived to kill his parents or children in order to ruin the fatherland, should be mourned; on the other hand, if someone killed his father or his son in order to save the fatherland, they held that the act was not a crime, and even that the killer should be rewarded. (*D.*, 11.7.35)

According to this new political configuration, parricide had lost its eminent place as a major crime. As, in the hierarchy of the unbelievable and the unspeakable, it had been supplanted by the crime of lese-majesty, it was now open to be perpetrated without any guilt being incurred – as long, that is, as it was perpetrated in the service of the emperor's majesty. Or, if one prefers, one can also say that from a certain point in time, parricides par excellence are those involved in conspiracies against the Roman Emperor, also qualified as the Father of the Fatherland. The oath made to the prince comprised for everyone the obligation to prefer the prince to one's own family. These oaths notably included the commitment to pursue, without any restriction, the emperor's interior enemies as true parricides of the state. Thus, for example, we find on a mutilated Umbrian inscription, *Corpus Inscriptionum Latinarum* XI, 5998a, the oath sworn to Caligula in 37 formulated in the following way: '. . . [whoever] has plotted [against Caligula and his sisters] or has put [them] in peril, I will pursue him with arms in an unappeasable warfare, and will not cease to hate or persecute him before they have paid the penalty for their crime of parricide; and anyone who is of a hostile mind to one or the other [i.e. Caligula and his sisters], I will treat him as an implacable enemy . . .'. A new career here opens up for heteronomy, of which the ban on parricide is, in my understanding, the ultimate expression: that of the political subject. A subject shaped by an entire hierarchy of prohibitions. They functioned as sanctuaries within whose limits the inviolability of power was instituted.

In order to understand the contemporaneous stakes of such a constitution of the subject, a constitution made of prohibitions, nothing offers more help than a glance at our own time. Consider, for example, the rule inscribed with the French penal code of 1807: 'Parricide is never excusable' (art. 323), as well as its abolition by the reform of the same code in 1992. What is the meaning of this postulate and, conversely, what is the meaning of its abolition in currently valid law? How are we to interpret, to make sense of, the equivalent treatment of the murder of the father, the mother, with murder generally? And, considering that this specific qualification is henceforth obsolete, on what grounds could one possibly imagine maintaining a more severe penalty for those who have killed their father or mother? I will content myself with a few brief remarks located in the field of legal history.

Structurally, the question of the father is a political one. For a very long time, we used to encounter, in the person that

was called the father, a construction of power which far transcended the closed precinct within which familial practices
took place. The meaning of this is simple enough. It means
that, in Roman law, but no less in the medieval and even
the modern West, nourished with Roman references as they
were, the father held a position that has nothing to do with
what today we call the 'family father'. The father was much
more the elementary institutional formula through which the
absolutely irreversible relation that we call sovereignty could
be apprehended. And it is I think following this line of analysis that we must locate the – legally constructed – person
of the father, in order to approach the question of parricide
without losing any of its essentials.

Up to the end of the *Ancien Régime*, the term parricide designated two closely linked transgressions: on the one hand,
the murder of one's father or mother, and on the other hand
an attack against the king. Parricide, then, became identified
with regicide or lese-majesty. It is precisely this close connection with political interdiction/repression that confers its
strong sense upon ancient parricide and that distinguishes it,
strictly speaking, from murder properly speaking. I would
like to make a few specific points on this topic. The ancient
jurists were aware of them. This necessary detour will allow
us to understand, beyond the historical facts, what is at stake,
in our days, in the requalification of parricide as a simple
aggravated murder. The de-qualified parricide is, in my
opinion, a mere epiphenomenon. We are dealing, all in all,
only with a distant effect, and yet with one that is perfectly
intelligible in terms of an institutional logic – of the in-depth
movement toward individualism that will put, in the *longue
durée* of modern social organisation, the political form of contract in the place of a structure of authority based on the
fiction of a subject *without* absolute autonomy.

We need to start from the following clear-cut state of
fact: attacks against the sovereign are qualified indifferently as lese-majesty and as parricide. Lese-majesty refers
to parricide, and majesty, *maiestas*, literally the 'greatness
of that which is greater', refers to the father. To begin with,
lese-majesty is among the oldest Roman qualifications; it
qualifies either a damaging of greatness – *laedere maiestatem*
– or a crime intending the death of the carrier of greatness

– *crimen maiestatis*. These notions were transmitted to the Middle Ages on diverse levels: empire, states, cities. They were, above all, adopted by canon law, in order to ground the proceedings against heretics upon the representation of an assault against God's 'greater Greatness': heresy is an amputation of divine majesty. But to what exactly should the notion of 'damaging majesty' be understood as referring? It refers to the act of amputating the superiority of an instance that has no other mode of existence than its very superiority itself. The crime perpetrated against the prince does not just damage the prince in person, nor even the prince in his function. That which is 'damaged', 'lowered', or 'violated', is the 'greatness' itself, taken abstractly as such. Greatness is the very institution of eminence, of highness, cast in the mode of a comparative – a comparative, but one that is invested with the value of an absolute superlative: this thing that is 'greater' (*maior* – *maiestas*) to the point of there being nothing greater than it. The murder of the king, then, is not really a murder. It is not even an attack against the royal institution. It hits something far more vital, namely the incommensurable measure. It challenges the sanctuary of inviolability that is presented in the abstract mode of this comparative that is staged as a superlative.[9] At the same time, regicide does admit of another qualification, that of parricide, which adds to it. Everyone knows that the attacks against the French Kings, of Ravaillac in 1610, of Damiens in 1753, have been qualified as parricide. The blow that weakens the absolute and incommensurable pre-eminence under whose aegis the institution of kingship is guarded by interdictions, also kills the father. The crime of majesty and the deed of parricide are but one and the same.

At first glance, everything looks as if the qualification of parricide metaphorically and ornamentally reduplicated the crime of majesty. The parricide perpetrated against the royal majesty appears to find its raison d'être in the title of a father, conferred upon the king. The kings of France, England and Spain were indeed the fathers of their subjects. But after the fourteenth century, in France, the kings, in the manner of Roman emperors, claimed the title of a father of the fatherland, as well. In construing the motif of an awesome coat of arms that was based upon a Roman reference, and that interweaved father, majesty, fatherland and crime (see, for example, Bodin, *République* II, 5), the jurists of the French *Ancien Régime* give proof of the acute vision they had of these titles and their *arcana*.

Going further back, one discovers yet more archaic connections. These lead beyond the all-too explicitly fatherly figure of the king – an image whose metaphoric transparency makes it look somehow obvious and immediately interpretable. The name 'parricide' applies also to the traitor to the Republic, of the city or the state. In these crimes against supreme obedience we find neither father nor murder; and yet they are qualified as 'murders of the father'. In the place vacated by any real referent, there surfaces a constitutive displacement of what the jurists had traditionally called the father. What they were calling father, was the political reference in itself. On that topic, we find countless references from antiquity, all objects of abundant quotations. They were taken up, during the Middle Ages, by the glossators especially. Huguccio of Pisa, writing toward the end of the twelfth century, cites, in one of his glosses on Gratian's *Decretum* (C 7, qu. 1, c. 41) the text *In apibus princeps unus*, drawn from a letter of Gregory the Great (Pope from 590 to 604). 'The bees have only one King (note the Queen bee's masculinisation!); so, too, the fleet follows the flagship; so, too, there is only one Emperor in the world; so, too, in each province, there is only a single Governor; so, too, finally, at the moment of the foundation of Rome, as there were two brothers and only one could be king, one of them committed 'parricide' against the other.' Dealing with the word *parricidium*, the gloss is adduced as a reference. It would have been better to write *fratricidium*, notes Huguccio, because 'parricide' strictly speaking is said of one who betrays his fatherland and who kills his father. Whereas one who kills his brother cannot be called 'parricide' except if one is prepared to take it in the sense of *suum parem occidit,* in other words, that he killed his peer (*parem*), his equal. One could not more clearly underline the difference in nature between the relation to *patria* and *pater,* on the one hand, and the relation to an equal, a *par*, on the other hand, than by means of this etymological pun. Likewise, as is noted in a gloss by Andrea de Isernia (on *libri feudorum* 2, 24), we owe the republic more love than one owes one's father (*rempublicam plus quam patrem*), while one owes one's father more love than we owe our equals.[10]

Therefore, in putting to death the king, it is far more than just the father who is put to death: it is *patria* itself, the *res publica* in person, that one is killing. In order properly to understand the fabric of these correspondences, one needs to fit them into their Roman references. In the French kingdom, the king embodied the *patria* of the *regnum Francorum* in the same way as, in the empire or the church, the emperor and the pope embodied the *communis patria*, which is to say the common and universal fatherland, Rome itself. A hierarchy of bonds of affection that coincides with one of political allegiances; the summit of this hierarchy is occupied by the public sphere, embodied in the monarch. It is the prohibition of parricide, in the form in which it has been construed by the jurists, that sanctuarises the public sphere. Yet, within this inviolable sanctuary, the father is accommodated in a place that is subordinated under another, primary one, that of public sovereignty: the *respublica*, the *patria*, the king.

This institutional construction belongs to the very long term. It is Roman to start with, it unfolds in diverse forms and obviously divergent historical contexts in the political structure of the Middle Ages and modern times. The founders of public law in the *Ancien Régime* build upon it the theory of royal absolutism. It is sufficient to re-read Bodin, Le Bret, or Domat in France, Filmer in England (*Patriarcha or the Natural Power of Kings*, 1680), in order to perceive that the legal relation to the father, a relation enclosed and sanctuarised in the prohibition of parricide, already represents for them the forge that will produce political rights. For, what is at stake here is something other than simply a patriarchal representation of power. What we are dealing with, more fundamentally, is the foremost constitutive element of power. The first, the irreducible subjection, the one to which all political subjection can be traced, is the subjection under the father. The theorists of absolutism postulated in their analyses an elementary legal relation – in the same manner, all in all, as will be done by the theorists of contract. Yet, this legal relation is characterised – contrary to that which prevails in the contractual realm – by the non-reciprocity and irreversibility that governs the relationships of the subjects that it unites. At the beginning stands the bond of paternal power. It not only provides what is called a 'model' that is useful in the realm of political metaphors: it furnishes the irreducible *nucleus* of heteronomy that determines the condition of every political subject.

It is, precisely, this *nucleus* that is tackled by the early theorists of liberalism in the seventeenth century, in England in particular. They are working against the backdrop of the market and the progress of a sweeping contractualisation of social exchanges. Today, it is still this *nucleus* of elementary allegiances – which have shrunk to the level of a vaguely educative role – that is deconstructed by the nascent thought of liberalism. By liberalism, but also by the deep social transformations that have been at work for centuries, by then, owing to an organisation of the market that postulates, and constructs, a subject that is no longer based upon majesty and power. Henceforth, paternal power is no more political, than political power is paternal – see on this point the perspicacious analysis offered by Locke (*Treatise of Civil Government*, ch. 6). Hobbes, too, writes pointedly that, if there is a primordial power in nature, it is the power of the mother, with which the child is immediately confronted, more than that of the father, who is only artificially constructed. The power of fathers presupposes the state, which in turn presupposes the pattern of contract or, in other words, the absolute autonomy of the subject (*Leviathan*, II, ch. 20).

We are, at the moment in which the thought of liberalism goes through this first shape, of course still far from the modern de-qualification of parricide. Even so, it is already at this stage that we witness the appearance of the first symptoms of an anthropology that inevitably leads to this de-qualification. The role played by the father is no longer a social role. Within the irreducible structure of authority, he has been divested of his political status. Now, as we have seen, the singularity of parricide, if we hold it against the backdrop of murder, is, from an institutional point of view, connected to the primordial status given to power. And from this point of view, it is the obsolescence of political power that has led to the disappearance of the paternal singularity. If one considers this politico-juridical structure over the *longue durée*, it is plain that – power having long since lost its quality as a forge of the political bond – the murder of the father, as the murder of the mother (which from this point of view, can be assimilated to the murder of the father) should eventually also abandon their inaugural field of meaning and their standing as a major political transgression. In this way, today we must transfer the question to a totally different register: a register where the singularity of the parental function is disconnected from its ancient ties with the core of a primordial power.

One will have understood the purpose of the present modest contribution: an invitation to reflect on the prohibition of parricide and its institutional modalities, starting from its historical footholds. Historically, no doubt, today's conditions are no longer of the same type. How is heteronomy to be thought of in a world where power has been divested of its core inviolability? How is prohibition – prohibition that uses words, or more precisely, interdiction – to be thought in the absence of those constructions of majesty and sovereignty that have underpinned it throughout the Western tradition, since its Roman origins? Investigating it is a work that can only be done without a safety net. What is sure is that the forms that *forbidding* have taken so far, have little to offer, if we ask them for help in imagining its future modalities.

The best thing that we might be allowed to expect from these constructions – if, that is, we prove able to consider them with enough historical objectivity to avoid trading desires and illusions for realities, especially for the illusions of a world that would be more human than our own (an illusion largely favoured by the infantile campaigns of the minimalist, retrograde type that has defeated more articulate ideologies) – would consist in correctly distinguishing these past forms, in order precisely to learn how to do without them. That is, in posing today's questions disencumbered from yesterday's answers, armed only with our own forces, and without forgetting the dangers that have haunted, and still haunt, those who attempt to behave freely.

Notes

1. J. D. Cloud, 'Parricidium: from the lex Numae to the lex Pompeia de parricidiis', 88 *ZSS*, 1971.
2. Cf. my study *Paura dei padri, violenza dei figli*, Rome, ed. Laterza 1984, published in French in an abridged version

under the title: 'La peur des pères et la violence des fils. Images rhétoriques et normes du droit' (*Droit et Cultures,* 1985).

3. Émile Benveniste, 'Deux modèles linguistiques de la cité', Jean Pouillon, Pierre Maranda (eds.), *Mélanges Levi-Strauss,* La Haye (Mouton), vol. 1, 1970.

4. Yan Thomas, 'L'institution civile de la cité', *Le Débat,* n°74, 1993.

5. André Magdelain, *De la royauté et du droit: de Romulus à Sabinus,* Rome 1995.

6. This is overlooked when – as e.g. in the works of Blandine Barret-Kriegel – one believes that Roman law is not political. One thereby disregards, on the one hand that in Rome 'the political' – that which belongs to the organisation of the city – grows on the soil of the 'civil'; and on the other hand, that the 'political law' of the West has, in its entirety, been cast in this mould.

7. Émile Benveniste, *Le vocabulaire des institutions indo-européennes,* I, Paris 1969, pp. 270 ff.

8. Yan Thomas, 'Parricidium: le père, la famille, la cité', *Mélanges de l'Ecole française de Rome, Antiquité,* 1981; Id., 'Droit domestique et droit politique à Rome', *Mélanges de l'Ecole française de Rome, Antiquité,* 1982; Id., '*Vitae necisque potestas*: le père, la cité, la mort', in: *Du châtiment dans la cité,* Rome, 1984 [Chapter 7 in this volume].

9. On majesty and lese-majesty in the western world, I refer to work in progress in common with Jacques Chiffoleau. Among the parts already published, cf. Yan Thomas, 'L'institution de la majesté', *Revue de synthèse,* 1991, pp. 331–86; Jacques Chiffoleau, 'Sur le crime de majesté médiéval', in: *Genèse de l'Etat moderne en Méditerranée,* Rome 1983, pp. 183–213. On the crime against the Reference, see the major study by Pierre Legendre, *Le crime du caporal Lortie: Traité sur le Père,* Paris 1989.

10. Cf. also Guillaume Durandus of Mende (end of the thirteenth century), *Speculum,* IV, 3rd part, §2, n.32: 'It is lawful to kill one's father in the defence of the fatherland'; Lucas de Penna (fourteenth century), writing on *Codex iustinianus,* 10, 31, 35, n. 2.: 'For the sake of the fatherland, the son needs to take arms against his father, the father against his son, the husband against his wife, the wife against her husband'.

Nine

Act, Agent, Society: Fault and Guilt in Roman Legal Thinking

Each time we refer to responsibility it seems to us that we use a concept that goes without saying, that we are dealing with a matter of plain psychological and moral unambiguity. Its function appears as necessary, to the point that in our opinion no legal system, however elementary, could possibly do without it. The universality of the arguments it involves, presents responsibility in the light, as it were, of a natural endowment.

For legal historians, responsibility is usually a matter of presupposition. It is true that, in dealing with certain societies – those they call 'archaic' – legal historians note its 'insufficiency' and lack of 'precision'. Once the mechanism of familial solidarity has disappeared or persists only vestigially,[1] once the empirical individual is recognised as the sole cause of its misdeeds and the only passive subject of social reactions,[2] and a fortiori once the 'intentional element' of the wrongdoing appears to be taken into account in the definition of crimes,[3] there is no doubt that one is confronted by a regime of responsibility. As soon as the remnants of primitive ages have been eliminated, as soon as the repression of acts of 'collective vengeance' and its folkloric vestiges – trials against animals, punishments imposed on dead bodies, etc.[4] – have been disposed of, one is inclined to admit the clear rationality in which the cult of *homo juridicus* can establish itself. For it is this *homo juridicus* that is effectively under discussion here: the one whom article 1382 of the Civil Code burdens with all damages that result from one's culpable action. The responsible person emerges, and is welcomed, within a dialogue in which the lawyer, under the duty of turning into a historian, claims that the language one speaks – but of which one would prefer not to be the sole speaker – has already been the language of one's predecessors.

'Under the duty of turning into a historian' – this is to be read as opposed to 'out of sheer intellectual curiosity'. Indeed, historically, our legal language would not have been able to constitute itself otherwise than through the reading of texts – of those legal texts from which every new generation of exegetes has drawn its references, adding theirs to the sedimentation of all earlier glosses, giving rise to the constitution of a body of common knowledge, and, moreover, to the aggrandisement of references to written law. Glossators, post-glossators, humanists, natural lawyers, pandectists, etc., all of them do achieve improvements – if slow ones, to be sure – in re-reading already read bits of text. Mind, however, that their discourses deal less with founding legal texts than with the totality of other discourses – the discourses to which, in our legal culture, a literature that is essentially tautological and self-referential, always returns. This explains the difficulty that we find ourselves confronted with, today, as soon as we try to inquire into the categories of Roman law. The main obstacle we encounter, is located, however – paradoxically – in something we do understand: namely in those texts which, in our eyes, look like so many milestones highlighting *the distance that separates* us from those categories, or in other words, the texts *that have enabled us to leave Roman law behind*.[5] Owing to some sort of an optical illusion, we tend to gauge these fragile virtualities by the yardstick of the accomplishment we believe we have reached. There are, today, specialists who, following their penchants, claim that Roman law epitomised, in the freshness of the early days, just those modes of legal thinking that our age has brought to perfection.[6] But law's thinking accomplishes its operations in a reversible type of time – from one insignificant but consequential event to another, giving rise to a unique progress or 'organic development'. In this view, responsibility appears, as much as and more than any other notion, like an exemplary legal item, that is born, gropes for some time, adapts to the situations it finds itself exposed to, and, finally, triumphs.[7]

What we would like to suggest, quite to the contrary, is to direct all our attention at the 'groping' stage – not because we believe that there is 'something missing' in the more recent forms, even less in order to find in it the negative origin of what responsibility will be one day, but rather because, as an object, it epitomises the meaning of a legal conception – one that has never ceased to evolve since.

Invested with the glory of its *taken-for-grantedness*, responsibility appears as related to a certain mode of conceiving the relationship between the individual, its actions, and society.[8] Article 1382 of the French Civil Code, which enshrines its most direct expression, establishes, starting from the 'fact' of 'man' – in other words, the notion of an agent posited as a universal, thus as such both necessary and equal – a necessary and balanced relation between a fault that results from the subjectivity of an agent, and a compensation for damages understood as the 'price' to be paid for it, as an objective quid-pro-quo. There is no rupture or discontinuity that would separate the deed and its cost: the faults involved and their compensations (damages) are equivalent, just like the objects of an exchange.[9] The thought that underlies the Civil Code sets up, between these various levels, a relation of transparency that makes of a human being, objectified and universalised by the law, at once the agent, the site and the object of a continuous exchange.

It is precisely this transparency that is problematic. It is, in other words, this opening of the act to the agent and of the agent to the compensation that we need to question. It is first of all a question of interpreting, throughout history, the provisions put in place by the repressive or remedial organs of society, to deal with various types of harmful acts. The legal sanction applying to such acts, whether punishment or compensation, is not some technical choice, in itself indifferent: rather, we find a coexistence of factors that are economic (e.g. monetary), political (relating to the role of the courts, the distinction between private law and criminal law, etc.) and ethical (which prevent the precise legal and procedural mechanisms from being observed, as long as they are analysed in isolation from their cultural context). Yet, what we find, further upstream, is the human being as an acting entity and as a complex of psychological functions that the juridical treatment of action reveals to us in a number of different lights. On their own, the categories of intention, will, wrongdoing, do not authorise any peremptory conclusions in this respect. They are not at stake in themselves, they count only in connection to the act. At stake is, in other words, only the qualification added by their existence to the action once it has been performed. We must get beyond the simple, and inaccurate, opposition between a type of responsibility 'for fault', based upon culpable wrongdoing, and an 'objective' responsibility, which attaches consequences only to the act itself, independent of the person of the agent. There has never been a society that has observed human actions through such naïve eyes: an act is always the sign of something. It is, conversely, neither always a culpable wrongdoing, even where it is confessed, that the assessment of responsibility refers to, nor does it do so always in one and the same way. In certain cases, the notion serves only to establish a causal link between a prejudice and the action of an individual, without requiring either the idea of subjective commitment or the presence of the culprit in the act; a fortiori, it can be excluded from any relevance as to the evaluation of punishment or compensation.

In dealing with responsibility, we thus need to consider a whole network of relations: a set of connections between various authorities, with its mix of the social, psychological and moral values of its era. The topic goes far beyond the legal sphere, yet it is cast in forms and configurations that are legally determined.

That a linguistic inquiry into the names of agents and actions is considered useful is no surprise. The important conclusions reached, on this point, by the work of Jean-Pierre Vernant, by taking up, in the Greek domain, the results of Emile Benveniste's pioneering work, are not a secret. The distinction between agent-names ending with -τηρ and -τύς, matching that of the action-names ending in -τύς and -τις, divides the field of human action into two zones: an area of subjectivity, in which the agent 'is identified with its action conceived as a function that the subject accomplishes' (here the action is considered as a tension), and an area of objective fact, where the agent 'has' or 'possesses' an act – an act considered as already accomplished or 'effected' by the action, and where, as a corollary, the action is 'represented as being realised outside or independently of the subject'.[10]

What we find here in a twofold mutually complementary definition, is, on the one hand, a world of being in which functions are accomplished by passing through the subject, i.e. by realising themselves in acts; on the other hand, a world of having, i.e. of created objects and finite forms, as external results of action.[11] There exist no comparable studies for the Latin world. We must limit ourselves to pointing to features of the juridical conception of action that allow us to relate them to the registers of having, on the one hand, and, on the other hand, mostly, that of 'a thing'.

There do exist, however, a very large number of operations that can be understood as 'a thing affected by an action'. They refer to a *res* (a material object, an estate, an incorporeal thing) understood as the passive subject of some predicate that is invested with an adjectival function. Examples include: a 'thing lent on credit', meaning a loan (*res credita*); a 'business deal', meaning an agreement (*negotium contractum*); a 'thing that has been judged', meaning a judicial decision (*res iudicata*); 'things received', meaning a deposit accepted by an innkeeper as a security; deposit of animals or carriages delivered to a stable attendant; a contract for maritime transportation; a deal for arbitration entrusted upon a third party (*res receptae*, and respectively: *receptum cauponum, stabulariarum, nautarum, arbitrii*); a 'slave appropriated' (from someone else than his master), meaning an illegitimately acquired slave (*servus corruptus*); a 'thing sold and delivered', meaning sale (*res vendita* and *tradita*); a 'sum of money disbursed', meaning payment (*pecunia pensata*). Sometimes, the predicate is not mentioned. For example, in numerous sections of the Praetor's edict, the verbal adjective, which in other contexts expresses the right or the obligation of an action, is passed over in silence: 'of drains' (to fix or to unblock): *de rivis* (*reficiendis aut purgandis*); same for 'of sewers': *de cloacis*; same for 'of sources' (that may be used): *de fonte* (*utendo*); same for 'what surmounts the ground' (=and may be the object of a right to enjoyment: *de superficiebus* (*fruandis*)), etc. The thought of the Roman jurists thus proceeds by incorporating the action (whether realised or potential) into the thing. In this association, which gives rise to a legal figure (i.e. to what the jurists commonly call a *causa*), one becomes the principal, the other the qualifying accessory.

Even if the act is independent from the thing and isolated in an abstract concept, the very general use of the substantive past participle, in preference to forms derived from verbs by means of a suffix indicating action (*-io*, as in: *solutio, obligatio, novatio*, etc.), reveals an objectivist vision; the emphasis is placed on the result rather than the process, on a thing that is accomplished rather than on the operation of its accomplishment. We can consider, under this angle, starting with *gestum, actum* and *contractum*, the entire vocabulary of juridical acts and contracts: *creditum, indebitum solutum, mandatum, commodatum, depositum*, etc.

In the field of *delicta*, of offences, whose lessons are for us the most relevant, Roman legal language insists far less on the perpetration of a criminal or harmful action than on what the incriminated act represents, once it is perpetrated. *Delictum* is not quite an 'offence' in the sense in which the word is used today. It is defined by the 'lack' to which it gives rise (corresponding to the first meaning of *delinquere*),[12] or by the fact of being 'no longer in its place', owing to the fact of the culpable action. *Furtum*, which for a long time referred to the stolen thing,[13] indicates, rather than the theft itself, 'the fact that something had been stolen'.[14] With respect to offences from ancient civil law, which go back, more often than not, to the law of the XII Tables and to certain *leges* from the time of the Republic, we can cite as examples the 'broken limb', the 'broken bone', also the 'joined beam' (e.g. the fact of incorporating in one's own building, supports belonging to another person), and the 'unjustly caused damage', etc.[15] The same is true of the offences usually referred to as 'praetorian delicts', which stem from a later epoch; such as the 'thing poured or thrown' (through a window, capable of killing or injuring a passer-by); or the 'thing placed or suspended' (same damage, if the thing fell by itself); or the 'lacerated poster' (what is meant here is the *album* on which the magistrates displayed all legal means and manners of procedure that had been authorised).[16] This degree of regularity in the choice of a passive expression for crimes is certainly not an indifferent fact. The terminology reveals a vision of action which, we believe, persisted in one perfectly explicit notion: *iniuria*.

At the outset, the word *iniuria* can designate a specific offence. In the XII Tables, it covers all slight injuries inflicted upon the person of a free man, as opposed to serious injuries, which were subject to talion or pecuniary compensation.[17] The comic theatre, in its particular context, gave the term a similar application: *iniuria* most often referred to marital offences, or to offences to the honour or reputation of the spouse (adultery, inadvertent repudiation, publicly circulated suspicions, etc.).[18] However, when used in the ablative case, *iniuria* could just as well refer to a modality of action. Romanists often translate it as an adverb: 'unjustly'. The *lex Aquilia* (third century BCE), for example, established a system for the reparation of damages from certain acts committed *iniuria*, as e.g. when a slave or a domestic animal is killed or wounded, or an inanimate good burned, broken or damaged.[19] What exactly does *iniuria* mean here? Or rather, what exactly is the level of action to which the circumstance expressed in the word *'iniuria'* relates? Does it qualify an agent's conduct – or is, what it qualifies, on the contrary, rather only the result thereof? Should we translate *'occidere iniuria'* as 'to unjustly kill', or as 'to kill in the process of committing an injustice'? In one case, the judge's investigation will lead him to inquire into anything that relates to the agent – motives, in particular; in the other case, he needs to consider to what extent and in what sense the situation produced by a homicide is objectively unjust, a non-right.

In the third century CE, when the casuistic analysis of Aquilian delicts had considerably advanced, and when the notion of a fault (*culpa*) – on which more later on – enabled Roman jurists to establish a generalised compensation for damages, *iniuria* will still be defined in purely objective terms, as something that is brought about, and that goes against the law *'iniuria . . . est quod non iure fiat'*.[20] In order to fully understand the expression, one must take *ius* in its traditional meaning of 'protected status', 'sphere recognised by others', 'jurisdiction', or 'reserved zone of action'.[21] To act *iure* is to recognise (or to not fail to recognise), the part that belongs to another; to commit an act *non iure*, or *iniuria*, is to trespass into what is 'proper' to another, no matter whether in relation to the sphere of the person, to honour, etc. (cf. the *iniuria* of the XII Tables), or to the goods belonging to the owner of a house and to the powers he holds over his house. This interpretation is corroborated by the consideration that the formula *iniuria vindicare*, which implies the reference to the idea of an assault against one's estate, an usurpation of one's power, in the archaic context of the *sacramentum in rem*.

This very ancient judicial ritual pits against each other two opponents in a trial about a thing which both claim to own. Both protagonists express, one after the other, their *ius* to the same good (a slave, a clod of earth representing a field, a person subject to the power of a head of family, etc.). By pronouncing the consecrated *verba* and carrying out the symbolic gestures of mastery, each of the two creates, for his benefit, a right – throwing it in the face of his rival as a challenge.[22] It is at this point that, after the mediation of the attendant magistrate, a genuine dialogue begins between the parties:

— I demand that you tell me the grounds of your claim (*postulo anne dicas qua ex causa vindicaveris*);
— I have exercised an *ius* in imposing my claim on you (*ius feci sicut vindictam imposui*);
— As your claim has resulted in an *iniuria*, I call upon you for a stake of fifty asses (*quando tu iniuria vindicavisti, quingentis assibus sacramento te provoco*);
— And I make the same call upon you (*et ego te*);

Contrary to what has sometimes been claimed, there is no mismatch here between question and answer: if the defendant invokes – contrary to all expectations – that what he did was the exercise of a right, *ius* (*ius feci*), he does so because the plaintiff's questioning most likely does not relate to any earlier title of acquisition or possession, but refers, instead, without naming any further source, to that which founds the action itself. Difficult to grasp for the contemporary jurist, and long since considered as a mysterious *aporia*, this coincidence of judicial action (*vindicatio*), foundation (*causa*) and law (*ius*) is clarified only if we remove, from the archaic procedure, a category without which we are unable to come up with any concept of law: the category of time.[23] Thus, the correlation between '*ius feci*' (I have realised my right) and '*iniuria vindicavisti*' (you have unjustly claimed) performs its functions on the objective, exterior level of a concrete reality (for a concrete reality it is, even if it is a performed one). It thereby sheds light on the meaning of *iniuria* as well. Neither the *vindicating* party, nor the party that *counter-vindicates*, has acted unjustly by relying in bad faith upon a title that does not exist. Being a modality of the act, *iniuria* is not situated on the side of the agent or his motives, but on the side of the result of his intervention, in the situation of an absence of right that has been created. One after the other, and reciprocally, each of the litigants challenges the other's *ius*, both charging the other party that, by invading their respective domestic sphere, they have infringed the limit. This is, by the way, why *iniuria*, where proven, received the same treatment as a criminal wrongdoing: the loser had to give up the amount of money he had deposited (*sacramentum* was originally the head of a sacrificial animal) and was condemned to pay double what would have been the fruits of the thing, had it been in his possession.

Numerous *leges* from the republican era attest to the omnipresence of *iniuria*, wherever employed in this sense: an example is the stylistic clause *quot sine privatorum iniuria fiat*, which can easily be translated by the juridical cliché: 'without prejudice to the right of particulars'.[24] Here again, we are undoubtedly dealing with a modality of the outcome, far from any consideration of the agent. The same applies, save for late subjectivist interpretations, to the expression *iniuria occidere*, which, in the case of the homicide of a slave, only considered the unjust loss of property that has thus been caused to the owner of the slave.[25]

This entirely external vision of acts becomes even more striking when one considers the fact that Roman law proceeds by catalogues, enumerations, lists. The generic concept of a fault that triggers an individual's responsibility in view of the harm it causes, is unknown to Roman law. There were offences known under specific names. Apart from them, there was a legal void. It is true that the Roman jurists provided interpretations which, over time, tended to multiply the cases, giving rise to the protection of victims of an injury. However, this continuous growth of the range of damage recovery, routinely highlighted by the specialists of Roman law, fails to bring about any essential innovation: the remedies of the *jurists* continued, as they ever did, to rely on defined *topoi*. It was the names, *nomina*, that provided the possibility of an analysis based on analogy and difference, and offered, as they had done at all times, the possibility of subsuming, fittingly or less so, this or that particular case. There was a *numerus clausus* of legal acts, not unlike that of ideas in the platonic heaven. Acts, hypostatised by law, were 'typical'. But that which was 'typical' was nothing other than that which was 'objective'. The efforts of distinction, of definition, of labelling, to which the Roman jurists subjected all acts – all existing acts, meaning, only those recognised and inventoried *as* acts – based upon the hypothesis that no matter which legally relevant action was conceived as a thing that was separate, neutral, and that fitted into a catalogue.

The approach taken by modern Europe goes in quite the opposite direction. On the one hand, any case-based proceeding, any effort of constituting reality out of cases, was gradually eliminated; on the other hand, the legal sphere was increasingly invaded by the individual, to whose subjectivity the entire spectrum of relationships ended up being subjected. The two conjugated phenomena worked to dissolve the world of acts into a small number of general categories, each of which represented, from a certain vantage point, the total activity of an agent: fault; will; responsibility. In the rationalist anthropology of the eighteenth century, including that of the Civil Code, the expansion of the notion of 'man' is followed by a comparable expansion of the notion of *le fait de l'homme*, the 'fact of man' (cf. art. 1382, Civil Code). The field of fault-based liability was thereby – like that of contract, and for much the same reasons – put on a track toward a promotion that endowed it with the universality proper to the subject. The praxis of *dealing with cases qua cases*, called *'casuistique'*,* has not disappeared; however, it now only serves to illustrate – and in this sense it is no

---

* Translators' note: The obvious way of rendering French *'casuistique'* would appear to be the English 'casuistry'. The divergent semantic evolution of both terms makes of this translation a no-go. Specifically in the case of the English term it refers to a history that is both essential and fascinating. The English word 'casuistry' has, since early modern times, placed centre-stage the meanings of chicanery, deceptiveness, equivocation, delusion, fallacy, lie, excessive speciousness, evasion, sophism, sophistry, spuriousness, trick, subtlety. None of these is to be found anywhere near the semantic centrality of the French term. Most decisively, the moral reprobation expressed in them is at the opposite of the meaning intended by the author.

longer a reality but, much rather, an image – those rare universals whose function requires that they are *not subject to a definition*.

And yet, nothing authorises us to say that in classical juridical thinking, action never refers to anything apart from some 'having'. Admittedly, there is no way around the connection between the act and the agent that has carried it out, but this in no way exhausts the point at stake. What is really problematic about it is modality. Our questions must focus on the degree of commitment shown by the person who perpetrates a criminal act; on the forms that qualify his presence in the action according to judicial experience; on the significance that attaches to the duty of finding out, in the course of a civil or criminal procedure, who has committed the deed; and, most of all, on the totality of questions that refer to his person.

'Responsibility' – today, for us, this implies 'personal commitment'. Accounting for one's own actions means accepting an eventual sanction in advance; it means to project into the future the indebted person of the agent. The institution of judgment – or of the obligation of compensating the harm we have caused – is accompanied by a psychological function that is its necessary correlate: the obligation triggered by its action, the subject does not perceive it as contingent; it perceives it as the condition of its freedom. In this sense the act enters into account only insofar it is an extension of the person; to the extent, that is to which our law offers us an ethics of behaviour.

The analysis of Roman legal language reveals a different conception. The very idea of binding oneself by one's acts is foreign to a thought for which the subject is only the accessory of its action. *Noxae se obligare*, 'to bind oneself to one's act' (as opposed to: *by* one's act), implies a reverse relationship to that which defines commitment, strictly speaking. Here it is the misdeed (*noxa*) that in some sense closes on the culprit and exercises its retro-action back upon him. He is not, strictly speaking, the agent of the crime, rather he is something like its included subject. Bound, or even better: tied to his action, he is not under the duty of responding for it; rather, he is fastened to it by the law: *actione teneri* is 'to be fettered by a legal action'.

In Roman law, therefore, the key relation is not one of the agent to the act, but of the act to the agent. It is an external, synthetic relation, that excludes the psychological and moral continuity, upon which responsibility is, already etymologically, grounded. The Roman expression of obligation derives in its totality from a thought of exteriority. *Obligare* or *nectere*, before coming to signify the legal relationship of which the debtor is the passive subject, referred to the bodily shackling of a hostage or a surety. Expressions such as *rem obligare* (to provide a property as security for a debt) and *obligare caput votis* (to commit one's own person as surety for a solemn vow) assume an entirely passive conception of the thing or the committed person at stake – the obligation being understood as an external bond, a constraint imposed from the outside.[26] There is no trace of a notion that would charge the debtor's personal resolve with any relevance at all, or indicate that, rather than being personally tied, the debtor could commit himself to some action or deed instead. One can raise in this respect a misinterpretation, and a widely shared one, of the way in which Justinian's compilation defines the concept of an obligation: '*obligatio est iuris vinculum, quo necessitate adstringimur alicuius solvendae rei, secundum nostrae civitatis iura*'.[27] According to the translation of numerous specialists of Roman law, the famous phrase has the meaning: 'obligation is a legal bond, by which we are compelled to the necessity of paying a certain thing, in accordance to the laws of our city'. But if one takes into account the grammatical impossibility of making of '*necessitas*' an indirect complement of the verb '*adstringere*' – which does not admit of an indirect complement – one finds oneself confronted with the fact that the ablative case '*necessitate*' imposes a different translation: 'obligation is a legal relation by which we are restrained to pay something, in virtue of the necessity that exists according to our civil law'. In which case, the debtor is no longer the site of a necessity toward which tends his whole person, and where the obligation of paying constitutes something like the internal mark of his state. He becomes, on the contrary, the doubly passive object of two constraints both of which weigh on him from the outside: the constraint of the obligation that debt imposes on him; the constraint of *iura civitatis*, of the city's rights, which found and justify any obligation. Contrary to modern legal thought, which is a thought of freedom and of commitment, the vision of the Roman jurists is consistent with the subject's passive status, its lack of 'integrity'.

But neither should any of this prevent us from taking a closer look at the agent. He seems almost detached from his action. The necessity of imputation imposes the need to search, behind the act, the agent who has produced it. It is, banal as it might appear, a search that supposes a whole procedural technique of verifying the facts and, more fundamentally, of manipulating the mental tools supposed by a rational practice of justice. This – as Louis Gernet has shown in the Greek context[28] – is not something easily accomplished. Above all, what is needed to be established in law, is a notion of time capable of staging procedural action within a duration;[29] Plus, one needs to add to the presence of this notion of what precedes the complement of an intuition of the distance that separates words and things (the distance that discourse must cross).[30] As to the discursive trajectory destined to lead to the author of the culpable act, the best source that is available to us is rhetoric. Rhetoric codifies most categories and figures of reasoning that are at work in a trial. It is courtesy of rhetoric that a continuity is instituted between the present and the past. The idea of causality was established thanks, precisely, to the elimination of the space separating both.

I refer to judicial rhetoric, to criminal rhetoric in other words. It deals for the most part with cases belonging to the conjectural genre (*constitutio*, or *status coniecturalis*), in which that which is in question is the existence of the thing (*an sit?*): did the accused really commit the facts alleged against him? The divisions of argumentation vary from one treatise to the other; the taxonomic oppositions, likewise, often do not correspond. And yet, what we can identify beyond all these nuances are two recurring types of *topoi*: those in relation to the facts (site of the crime committed, its circumstances, its duration, etc.),[31] the others in relation to the person involved.[32] The latter warrant a closer examination. What becomes visible through them is a phenomenology of behaviour and a criminal pathology, both of which are those that are in use in our criminal courts still today. Yet these themes do not aim at doing what they do today, i.e. reveal the intimate sources of an action or the forces present in the inner world of an agent, in view of precisely circumscribing responsibility. And the purpose of psychological inquiry is neither to distinguish the degrees of fault, nor to nuance culpability, considered as uncertain anyhow. Its logic is not a logic of more or less, but one of all or nothing. The guilty man is considered, globally and from the outside, as it were, as the cause that produces an act. The function of debate reaches its goal at the point where a personal causality is established.

Moreover, it is the accuser of a crime who will invoke passion (*impulsio*) to confirm that a person is the probable culprit, whereas it is the defence lawyer who will endeavour to prove that his client was *not* under the influence of a passion: the allocation of roles and arguments is thus the opposite of the one familiar to us.[33] Premeditation (*ratiocinatio*) is used as evidence that the accused is guilty, not (as with us) that the sentence needs to be harsher.[34] It also strikes us as strange that a person's mental disorder (*affectio animi*) should be part of the same argumentative arsenal as a person's discernment and carefully studied project (*diligens et considerata faciendi aliquid aut non faciendi excogitatio*).[35] From the point of view of causality and imputation, which is that of the orators, both provide proof of the same thing. What further consolidates this account, it seems to us, is the intellectualist conception of action and decision prevailing in Rome; the vocabulary of these functions is a matter less of will than of knowledge.[36] Now, if deliberation and passion have opposite effects on the will, if they pull it towards either 'more' or 'less', weaken it or strengthen it, their effects on knowledge are always identical, and always negative. And neither is there anything paradoxical about this. One has simply to take into account that knowledge, applied to the pragmatic realm of moral and juridical activities, aims at reasonable and average ends. The *recta ratio*, which is not just a Stoic theme, implied more than just a cognitive claim about a point of knowledge: it referred to the recognition of the values shared, either by all human beings, or by the city.[37] Seen from this vantage point, 'passion' and 'underlying criminal intent' did not constitute a 'plus' or a 'minus': they draw a boundary as to what lay 'this-side-of' and what 'beyond'. And yet, both come to nothing, as neither of them succeeds in touching the middle ground, in which alone morality and law are located. Thus, any venture of distinguishing between these apparently contrary circumstances appears as marred by irrelevance, with respect both to ethics and to proof.

Notwithstanding this, the person guilty of a wrongdoing exceeds the sphere of motives and impulses that the orators locate under the rubric *causa*.[38] Add to this arguments drawn from *proper name* (e.g. the fact that one culprit *Caldus*, whose name thus means 'hot', does not carry his name by coincidence, given his fiery and violent nature); from wealth or fortune (that someone is rich or poor, free or a slave, well known or obscure, independent or under the power of a master, etc.); from luck (*felix/infelix*: that the gods have shown their favour to the person, or less so); from nature (sex, age and moral qualities and defects, place or region of birth, kinship); from acquired qualities (physical skills, knowledge etc.); from usual occupations (*studium*); from earlier deeds done (*facta*), or facts that have happened to the person (*casus*); speeches that they have delivered (*orationes*).[39] This is a surprising list, if looked at through contemporary eyes. The interior mixes with the exterior, the contingent with the necessary, the permanent with the fortuitous, nature with nurture, the individual with the social. No inner structure or psychological unity of the agent emerges from criteria such as these. The logic here is one of contiguity: the *persona* is an inventory of so many adventitious elements, through which, starting from one, adding the next, be it a name, a family, a city, a story, will, in the end, take shape. The individual is not defined as a separate being.

In such a perspective, the crime committed will never be the manifestation of an agent considered as an autonomous centre of decision making; it cannot be a sign that secretly refers to a psychic entity invested with the status of the ultimate seat of all meaning. Attached to its author as to its cause, the act entertains with the person a dual relationship: in one sense, the act is added to its other acts, its previous *facta*, and constitutes the person along with them; in another sense, it is the confirmation of a totality of facts, behaviours, words, which are unique to an individual: the individual to whom we must attribute it. The decisive proof that the accused had committed the crime is that it cannot be imputed to any other: the crime designates the culprit.[40]

Apart from these conjectural questions, where the imputation of a crime to its author is the only issue, there exist the questions designated 'of quality' – about the person's *status qualitatis*. The debate here centres on justifying an action that as such is already recognised. One ventures to prove – or, on the contrary, refute – that the accused had a good reason to act the way he did. Now, the most significant of these causes were to be found in what Cicero calls the *pars assumptiva*. The argument is here external, insofar as it draws on (*assumere*) elements that are extrinsic to the agent.[41] Thus, comparison (*comparatio*) consisted in comparing the advantages of committing an act with those that would have resulted from not committing it: accused of lese-majesty for having abandoned the equipment of his troops, arms and all, to the enemy, a defeated Roman general pleads that to refuse to negotiate would have led to the loss of his men.[42] This transfer (*criminis translatio* or *relatio*) shifts the reason for acting (*ratio facti*) to another individual than the author of the criminal deed at stake in the controversy: thus, Horace vindicates the murder of his sister, invoking the patriotic and familial treason of which she had been found guilty; Orestes justifies his matricide by invoking the assassination of Agamemnon.[43] This is not really about the motive of the deed: there is, for example, no question of some inner state 'explaining' an outward action, such as 'legitimate anger'; nor, for example, does provocation make any relevant difference. Arguments address the crime as such, rather than the measure of the subject's responsibility. The only culprit was the one '*in quem crimen transfertur*', i.e. the crime as such, *en bloc*, was transferred from one agent to another.[44] The same is true of the 'rejection' (*remotio criminis*), a related proceeding which applies to cases where the deed is presented as merely the execution of a higher order or the result of an operation of force majeure:[45] the accused, in this case, limits himself to revealing that the deed he has accomplished has been beyond his power or attributions.[46] In no case is there question of a justification drawn from anything like a motive present within the individual agent that would potentially mitigate one's responsibility from the inside. Neither the will to commit a crime, nor the conscience of committing a crime are decisive factors. The subjective viewpoint, as is present, for instance, in the theory of extenuating circumstances, is absent from all and any of these figures of argumentation. The prevalence of the *spatial* dimension in them (cf. *comparatio, relatio, remotio . . .*) shows that we are dealing with a *topical* ordering of acts, and acts alone.

One category reveals itself as problematic throughout this whole region: that of the fault, *culpa*. What is *culpa*? Even at this level, we need to be wary to keep clear of a subjectivist interpretation. It has succeeded in definitively imposing itself only through a Christian reinterpretation of the texts, one that was inspired by the notion of sin. This being said, it would be an exaggeration to claim that judicial experience has not represented a decisive step towards the constitution of 'subjective' being. At the forefront of the stage of Roman citizenry, of civic life – at the forefront, in other words, of reflections on law and morals – one finds the much-debated issue of a person's agreement with the wrongdoing they commit. What one sees dissected by the *accusatores* and the *defensores*, under the gaze of the jury, is just as much a man as it is a crime. We have already encountered this in view of arguments *a persona*. What criminal law demands, however, is the intelligence of what is at stake and nothing more. That it makes of the necessity of being conscious of the act a constitutive element of certain public offences goes back to times as early as those of archaic law.[47] It is in reference to those same criteria that one needs to understand the ways in which the orators treat the problem of ignorance.[48] It is not without importance to note that the moral requirement that the author of a crime was lucid enough to grasp what he was doing, applied initially, and for a very long time, to such offences that escaped treatment based upon reciprocity (e.g. the law of talion, pecuniary compensation, monetary penalty) and thus, concerned exclusively punishment meted out by the political powers.

Yet it is precisely not this intellectual dimension of the act that constitutes *culpa*, guilt, in Roman judicial rhetoric. Instead, what is *culpa* is the act itself. *Culpa* is synonymous with *peccatum*, which meant 'guilty act',[49] or with *maleficium*, which denoted the misdeed as such.[50] Its most frequent uses are connected to *relatio criminis* or *remotio criminis*: *culpa* served here to refer to another person's action, i.e. to the claim of the accused party not to be considered as accountable. It served to find a cause why this is so.[51] *Culpa* – this is here nothing other than a *causa peccati* foreign to the accused, a guilty act transferred onto a person (conferred *in hominem*) or a thing (*in rem*), as e.g. in the case of *force majeure*.[52] But *culpa* also intervenes in cases where the accused claimed to have acted out of ignorance: here, one must distinguish between acting out of an accidental ignorance (*casu*) and an ignorance that could have been avoided (*culpa*).[53] Note that in all of these cases, the fault appears to be linked to a problem of causality. *Culpa* indicates another person's action, of which the accused's act is the result or the consequence. It is there to indicate that, where it is not the result of an accident, the act is the accused's own act. A fault, in Roman law, is thus an act the author of which is its sole cause. Once again, a purely external relation of which the agent's subjective dispositions have once again, or so it seems, been excluded.

The same applies to the case when the notion of fault is mobilised to determine the fallout of a person's behaviour on the occurrence of a damage. As we know, it is in civil law that the notion of *culpa* finds its most important application, most specifically in the interpretation of the formula *damnum iniuria datum*.[54] I shall limit myself to two brief remarks. First, the use of the formula is admitted, if only at a relatively late date, only in the rare cases in which the causal role of the agent seems problematic. This is why the action of the *lex Aquilia* is, according to Ulpian, as inapplicable to the infant (*infans*) and the insane (*furiosus*), as it is to an animal: one cannot attribute *culpa* to one who is not master of their own mind.[55] Note that this is a rather original genealogy. The Emperor Marcus Aurelius, as well as the jurist Modestinus, invoked purely humanitarian considerations: the insane, no matter what has been their crime, are sufficiently punished by their madness (*cum satis furore ipso puniatur*).[56] We find here the archaic view according to which *furor* is a blindness inflicted by the gods, which constitutes a punishment in itself – one which men had no business to interfere with.[57] The casuist approach of Aquilian crime also provides numerous examples in which the *culpa* refers to the action of another person, or to that of the victim himself, where in other words it allows the criterion of accountability to be shifted: an eye that is punctured during a brawl in which the victim took part;[58] a throat that is sliced by the razor of a barber having his shop near a play-ground and whose hand had been struck by a ball;[59] branches that were cut and that, in falling, killed a passer-by, in a location where pruning work had been announced,[60] etc.

On the other hand, it needs to be stressed that, even apart from these narrow limitations, *culpa* is never considered as a subjective matter. There is, from the viewpoint it offers, no access to a intra-personal differentiation; rather, the agent is defined overall, in counter-distinction to that which happens merely accidentally: *'casu magis quam culpa videtur factum'*.[61] Fault is considered in all cases where an action turns out to be, undeniably, the cause of the damage. The assessment of causality is grounded in the purely objective criterion of 'normal activity', or in other words, of what we would expect from an attentive man (*diligens*): *'culpam autem esse, quod cum diligente provideri poterit, non esset provisum'*.[62] The notion of *diligentia*, which connotes correctness, propriety and normality, refers us to a moral and juridical conception of action that has its centre in a vigilant adherence to social models, rather than in the supposition of the autonomy of a will conceived as infinitely free.[63]

The various acts here considered involve law/right in various respects. In Rome, most offences are private offences. Until the second century BCE, public criminal law is limited to certain crimes that directly affect the city (as is treason, *perduellio*), or are related to the ancient idea of defilement (as with parricide, whose repression would eventually expand to include the murder of any free man). The punishment pronounced by criminal juries most often consists in an act of cleansing. Looking at atrocious rites, such as the *arbor infelix* (gallows), the *poena cullei* (where the parricide is thrown into the river Tiber tied in a sack together with a dog, a snake, and a rooster), or the consecration to Ceres (hanging from a tree), one perceives how the repellent mechanism of *sacertas*, which functioned in pre-civic Roman ages within the narrower framework of families and *gentes*, had been widened to the whole city.[64] For the most part though, and until the development, at a much later date, of specialised juries (*quaestiones*),[65] crimes continue to be subject to a prosecution in which both the initiative and the benefit are matters that concern the victim alone. A whole section of our criminal law, including theft and various types of physical and moral violence exercised against a person, is dealt with under the heading of *delicta,* in one go with what today is called civil responsibility.[66]

It would be interesting to have a closer look into the massive presence of legal efforts focusing on punishment in the world of the classical city – as long, that is, as one manages to avoid the evolutionary patterns that have become traditional. To start with, punishment is, more often than not, located outside the range of action of the state's repressive authorities. The task of regulating violence in all its forms was discharged through a mechanism of reciprocity (either the principle of *lex talionis* or pecuniary penalties) and of exchange (reparation, compensation). To understand this mechanism, one has to keep in mind that it is part of a compassing system of exchange between equals, i.e. 'co-citizens'. In turn, the study of criminal law can do justice to its object only if it includes an analysis of all the other services involving non-reversible relationships between hierarchically ordered actors – as in the case of punishment. This analysis is as indispensable as it is insufficient to suppose, as many legal historians do, the presence of the state as if it were an invariant whose presence is to be taken for granted once and for all. From the evolutionist perspective – which incidentally carries the hallmark of myth rather than of history – the passage from 'private vengeance' to punishment corresponds to the passage from societies without states (generally understood as anarchic and violent, although this is contradicted by ethnographic evidence) to state societies regulated by law. But these evolutionist concepts are themselves pure legal forms, i.e. fictions that screen, behind the hollow notion of the state, the infinitely more complex historical reality that is at the origin of criminal law. The regulatory phenomenon appears with the emergence of a political centre whose essential function lies in the absorption and redistribution of a surplus, just as it has been observed for ancient Mesopotamia, for Cretan and Mycenaean palatial civilisations.[67] A more acceptable hypothesis is to claim that criminal law is born at the same time as and together with all the other functions that arise from the emerging of a unique centre of redistribution and regulation: together with taxation (though not with archaic forms of membership contributions or fees, nor with the equal participation of 'fruits' commonly raked in); with conscription; with the distribution of land and food (which has nothing to do with the sharing of a booty or with the benefits emerging in the context of a patron-client-relation), etc. The mechanism of the 'distribution' of punishments should be reinterpreted by bringing it within the compass of levies and benefits. The progress of each of these various systems derived structurally from one identical cause, namely the presence of a centre, autonomous and permanent, around which relations of power came to be organised. From this perspective, the extension of the sphere of private offences should not be placed on the line of an evolution that leads from societies without a state towards state societies. Rather, this extension should be seen as a feature peculiar to the world of the city, a world in which the relations between free men were not covered by legal and judicial organisation, but rather, at best, *mediated* by it. In Rome, justice dispensed in the name of the collective starts only late – with the crisis of the Republic – and imposes itself, only slowly, under the imperial state.

As I shall deal separately with the sociological interpretation of the Roman modes of regulating violence, I limit myself here to a brief overview of the legal sanctions accompanying private offences, where they can clarify the ancient conception of the act, as already outlined.

In this field, as in most, Roman law, considering the depth of the evolution between the XII Tables and the compilations of Justinian, presents an extremely difficult case for whoever tries to achieve results which do not involve vast layers of relativity. Only one feature remains constant: the fact of committing a *delictum* gives rise to an obligation to pay its victim a *poena*.

Mind however that this *poena* is not exactly a reparation. It is originally only a voluntary compensation, the price paid to the victim for their withdrawal from the pursuit of retribution. The culprit is thus able to escape reprisal.[68] From very early on, the law – and later, the *praetor*'s edict – comes to specify the amount to be paid in these private penalties, fixed in silver or evaluated as a multiple of the thing (e.g. in case of theft, or when a sale of land was consented under duress). Yet, slowly, and always imperfectly, *poena* starts to assume the function of a reparation. With the use of money, monetary estimation tends to replace the loss sustained with a value, a *res*. When the *Lex Aquilia* determines the amount of a *poena* as *quanti ea res est* (as the amount of money equivalent to the thing's worth), what we are dealing with is clearly not a true assessment of damages, but an approximation that can result, depending on the case, in a victim's enrichment, as well as in their impoverishment.[69] What is certain, on the other hand, is that the circulation of money and the emergence, in certain sectors, of a genuine market economy – notably that of the slave trade – made it possible both to specify the exact value of a *res* and to integrate this trade, based upon juridical assessment (thus 'negative') within the general circuit of exchange. The notion of an incorporeal thing (*res incorporalis*), directly related to that of value, was probably born on the legal terrain where the estimation of *quanti in res est*/what the thing is worth constituted the key task of the arbitrator or the *iudex*.[70] In the same way, in matters of *iniuria* (in the sense of violence against a person) as well, talion and fixed penalties will come to be replaced, at a historical juncture difficult to gauge, by an *actio* based upon an estimate allowed by the *praetor*, and subject to be decided upon by the tribunal of *recuperatores*. The magistrate would then draft an *actio* formula containing an *aestimatio* that the judge cannot exceed.[71] Once again, this was not really compensation: the victim would in fact give an *aestimatio* from which the judge would generally not deviate, least of all in dealing with a matter of *iniuria atrox*.[72] To establish the amount of the penalty was somehow allowed to be measured by the victim's resentment. This mechanism is infinitely more flexible than the old system of talion or legal compensation; yet, above all, it reveals the process by which delicts were subjected to monetarisation – a process that cannot be traced further back than to the second century BCE.

That this is an ongoing evolution, and one that is still not completed by the time of Justinian, is sufficiently proven by the classical distinction between criminal actions and actions for the recovery of a specific thing ('reipersecutory actions').[73] The Romans perfectly felt the distance that separated the pursuit of a *poena* from the pursuit of a value reduced to its monetary translation, *res*. The latter category included all contractual actions aiming at obtaining a price, a thing, or a service. In contrast, we find delictual actions, which, beyond the issue of *poena*, were looking at moral satisfaction.

When one considers the Roman system of *delicta* in its totality, one sees that it is grounded in two interpretative models.

The first model corresponds to what was imperfectly called 'objective responsibility' by the jurists. The legal system provides a uniform answer to a specifically defined type of act. In such a system, the agent completely vanishes behind the act. Correlatively, the victim does not obtain a remedy that is proportional to the damage they suffered, but a satisfaction that is equivalent to the social value that has been violated by the action that has led to the damage. In the procedure to which the culpable action gives rise, the primary role does not fall to the actors, to the author and the victim of the offence, or to the debtor and creditor of the penalty, but rather to the act: the normative order responds to a *delictum* directly with a *poena*. What is remarkable and paradoxical about this type of regulation, is that political power hardly ever takes any practical role in it at all. Whatever happens, happens in the context of an exchange between citizens. Those who are the partners in this process, albeit excluded from judging the act and the penalty, are nonetheless the only poles of the interaction dealing with the punishment. The state remains absent, except where it is subject to judicial mediation: it neither brings the action, nor does it benefit from the condemnation. Moreover, the legal mechanism obeys one single principle: that of reciprocity. In the same way in which goods are in circulation, and the way in which this peaceful circularity does not spring from economic rationality alone, but brings into play, given its location in ancient economies, such other levels as religion and family, we can say that there is a negative circulation of offences and penalties, and that this penal exchange conforms not only to the simple and rational law of substitution or compensation, but involves several further factors, which such an elementary equilibrium cannot satisfy, and some of which are related to the idea of a transgressed social value.

A second model exists, although it has never reached the point of completion. According to this model, the crime is not merely an act, but also the manifestation of a person. *Culpa* here supposes, if only to a modest point, a more intimate presence of the agent. Correlatively, the victim is no longer considered just in their social role as value embodied, but in their individual situation as a harmed person. What the victim is pursuing is less and less a punishment, more and more a compensation. The principle of reciprocity is refining itself and ends up limiting itself at the level of an exact substitution. And by the way, this penal exchange evolved simultaneously with the trade of goods. Just as contracts, in losing their formal character, as linked to domestic and religious prescriptions, ended up being reduced to pure economic operations, in the same way crimes appear, in a money-based economy, under the aspect of a patrimonial imbalance that must be deciphered and repaired.

This evolution finds its complement in the progressive expansion of the sphere of public criminal law. Since the second century BCE, the number of crimes publicly prosecuted and tried by specialised criminal courts is on the increase. Punishment moves out of the realm of reciprocity and private exchange and tends to serve as a retribution. The distribution of sanctions becomes a matter of the jurisdictional organs of the city, who follow their hierarchy. It is in the field of *iniuriae* that this development becomes most clearly apparent. Indeed, it is here that we see the state taking over what has hitherto been a role taken by individuals: after Sylla's *lex Cornelia de iniuriis*, one encounters more and more criminal proceedings in response to acts of physical violence and personal injury.[74] There are good reasons to assume that the increase in the publicisation of this type of *delicta* follows closely upon the emerging of a monetary appraisal of corporeal damages, which is to say of an estimation of *iniuriae* delivered by the *praetor*. Concomitantly with the trivialisation of delictual acts that resulted from the fact of handling them by way of estimating their monetary equivalent, Roman society searched and found help in the function of vindication, of vengeance, as legal punishment offered it. Imperceptibly, out of what constituted the law's irreducibly *affective* core, we see a state monopoly evolve.[75]

* * *

There is, however, one thing that these evolutions do not do: they do not give rise to any form of logical necessity. There is not a single point in its history at which Roman society conceived of the notion of a universal agent, of the notion of an abstract being responsible for their acts and accountable for their faults as a matter of principle. The fact is that the universality of the subject, though effectively emerging upon juridical premises, is, in modern Europe, the formal expression of the universality of the market economy: the legal subject is the juridical form of the economic agent; as such, in effect, it is naturally free to contract infinite relations, though it is under the natural duty of being liable for all damages it causes. The reduction of things to values that can be realised in exchange, and the reduction of persons to inter-exchangeable subjects, gives rise, by necessity, to a universal vision of man. It is from these grounds, both economic and philosophical, that emerges the modern notion of responsibility, plus its historical complement: the state as exclusive holder of the penal function.

The conditions that correspond to this notion cannot, obviously, be found in Rome (or any other ancient society); in particular the universe of urban Rome only knows of singular, exactly circumscribed relations. The citizen has, a priori, not a 'juridical capacity,' but a *status*. He is not the holder of subjective rights inherent in the individual; he only possesses goods that are occasionally the focus of a legal interest. One does not freely enter into any desired relations: one remains subject to a limited number of 'typical' contracts. There is no single action one is liable to respond to, as a matter of principle; yet, there exists a list of precisely defined acts for which one would have to pay a *poena*. These acts can never be reduced to the generic notions of fault or damage. The law does not acknowledge, in advance, a leeway to do or not to do something, or indeed an obligation to repair a harmful action against another. The human person and its acts are not separable from the specific definition that they receive from society. These concepts, in the universal form that they will assume later on in history, remain foreign to the world of law.

Notes

1. Paul Collinet, 'Les vestiges de la solidarité familiale dans le droit romain', in: *Mélanges Gustave Glotz*, Paris (PUF) 1932, pp. 249 ff.; Fernand de Visscher, *Le régime romain de la noxalité*, Bruxelles (A. de Visscher) 1947.
2. F. de Visscher, op. cit.; Arlette Lebigre, *Quelques aspects de la responsabilité pénale en droit romain classique*, Paris (PUF) 1967.
3. Bernard Perrin, 'Le caractère subjectif de la répression pénale dans les XII Tables', *Revue historique de droit français et étranger*, 1951, pp. 383 ff.
4. On the responsibility of animals, see A. Lebigre, op. cit., pp. 18 ff.; on the responsibility of the dead, see E. Volterra, 'I processi penali contro i defunti in diritto romano, *Rivista Internazionale di Diritto Romano ed Antico*, 3 (1949), pp. 405 ff.; Id., 'Sulla confisca dei beni dei suicidi', *Rivista di Storia del Diritto Romano*, VI,3, Bologna, 1933.
5. On this history of successive reinterpretations, see Riccardo Orestano, *Introduzione allo studio storico del diritto romano*, Turino, 1971.
6. For insightful metaphors in this connection, see the works of Emilio Betti and Biondo Biondi listed in B. Biondi, *Scritti giuridici*, Milano (Giuffrè) 1965.
7. 'Despite occasional fumbling, the notion of responsibility has not ceased to assert and refine itself throughout the Republic and the Principate, although some archaisms do resist and remain powerfully in place, and although even if some difficulties of adaptation can be observed . . .' (Jean Imbert, 'Foreword', in A. Lebigre, op. cit.).
8. Jean Gaudemet, 'Le problème de la responsabilité pénale dans l'antiquité', in *Studi in onore di Emilio Betti* (1962), pp. 483 ff.
9. It is clear that the amount of the damages determines that of the compensation. But that which counts, from an anthropological viewpoint, is the fact that it is the fault that qualifies this relation. The fault plays, in matters of *delicta* or *quasi-delicta*, the same role as the will does in matters of contract. The individual, understood as free essence, supposedly 'monetises' all forms of freedom in goods and in values.
10. Émile Benveniste, *Noms d'action et noms d'agent en indo-européen*, Paris (Adrien-Maisonneuve) 1948; Jean-Pierre Vernant, 'notice', in *Annuaire de l'Ecole Pratique des Hautes Etudes, V^e section*, 1971–2, pp. 259 ff.; about the categories applying

to work and technical functions, id., *Mythe et pensée chez les Grecs*, Paris (Maspero), 1972, vol. 2, pp. 5 ff.

11. It would be interesting to revisit the study of the Latin moralists on the basis of these hypotheses. The world described by Cicero's *De officiis* is essentially a world of acts, of social behaviours that are rather *types* of behaviour, and are thus considered in an 'objective' way.

12. See Festus, p. 64, '*Delinquere ist praetermittere, quod non oportet praeteriri; hinc delinquere et delicta*'. (Also, *deliquum*, in Plautus (cas. 207), carries the meaning *minus*.)

13. Paul Huvelin, *Etudes sur le furtum dans le très ancien droit romain, I. Les sources*, Lyon and Paris, 1915, pp. 487 ff.

14. Even if it imposed itself only late, the notion of theft used as referring to an action has been present since the XII Tables (VIII, 12 and XII, 2). See generally Lelio Lantella, *Il lavore sistematico nel discorso giuridico romano*, Turino, 1976, pp. 41 ff.

15. Respectively: *membrum ruptum, os fractum, tignum iunctum* (=decemviral delicts), *damnum iniuria datum* (*lex Aquilia*).

16. *Effusum et deiectum, positum et suspensum, album corruptum.*

17. XII Tables, VIII, 3. Gaius, III, 320 f.

18. E.g. Plautus, *Aul.*, 794; *Cist.*, 180; *Cas.*, 948. Terentius, *Eun.*, 49; *Hecy.*, 165, 401.

19. Gaius, III, 210 f., to be completed with Ulpianus, *D.* 9, 2, 27, 5 (on *iniuria*, where damages are inflicted upon things).

20. Ulpianus, *D.* 47.10.1 pr.

21. Georges Dumézil, 'A propos du latin *ius*', in id. *Idées Romaines*, Paris 1969, pp. 41 ff.

22. Gaius, IV, 6: '*qui vindicabat, festucam tenebat; deinde ipsam rem apprehendebat, velut hominem, et dicebat: hunc ego hominem ex iure quiritium meum esse aio. Secundum suam causam, sicut dixi, ecce tibi, vindictam imposui, et simul homini vindictam imponebat; adversarius eadem similiter dicebat et faciebat.*'

23. Louis Gernet, 'Le temps dans les formes archaïques du droit', in id., *Anthropologie de la Grèce antique*, Paris 1976, pp. 261 ff.

24. Most of the relevant contexts are part of the sphere of public industries, in the charge of urban magistrates. Cf. *Lex coloniae Genetivae iuliae*, ch. LXXVII (*quod eius sine iniuria privatorum fiat*). Lex Tarentina, 39f. (*quod eius sine iniuria fiat*). Senatus Consultum de rivis specibus (Frontinus, *De aqueductu urbis Romae*, 125): *Per agros privatorum sine iniuria eorum itinera actus paterent darentur.*

25. The concept of *iniuria* is thus connected to the interdiction *neminem laedere*, through which Ulpianus defines the

ius (*D.* 1.10.1). The uses of *iniuria* as subjective modality on a person's behaviour are rare in the legal context. Sandro Schipani, *Responsabilita 'ex lege Aquilia'. Criteri di imputazione e problema della 'culpa'*, does not succeed in proving the opposite: in particular, his interpretation of *iniuria vindicare* remains unsatisfactory.

26. François Dumont, 'Obligatio', *Mélanges Philippe Meylan*, Lausanne 1963, I, pp. 77 ff.
27. Justinian, *Institutes*, 3,13, pr.
28. Louis Gernet, 'Droit et pré-droit en Grèce ancienne', *Anthropologie* . . . (op. cit.), pp. 217 ff.
29. Louis Gernet, 'Le temps', op. cit.
30. Cf. my lecture at the Centre de philosophie du droit (1977), 'Rationalité du discours et nature des choses dans la jurisprudence romaine' (Cf. also, Yan Thomas, Le *droit entre les mots et les choses* (Chapter 4 in the present collection)).
31. Cicero, *De inventione*, II, 38 ff. We find the same type of charts in the theory of indices (*signa*) developed by the *Rhetoric to Herennius*, II, 6 ff.
32. Cf. *De inventione*, II, 17. Quintilian, *Institutiones oratoriae*, V, 10, 23f. It is remarkable that Cicero and Quintilian – both following Hermagoras of Temnos, the model of Latin orators from the second century BCE onwards – distinguish from the person anything that refers to mobiles (*causa*). Which means that they stop short from recognising, in the psychological infrastructures of action, a decisive component of the person.
33. Cf. *Rhetoric to Herennius*, II, 3,4; Cicero, *De inventione*, II, 19, 25.
34. Cf. *De inventione*, II, 18; 20; 22.
35. *De inventione*, ibid.
36. The point would need clarification by a specific study, but prima facie legal and rhetorical sources convincingly argue in favour of a predominance of intellectualist vocabulary (*scire, discernere, intellegere, mens, animus, sciens, sciens prudensque*, etc.) over that of the will (*voluntas*). In addition, the category of the will has no standing in the psychology of the times. Generally, in Cicero as well as in Seneca, it is defined as an interiority, some kind of autarchic movement of the agent, as opposed to an action that follows external constraints. Accordingly, the instinct of animals belongs to *voluntas*. (Cf. Seneca, *Epistles*, 36, 8; 82, 15; 121, 24).
37. Cicero's *De officiis* as well as his *De finibus* both argue integrally in this sense.

38. Cf. Quintilian, V, 10, 29.
39. Cicero, *De inventione*, II, 28f.; Quintilian, V, 10, 23 f. The latter adds further external criteria (*natio, patria, educatio, disciplina,* etc.) and formulates poignantly that passion is an element that is foreign to the person, as it only remains a temporary movement of the soul (*temporarium animi motum*).
40. *De inventione*, II, 24; *Rhetorica ad Herennium*, II, 5 (*conlatio*).
41. *De inventione*, II, 69; Quintilian, VII, 4, 7: *genus . . . in quo factum per se improbabile adsumptis extrinsecus auxiliis tuemur.*
42. *De inventione*, II, 72; for other examples, *Rhetorica ad Herennium*, II, 21.
43. *De inventione*, II, 78 f.; Quintilian, III, 11, 11.
44. *De inventione*, II, 80.
45. *Rhetorica ad Herennium*, II, 23; *De inventione*, II, 87 f.
46. *De inventione*, II, 92: *In hoc autem non accusare alterum nec culpam in alium transferre debet, sed demonstrare eam rem nihil ad se nec ad potestatem neque ad officium suum pertinuisse aut pertinere* (In this type of case, the accused ought not to accuse another and transfer his own guilt to him, but to demonstrate that the deed was or is neither part of his powers nor of his duties).
47. Cf. *Leges regiae*, Numa 16 (Festus, v° *Parricidi*): *Si quis hominem liberum dolo sciens mortui duit parricidas esto* (cf. Servius, *In Vergilii Ecl.*, 4, 43). XII Tables, 8, 24: *Si telum manum fugit magis quam iecit . . .* The formula *dolo sciens*, which obviously has its origins in early times, can be found in epigraphic laws from the republican period, such as the Latin law of Bantia, or the *lex Acilia repetundarum* (cf. Riccobono, *Fontes Iuris Romani Antiqui*, I, 82, 90). The so-called 'intentional' element of the wrongdoing has nonetheless been exaggerated, especially by Bernard Perrin, op. cit. (cf. note 4), and Arlette Lebigre, op. cit. (cf. note 3). To take but one example, the *malum carmen*, a recitation of magical *formulae*, does not contain any trace of an intent to commit a *delictum*, even if 'the distinction between good magic and evil magic existed at this point' (Lebigre, op. cit., p. 57); this distinction existed everywhere and at all times, and the criterion of the distinction is obviously only formal, being a matter of the *formula* that happens to be chosen in each case.
48. The argument of ignorance comes up when the accused, without taking the defence of the act they have committed, denies his *voluntas* or, in other words (cf. *supra*, note 36), denies that his act was spontaneous or free: They will refer, in this case, alongside accident (*casus*) and 'force majeure'

(*necessitudo*), to his own *imprudentia* (*cum scisse aliquid is qui arguitur negatur*). Cf. *De inventione*, II, 95; *Rhetorica ad Herennium*, II, 24.

49. Cf. *De inventione*, II, 78.

50. Cf. *De inventione*, II, 82.

51. Cf. *De inventione*, II, 88; 90; 92.

52. *Rhetorica ad Herennium*, II, 26.

53. *Rhetorica ad Herennium*, II, 24.

54. This is a question that has frequently been discussed. See especially Wolfgang Kunkel, 'Exegetische Studien zur aquilischen Haftung', *Zeitschrift der Savigny-Stiftung für Rechtsgeschichte*, 49, 1929, and Sandro Schipani, Responsabilità 'ex lege Aquilia', *Criteri di imputazione e problema della 'culpa'*, op. cit.

55. Pegasus-Ulpianus, *D.* 9.2.5.2: *quae enim in eo culpa sit, cum suae mentis non sit?*

56. Marcus Aurelius, rescript quoted by Macer, *D.* 1.18.14; Modestinus, *D.* 48.9.9.

57. Cf. Louis Gernet, *Recherches sur le développement de la pensée juridique et morale en Grèce*, Paris 1917, 313 f.

58. Alfenus, *D.* 9.2.52.1.

59. Ulpianus, *D.* 9.2.11 pr.

60. Paulus, *D.* 9.2.31.

61. *D.* 9.2.53.4.

62. *D.* 9.2.31.

63. *Diligentia* is a decisive term of the *action*-vocabulary. It always supposes a pre-constituted object, with which the subject is endowed from outwards. Military activity (example: Caesar, *Bellum Gallicum*, I, 40, 4; VII, 4, 9; *Bellum civile* I, 31, 11); judicial activity of an attorney (example: Cicero, *Pro Caelio*, 70; id., *Orationes in Verrem* II, 1, 15; Brutus, 237); electoral activity; Quintus Tullius Cicero, *Commentariolum petitionis ad M. fratrem*, 16; 24; 33); activity within relations between client and patron (Cicero, *Pro Cluentio*, 188; *Orationes in Verrem* II, 2, 179). All these 'activities', being heavily socialised, are regulated by strict rules. The *'diligentia'* is nothing other than the fact of observing these rules, and showing this in one's actions.

64. The *sacratio* of those guilty of having laid hands on their parents (cf. the *lex* of Servius Tullius, V. *plorare*); the *sacratio* of the patron who has failed in his obligations of *fides* in relation to his client (Plutarch, *Romulus*, 13; Tab. 8, 21); the *sacratio* of him who has removed or displaced the limitations of a field (*lex* of Numa, Dionysius of Halicarnassus, Festus L.,

p. 506). Doubtless, the formula *paricidas esto* also needs to be understood as a *consecratio* of the culpable. See on this Louis Gernet, 'Paricidas', *Revue de Philologie*, t. 63, 1937, pp. 13 ff., and generally, on the rules of banishment in archaic laws, id., *Anthropologie*, op. cit., pp. 288 ff., pp. 302 ff.

65. These commissions charged with public inquiries have been put together, for the largest part, during the end of the Republic, from the times of the Gracchi brothers onwards. For an overview, see Erich S. Gruen, *Roman politics and the criminal courts*, 1962.

66. Delicts are defined as all of those deeds causing damage according to civil or praetorian law: *damnum iniuria, pauperies* (=damage caused by animals), *effusum and deiectum, positum et suspensum.*

67. Concerning the problems related to the 'birth of the state', the only coherent explanations are, to date, those of economic anthropology. Historians of institutions have much to learn, for example, from M. Sahlins (*Tribesmen*, Prentice Hall, 1968), and from the works of K. Polanyi (NY, Farrar & Rinehart, 1944).

68. In the XII Tables, *poena* is subject to a gradation of tariffs (e.g. 8, 3: *os fractum*; 8, 4, *iniuria*). Gaius, III, 223, uses the word *poena* in a generic way, in order to refer to talion and compensation.

69. Where, for example, a slave is killed, it is the highest value the slave has attained during the last year that will serve as a yardstick of estimation: no allowance will be made for a situation where the slave has been the victim of severe physical impairment some months before his disappearance. Conversely, the pecuniary injury caused by the loss of a slave acting as salesman, shopkeeper or comedian, is not taken into consideration either. It should be added that the *actio* resulting from the *lex Aquilia* is a noxal *actio*: I might thus content myself to abandon my one-eyed and impaired slave, if he has caused the death of a slave worth a fortune.

70. On this, though from a less general vantage point, see Giuseppe Grosso, 'La distinzione tra res corporales e res incorporales et il secondo capo della lex Aquilia', *Synteleia Arangio-Ruiz*, Naples 1964, pp. 791 ff.

71. Gaius, III, 186.

72. Gaius, III, 187.

73. Gaius, IV, 6 ff. Justinian will propose the intermediary category of mixed *actiones*, of which the *actio legis Aquiliae* is an

example. This indicates that, despite all evolutions, *poena* has remained irreducible to reparation properly speaking.

74. Cf., for instance, the *lex Cornelia de sicariis et veneficis*, the *lex Cornelia de testamentis*, the *leges Iuliae de vi privata, de adulteriis*, etc ... All of these delicts are rules by the mechanism of the *publica accusatio*. The Empire, especially the late Empire, will increasingly subscribe to criminal persecution *extra ordinem*, in other words, it will increasingly choose forms according to an administrative-style procedure (cf. *D.* 47.10.45; *Sententiae Pauli*, 5, 4, 8; *Institutes*, 4, 4, 10).

75. An ideological vestige of this evolution can be found in the condemnations of resentment and vengeance which, around the time of the end of the Republican era, have become a common theme, of which Seneca will make one of the favourite topics of his moral reflection. Cf. Cicero, *De inventione*, II, 83 ff., and Seneca's *De ira* in its entirety.

Ten

The Slave's Body and its Work in Rome: On Analysing a Juridical Dissociation

The historians or philosophers who, in the horizon of our time – a time in which liberal and Marxist ways of theorising still loom large – have most contributed to the reflection on work in antiquity (M. Finley, J.-P. Vernant, H. Arendt),[1] have, oddly enough, removed from their scope the entire realm of lawyerly operations dealing with work. Practically all of them have disregarded the contracts relating to *operae*, focusing their attention instead on a model of *labor* that was almost entirely based upon slavery. The word *labor* is, as we know, largely associated with a wearying effort, even with a suffering of the body, rather than with an activity that is positive insofar as it is productive. Like Greek *ponos*, Latin *labor* designates work – especially agrarian work – as much as the suffering of soldiers in war and the throes of women giving birth; it designates, in short, an ordeal inflicted upon the labouring body.[2] This is why, in its typical representation, work is associated with the very body of the slave. To such a point that the 'mercenaries' who sold their *operae* appear to have submitted themselves to a state of quasi-servitude. Often it is question, as well, of a 'power' – *imperium* or *potestas* – exercised on free wage earners as well as on slaves,[3] which, in agricultural enterprises, was delegated to their slave foremen.[4] According to these accounts, the work relation finds itself entirely absorbed in a form of statutory subordination, which, in turn, is rooted in physical control. In such a view, an employment contract can finally appear as a contract that relates mostly to status. In other words, the work relation itself appears as being entirely absorbed in a statutory subordination rooted in physical control. Thus, an employment contract can end up appearing as a type of status contract, as shown in a legal text from the end of the third century, in which the workman places his own status as a free man at the disposal of another: 'the free man who controls his own situation (*homo liber qui statum suum in potestate habet*) has also the power to downgrade it . . . by leasing his work by day, or by night'.[5]

Slavery, work of the body, subordination of the body of a free person under the status-defining control of another person: what we find at stake in all of this, is a work relation. In summary, the fact that productive tasks were assimilated, in the Roman world, from the second century BCE onward, to slave status, and that, hence, it was more often than not a property relation that determined producers and products, seems to indicate that something prevented Greco-Roman culture from thinking of work according to its modern form: that of value. For reasons that relate as much to the slave-based social structure itself as to the representations involved in work (work as physical subordination), we are dissuaded from finding any correspondence to the functional – and a fortiori the juridical – autonomy that defines what, today, we call work.[6] As it has frequently been noted, it is no coincidence that the only properly theoretical text on work in antiquity is the first book of Aristotle's *Politics*, which is devoted, precisely, to slavery.[7]

And yet, *labor* does not feature in our jurisprudential or legislative sources until the very last years of the third century CE, and then only in contexts where what is at stake are not contracts but the carrying out of imposed services.[8] What is decisive is the analysis that Roman jurists contributed to the hiring of work, *locatio operarum*, which precisely served as a form whereby a certain quantity of work-time is exchanged for a salary. Work is here considered in a unified and abstract manner. Unified, because in such cases the lawyers' lexicon knows the term *operae* alone – exclusive of all other terms, including *labor*. Abstract, because – even though this contract may cover a certain kind of service (the work of a fuller, a painter, an architect, a teacher, etc.) – the salaried workman's obligation does not relate to a specific result, but instead to a divisible and measurable quantity of work, a quantum whose value is indifferent to the objects in which it invests itself.

The documentation from Greco-Roman and Byzantine Egypt is abundant.[9] The indispensable source, however, remains Roman jurisprudence of the imperial period, the only one that is known to devote remarkable efforts of theorisation to work as such. This type of contract has hardly attracted the attention of historians of ancient economy. And yet, it is the structure of the contract of *operae* that invites us to analyse work on the terrain of commercial exchange, which is where, precisely, the classical economists analysed it, but where we do not generally assume that antiquity had succeeded in developing any relevant thinking, considering that the reflection on the division of labour remained blocked by the unequal distribution of the natural qualities proper to each task, and by its purely political approach both to social complementarity and the origin of the city.[10] Legal historians are no doubt familiar with the figure of a *locatio operarum* – a figure whose least distant relative in the French *Code Civil* is a contract for hiring services, the '*louage*' of the *gens du travail*. But what interested French legal historians was the nature of this particular hiring relationship, i.e. the exchange of a service for a price in general terms, rather than for *operae* in particular. That, from the first century BCE to the third century CE, the jurists were able to circumscribe and model work as an autonomous object, is rarely admitted. The fact that work as such has attracted scarce attention from specialists of Roman law is also owed to the opinion that those free Romans who had no other choice but to sell their efforts in return for a salary, were rare and, owing to their low position, similar to slaves, an opinion widely shared (despite the studies of F. M. de Robertis).

As the object of a contract, work struggles to attract the interest of legal historians, except in those cases where the person who hires out his labour is a free person. Moreover, as, according to the preconceptions prevailing in antiquity, he who receives a salary is in a quasi-servile position – the presence of a contract[11] is a mere facade that does not change anything about this – work seems to lend itself inadequately to an autonomous analysis, or at best only in view of the personal subordination and status it entails. What one was keen to look into were such free relationships which subscribed to the servile model; whence a focus on the personal condition of the worker, rather than on work as a specific value in view of a market.[12]

Yet, in our sources, employment contracts do not refer as much to free persons prepared to abandon their free status in order to embrace a servile condition, than to slaves whose masters (or other slaves who act as managers for these masters),[13] rent a certain amount of their work-time to third parties. By way of a paradox that I will try to explain, it is precisely in connection with the renting of such servile *operae* that the Latin jurists have most contributed to thinking work as determined by contract and as detached from status. We are dealing with slaves rented out by their masters to third persons. A superficial, but common view of things tends to consider such a work arrangement as unproblematic and self-explanatory – as a truism that the law has no motive to further expand on. Since, as a matter of course, slaves are tools used for productive tasks, all one needs to know in order to understand their leasing is, first, what is this contract, and, secondly, what is a slave. True, these slaves are doing work, being placed outside their homes: this is what their lease imposes its distinctive legal form on. And yet (and even if the sources are perfectly clear), a look into the specialised literature on Roman law reveals an extraordinary difficulty at distinguishing between, on the one hand, a slave, and, on the other hand, the price due in exchange for his service. Everything looks as if the contractual obligation had no other object than the very person of the worker, as if, in other words, the operation concerned the worker's body in its entirety.

It is true that a small number of texts also attest to cases in which the slave himself is rented out, the work then being not disjoined from the man 'placed' in the manner of a corporeal thing: 'if you have leased my slave mule driver', 'if you have leased a vehicle . . .', 'if he took a slave to ride a mule . . .', 'if I rented you a house . . . or a slave to keep your tavern . . .', 'if you wounded the slave who has been leased to you . . .', 'if you have not returned the leased slave or any other movable thing . . .', 'If you take away the slave that has been rented to you', '. . . then actions, either of leasing or for theft, may be brought against you . . .', etc.[14] Such texts prove that Roman law was aware that work could also be thought of as included in the body of the rented person (or of him who rents himself out); or in other words, they show that work could also simply remain unconsidered in law. Yet, from the existence of these two competing representations, we cannot postulate a necessary evolution that would have led from an original regime – in which work, being inseparable from the worker's own body, was a material, bodily thing, which its owner alienated by renting his slaves or by renting himself – to a newer, more sophisticated regime in which the contract isolated the *operae*, objectifying them, allowing to rent a certain quantity of work, whether servile or free.[15] There is, first of all, no evidence of such an evolution. The jurist Labeo, a contemporary of Augustus, was aware of both regimes: renting a slave, and renting his work.[16] And already half a century earlier, Varro and Cicero knew that the object of a lease is not necessarily a person but, rather, their work.[17] In the first half of the second century BCE, contract forms compiled by Cato the Elder juxtapose leasing of work and leasing of salaried workers.[18] Even earlier, at the turn of the third and second century BCE, Plautus's theatre shows that the *locatio operarum* was already familiar to Roman audiences.[19] It is pointless to go further back, as there are no sources. Moving forward in time, nothing supports the hypothesis that what is taking place is an evolution. The lease documents use the formula: 'he acknowledged having rented out himself . . . he has leased his work . . . to so-and-so'.[20] The expression 'to let/lease/rent', whether meant to refer to oneself or to a slave, is, then, most likely, an elliptical formula to be applied to work, rather than to a thing. What we find in the remarks of Roman jurists about their thought on statutes turns out to be perfectly in keeping with that objectification of abstract labour that can be found in contracts: texts that compare the free wage earner to the slave refer to a lessor who alienates, not his person, but his *operae*.[21]

We need to get used to the idea that, as far back as we can go in time (until around 200 BCE), Roman jurists based themselves upon the notion of work as perfectly autonomous and construed as an object of its own kind. Such an operation invites us to consider work as one among the 'things' subject to exchange and freely alienable, and to unfetter the notion of work from the sphere of a person's status, opening it up to that of its transactions. Law is thus at the origin of certain basic components of the market. It defines a commodity. An oft-used formula expresses this in the most trivial way: 'If he has rented a slave's work, or a lodging . . .'[22] It creates an adequate mode of exchange, an instrument for bringing together the actors of supply and demand – proof of how important it is to pay attention to the legal morphology of social objects. In a world where the legal art provides human activities, such as work, with means of their formal definition (and the Roman world from the second century BCE until the third century CE certainly does belong to such a world), we lose sight of the meaning of this fact, even of its very existence, if we fail to use the arsenal of tools capable of qualifying such activities and, thereby, of producing them as objects – as objects of dispute and of exchange.

II.

In Roman law, the master who leases his slave's work for a price is at once: owner of a man; debtor of work; and creditor of a salary. In his single person are concentrated all the rights that divide the work relation: property, debt, credit. This is why the *locatio operarum* does not provide all the keys to understanding the legal nature of work as contract, obligation and value. In order to define such an object, the jurists do not consider the case in which the master himself is entitled to enjoy the *operae* of his slave in the form of a salaried income and thus embodies all three positions of proprietor, debtor and creditor. In defining such an object, the jurists abstain from using as their paradigm the case that is doubtlessly the simplest and the most frequent: the case in which the master himself is entitled to the enjoyment of the *operae* of his slave in the form of a salaried income, thus piling up in his person all three positions – owner, debtor and creditor. This is the simplest case, yet because of its very simplicity, it is also the one that is the least suitable to an analysis and distinction of the different rights involved – among which, in particular, are the owner's right in the property of the body of the slave, and the personal creditor's right to be paid a salary for the slave's work. In order to conduct such an analysis, Roman case law prefers to dismember ownership between a bare owner, and a usufructuary to whom the slave's work belongs, or more exactly the unrestrained right to dispose of it by leasing it to third parties. This choice certainly corresponds with existing and well-documented practices showing how the usufruct of slaves has been dealt with, notably by bequest.[23] Yet, this distribution of rights between two right-holders also makes it possible to think differently and to construct bare ownership and the fruits of activity; property and obligation; the body and the yield that it produces. One owns a man's body as property, another has a title to his work.

This dismemberment makes it possible to consider work under the jurist-made category of 'fruit': 'in the usufruct of a slave, there is his work plus the wages of his work'; '[t]he fruits of a slave are his work; conversely, the slave's work are his fruits', etc.[24] *Operae* are, therefore, specifically defined as a resource, an income: *fructus*, in law, abstractly refers – well beyond the realm of the physical fruits of land or cattle – to the pecuniary yield derived from a good; in particular, it refers to work-derived wage income.[25] Thus isolated as a distinct category, and thanks to this separation of bare ownership and fruit, work becomes comparable to an income or a rent (*pensio*).[26] The rent is precisely what is branched off to profit the holder of the usufruct. The usufructuary is the sole beneficiary of the promise that the slave receives from the taskmaster-employer in exchange for the verbal act of 'stipulating his work'.[27] He alone holds the right to receive the wages owed to the worker by the taskmaster-employer. Only when the usufruct ceases, does the slave-owner recover this income for the time remaining until the end of the contract: 'If a fructuary slave has rented his work and the usufruct has ceased before the end of the lease period, the remainder belongs to the owner of the slave'.[28] Bare ownership v. income (and therefore, wages): the worker is split between two areas of law corresponding respectively to what he is as a body and what he represents as an income, an incorporeal asset. Work also involves physical control over the worker, a power of supervision and coercion, which belongs to the owner of the work, rather than to the bare owner of the worker's body – except where the latter has agreed with the usufructuary a lease entitling him to the *operae* of his own slave, leading to a cumulation of ownership rights and what is entailed by subordination.[29] The last of these is a borderline case, whose speculative interest is obvious: the legal operation at first disjoins the thing and the fruit, a right to the body and a power over the person, before subsequently bringing together abstract right and concrete power, bare ownership and disciplinary control.

The dismemberment of property into bare ownership and usufruct allows work to be isolated as such and give it a proper legal standing. But the jurists add one more level of specification when they further divide the category of usufruct into a right to use (*usus*) and a right to reap fruit (*fructus*). The opposition here is no longer between body and work but, within work itself, between object of use and source of income, between service and profit. The opposition, then, is not only one of body and work. It is, within work itself, one between what it is as an object of use and what it is as a source of income – between a service and a profit. Note immediately that this distinction is not only a doctrinal one. There are cases where what is awarded is pure use, which excludes by hypothesis any fructification of work by means of a salary. So, for instance, in the case when a slave can manifestly only serve his master's amusement: 'with respect to a small child, one has bequeathed only its use'.[30] Moreover, the Roman jurists understood the concession of *operae* to be, either, according to the particular case, a transfer of fruits without use, which is to say the award of a salary, or a transfer of use without fruits, which is to say, the concession of a service.[31] They regularly asked the question of whether the holder of the *usus* alone could, or could not, lease the work of his slave, as could the person who possessed the fully-fledged usufruct. Does use include the commercial alienation of the *operae*? It is at this juncture that the distinctions of Roman case law – between use and fruit, to be precise – provide, apart from practical solutions applicable in this or that particular case, theoretical tools which operate on the categories themselves and on the objects which they determine. This leads the jurists to the opposition between the direct enjoyment of work and the fact of placing it on the market.

> If someone has received by bequest the use of service staff (*usus ministerii*), he can use it for himself and, as well, for his children and his spouse. If he makes use of it at the same time as they, he will not be considered as having

conceded it to others . . . for, as Labeo has it, he will not lease the work of the slave whom he has the use of, nor will he concede this use to another person. How, indeed, can he concede to others a work that he can only use himself?[32]

The jurist Labeo, a contemporary of the Emperor Augustus, quoted two centuries later by Ulpian, considers the work here at stake from two complementary angles: (1) as work that forms part of the service of the person who has the use of it, and that can be extended, as a service, to his relatives; (2) as work that is rented to a third party for an income. In order to respect the limits of his right, the owner of the *usus* must realise his entitlement himself and concretely; in other words, he must realise it in kind. Such direct enjoyment extends to, but cannot exceed, the circle of the close members of his household, spouse and descendants. Outside the confines of the immediate family, the leasing of work would exceed its reserved sphere, an alienation that would be contrary to the very notion of *usus*, as it would transform it into a commodity mobilised in the circuit of exchange. To sell, lease or otherwise exchange this servile work for money would transform it into a commodity. If the legatee separated the *operae,* to which corresponds the value of an income, from the slave of whom he possesses full *usus*, what would be destroyed is the very unity of the right he holds. Such an operation would constitute a transgression of the limits in which his right is contained; it would contradict its concept and violate its regime. It would dissociate the elements of the totality constituted by personal service and economic benefit.

Work is attached to usufruct as opposed to bare ownership; but then, work is, in relation to simple use, also associated with an income and, through this alliance, with the sphere of market mediation. Thus, work finds its proper place within a disjunction between use and fruit. But how is the jurist to distinguish accurately between a service and a rent within a social organisation where slavery was employed, not just for domestic tasks, but also in production, either through direct exploitation, in the form of the ownership of workforce, or through indirect exploitation, in the form of contracts with slave owners? On a first level of analysis, one might expect that service to correspond to domestic activities, profit, on the contrary, to productive activities; one might think of enterprises agricultural, pastoral, and artisanal, whose owners exploited not only the work of the servile members of their own *familiae*, but equally the salaried work of other slaves, and even of free men hired on the market. This is not so, however. What is enlightening in this respect is how the text quoted above continues. Labeo considers the fact that, while being committed to use, slaves can also be employed in production, and while indeed this production can, in turn, be destined for the market, this does not mean that such work needs to be recognised itself as involving a commercial dimension:

> Yet, Labeo thinks that, if one has an estate in leasehold, one also can let a slave work on it, provided one possesses his use: what difference, after all, does the type of work for which the slave is employed make? Thus, if the holder of a use has contractually agreed to provide weaving work, he is entitled to have this task be performed by the women in his use; in the same way, if the agreement mentions cloth-dying or ship-building, he may utilise for that purpose the work that corresponds to the use he possesses. This solution is not disputed by Sabinus, who holds that he who has been conferred the use of a slave woman, cannot make her the object of a lease to have her do wool-work and enjoy an income from her wool-work, nor collect the price of that work. Since he has not rented out her work, he is in effect meant to make her work for himself, unless he assigns her a task and this task is mentioned in the contract he has agreed.[33]

Whether an artisan sells his production or is remunerated according to a commercial contract (*locatio operis faciendi*), the hypothesis envisaged here suggests that the manner in which he employs servile *operae* still fits the notion of use as long as he puts on the market the *product* of the slaves' work for a price, rather than putting their *work* on the market for a wage. Note that using a slave for the production of a commodity is not in itself contrary to *usus*. What is contrary to use, is to transform his workforce as such immediately into a commodity. Such would be the case if the *holder of the use* employed the slave's workforce as an object of commercial exchange, or of another's production, against a salary. This would disrupt the unity, which supposes that, within the use, a human being and their work are only one and the same thing, and where the economic advantage that the worker provides is indistinguishable from the personal service that he renders. In this respect, the doctrine that Labeo had formulated under Augustus is not called into question by that of Sabinus writing in the years of Tiberius. This was the doctrine followed by all jurisconsults of the first three centuries of the Roman Empire: by Ulpian, who endorsed it at the time of the emperors of the Severan dynasty, but before that, by Pomponius, prior to the years 150,[34] as well as by Marcellus, in the same period.[35]

The same distinction clearly appears again in the following scenario. A slave cannot acquire, for the person who has a right of use over him, the salary for his work. And neither can he sign an employment contract in the name of the latter. Nothing, however, forbids the same slave from managing his master's estate and, in this capacity, receiving other types of commitments or debts. Think of a slave employed as the keeper of some shop or business. In the name of the owner of the *usus*, who has initially provided him with a sum of money, he acquires rights and property. These are, however, in no way a corollary of any contractual agreement on *operae*. The slave is like an extension, an organ of his master's assets: 'Do I acquire rights, when I stipulate . . . by the intermediary of a slave of whom I have the use? This depends on whether it is stipulated of my estate or of his work. If it is stipulated of his work, the operation is invalid, since we have no right to rent the work of this slave; if, however, it is stipulated of my estate, we say that the slave who stipulates X makes me acquire rights, since I have the use of his work.'[36]

Such are the operations that the text relates to the estate: by means of the slave, the right-holder engages in an activity that is deployed for himself. The lesson is perfectly clear. Work is the direct cause of the advantages it provides only where it is itself a commodity.

The distinction between the slave and his work, which is understood in Rome as one of the slave's features, corresponds exactly with the dissociation of bare ownership and fruits. Fruits are always considered as a pecuniary value since, for he who is entitled to them, work is not only an asset in nature. Think of someone who receives the usufruct in a slave as a bequest. Suppose the heir bars the legatee from collecting the fruits by fraudulently creating a legal situation in which the slave no longer has to work for the legatee. For example, he sells the slave, who, as a result, now belongs to another master. Or alternatively, he frees him. Even in this case, the heir remains liable to an action that forces him to pay the bequest, since what is owed is not the factual employment of the slave's know-how but its pecuniary equivalent, the amount of which is precisely determined at the value of the *operae*. Such an assessment is possible, since the beneficiary of the usufruct could always rent out the slave's labour, or, if he does not do so, the slave could even rent himself in the beneficiary's name: 'The legacy of a slave's labour is not lost through a change of status or a loss of use: the legatee may receive a salary; he may also rent this work himself. The heir fails in his attempt at thwarting the legatee's right. Same result, if the slave rents out his own work [on account of this legatee].'[37]

Such texts show that Roman jurists, in dealing with servile *operae*, succeeded, from the first to the third centuries, in developing a genuine reflection on value. It is genuine, and what is most remarkable about it, it is a reflection that unfolds within the field of the wages of slaves. It also supposes, if not the existence of a labour market, at least the intellectual operations that make its existence thinkable and, therefore, possible.

The entire juridical issue of work is polarised around the matter of usufruct, more precisely around that ramification of the usufruct that is the fruit. It is truly striking that work contracts about slave work are almost never considered in the most ordinary case: that in which the lessor is the master, but almost always in the (undoubtedly rarer) cases in which the lease appears as the prerogative of the usufructuary, or indeed as the prerogative of the owner of the fruits, as opposed to that of the mere use of the slave. If we were content to count the textual examples, we would arrive at the conclusion that the income from renting servile work represented a lesser interest to the bare proprietors than to the usufructuary – an obviously absurd conclusion and as such proof that a purely empirical approach to case law is insufficient. The social impact of such analyses can be precisely appreciated only in hindsight, and after a detour through legal and formal analysis. And yet, this essential component of the Roman sources on work has been grossly neglected. All that has been concluded from the insistence with which case law attempted to establish a correspondence between work and fruit, is the insight that the human being is a fruit-producing thing, as such barely helpful.[38] Some scholars, following a typically empirical approach, went as far as to imagine that the usufruct of slaves was based upon the usufruct of a rural property, a *fundus instructus*, complete with its instruments of exploitation – the slaves counting among these. Defying straightforward textual evidence to the contrary, they judged it improbable that there could be such a thing as a practice of establishing a usufruct on slaves taken individually, without any relation to owned land. This is how the Roman reflection on the work contract, located as it was in the opposition between bare ownership and usufruct, or more precisely between *usus* and *fructus*, has been nullified. From the outset, the operations allowing a juridical analysis of work disappeared behind the dubious presupposition that it all boiled down to a simple question of fact.[39]

If the Roman jurisconsults chose to interpret servile *operae* through the grid of use and fruits, they undoubtedly did so because this opposition represented the most suitable tool to isolate work as an autonomous object. These two poles categorically distinguish two modes of work exploitation: as a service and as profit. The work to which the *usuarius* (holder of use) is entitled is one and the same as the personal or domestic use he has of his slave and which excludes commercial profit. On the contrary, the *fructuarius* is entitled to a work that can be alienated for a price on the market: it can be rented out. In both cases, whether the slave is the object of a use or that of a usufruct, concretely speaking, he works. Only, the slave's activity, in everyday language his labour, does not have the same legal value in both cases. There are two possibilities: Either the slave remains at the personal disposal of the *usuarius* in person. This is what I would call a service *'en nature'*. One could also call it 'use work', as one speaks of 'use value'. Or the slave's *operae*, separated from him, are a 'thing' sellable to a third party through the legal form of the contract. What the usufructuary receives, is only a pecuniary income. To the slave's 'use work' is added work that we could call commercial, as it has market value.

Work is defined as a resource, a revenue, also a value: it can always be substituted for with money.[40] In the slave, apart from his body, only his work admits of a pecuniary estimate. This is why the usufructuary of a child under five, unfit for work, is not eligible to be reimbursed with the monetary equivalent of an entertainment (*voluptates*) derived from it, for example.[41]

Similarly, the claim to an amount of work is an asset, and as such part of an estate, which can be sold on the market like any other good: the patron to whom a freedman has promised a certain number of working days, can always, if his services are not exclusively tied to the former's person, lease this work to a third party for a price.[42] This is, finally, why the damages and interest owed to his former master by a former slave who, after having been freed, has engaged in unfair competition against him, are not calculated on the basis of a loss of earnings and by taking into account the negative interest, but on the basis of the fruit, that is to say of the salary that the freedman would have had to repay the patron had he worked for him, rather than on his own account.[43]

The jurists of the Republican era already conceived usufruct generally as an incorporeal good and consequently indivisible materially: it could only be shared by virtue of a monetary estimate. The jurists of the imperial age extended this notion to work, which they analysed, as we have seen, on the basis of the category of usufruct. Thus, in exactly the same way in which the heir who wanted to take his legitimate share before paying out the bequest of a usufruct, could not keep for himself, in kind, a quarter of the use and a quarter of the fruits, but rather had to evaluate the overall amount of the bequest to pay three parts in cash, so equally the heir, debtor of an *operae* legacy, could not share concretely this work in two portions of one quarter for him and three quarters for the legatee, but rather was to pay the legatee the pecuniary value of his share:

In the case where the usufruct is the object of a legacy, the ancients thought that it was necessary to estimate the global value of the usufruct and thus establish the amount of the legacy . . . When bequeathing the work of a slave . . ., the opinion of the ancients is proven right: what is decisive is the overall amount of the legacy, for if it is true that, for any bequests of an obligation involving an action, what is owed needs to be diminished by a fourth, it is hard to determine what a fourth of a duty of work is supposed to be.[44]

That we are dealing here with a coherent effort of legal thought, is what we learn from the fact that, as soon as it is no longer defined as usufruct or as income but rather as use, work becomes once again concrete and divisible in nature. With respect to the work that freed slaves owed their patrons, Celsus (consul in 129 CE) insists on the irreducible and singular nature of each task,[45] while Gaius (about 160) considers that the freedman of two patrons can exercise the trade of copyist for one, while tending to the house of the other, tasks that are performed at the same time rather than subjected to an assessment, followed by a division, of their value.[46]

III.

Roman law, therefore, provides access to certain specific operations that allow, in part, the correction of the traditional approach to work in ancient societies. In these technical contexts, it is of relatively little importance that the Greek and Latin vocabulary convey the notion of productive work along with a painful effort of the body, or along with a movement directing human activity towards the fulfilment of forms inscribed in nature. What is essential is rather, on the one hand, the manner in which human work has been integrated into a logic of the estate and, on the other hand, the ability of the jurists to conceive of it as an abstract value, at odds with what one might guess antiquity thought about work, if one only considers it through the makeshift analyses provided by historical anthropology.

Work, as a value, is measured by time. The time at stake is an abstract one. Work as a concrete process remains, of course, subject to natural constraint, that of the duration necessary for the accomplishment of a given task. In which setting, law can neither construct time, nor transform it into a measuring instrument. The jurists know just as well how to distinguish between time as a mode of the quantification of work, and time that has really elapsed, as they know how to distinguish between work, understood as pecuniary income (as a value that finds its place in the theory of fruits), and work as an irreducibly concrete work, as it is envisaged in the theory of use. This concrete time is evoked above all in relation to the time limit within which the accomplishment of a task, insofar it is possible to accomplish it, can be imposed: 'When one promises a certain type of work, such as painting, its delivery cannot be demanded before the necessary time has passed, because, even if it is not specified in the verbal formula of the contract, the passing of time is an integral part of that obligation'.[47] Better still, *operae* depend so much on their temporal condition that they are supposed to have no existence before the expected end: 'Certain things, in view of their nature, cannot be accomplished within a single moment. They necessarily involve a division of time, as e.g. if one has committed oneself to ten days of work, considering that the work keeps being realised throughout this time span'.[48] 'Before that date', the jurist Paul writes at the beginning of the third century, 'the work at stake, which is an act, has no natural existence'.[49]

Yet, a wholly different issue is that of time insofar as it determines the monetary value of work. Here we are dealing with a homogeneous duration, divisible and measurable in number. In all likelihood, the practice of usufruct has its stakes in this temporal quantification of waged work: the man who works generates a yearly revenue – as do land or animals. We have seen above that, at the expiration of the usufruct in a slave, any outstanding wages due for his work belong to his owner. In this case the unit of accounting is the year. This is also the case where, after the breakdown of the marriage, the husband must return the dowry goods of which he has the legal usufruct: revenues from the current year, fruits of the land and the herds, as well as wages for the slaves, are divided between the usufructuary husband for the time before the divorce, and the female proprietor for the time after the divorce: 'For the slave, too, the calculation of the *fructus* is done by year. If his work has been rented for the length of a year, this work belongs to the husband for the time preceding the divorce and to the woman for the time that follows it'.[50]

Just as the usufruct's income was calculated by year, so too was the usufructuary slave's work rented out by year: 'A usufructuary slave leases his work, stipulating in exchange a certain amount of money per year. Iulianus wrote that when the usufruct ceases, the master acquires the debt arising from that stipulation for the rest of its duration. This opinion seems to be supported by perfectly sound reasoning. For if the lease had been, for example, concluded for five years, since one does not know how long the usufruct will last, money will be claimed by the usufructuary at the beginning of each year. This way, the stipulation does not benefit another, but ensures that everyone acquires his due according to the reason of the law.'[51]

Stipulated on a yearly basis (*in annos singulos*), the wages are precisely connected to the usufruct: it was a way of calculating the yearly gain from work.[52] The jurists mentioning contracts concluded for periods of one year, three years, five years, or ten years, do so always with respect to usufructuary slaves.[53] Let us note that the duration is never indeterminate, and that the annuity of work is neither perpetual nor established until the death of the slave or of the parties to the contract:[54] The disposal of the fruits of work by the owner or the usufructuary is necessarily a temporary one. Also, whatever relevant documents of transactions have come down to us always set the obligation to work within a limit of less than a year.[55] In reality, these contracts extended either to a time-span that was specified by precise dates, e.g. from 20 May to 13 November 164,[56] or on a day-to-day level, as Cato the Elder advised to proceed in dealing with the harvest.[57] One called a day of work *una opera* or *operae singulae*, i.e. work units;[58] contracts were usually written as a multiple of this unit: four, five, ten, a hundred, one thousand.[59] In all cases at hand, work was only measured in time, so that one could rightly call a wage the 'price of time', *temporis merces*.[60]

Being agreed by contract and thereby rendered autonomous, work is not an immediate given, whether as income or as value measured by time. It has no reality outside of the artefacts through which the law isolates, organises and constructs it. It is then *abstract*, in the full sense of the term. It is seen, if not as a measure of the value of commodities in the manner of classical economics, at least as a commodity, whose value is object of quantification. In this sense, it can be said to be a 'thing'. It is a thing whose particular content is the contract that institutes it.[61]

What is most remarkable is that this reflection has been engaged mainly on the terrain of servile *operae*. The categories that conceive work as an object of exchange show their profile especially in cases such as that of a contract agreed between a slave master earning an income from the wages (*merces*) of his slaves, and an employer who rents their work. If slave ownership proved to be a paradoxically fertile ground for the elaboration of abstract labour, this is because it forced the jurists to distinguish between the worker himself (who remains part of the bare property of his master), and, on the other hand, any activity of the slave that can be branched off from it without affecting this reserve. Just as the labour of a slave who remains in his master's use as an object of his domination might remain completely undefined, so is there an obvious need to precisely circumscribe the activity of the slave whose work is rented out, thus excepted from the master's *dominium* without being transferred to the *dominium* of the work-renting employer. An object of exchange under the title of *fructus*, this activity exists as an autonomous contractual item. Whence the necessity of tracing its precise contours.

Hence defined, work as such is separated from a body that is, as such, protected. Necessary limits to exertion are contractually defined. So are scheduled work hours (e.g. work during daytime, stopping at sunset),[62] the lunch-break,[63] the time spared for food and bodily care,[64] the suspension of work in case of illness.[65] Neither do these protections respond to an altruistic concern, nor are they limited to free workers.[66] They simply respond to the need to protect existing property rights in the body. The very idea of work – an idea that can be found, formulated distinctly as such, only within the field of *locatio operarum* – implies a separation between work and body. The separation is legal: it supposes a disjunction between bare ownership and fruits. Independently from any notion of social law, the category of work, once it acquired juridical standing, once it escaped the sphere of domestic subordination to become autonomous in the contract, implied a limitation and, therefore, a protection. The relevant texts pinpoint the fact, that, whatever can be demanded of the slave finds its limit in what his master has trained him for, unless the usufructuary has taught him some other skill.[67] However, this question of matching the type of work that is demanded from a slave with the training he had received, is directly part of the problematics of the abuse against another's right:

> We must not abuse the usufruct of slaves that has been bequeathed to us, but use them according to the condition of each. For it will appear to be an abuse of [the master's] property if one sends a scribe to the countryside forcing him to carry bags of pebbles, if one makes an actor a bath boy, if one employs a musician as a caretaker, or a gymnast to clean the latrine.[68]

Excruciating types of work that could put the slave's health at risk, as well as ill-treatment that could disfigure his body, are equally counted among the abuses against bare ownership: 'The usufructuary cannot damage a master's workman by requiring services from him that are contrary or unrelated to his duty, nor can he disfigure him with scars',[69] referring to disciplinary corrections which might risk the slave's physical integrity or life:

> Since what is acquired through the slave's work benefits the usufructuary, one needs to keep in mind that a slave can also be forced to work. In fact, Sabinus indicated that the usufructuary had the right to exercise light punishment, while Cassius, in Book Eight of his Civil Law, wrote that this right could be exercised within the limits of torture and death by flogging.[70]

Upon the expiry of a usufruct or after the contractually fixed duration of his work, a slave must be returned to his owner in the state in which he had been hired. In sum, the legal divisions from which the category of work emerges, translate, from the viewpoint of behaviour and practice, into an obligation to keep intact the property of he who has the bare ownership in the slave.

I have tried to analyse the exercises that the Roman jurists put into operation in order to develop an appropriate concept of the work of slaves, by abstracting it from the power that was held over their persons. I have shown that they succeeded in isolating a genuine category of work as commercial value, despite the fact that the appropriation of this work was ensured in the legal form of ownership over the worker's person. Slavery makes it difficult, a priori, to distinguish between the appropriation of the slave and the appropriation of slave work. Yet, it is, on the contrary, because (rather than despite, as one might be tempted to believe) of ownership and its ramifications, that Roman law succeeded in developing something that is equivalent to what liberal theoreticians have called work. The reason why the master, who places his slave in the hands of a third, retains the property of this tool, is indeed that work needs to be defined as an object dissociated from the servile body. Right from its origin, the juridical category of work is the result of an operation through which the human body is separated from the income to which it gives rise.

Notes

1. M. Finley, *The Ancient Economy*, London, 1973; H. Arendt, *The Human Condition*, Second edition, Chicago, 1989; J.-P. Vernant, *Myth and Society in Ancient Greece*, Second edition, New York, 1990.
2. The basic text here is Cicero, *Tusc.*, II, 15, 35ff., in a development dedicated to the difference between *labor* and *dolor*: there is labour when the soul and the body realise a most painful work, examples: military service, hunting, the exertion of gladiators.
3. Cic., *De off.*, II, 6, 22, Javolenus, *D.* 4.22 pr.; Schol. II, *Bas.*, IX, 3, 35.
4. Varr., *Rust*, I, 17, 4; cf. *Colum* 1, 8, 10; Sen. *Contr.*, V, 5; IX, 30, 28.
5. Paul., *Sent.*, II, 18, 1. Later contracts about work systematically contain express clauses of subordination, cf. R. Taubenschlag, *The Law of Graeco-Roman Egypt*, Warsaw, 1975, pp. 375 ff.

6. M. Finley, 1973; A. Schiavone, *La storia spezzata: Roma antica e Occidente moderno*, Rome, 1996, pp. 130 ff.
7. M. Finley, 'Aristotle and Economic Analysis', *Past & Present*, 17 (1970); id., *Studies in Ancient Society*, London, Boston, 1971, pp. 24 ff.
8. Interpolated passage in Ulpian, *D.* 47.10.13.5, and Arcadius Carisius, *D.* 1.16.5.1; *Cod. Theod.*, 1, 26, 11; 27, 13; 15, 1, 49; 16, 2, 1; *Cod. Iust.*, 5, 37, 22, 4, etc.
9. O. Montevecchi, *I contratti di lavoro e di servizio nel Egitto greco-romano e bizantino*, Rome, 1950.
10. Plato, *Republic*, 370b–c; Aristotle, *Pol.*, 1252b, 1–5; Xenophon, *Cyr*, 8, 2; See J.-P. Vernant, *Myth and Society in Ancient Greece*, op. cit., New York, 1990.
11. To the references given above, note 3, add the prohibition, in relation of work-related contracts, that is reported by Ulpian, *D.* 19.2, on *locatio conductio* 44, 'no one can hire his own servile status'.
12. A. Maschi, 'Locatio rei, operis, operarum, e contratti di lavoro', *Bollettino della scuola di perfezionamente in diritto del lavoro dell'Università di Trieste*, I, 1954; A. Macqueron, 'Réflections sur la *locatio operarum* et les *mercenarii*', *RHD* 37, 1959, pp. 600 ff.; F. M. de Robertis, 1963; D. Nörr, 'Zur sozialen und rechtlichen Bewertung der freien Arbeit in Rom', ZRG 82, 1965, 67 ff.; E. Schlechter, 'A propos de la *locatio operarum* en droit romain et en droit babylonien', *Atti di Seminario di diritto romano di Perugia*, 1952, 254 ff.; P. Garnsey, 'Non Slave Labour in the Roman World', in *Non Slave Labour in the Greco-Roman World*, Cambridge 1980, 34 ff.; O. Diliberto, *Ricerche sull' 'auctoramentum' et sulla condizione delli 'auctorati'*, Milan, 1981.
13. *D.* 14.3.11.8 and 12; I. Butti, *Studi sulla capacità matrimoniale dei servi*, Univ. Giur. Camerino, 1976, 107; F. Redozzi Merola, *Servo parere*, ibid., 1990, 217 ff.
14. Cf. respectively, Labeo, *D.* 19.2.60.7; Mela, *D.* 19.2.27.34; Paul., *D.* 19.2.45.1; 2.43; Marcellus, ibid., 2, 48; Paul, 2, 42.
15. Cf., in this sense, E. Deschamps 'Sur l'expression *locare operas* et le travail comme objet de contrat à Rome', *Mélanges Girardin*, 1906, pp. 57 ff; F. M. de Robertis, 1946; id., 1949; id. 1963, 9ff. V. Arangio-Ruiz, *Istituzioni del diritto romano*, Naples 1960, 216 ff.; J. A. C. Thomas, 'Locatio et operae', *BIDR* 61, 1961, pp. 231–47.
16. Respectively, *D.* 19.2.60.7, and *D.* 7.8.12.6.
17. Varr., *Ling.*, VII, 105; Cic., *Off.*, 42, 150.
18. Cato, *Agr.*, 1, 6, 4.

19. Plaut., *Vid.*, 20–30.
20. Tartaria tablets (164 CE), *FIRA*, t.III, p. 150.
21. Ulpian, *VII ad edictum*; *D.* 19.3.44; Paul., *Sententiae*, II, 18, 1; cf. already Cic., *off.*, I, 12, 150; Varr., Ling, VII, 105.
22. Ulpian, *D.* 19.2.9.1; cf. *D.* 7.9.5.3.
23. For example: Gaius, 41, 32; *D.* 33.2.2; 7.20; 24.1; *D.* 35.21.9; etc.
24. Cf. Gaius, respectively 7, *ad ed. provinciale*, *D.* 7.7.3; II, *de liberali causa edicti urbici*, *D.* 7.7.4.
25. Labeo, *D.* 6.1.79; Alfenus Varus, *D.* 38.1.26.1; Paul., *Sent.*, 14, 17, 7 (labour in comparison to harvest, to the growth of the herd, to the reproduction of slaves), cf. de Robertis, *Lavoro e lovoratori nel mondo romano*, Bari 1963, pp. 22 ff.; M. Bretone, *La nozione romana di usufrutto*, Naples, 1962, p. 44.
26. Ulpian, *D.* 5.3.29; *D.* 30.39.1.
27. Ulpian, XVII, *ad Sabinum*, XVII, 1, 21; *D.* 45.3.24.
28. Paul., II, *ad Sab.*, *D.* 7. 1.26; also, Iulianus ap. Papinian, XXVII, *quaest.*; *D.* 45.18.3; Ulpian, *ad Sab.*, eod. loc., 27, 2.
29. Paul., XXII *ad ed.*; *D.* 9.4.19.2.
30. Pomponius, XVI as Q. Mucium, *D.* 17.1.55. There is a body of evidence showing that small children of less than five years of age were rented out, or left to use, for pleasure or pastime. Cf. Ulpian *XIV ad ed.*, *D.* 4.19.2.
31. Respectively, Paul., *libro singulari ad legem falcidiam*; *D.* 35.21.9: if one bequeaths the labour of a slave, the bequest includes neither a right to use, nor a ususfructus (in the sense of the totality of fruits and uses to which the slave gives rise) . . . In such a way that one needs to assess the value of the bequest (to enable the heir to subtract the monetary equivalent of his legitimate part); Iulianus, ap. Terentius Clemens, XVIII *ad legem Iuliam et Papiam*, *D.* 7.7.5: 'If one makes a bequest of the work of a slave, what is deemed to be conferred is the use value, according to my teaching and that of Iulianus'.
32. Ulpian, XVII *ad Sab.*; *D.* 17.8.12.5.
33. Ulpian, eod. loc., 6.
34. Pomponius, *V ad Sab.*; *D.* 7.8.16.2. 'When we hold only the use of a slave and not his fruits, we can hand over to him some good or even keep a business that is part of our funds; and everything that he has gained in this fashion, will be part of our assets'; cf. also *D.* 15.1.2.
35. Marcellus, *D.* 7.8.20: 'The slave the use of whom I have received by bequest, acquires for me, if I have made him a shop-attendant or a tavern-keeper. What he acquires by selling and buying goods, it is for me that he acquires it.'

36. Ulpian, XVII *ad Sab.*, *D.* 7.8.14 pr.; cf. *D.* 7.8.15 pr.; *Inst.*, 2, 5, 3. In Gaius, ad *ed. prov.*, *D.* 7.8.13 (Lenel, *Palingenesia iuris civilis*, Leipzig 1889, n° 172), what we probably need to understand is that the titulary of the use allows the slave to himself dispose of the product of his work, in exchange for a sum paid by a *peculium* that he has been allowed to hold. (See W. W. Buckland, *The Roman Law of Slavery*, 1908, p. 370.)

37. Papinian, XVII, *quaest.*; *D.* 33.2.2; cf. equally Ulpian, *D.* 7.7, *de operis servorum*, 2, 2.

38. Cf. F. M. de Robertis, *I rapporti di lavoro nel diritto romano*, Milan 1946, pp. 22 ff.

39. Buckland, op.cit., pp. 356 ff.

40. Celsus ap. Ulpianum, XXVI *ad edictum*, *D.* 12.6.26.12; on estimating the value of operae: Labeo VI, *pithanon a Paulo epitomarum*, *D.* 6.1.79; Alfenus Varus, VII *digestorum*; *D.* 38.1, *de operis libertorum*, 26, 1; Papinian, XVII *quaest.*, *D.* 33.2.2.

41. Ulpian, IV *ad edictum*; *D.* 7.7.6, 1–2.

42. Iulianus, *D.* 38.1.23 and 25; Ulpian, *D.* 38.1.9; Terentius Clemens, *D.* 40.9.32. As to the much discussed question of whether the *operae fabriles* and *officiales* were subject to sale, see L. Mitteis, 'Operae officiales und operae fabriles', *ZRG* 23, 1902, pp. 143–8; Jean Lambert, *Les operae liberti: Contribution à l'histoire du patronat*, Paris 1934, pp. 232 ff.; G. Lavaggi, *La successione dei liberi patroni nella successione nelle opere dei liberti*, *SDHI*, II, 1945, p. 245; C. Cosentini, *Studi sui liberti: Contributo allo studio della condizione giuridica dei liberti cittadini*, Catania, 1948, pp. 125 ff.; W. Waldstein, *Opera libertorum: Untersuchungen zur Dienstpflicht freigelassener Sklaven*, Stuttgart 1986, pp. 247 ff.

43. Alfenus Varus, *D.* 39.1.26.2.

44. Paul., *D.* 35.2, *ad legem Falcidiam* 1, 9; *Fragmenta Vaticana* LXVIII (see the *Index interpolationum* ad loc., and M. Bretone, 1962, pp. 55 ff., on the indivisibility of the *ususfructus* as an entity). Iulianus also thought that work is not divisible corporeally, but only as to its number, *in numero*, meaning: it can be divided into quota shares of its value. Iulianus, *D.* 22; *D.* 45.1.54.1.

45. XXVI *ad ed.*; *D.* 12.6.26.12.

46. *Libro singulari de casibus*; *D.* 38.1.49.

47. Iulianus, *D.* 38.1.24; cf. Ulpian, *D.*, XXXVIII *ad edictum*, 11; *D.* 38.1.13.2.

48. Paul., *ad Plaut.*; *D.* 40.7.20.5.

49. *D.* 7.7.1; on the conditions of a work that cannot be demanded before its time, cf. also XXII *ad ed.*, *D.* 45.1.73 pr., where one's

commitment to undertake *operae* equally obeys the rule according to which 'an action cannot be brought before the relevant performance could have been delivered, in accordance with the nature of the things at stake'.

50. Ulpian, XXXI *ad Sab.*, D. 24.3.7.10.
51. Iulianus, *ap. Papinian*, XXVII, *quaest.*, D. 45.3.18.3.
52. Iulianus, as quoted in n. 51; also Africanus, *V. quaest.*; D. 12.1.37; Ulpian, XVIII *ad Sab.*, D. 12.1.25.2.
53. One year: D. 24.3.7.10 (D. 19.2.19.9, dealing with a free man who leases himself out: this text does not speak of a contract over a year, but instead of a salary that has not yet been paid during the current year); three years: D. 11.7.14, pr.; five years: D. 14.3.18.3; ten years: D. 7.1.37.
54. The opposite is the case of other *stipulationes in annos singulos*, which fail to mention any term. On these operations, cf. R. Sotty, 'Remarques sur les stipulations *in annos singulos*', in M. Humbert and Y. Thomas (eds.), *Mélanges à la mémoire d'André Magdelain*, Paris 1998, pp. 435–45.
55. Ref. in de Robertis, 1946, p. 141.
56. Tartaria tablets (164 CE), *FIRA*, t.III, 150.
57. Cato, *Agr.*, V, 4.
58. *Una opera*: Colum., 11, 2, 44; D. 45.1.54.1; *singulae operae*: D. 19.2.51.1, etc.
59. *Quaternae operae*, Varro, *Rust.*, 1, 18, 2; *operae quinque*: D. 35.14.6; *decem*: D. 38.1.7.1; D. 40.7.20.5; *centum*: D. 37.14.6; D. 38.1.24; D. 40.7.44; *mille*: D. 38.1.15.1.
60. D. 19.2.38.
61. Gaius, XIV *ad ed.*; D. 38.1.22 pr., dealing with the claim to an amount of work that the former patron can cash in from the former slave who had contractually agreed to it.
62. Lex metalli Vipascensis, *Corpus Inscr. Lat.*, II, 5188, 1, 9: 'From sunrise to sunset'. The works that the former slave promises to his former master are qualified as 'day service', D. 38.1.1 and 3; contracts for night-time work are known only for free men who rent out their own services; Paul., *Sent.*, 11, 18, 1; Vergil, *Georgica*, I, 287; Plin., *Nat.*, 18, 10. Cf. on the workday, F.M. de Robertis, 1963, pp.169 ff.
63. Alfenus Varus, D. 38.1.26. Mart., IV, 8.
64. D. 7.1.15.2 on the usufructuary's duty of nourishing and dressing the slave, D. 38.1.50.1 on food and body care of former slaves and workers of any status. D. 38.1.15 explains that former slaves are not under a duty to work when they are in ill health, whereas the *operae* contracts signed by free men state the condition that, what is asked, is asked from

someone who is physically fit, *operas sanas valentes* (*CIL* III, 958, 1, 5, 949, 1, 10).

65. *D.* 38.1.15.
66. See the texts quoted in footnote 62.
67. *D.* 7.1.27.2.
68. *D.* 7.1.45.1.
69. Ulpian, XVIII *ad Sab., D.* 7.1, *de usu et fructu,* 17.1; cf., in the same vein, regarding limitations in view of physical integrity and life-endangering services in connection of work stipulated by former slaves, *D.* 38.1.6.17 and 38 pr.
70. Ulpian, XVIII *ad Sab., D.* 7.1, *de usu et fructu,* 23.1; cf. Labeo, *D*, 7.1.15.3; and Paul., *D.* 7.1.66.

Afterword
A Knowledge Apart

Alain Pottage

Speaking of Yan Thomas's early article on *La langue du droit romain*, Niklas Luhmann observed that the argument was 'not fully thought through'.[1] Given the topic of Luhmann's own paper – law and structural coupling – it is obvious what he meant. He would have been intrigued by the proposition that Roman law 'coded' everyday Latin, turning it into the medium of operations that were intelligible only to those schooled in the code.[2] But for a theory of structural coupling there is always more to legal operations than legal operations. Luhmann's preferred examples of the co-implication of law and collateral systems are contracts and constitutions. In the case of contract, '[a] payment can be at the same time (but *only* at the same time) the fulfilment of a contractual obligation in the legal system and part of an economic transaction which transfers the capacity to make further payments in the economic system'.[3] The qualification – 'only at the same time' – is necessary because systems are autopoietic, which means that each of these operations unfolds within the immanent temporal structuration of its home system, law or economy. The only 'time' in which the operations coincide is that of the system inhabited by the observer, in this case the sociologist. But for Luhmann the point of the paradox of openness through closure is that it turns differentiation into connection. The participation of systems in society might have a peculiar form – systemic operations connect with society at large by registering external events as confirmations or perturbations of self-generated expectation structures – but legal operations are still wired into society. To think law through means to reveal the ways in which its qualities of autonomy and technicality participate in the social; or, to switch idiom, how law is articulated into reciprocally 'collateral' relations.[4]

Thomas's analyses of legal form prefer not to think law through in this way. And in their imperturbability they invite one to query Luhmann's observation: what does it actually mean to think law through . . . fully? If the standing imperative of contemporary social theory is to connect, always to seek further connection, then at what point will law have been thought through fully enough? There is no metric for extension. But perhaps thinking things through (more) fully is not a matter of giving sufficient extension to ramifications but rather a matter of revealing the fullness of a potentiality for connection. In other words, perhaps the point is just to understand that there is more to law than can be revealed in even the most densely textured example, that any instance of law is always already social, and that this sociality might be unfolded almost infinitely. In any case, whatever we mean by 'fully' or 'more fully', we understand that law is 'thoroughly' articulated into society. This is precisely the mode of understanding in which Thomas's reconstructions of Roman legal forms and operations prefer not to participate. Roman law functioned in society, it parasitised the social energies that set the machinery of casuistic reasoning in motion, and its forms and formulae were appropriated in society at large.[5] But there was nothing social about the operationality of legal operations: law was not made of sociality, it was not made in the same way and of the same stuff as other social productions, it did not employ the same schemes or semantics. So it did not function as the exemplar of some more generalised engine of sociality, whether it be called *agencement*, translation, or Luhmannian differentiation.

Legal operations were radically alien to the society in which they operated, and it is important to be clear about this quality of otherness. In 1998, Thomas contributed a brief foreword and a study on the labour time of slaves to a journal issue dedicated to analyses of 'law's objects'. His colleague Marie-Angèle Hermitte contributed an essay entitled 'Law is another world' (*'Le droit est un autre monde'*), in which she explained how law constructs its own objects: 'The law transforms objects from other worlds so thoroughly as to make them unrecognisable. For example, in private law, an elephant tusk that was lawfully acquired will be protected as private property, or as a work of art if it was turned into a sculpture. But the same tusk will be seized and remorselessly destroyed by customs authorities if it was acquired in breach of legislation protecting endangered species'.[6] For Hermitte, law's capacity to reconstruct objects offered an insight into constructivism as a more generalised social operation: 'legal operations are powerful disclosing agents [*des révélateurs puissants*] which reveal the complexity of objects and the shifting and paradoxical quality of the constructions that society applies to them'.[7] This was not how Thomas construed legal operations. Law is not one of a number of more or less symmetrical social worlds, which reconstruct their environments in similar ways.

Nor, again, did law exemplify some more generalised engine of sociality. This point can be illustrated by reference to the question of media and 'middles'. In her take on law as cultural technique Cornelia Vismann suggests that the grammatical form of the middle voice in ancient Greek articulates the mode of agency that makes law social: 'Unlike active and passive constructions, this particular verb form signals that the acting subject is, grammatically speaking, dependent upon a third element. In the medium voice, an action does not derive from someone and encounter something; nor does it work the other way around'.[8] So, in the case of law, the process of retracing an event to the person who originated it depends on a cultural technique of attribution, which conditions the existence of both the person and their actions: 'From the perspective of cultural techniques, the category of personal subjecthood is the object of an act of assignation, and that act, in its turn, is itself a technique, one that occupies a central place in our legally defined culture'.[9] If we understand the legal operation of ascription or imputation as one that is articulated in the middle voice, then the effect is to make the existence and agency of the legal person contingent upon the operation of cultural-technical procedures and 'bureautechnical' affordances of the kind that were explored in Vismann's earlier work.[10] These procedures and affordances are exemplary of cultural techniques more generally, and of their capacity to produce the elements of the social. This is the basis of the recent convergence between post-Kittlerian cultural technique theory and Latourian actor-network theory. Latour had already asked how we might 'do justice to what the Greeks called the "middle voice", a verb form which is neither active nor passive'? And he focused that question on the crucial part of Benveniste's linguistic archaeology of the middle voice, namely, the proposition that in this verb form the subject *'effectue en s'affectant'*.[11]

There is some resonance between the cultural-technical take on law and Thomas's understanding of legal operations. Thomas's extraordinary essay on the figure of liability (*responsabilité*) in Roman law, which was published in 1977,[12] casts law as a 'medium' of a certain kind. Contra the assumptions of orthodox legal history, which imagines a process of enlightenment which gradually disposed of irrational notions of magical or collectivised responsibility to leave responsibility where it properly belonged, with the individual human being who is psychologically competent and morally habilitated to assume the consequences of their actions,[13] Thomas highlights the agency of impersonal operations and artefacts. He draws on another of Benveniste's studies of grammatical agency to make a distinction between two spheres or modes of agency: 'a world of being, in which are performed functions that in a sense pass through the subject so as to realise themselves in actions, and a world of having [*avoir*], a world of fabricated objects and finite forms [*monde d'objets créés et de formes finies*], which might be seen as an eclipse of agency [*un dépassement de l'agir*]'.[14] Agency in Roman law belonged to the second of these dimensions, to the world of having rather than the world of being.

Actions were not the spontaneous expressions of the will or the psychological motives of a subject. To begin with, they existed as off-the-shelf items in a juridical inventory, as forms which had the finite, bounded, and always-already-completed quality of an object. An act that entailed liability might be formulated in terms of the adjectival state or condition of an object – *membrum ruptum, os fractum, effusum et deiectum,* etc.[15] – the wrong being identified with the diminished or corrupted aspect of that object. In the more general sense of *iniuria,* an actionable wrong was identified with some materialised incursion into the personal or patrimonial 'propriety' of the plaintiff. Second, the relation between the defendant and these act-objects was not made by unwinding the consequence back to the originating force of subjective will, but by attaching the defendant to the action: 'the wrong (*noxa*) closes around the guilty person and captures him retroactively. The latter is not truly the agent of a wrong, so much as the subject included in it. Tied or bound to his action, he is not required to answer for it, but he is, strictly speaking, 'held' by law; *actione teneri* means 'to be held by a legal action'.[16] So the formula of a legal action – in the procedural sense of a cause or form of action – was the medium in which the agency of the person took shape, and precisely because the formula agency in register of 'having', an act became an object.[17]

For Vismann, the agency of the middle voice finds expression in the procedures, routines, and quasi-algorithmic practices of law: 'written directions, notations, codes of procedure, rules of application, annotations, and other systems of signs'.[18] In these terms, dogma is another word for cultural technique. 'All disciplines grounded in transferable praxis deal with cultural techniques. That is clearly the case with the classical dogmatic disciplines of theology, medicine and law, where dogmas ensure that operations are performed independently of persons.'[19] In the milieu in which Thomas was working and writing, 'dogma' had taken on the meaning given to it by Pierre Legendre: it evoked the capacity of law, by virtue of its specific technicality, to fulfil the grand 'anthropological' mission of instituting subjectivity.[20] But although Thomas might have been happier with Vismann's sense of dogma as a mode of operationality rather than a technique of subjectification, there is a crucial difference between his and Vismann's sense of the operationality of law as an impersonal 'middle'.

Vismann's characterisation of attribution as one of law's cultural techniques echoes Thomas's description of the subject 'held' by a legal action: 'Instead of an investigation of causes, which presupposes a search for an individual culprit in the matter, here the doer is deduced from the instrumentalities of the action and the agent is derived from the medium itself'.[21] But there is a difference between the constitutions of these two procedures. However routinised or algorithmic they become, the cultural techniques of law are historically emergent, their constitution and operation are referable to their 'conditions of production, material properties or spatial circumstances',[22] and for that reason they cannot be the products of self-directed human knowledge and action. Given his allusions to the transhistorical persistence of legal technique,[23] Thomas would presumably have acknowledged the sense in which legal operations depended upon tacit knowledge, or upon practices that were part of an impersonal language game, but he preferred to leave this dimension of law unexplored. The point at which a cultural-technical analysis would really get going, and at which Thomas's work almost invites it to get going, is precisely the point at which he himself stopped. There is no discussion of the media of Roman law, of tablets, parchments or albums, of architecture, clothing, bodily hexis, wands and other accessories, or of the scriptural practices of the glossators. And there is certainly no sense of the capacity of media or materialities to move things forward in the way that perforated sheets and lever arch files cue up and impel human agency by creating a bureau-technical expectation of further action – in the banal form of the blank entry that awaits completion.[24]

Thomas stops short of cultural-technical analysis because he refuses to engage in what might be called '*dispositif*-thinking' (a refusal which makes his work all the more attractive to those who do engage in this mode of thinking). He does not seek to elicit from Roman law the modes of emergent connectivity, inflection, and production that are generated by theories of *dispositifs*, *agencements*, rhizomes, epistemes, networks, materialities, or *Kulturtechniken*. If the question of what it means to think law through 'fully', or 'fully enough', is problematic it is because the orderings and artefacts that this way of thinking conjures up are so spectral and evanescent. The difficulty with *dispositif*-thinking is summed up in the proposition that the *dispositif* is 'what takes the place of universals in Foucauldian strategy'.[25] To ask a figure of emergence to 'take the place' of the classical notions of power or sovereignty is to create a duplicitous relation in which one denies the conceptual content of the classical notion of power while at the same time seeking to recreate its performativity in revealing our condition of subjection. This kind of *dispositif* turns out to be animated not by the immanent 'liveliness' of emergent forces and inflections but by the spirit of a conceptual figure – power – which is supposed to have died when we cut off the king's head, but which now haunts the materialities of the *dispositif*. Foucault might be the central case, but there are other modes of *dispositif*-thinking, and hence other modes of spectrality: for example, the evanescent quality of networks that are made by following the actors themselves so as to evolve a tracery that is illuminated only for the moment, within the time of the analysis. Those of us who engage in *dispositif*-thinking of one kind or another might celebrate its vitality, but from the perspective of Thomas law is precisely not thought through in terms that track its own mode of fabrication.

Here the aesthetics of Luhmann and Thomas coincide, if only momentarily. Even if we include Luhmann's systems theory in the broad twentieth-century 'cybernetic imaginary'[26] that produced *dispositif*-thinking, and even if the belief that law can be thought through more or less 'fully' belongs to that imaginary, Luhmannnian connections do not replicate as freely as do kindred forms. First, Luhmann does not allow communication to unfold into an infinite cartography of material or medial relays: 'Communication (which is to say, society) is coupled to consciousness, but not to the immense mass of physical, chemical, and biological facts. These facts can prevent communication and they can destroy it, but they cannot irritate communication'.[27] So, however lively it might become, materiality can be externalised from the process of communication. Second, for Luhmann a theory could only be what he called *gut gemacht* if it clearly acknowledged and articulated the paradox of order and emergence, or unity and multiplicity, in a way that *dispositif*-thinking neither wants nor allows; hence his interest in the mediaeval figure of *unitas multiplex*.

Thomas's artefacts are also made in a way that avoids *dispositif*-thinking. As Thomas describes them, the operations of Roman law did not consist in movement, process or transitivity. Precisely because legal forms existed in the register of 'having', operations were figured as objects. Temporality was wrapped into the form of a status or a *res*. So, to return to the example of responsibility or liability, Roman law penalised a wrong by recomposing an object. In the course of the trial, the plaintiff would try to persuade the court that the facts warranted putting the prefabricated elements of the act-object (back) together so as to bind the defendant. Persuasion was not a matter of proof in the sense that we understand it now: each side formulated the 'facts' in such a way that they already replicated the relevant part of the act-object; so that, in other words, they already appeared as exemplars or tokens of the formula that defined the *noxa* or *iniuria*. The point was then to make these constructs hold by force of argument, by rhetorically defeating one's adversary within the temporally and spatially defined forum of the trial. Where the process of recomposition became casuistic, in the sense that existing formulae were adapted to new questions, the *res* or status that was in question had to be able to change while remaining the same. By implication, the metaphor that Roman lawyers adopted to explain the persistence and stability of collective entities such as flocks, legions, or cities – Plutarch's image of the ship of Theseus, in which the boat remained the same through and despite the progressive substitution of all of its constituent timbers – also applied to the mode of argumentation that deployed the metaphor.[28] A legal form remained the same thing – the same object – throughout the process of its evolution and adaptation.

For the most part, the operations and artefacts studied by Thomas were objects of this kind: in the legal form of the institution, a city was a thing;[29] so too was the family,[30] the person, or the labour of a slave.[31] And each of these objects, in its own way, was generated and maintained by a mode of fabrication that found the necessary materials and techniques within legal knowledge itself. The work of fabrication was involuted in a double sense: first, it produced legal knowledge from out of legal knowledge through a movement that proceeded by first turning backwards and inwards; second, it generated forms with an intricacy that was peculiar to law. This strange art of intricacy is emphasised in Thomas's studies, which often engage our attention precisely through their recounting of an aesthetic that cuts and compiles in ways that are alien both to common sense and to the ways of *dispositif*-thinking. Consider, for example, the way in which Roman law divided the structure of an urban building from the 'ornaments' of its façade, which as *adjuncta* could be detached from one building and moved to another so long as they remained within the same patrimonial fund.[32] Or consider the construction of a tomb as a *locus religiosus*. A tomb had to hold a body if it was to be protected as a *res religiosa* but what was protected in law was the tomb rather than the body: 'the law sanctuarised the tomb rather than the deceased. It protected a thing which in turn contained another thing. A status of inviolability was attached not to the contents but to the container, not to the relics but to their shield.'[33] The container was a material edifice, made of stone and marble, but the status of *res religiosae* was produced by the legal operation of instituting the edifice as an envelope or perimeter which derived its prohibitional force from the fact that it was in contact with the body. What is important here is that the fabrication of these artefacts did not exemplify a more generalised mode of constructivism, and in their self-sufficiency they do not participate in any of the modes of agency that are central to *dispositif*-thinking.

This way of making artefacts is manifested in the form of Thomas's publications. As the notice on the back cover of the first posthumous collection of his works observes, he favoured the concision and density of the article form [*la concision et la densité de l'article*].[34] His peers in the social sciences were alert to the peculiarity of this preference: 'he writes articles, not books!'[35] But the article form suited Thomas because each of his studies is as involuted and self-sufficient as the legal artefact that it reconstructs. Each study unfolds the architecture of an artefact or operation as if it were merely recapitulating an ontogenetic principle that was immanent in the artefact in question and which was sufficient to explain its making. Thomas rarely felt the need to import concepts drawn from philosophy or the social sciences into this process of explication, nor did he seek to develop analogies or comparisons that would situate juridical artefacts in a broader social or cultural fabric. Whereas the book form lends itself to the cultivation of interdisciplinary conversations, the aesthetic of Thomas's scholarship was one that highlighted the alien and anachronistic nature of Roman law. Of course, the work of reconstruction had to draw air from the world in which these articles were written and read, and Thomas very adroitly exploited the aesthetic of apartness to position (almost in the media-marketing sense) his studies in relation to contemporary interdisciplinary conversations. This positioning was rarely made explicit,[36] but his chosen operations and artefacts were selected and curated in such a way as to interpellate these conversations from a locus whose very indifference granted it a certain epistemic privilege.

The artefacts that Thomas found in Roman law – person, labour, *res* – are compelling because they are so well made. Each gave shape to a fundamental category of human existence: the person, the family, gender, nature, labour, power, religiosity. And each was fabricated by operations that have their counterparts in contemporary epistemes; techniques or subroutines of individuation, reification, derivation, representation and classification. As they are reconstructed by Thomas, the artefacts and operations of Roman law become creatively, productively, anachronistic; they captivate the contemporary from a moment of non-contemporaneity. This way of positioning Roman law became explicitly politicised in the context of the emergence in the 1990s of biotechnological and biomedical techniques which seemed (to a number of French private lawyers) to engage precisely those categories of existence that were to the fore in Thomas's work. A particular focus for these discussions of the nature of the legal person was the question of the 'ownership' of human genes, a question provoked by the European Commission's proposal for legislation relating to biotechnological inventions.

A particular flashpoint was a decision of 1992 in which the Cour de Cassation held that a person with the 'syndrome of transsexualism' who had undergone surgery for 'therapeutic reasons', who no longer possessed their 'original sexual characteristics', and who had taken on the 'physical appearance' and 'social behaviour' of the 'other sex', had the right to change the determination of their sex in official documents.[37] As the phrases picked out in quotation marks suggest, the premises of the decision were thoroughly patriarchal and heteronormative, and, even by the standards of the time, it was obdurately unimaginative in its appreciation of what is at stake in being trans. But even this reluctant recognition of a right to change the official record, which was compelled by a decision of the European Court of Human Rights, was sufficient to provoke a constituency of French legal academics to take to the media to denounce the court's decision. They argued that the legal person was a normative artefact which had the 'anthropological function', as it came to be known, of securing identity and kinship, and of protecting the dignity of the human person; the decision had allowed this foundational artefact to become a vehicle for the affirmation of subjective desires or fantasies which eroded the armatures of kinship and identity. Thomas responded to this conservative reinvention of the legal tradition and to the dogma of human dignity with which it was associated in an article published in *Le Débat* in 1998.[38]

Thomas began by noticing the hypocrisy of a politics that in seeking to suppress the 'desire' of alternative subjectivities overlooked the psychic life of the propertied capitalist: 'These psycho-jurists, concerned as they are with the constitutive "limits" of the "logical structure" of the subject, have to explain why the right to extend one's possessions and bequests infinitely, without restriction as to value or duration, and hence to deprive the world an ever-increasing share of its value, to the detriment of others, is any less a fantasy of omnipotence [*fantasme de la toute-puissance*] than the right accorded to transsexuals to change their own body and their own identity'.[39] But his critique was centred on the artefact of the legal person, and on the question of its relation to desiring 'subjects'. He pointed out that there was a radical difference between the legal person and the psychic subject; the form of the *persona* in Roman law was entirely detached from the reality of the flesh and blood persons, so that a single *persona* could be ascribed to two bodies, or so that an individual might be attributed personality for some purposes but not for others, and so on. The person was a logical function rather than a 'real' subject. One of the examples Thomas chose to illustrate that point was the agency of a slave owned in common, which also, from the perspective of a commentary, illustrates the way in which he aestheticised the autonomous logic of Roman legal operations so as to present casuistic reasoning as a knowledge apart, as a knowledge alien to any other social discourse or technique.

Thomas asks us to imagine two masters, A and B, each at the head of a patrimonial estate, and each owning a slave in that capacity, slave (a) and slave (b), respectively, and each of these slaves represents their master by making contracts with third parties on his behalf. But they also own a slave in common, slave (a'/b'):

These slaves manage the property of their masters, contract in their name, and make binding agreements between their masters and third parties and receive commtiments from third parties according to a mechanism of agency [*représentation parfaite*] that was developed by Roman family law. But these two masters also own a slave in common. What happens if the common slave (a'/b') makes a verbal promise to (b), the slave of B? In what capacity does the actor (a'/b'), who is divided between two domestic spheres, divided between two estates and split into two statuses, pronounce the formula that makes the contract? Does he do so as slave (a') of master A, whom he does not have in common with his contractual partner, slave (b)? Or does he do so as slave (b') of master B, whom he does have in common with his partner (b)?

More interesting than the answer – given that a person cannot contract with themselves the divided slave could speak only for the master that he did not have in common with his addressee – is Thomas's reconstruction of the question.

The text of the *Digest* is rather straightforward: it presents the agency of the common slave quite economically, as a compilation of settled rules as to the effect of stipulations made by slaves.[40] By translating the language of the text into a schema of quasi-algebraic letter symbols, Thomas draws the contemporary reader into an aesthetic of problematisation and resolution that performs, of itself, the abstraction of law from society. Inducted into this aesthetic, the reader finds themselves in an alien world, a world that has already begun, with units of accounting and ways of reckoning that are starkly different from the familiar currencies of subjectivity. Thanks to the aesthetic of brackets and prime symbols – (a), (b), and (a'/b') – the reader immediately understands that this is a system that reckons not with persons but with 'person-functions', and that these functions do not decline or decompose the capacities of 'whole' persons: they operate without reference to the 'reality' of individuated embodiment. Thomas also turns the prescriptive 'if, then' modality of the original text into a hypothetical 'what if?' modality: *'Que se passe-t-il si . . .?'* The effect is to induct the reader into the dynamic of a problem, which, like all problems, sets up a particular kind of subjective attitude, a very specific habitus. The reader finds themselves in the position of having to find a solution to a problem where the rules of the game are not just unknown but also of an incomprehensible logic. The habitus of perplexity involves not only reaching forward towards a solution but also looking back to the rules of the game and to the permutations that are possible, given the competences that each piece (person-function) has accrued in preceding problem scenarios. Framed in terms of a *what if?*, the analytic of the common slave puts the reader in the position of having to make sense of a logic that is thoroughly alien, and which has realised the world into elements and functions that elude all known coordinates, but which the reader knows must make sense in its own terms, if only because in adjudication (or casuistics) all problems are supposed to be amenable to solution.[41]

Few readers will know Roman law well enough to unwind the problem into its solution, but they are primed for the interpretive guidance that is interjected by Thomas: 'To resolve the question into its basic legal elements, one has, within the promissor, to distinguish two persons . . .'[42] And the explanation unfolds from there into an eloquent statement of the difference between the flesh and blood individual and the legal artefact of the person: 'What nature brings together in a single body, a single mouth, a single voice, the law cleaves into two distinct legal formulae and two irreducible persons'.[43] By this point the reader, and hopefully the 'psycho-jurists', understand that the difference between the artefactual person and the 'real' person is stranger and more complicated than the difference between role and role-player. In the process of subdividing and aggregating what common sense sees as 'real' individuals, the law creates entities and competences that are modelled not on what psychic subjects can do, or even on what a particular part of a psychic subject can do, but on what is required for a particular legal operation to be effected. So, by translating the formulations of the *Digest* into the form of a pedagogical thought experiment, Thomas causes the reader to experience in Roman law a logico-discursive machine that would otherwise have remained invisible, and which is not revealed by other histories of Roman law.

Thomas's reconstruction of this particular use of the person is more significant and more enduring than the political argument in which it was deployed (even if the ideology of the 'anthropological function of law' has not disappeared from the French legal academy). What is important about Thomas's work, and what makes it so engaging and thought-provoking for scholars in all reaches of the human and social sciences, is precisely the originality and meticulousness with which he re-engineered Roman legal artefacts and operations. And one should emphasise the work of *re*-engineering. Obviously, the point of his aestheticisation of questions such as that of the common slave was to elicit the 'code' that Roman law wrote into everyday Latin, or to make explicit the schemata and techniques which Roman lawyers assumed and practised as tacit knowledge. But in the guise of merely revealing what was always already there, Thomas's own presentational strategies do something quite profound to Roman law. He fashions Roman legal artefacts and operations into 'works' or artefacts that fascinate the scholar because they so rigorously unfold a logic that is at once alien and compelling. Like a geological or archaeological 'find' that challenges our understanding of an epoch or period, these artefacts are engaging and unsettling because their intrigue is solidified into their construction; they are available to social-scientific analysis, they stimulate social-scientific analysis, but only because in their materiality and conformation they are not already creatures of social-scientific analysis. And this effect of geological[44] or archaeological alterity was a result of the singular imagination of Thomas, of the precision and rigour with which he pursued his preference not to think law through in any of the usual ways, and of his ability to manufacture such foreign bodies from within the human and social sciences. If the argument in his early article on *La langue du droit romain* was not fully thought through, it was not because he had not yet managed to connect his approach to the paradigm of 'law in society' scholarship, but because he had not yet perfected his own technique of constructing legal artefacts.

Notes

1. This particular formulation did not survive the editorial process of the US law review. The footnote of the printed version says only that Thomas asks for 'more refined semiotic analyses' of the modalities of law's internal operations; see Niklas Luhmann, 'Operational Closure and Structural Coupling: The Differentiation of the Legal System' (1992) 13 *Cardozo Law Review*, pp. 1419–41, at p. 1431. A copy of the original text is, to borrow the language of law review editors, 'on file with the author'.

2. Thomas asks of *fides*, the term with which Luhmann was concerned in his own article, whether 'legal terms that are derived from ordinary language (words from the vocabulary of religion, morality, social relations, propriety, etc.) retain their original meaning in their new legal context, or [whether] they are not instead, as soon as they enter the legal field, transformed by what one might call a neologism of meaning [*un néologisme du sens*]?'; Yan Thomas, 'La langue du droit romain. Problèmes et méthodes' (1973) 18 *Archives de Philosophie du Droit*, pp. 103–25, at p. 108). The answer is spelled out at p. 111: 'A legal statement can only be read juridically with the help of rules that are specific to the metalanguage of law'.

3. Luhmann, 'Operational Closure and Structural Coupling', op. cit. n. 1, at p. 1437.

4. Annelise Riles, 'Collateral Expertise' (2010) 51:6 *Current Anthropology*, pp. 795–818.

5. Thomas says very little about the ways in which legal forms were construed and practised outside the legal system.

6. Marie-Angèle Hermitte, 'Le droit est un autre monde' (1999) 7 *Enquête*, pp. 17–37.

7. Ibid., at p. 18.

8. Cornelia Vismann, 'Cultural Techniques and Sovereignty' (2013) 30:6 *Theory, Culture & Society*, pp. 83–93, at p. 84.

9. Ibid., at p. 88.

10. See Cornelia Vismann, *Files Law and Media Technology* (Stanford: Stanford University Press, 2008).

11. Bruno Latour, 'Factures/fracture: de la notion de réseau à celle d'attachement' in André Micoud and Michel Peroni (eds.), *Ce qui nous relie* (Paris: Aube, 2000), pp. 189–208. The original reference is Émile Benveniste, 'Actif et moyen dans le verbe' in Id. *Problèmes de linguistique générale*, vol. 1, (Paris: Gallimard, 1966), pp. 168–75, at p. 173. See now Isabelle

Stengers, 'The Earth Won't Let Itself be Watched' in B. Latour and Peter Weibel (eds) *Critical Zones: Observations for Earthly Politics* (Cambridge MA: MIT Press, 2020), pp. 228–35.

12. Yan Thomas, 'Acte, agent, société. Sur l'homme coupable dans la pensée juridique romaine' (1977) 22 *Archives de Philosophie du Droit*, pp. 63–83; see Chapter 9 in this volume.

13. Cf. Vismann, op. cit. n. 8, at p. 84: 'The default positions of media and things that set cultural techniques into motion contradict a legally sanctioned, and thereby particularly widespread, notion: namely, the claim that only the subject can carry out actions and rule over things'.

14. Thomas, op. cit. n. 12, at p. 66.

15. Ibid., at p. 67.

16. Ibid., at p. 71.

17. See my 'Law after Anthropology. Object and Technique in Roman Law' (2014) 31: 2 and 3 *Theory, Culture & Society*, pp. 147–66.

18. Vismann, op. cit. n. 8, at p. 88.

19. Vismann, op. cit. n. 8, at p. 87.

20. Maximilian Herberger's *Dogmatik: Zur Geschichte von Begriff und Methode in Medizin und Jurisprudenz* (Frankfurt: Klostermann, 1981) is an essential reference for both Vismann and Legendre, but in crucially different senses.

21. Op. cit. n. 8, at p. 85.

22. Ibid., p. 84.

23. See notably Olivier Cayla and Yan Thomas, *Du droit de ne pas naître. À propos de l'affaire Perruche* (Paris: Gallimard, 2002).

24. See Vismann, *Files*, op. cit. n. 10, esp. Chapter 5.

25. Giorgio Agamben, *What is an Apparatus?* (Stanford: Stanford University Press, 2009), at p. 7.

26. Erich Hörl, 'Luhmann, the Non-trivial Machine and the Neocybernetic Regime of Truth' (2012) 29(3) *Theory, Culture & Society*, pp. 94–121.

27. Luhmann, 'Operational Closure and Structural Coupling', op. cit. n. 1, at p. 1433.

28. See Yan Thomas, 'L'extrême et l'ordinaire. Remarques sur le cas médiéval de la communauté disparue', in Jean-Claude Passeron and Jacques Revel (eds.), *Penser par cas* (Paris: Éditions de l'EHESS, 2005), pp. 45–73, esp. at p. 58: 'what mattered to Roman lawyers was not so much the permanence of form as the substitutability of the component pieces'.

29. Yan Thomas, 'L'institution civile de la cité' (1993) 74:2 *Le Débat*, pp. 21–40.

30. On the *familia* as *res*, see Yan Thomas, 'Res, chose et patrimoine. (Note sur le rapport sujet-objet en droit romain)' (1980) 25 *Archives de Philosophie du Droit*, pp. 413–26.
31. Yan Thomas, 'L'usage et les fruits de l'esclave. Opérations juridiques romaines sur le travail' (1999) 7 *Enquête*, pp. 203–30.
32. See Yan Thomas, 'Les ornements, la cité, le patrimoine', in Clara Aussay-Assayas (ed.), *Images romaines* (Paris: Éditions rue d'Ulm, 1998).
33. Yan Thomas, '*Res religiosae*. On the Categories of Religion and Commerce in Roman law' in Alain Pottage and Martha Mundy (eds.), *Law, Anthropology and the Constitution of the Social. Making Persons and Things* (Cambridge: Cambridge University Press, 2004), pp. 40–72, at p. 66.
34. Yan Thomas, *Les opérations du droit* (Paris: Seuil: 2011).
35. Personal communication from a leading French social scientist.
36. Here, one might think of Thomas's article on *patria potestas*, which corrects Michel Foucault's presentation of *patria potestas* as the archetype of the sovereign power to *faire mourrir/ laisser vivre* (see Chapter 7 in this volume), or his references to Arendt and Finley in his study of the labour time of slaves ('L'usage et les fruits de l'esclave', op. cit. n. 31).
37. '[L]orsqu'à la suite d'un traitement médico-chirurgical subi dans un but thérapeutique, une personne présentant le syndrome de transsexualisme ne possède plus tous les caractères de son sexe d'origine et a pris une apparence physique la rapprochant de l'autre sexe, auquel correspond son comportement social, le principe du respect dû à la vie privée justifie que son état civil indique désormais le sexe dont elle a l'apparence' (*Cour de cassation*, Ass. Plén., 11 déc. 1192, *JCP* éd. G. 1993, II, n° 21991).
38. Yan Thomas, 'Le sujet de droit, la personne et la nature. Sur la critique contemporaine du sujet de droit' (1998) 100 *Le Débat*, pp. 85–107. See Chapter 6 in this volume.
39. Ibid., at p. 92.
40. 'A common slave bears the character of two slaves. For that reason, if my own slave has stipulated for a slave common to me and to you, the legal effect of this form of words will be the same as it would have been if two separate stipulations had been made: one in the name of my slave and the other in the name of yours; nor ought we to think that I acquire only a half share, and the other half goes to no one. For the character of a common slave is of such a nature that in a case where one of his masters can acquire and one cannot, he is

considered as if he belonged only to the one for whom he has the capacity to acquire'; *D.* 45.3.1.4, in Alan Watson (ed.) *The Digest of Justinian,* book 4 (Philadelphia: University of Pennsylvania Press, 1985), at p. 194.

41. Kittler observes of the Napoleonic prohibition on the denial of justice that 'A new law decrees hermeneutics and with it readers/writers who apply it in all its senselessness, and in so doing surround it with a cloud of meaning'; Friedrich A Kittler, *Discourse Networks 1800/1900* (Stanford: Stanford University Press, 1987), at p. 21.

42. Thomas, 'Le sujet de droit, la personne et la nature', op. cit. n. 38, at p. 99.

43. Ibid.: '*Ce que la nature réunit en un corps, en une bouche, en une voix, le droit le disjoint en deux formules juridiques distinctes et en deux personnes irréductibles*'.

44. Of course, theories of the Anthropocene have now brought geology into the human and social sciences. So, for example, the 'geology' of the Earth might itself have a sociality or historicity based upon a cybernetics of matter or conformation rather than 'information'. See Bronislaw Szerszynski, 'Planetary Mobilities: Movement, Memory and Emergence in the Body of the Earth' (2016) 11:4 *Mobilities,* pp. 614–28.

Biographies of Contributors

Cooper Francis is a translator, writer and researcher based in London. He is currently studying at the Center for Research in Modern European Philosophy, Kingston University towards the completion of his doctoral dissertation.

Alain Pottage is Professor of Law at SciencesPo, Paris. He was previously Professor of Law at the London School of Economics. His work focuses on the history and theory of intellectual property and questions relating to law and the Anthropocene.

Anton Schütz is an Honorary Fellow of Kent Law School, University of Kent. Topics of recent interest and research include legal and political history, the politics of legal historiography, the articulation of law-centred and right-centred normative thinking. He is the co-editor (with Thanos Zartaloudis) of the Book Series Encounters in Law and Philosophy (EUP).

Chantal Schütz is Assistant Professor of English at École Polytechnique, Head of Department of Languages and Cultures. Head of the Academic Council of Institut Polytechnique de Paris, and member of the Prismes research team at Université Paris 3-Sorbonne Nouvelle. Her Ph.D. was supervised by François Laroque, on Thomas Middleton's *A Mad World, my Masters* (Bilingual edition published by Garnier, 2013). Her recent work has been dedicated to early modern broadside ballads; Thomas Middleton; Shakespeare and music; Shakespeare in performance at the Globe.

Thanos Zartaloudis is Reader in Legal Theory and History at Kent Law School, University of Kent. His most recent book is *The Birth of Nomos* (EUP, 2019).